Praise for *The Beloved Community*

"[An] ambitious, wide-ranging book . . . " —*Publishers Weekly*

"'The revolution begins in the pews.' So opens this closely reasoned study of the faith expressed in good works like the Civil Rights Act and antipoverty movement . . . the great service of Marsh's book is to introduce readers to inspiring figures they may not have heard of." —*Kirkus Reviews*

"This fascinating, compelling book will appeal to readers with broad interests in religion and social justice." —*Booklist*

"What a magnificent book! Charles Marsh writes eloquently about 'lived theology' in the context of the civil rights movement and related social and religions endeavors such as Koinonia Farm near Americus, Georgia which emphasized social justice, racial reconciliation and redemption. Read every word. You'll be enlightened, revived, and blessed."

—Millard Fuller, Founder and President,
Habitat for Humanity International

"Charles Marsh is one of our best theologians, one of our best historians, one of our best storytellers. In this book—his most expansive and ambitious one to date—he places the Christian faith of the civil rights movement in a larger context: he shows us the faith that drove that movement, but also shows that its energy is still potent today, among places and people that we pay insufficient attention to. Most important, Marsh articulates a vision for renewal, a way that the larger community of faith can recover its passion for true social justice. This is a vital book by a major American thinker."

—Alan Jacobs, author of *Shaming the Devil* and *A Visit to Vanity Fair*

THE
BELOVED
COMMUNITY

THE
BELOVED
COMMUNITY

How Faith Shapes Social Justice,
from the Civil Rights Movement to Today

CHARLES MARSH

A Member of the Perseus Books Group
New York

Published by Basic Books,
A Member of the Perseus Books Group

Books published by Basic Books are available at special discounts for bulk purchases
in the United States by corporations, institutions, and other organizations. For more
information, please contact the Special Markets Department at the Perseus Books
Group, 11 Cambridge Center, Cambridge, MA 02142, or call (617) 252-5298 or
(800) 255-1514, or e-mail special.markets@perseusbooks.com.

Text design by Brent Wilcox
Set in Janson Text

Cataloging-in-Publication data for this book is available from the Library of Congress.
ISBN-13: 978-0-465-04416-0 (pbk)
ISBN-10: 0-465-04416-6 (pbk)

06 07 08 / 10 9 8 7 6 5 4 3 2 1

For my students
Restorers of hope

What is it, namely, that connects the temporal and eternity, what else but love, which for that very reason is before everything and remains after everything is gone.

SØREN KIERKEGAARD

Contents

Souls on Fire

In the final days of the Montgomery Bus Boycott, a month after the U.S. Supreme Court had assured black organizers the victory in their yearlong protest of city segregation laws, the Montgomery Improvement Association held a weeklong Institute on Nonviolence and Social Change at the Holt Street Baptist Church. In his address to that December 1956 gathering, Martin Luther King Jr. cast the achievements of the year in theological perspective. "It seems that God has decided to use Montgomery as the proving ground for the struggle," he said; the "old order" is passing away, and "our church is becoming militant, stressing a social gospel as well as a gospel of personal salvation." [1] Then he spoke with greater specificity of the lessons learned: "We have before us the glorious opportunity to inject a new dimension of love into the veins of our civilization. There is still a voice crying out in terms that echo across the generations, saying: 'Love your enemies, bless them that curse you, pray for them that despitefully use you, that you may be the children of your Father which is in Heaven.'" Although a boycott was necessary in Montgomery to bring an end to discriminatory laws, King urged the church people in the movement to keep in mind that a boycott and its achievements do not in themselves represent the goal. "The end is reconciliation, the end is redemption," he said, "the end is the creation of the beloved community." [2]

In Montgomery, Dr. King caught a glimpse of a new social order. The pursuit of civil rights for African Americans would be part of a larger spiritual journey in which people divided by centuries of oppression and hatred might come to live together peaceably in beloved community, envisioned in King's 1963 address at the March on Washington as a banquet feast in the red hills of south Georgia, where the children of former slaves share table fellowship with the grand-children of former slave owners.[3] When King boarded a city bus three weeks later to mark the return of black Montgomerians to public transportation, he told reporters, "Now is the time to move from protest to reconciliation."

The Catholic monk and writer Thomas Merton once described the civil rights movement as the greatest example of Christian faith in action in the social history of the United States.[4] This book tells the story of how Christian faith gave rise to and sustained the civil rights movement and its vision of beloved community. The logic of King's dream was theologically specific: beloved community as the realization of divine love in lived social relation. To be sure, King's concept of love was surely not the platitudinous "all you need is love"; it was rather the passion to make human life and social existence a parable of God's love for the world. It was *agape*: the outrageous venture of loving the other without conditions—a risk and a costly sacrifice. "If I respond to hate with a reciprocal hate," King said, "I do nothing but intensify the cleavage in broken community. I can only close the gap . . . by meeting hate with love."[5] Indeed it was the movement's genius to illuminate with unforgettable beauty, and with the "fierce urgency of now," the truth that beloved community is not self-generating; that behind it stands the event, and the power by which it lives and is nourished; that patient, passionate worldliness opens always onto larger vistas.

Despite the rejection of white liberals, black militants, segregationists, and evangelicals, King held on tight to Christ-shaped love. No doubt, the pursuit of beloved community inhibited those visceral energies that would put some heat on the white man and offer the catharsis of a much-deserved payback. But King accepted this inhibition and made it a spiritual discipline, the discipline of bearing peaceful witness to the cross of Jesus Christ in a violent nation.[6] The pursuit of beloved community gave the civil rights movement its sustaining spiritual vision.

Although organizations such as the Student Nonviolent Coordinating Committee (SNCC), the Congress of Racial Equality (CORE), and the Council of Federated Organizations (COFO) have been described as secularized waves of the civil rights movement, religious language saturated even the early literature of the youth movement. In Albany, Georgia, SNCC advertised its first mass meeting on November 9, 1961, by announcing, "To those who love the Lord and Freedom: COME; LISTEN; LEARN; LOVE!"[7] The handbill, drafted by SNCC's Charles Sherrod, read like the confession of the church militant in the segregated south:

We believe in the Fatherhood of God and the brotherhood of man. We believe that God made of one blood all nations for to dwell on all the face of the earth. If we are of one blood, children of one common Father, brothers in the household of God, then we must be of equal worth in His family, entitled to equal opportunity in the society of men. . . .

We are called upon, therefore, to love our fellow men, all of them, with all the risks that that implies and all the privileges that it promises.[8]

The theological language could not have been more unapologetic in its specificity and scope, or more subversive of the racial status quo.

In the staff meeting on April 29, 1962, SNCC staff members resolved their firm commitment to the creation of "a social order permeated by love and to the spirituality of nonviolence as it grows from the Judeo-Christian tradition."[9] Love was affirmed as the "central motif of nonviolence," the "force by which God binds man to himself and man to man" which "remains loving and forgiving even in the midst of hostility."[10] "Peace dominates war; faith reconciles doubt," read the mission statement. No doubt, there were many SNCC activists whose moral energies were driven by secular ideals, as there were those who considered the faith of black people altogether quaint. Nevertheless, student-based organizations like SNCC and COFO, as well as the larger movement itself, were initially anchored in the language, imagery, and energies of the church, in search of a "circle of trust, a band of sisters and brothers gathered around the possibilities of agapeic love, the beloved community."[11]

The story is told of a minister who was picketing at the county courthouse. When a white bystander said to him, "You shouldn't be doing that; you should be preaching the gospel!" a SNCC worker marching with the minister replied, "He is preaching the gospel!"[12] With a greater sense of eclecticism and imaginative freedom than King's own Southern Christian Leadership Conference (SCLC), SNCC proffered a theology for radicals. Its Christian commitments may have been "gentle" and "unashamed," as the writer Os Guinness once observed, but SNCC's theology for radicals allowed itself to be stretched by the uncertainties and energies of lived experience; to be invigorated with the rough-hewn wisdom and unguarded testimonials of the untrained.[13] One of King's young associates, John Lewis, the freedom rider and chairman of SNCC, described the movement's moral shape as "nothing less than the Christian concept of the Kingdom of God on earth" and as a "redemptive society" that heals social wounds and divisions. Beloved community gave expression to all that Lewis was longing for as a young seminarian devoted to the venture of making the teachings of Jesus come alive in the segregated South.

Too often historians and scholars have recast the civil rights movement as a secular movement that used religion to its advantage. In this reading, the movement leaders were crafty politicians invoking religion to inspire the troops into action and fortify social hope. Indeed, efforts to secularize the movement were already present in the 1962 Port Huron Statement, drafted by the white radical organization Students for a Democratic Society. The statement demythologizes black piety for the consumption of the New Left by articulating the modernist conceit that what black people do and say in church cannot possibly be taken seriously; the actions and speech of black Christians must be recast in terms amenable to enlightened secular interests. As such, the movement is about "human independence," "a quality of mind not compulsively driven by a sense of powerlessness," living life free of repression, "full, spontaneous access to present and past experiences," and nurturing an "intuitive awareness of possibilities, an active sense of curiosity, an ability and willingness to learn." The Port Huron Statement offers a thoroughly desacralized affirmation of human dignity, laying claim to the moral convictions of the southern civil rights struggle while deracinating them completely from their home in the black church. Christian conviction is stripped away in an existentialist-therapeutic rendering of humanity's "potential for self-cultivation, self-direction, self-understanding, and creativity." The goal of social struggle is neither "reconciliation, redemption, and the creation of beloved community," nor achieving legal equality through piecemeal social reform, but "finding a meaning in life that is personally authentic."[14]

In late 1964, and despite an impressive slate of civil rights legislation enacted that same year and the following, the vision of the beloved community began to fragment in ways that continue to shape and frustrate racial peace in America. The reasons are complex and disputed. Nonetheless, the factors include an emergent black separatism, the mobilization of white student energies toward antiwar activism (and away from racial matters), the burgeoning women's liberation movement, the search for new religious experiences and an alternative consciousness, and the persisting segregationist views of the white church in the South. At the end of 1968, Martin Luther King Jr. was dead, and SNCC, having fired all remaining white members the previous year, was (as historian Clayborne Carson writes) "scattered like seed to the wind after [its] radicalism could no longer find fertile ground in the southern struggle."[15] The story of the civil rights movement in America concludes with this final period of fragmentation and disillusionment.

Yet there is a different story of the search for the beloved community that has not been fully appreciated. This story centers on the more modest, yet more enduring and more focused pursuits in particular contexts of shared confessional or religious beliefs. The story of these initiatives in building beloved community reads as a kind of parallel history (and at times an overlapping one) to the story of the American civil rights movement and racial policy of the post–civil rights years. This story includes, but is not identical to, the widely misunderstood faith-based movement, recently seized upon by "compassionate conservatives" to exemplify the socially transformative power of religious institutions and to justify cuts in federal social spending. In fact, the faith-based movement has radical roots in the civil rights movement—and in many of the civil rights years' most creative experiments in community organizing. The founder of the community development movement—as the faith-based movement is more likely to be called by participants—is a black Mississippian named John Perkins, "a Bible-believing fundamentalist for black power," as he was once described, who came of age in the Jim Crow years and has lived among the poor for more than five decades. At its best, the community development movement seeks to reclaim, and to make more explicit, the theological commitments that animated the civil rights movement—"redemption, reconciliation and the creation of beloved community"—and to put these commitments to the test in building community among the poor and the excluded. The new legions of Christian radicals working in rural and urban areas remind us of the sobering fact that beyond the difficult work of achieving legal equality awaits more difficult work, indeed the daily disciplines and sacrifices required to sustain beloved community.[16] The revolution begins in the pews, as the movement of the sixties learned, and in a whole lot of waiting around for car rides, in tedious organizational meetings and arguments about strategy, around the mimeograph machine. The hardest part is not envisioning the end but living in the sluggish between.

This book may sometimes appear to be a defense of religion's utility, but it is not that.[17] It is rather a portrait of the Christian faith as a set of social disciplines shaped by gratitude, forgiveness and reconciliation. Biblical religion offers peacemakers and activists much more than pep talks and consolations, indeed a potent arsenal for imagining freedom, energizing social reform and forging solidarity with the poor. It is all well and good for Anthony Appiah to advise us, "live with fractured identities; engage in identity's play; find solidarity, yes, but recognize contingency, and above all practice irony." But what might it mean to settle down after all the fracturing and decentering and assaults on identity have run their course, to build community among the hopeless and excluded in places where irony is a condescending shrug? It is unlikely that anyone has ever read Friedrich

Nietzsche's *Thus Spake Zarathustra* or Jacques Derrida's *Disseminations* and opened a soup kitchen.[18] But the Christian peacemakers who yesterday and today build beloved community with the poor and excluded "drink the earthly cup to the dregs" and bear glorious witness to the spirit of life in concrete and practical ways.[19] In fact, the women and men encountered in the story of the beloved community provide such compelling demonstration of the mercy and kindness of God as to offer, perhaps unwittingly, an apologetic of their peculiar theological claims. Contrary to the caricatures of secularists and civil religionists, the ascent to God expands the horizons of worldliness. Thus, this book seeks to reinvest the civil rights movement of its deep soul by interpreting the civil rights movement as theological drama; herein lies a plotline that far exceeds the movement's significant political or economic achievements.

Please do not misunderstand my intentions. I am not seeking to claim the civil rights movement as an exclusively "Christian movement"— though this is precisely what King called the Montgomery bus boycott. I do not wish to divide what came to be spontaneously, if briefly, united: Jew and Christian, atheist and believer, southerner and northerner, nor do I wish to impose the name of Christ on every action intended for the sake of the poor and the excluded. Still, no one is well served by easy syncreticisms, especially when these become affirmations made into slogans that forget their origins. King's vision of beloved community was grounded in a specific theological tradition, and no amount of postmodern complexity can remove that intention and claim. "I am many things to many people," King said of himself in 1965, "but in the quiet recesses of my heart, I am fundamentally a clergyman, a Baptist preacher. This is my being and my heritage, for I am also the son of a Baptist preacher, the grandson of a Baptist preacher and the great-grandson of a Baptist preacher."[20] While the movement is often celebrated in the public sphere as a great civics lesson of a nation's common hopes, it teaches us equally important and urgent lessons about the integrity of our differences. The black churches of the civil rights movement did not relinquish their specific theological commitments when the student volunteers arrived, many of whom were not Christian; but they found ways of including new friends in their worship without erasing the real differences between them.

Thus, we would do well to accept the words, actions, and sacrifices of these lived theologies as a bold retrieval of the spiritual disciplines of forgiveness, reconciliation, and the preferential option for nonviolence, which have always shaped the social vision of true Christianity. The Christian peacemaker engages the world out of a passionate sense of gratitude for life—and for all who share in the work of redeeming creation. The story of the beloved community may also serve to remind us that authentic faith always finds a way to break free from incarceration in ideological and political gulags.[21] American Christians can blame secularists for many things but surely not for the trivialization of faith in the modern world: Christians in North America have surpassed all competitors in that booming business. Our patriotism has become a cult of self-worship consecrated by court prophets robed in pinstriped suits. Forgetting the difference between discipleship and patriotism, the God most Americans trust is a simulacrum of the holy and transcendent God, a reification of the American way of life. "The Church has an obligation not to join in the incantation of political slogans and in the concoction of pseudo-events," Thomas Merton wrote in his 1968 book, *Violence and Faith*, "but to cut clear through the deviousness and ambiguity of both slogans and events by her simplicity and her love."[22]

When we look at the story of the civil rights movement in the South, of those women and men who risked everything for beloved community, we see illuminated a rich and compelling way of life; but we also see an invitation.[23] The good news of the story—though it is hard to believe in our violent time—is that the same spiritual vision that animated the civil rights movement remains a vital source of moral energy and social discipline for the present age. The invitation says: Accept that vision as a gift and as a guide.

PART ONE

CHAPTER 1

~

From Church Budgets to
Beloved Community: King in Montgomery

Martin Luther King Jr. arrived in Montgomery in late summer of 1954 with his eyes set on denominational fame and fortune, eager to deliver on his promise to raise the Dexter Avenue Baptist Church "to such heights as will stagger the imagination of generations yet unborn, and which God himself will smile upon."[1] Civil rights activism was not high on the agenda.

Earlier that year, King had preached his trial sermon at Dexter, a cool affirmation of moral religion entitled "The Three Dimensions of a Complete Life." The sermon, which recalled Harry Emerson Fosdick's mannered presentation of the Gospel, proceeded as an exegesis of St. John's vision of the heavenly city, but all fears of a coming apocalypse had been removed.[2] King said:

> [There] are three dimensions of any complete life to which we can fitly give the words of this text: length, breadth, and height. Now the length of life as we shall use it here is the inward concern for one's own welfare. In other words, it is that inward concern that causes one to push forward, to achieve his own goals and ambitions. The breadth of life as we shall use it here is the outward concern for the welfare of others. And the height of life is the upward reach of God. Now you've got to have all three of these to have a complete life.[3]

There was no mention of race, no challenges to the status quo, no proposals for change, no irascible Hebrew prophets, no rebel Jesus.[4] The young preacher surmised that good religion makes a life balanced, whole-some, and complete.

The sermon was a hit. "The people would have voted him in that Sun-day, if a vote had been taken," said Robert D. Nesbitt, church clerk and preeminent deacon. The Dexter Avenue congregation considered itself temperamentally more restrained than most of the other twenty-seven black Baptist churches in Montgomery, and appreciated King's steadiness. Racial crusading was not a priority for Dexter Avenue Baptist Church. Church members shared a hope of a future without Jim Crow, but they were not going to be the ones to ignite the fires of dissent.

Dexter had long prided itself on its political power and access to white elites. Regarding the soon-to-be-famous bus system, most parishioners re-mained blissfully ignorant. An educated clergy and parish were still chief con-gregational virtues.[5] Dexter Avenue traced its history to a nineteenth-century Sunday school and regular school named Langridge Academy, and its current membership included not only schoolteachers and college faculty, but busi-ness leaders, lawyers, physicians, and railroad porters. Dexter's first pastor was the former slave Charles Octavius Boothe, who taught in the Freedman's Bu-reau—having learned to read and write in the home of a plantation master—and authored four books, including *The Cyclopedia of the Colored Baptists of Al-abama*, a chronicle of "Negro progress from 1865–1895 for black people, white people—friend and foes."[6] Boothe liked to describe his church mem-bers as "people of money and refinement," "owners and managers of large af-fairs, involving thousands of dollars."[7] Less than a century later, Sunday mornings saw late-model automobiles bringing well-dressed Negroes to the redbrick church prominently located across the street from the federal judi-ciary building and a stone's throw from the state capital. As historian Houston Roberson says, "Rather than challenge a system that seemed so trenchantly inexorable, [Dexter parishioners] chose to try to create good lives for them-selves within the circumscribed sphere of racial segregation."[8]

When Martin Luther King Jr. arrived back in the Deep South, he was twenty-five years old and still working on his doctorate in philosophical theology, though he had recently completed his residency requirements and attained the relative freedom of the dissertation stage. Two weeks be-fore the trial sermon, King had passed his comprehensive exams at Boston University, receiving "very good to excellent" marks (an overall A-), for his pithy summaries of modern religious philosophers Kant through Hegel and classical thinkers Miletus, Pythagoras, the Eleatics, and the Atomists. King's professors in the Department of Religious Studies, Harold Dewolf and Paul Schilling, were impressed with his well-furnished mind and his flair for rhetorical refinement, and they had nominated him for teaching positions in several black colleges.

The prospect of an academic post was no doubt flattering to the doctoral candidate. He had entertained hopes of one day becoming a college president, perhaps at his alma mater, Morehouse.[9] A teaching position would have put King on track toward a college presidency. Yet as he considered his options, seeking to balance his desires and his talents, he gravitated toward the greater prestige of the pastorate in a black church.

The spring of 1954 is a study of surprising contrasts. As white liberals, black intellectuals, and southern segregationists eagerly awaited the Supreme Court's decision in *Brown vs. Board of Education*, King was weighing the pros and cons of the Dexter situation. Six weeks after his first visit, Nesbett and the chairman of the deacons, T. H. Randall, telegrammed King in Boston and extended a formal offer from the pulpit committee. Wanting another look, King visited Montgomery again on April 4. Although he would not preach during this trip, he served communion and afterwards met with the committee to talk over details. King left Montgomery that afternoon without making any commitments. The church's modest size gave him pause—365 members as compared to Montgomery's Holt Street Baptist (1,200), the First Baptist in Chattanooga (1,500), or his father's congregation at Ebenezer Baptist in Atlanta (4,000).[10] King was still holding out for an offer from the First Baptist Church of Chattanooga, but nothing ever materialized.

There were other issues to work through as well. King had lived outside the region for six years and accustomed himself to the less confining social spaces of the northeast. He had recently married Coretta Scott, a talented musician who understandably worried that opportunities to develop her considerable skills in voice would decline dramatically in Montgomery, where the town's most popular musical event was the all-night sing with Hovie Lister and the Sensational Statesmen at the City Auditorium. When Coretta left her hometown of Marion, Alabama, to study music at Antioch College in Yellow Springs, Ohio, she took with her the determination, widely shared by many of the talented blacks who left the South for study and career, to unlearn the humiliating tutelage of Jim Crow.[11] "I wanted to go back South *someday* . . . but not yet," she said.

In March of 1954, King received an encouraging letter from an old Morehouse friend named J. C. Parker, who had recently moved to Montgomery to pastor the Hall Street Baptist Church. Parker hoped King would accept the offer. Parker liked the idea of Morehouse men in control of the influential pulpits. His encouragement no doubt masked certain territorial worries, but was impressive nonetheless. The two ministers had shared many enjoyable times together and knew each other well enough to let down their pastoral guard. Parker confessed his annoyance that the Dexter church leaders had taken the liberty of approving a full year's slate of programs without King's approval, padding the church calendar with a men's day, a women's day, a homecoming day, and a youth day. If King took the position, he would need to make some clarifications about pastoral authority, namely, that these were his decisions to make. Still, Parker told King he would be hard pressed to find a better salary than Dexter's—somewhere in the four thousand dollar range, "the highest salary of any minister in the city."[12] Parker had no doubt that King could "master the situation."[13]

Closer to home, however, King's father had nothing good to say about the tony congregation in Montgomery. Mike "Daddy" King, the pastor of Ebenezer Baptist Church in Atlanta, tried to alert his son to the dangers of a "silk stocking church" run by "big shots" where the chairman of deacons had earned himself the nickname of "preacher killer."[14] Daddy King had also hoped that his son would return to Atlanta to work as his pastoral assistant; his son's interest in the Alabama church was not the kind of flattery the father appreciated. Further unsolicited discouragement came to King from a former Crozer classmate and editor of the *National Baptist Voice*, J. Pious Barbour, who tried a different tack, hoping to disabuse his former classmate of the notion that a theologian might be welcome in the pulpit. "I feel sorry for you with all that learning," writes Barbour in a letter. "I wrote a two hundred page thesis on RELIGION AND PHYSIOLOGICAL PSYCHOLOGY and with the exception of lectures to colleges have been unable to use ONE SINGLE IDEA in the Baptist Church."[15] "Don't get stuck there," he insisted, "move on to a big metropolitan center in the North, or some town as Atlanta. You will dry rot there."[16] But neither man proved persuasive. With his recent conquest over doctoral comps and an arm full of accolades, King was not worrying about preacher killers, small-minded Baptists, or his father's insecurities. He was confident he could handle whatever congregational difficulties came along.

Despite these words of caution, there was finally no question that King's future, whatever it would bring, would be lived in the company of the church. He had accepted his schooling as a necessary stage in the attainment of ministerial freedom, which the Baptist church accorded its pastors to an extent unparalleled in other Protestant traditions. For all its benefits and pleasures, academe still put a man under the authority of state education boards, in the case of public institutions, or of trustees with sizeable white representations.

No one but the pastor and the Negro congregants themselves could influence church decisions. Being a black Baptist preacher meant doing the Lord's work, and, as a result, promised autonomy and self-determination.

King accepted the Dexter offer with three conditions: that he be allowed to finish his dissertation at Boston University and preach only once or twice a month until September; that his starting salary of $4,200 be raised "as the Church progresses;" and that the parsonage at 309 South Jackson Street be refurbished.[17] King's decision to move to Montgomery turned on these rather ordinary pastoral negotiations. The church leadership was happy to accept his conditions, adding as further incentive that a new organ would be installed the following week. With the offer finalized, King announced to his skeptical father and his unconvinced wife, "I'm going to be pastor, and I'm going to run that church."[18]

God set a dramatic stage in Montgomery. Dexter Avenue Baptist Church occupied a handsome redbrick building on a corner lot downtown, across a piazza from the state capital. The massive federal judicial building stood directly across the street from the church, sometimes shimmering in sunlight when the front doors of the church were swung open after the morning service. Above the pulpit an illuminated cross hung on a bronze chain just above the head of the preacher. The sanctuary had been designed in the early 1880s by the white architect Pelham J. Anderson, whose granddaughter half a century later—in a genealogical twist typical of the dense computations of life in the South—would marry a man named William A. Gayle, the mayor of Montgomery during the boycott year.[19]

In his first week at Dexter in September 1954, King presented his new congregation with a six-page pastoral letter called, "Recommendations to the Dexter Avenue Baptist Church for the Fiscal Year 1954–1955." Despite the prosaic title, the letter reads as a kind of manifesto of the young preacher's ambitions. King began by affirming his pastoral authority, reminding—if not informing—the laity, that "the pastor's authority is not merely humanly conferred, but divinely sanctioned." The letter detailed plans for fundraising, organizational innovations, and church renovation and expansion, and concluded by stating his need for a full-time secretary.

Buried in the middle of the letter was mention of the Social and Political Action Committee, created for the purpose of keeping the congregation "intelligently informed" about "the social, political and economic situation."[20] King would later cite the committee as an indication of his active interest in "current social problems," and some scholars would read into it evidence that King was already earning himself a reputation as a social activist.[21] But the committee long predated King's arrival, and whatever discernible tremors of dissent radiated from the Dexter congregation were a result of a handful of socially active parishioners, mostly women, who had been working quietly behind the scenes for more than a decade. Throughout the early 1950s, the Women's Political Council had issued numerous formal complaints to officials of the Montgomery City Lines regarding disrespectful bus drivers and unfair seating arrangements. Nothing in King's recommendation, or in the otherwise decidedly moderate Dexter Avenue ethos, encouraged opposition to legal segregation or even challenged the church's time-honored conservatism.

This is not to say that King was indifferent to civil rights concerns. In making his decision to return south, he had not sloughed aside the harsh realities of segregation, nor had he failed to appreciate the quiet stirrings of dissent in black Montgomery, the "slow fire of discontent," which he described in his memoir of the boycott year, *Stride Toward Freedom*.[22] King realized that "something remarkable was unfolding in the South," not as a result only of the WPC but of other organizations as well: the Voter's League of Montgomery, which had worked for black voting rights for two decades, and the NAACP in Montgomery and its steady preparations to test city buses.[23] Still, King did not come to Montgomery with an interest in social protest. In her memoir, *The Montgomery Bus Boycott and the Women Who Started It*, Women's Political Council founder Jo Ann Robinson described the evolution of the activist infrastructure in Montgomery in terms that largely excluded King and his fellow clergymen.[24]

In his first sermon at Dexter, "Loving Your Enemies," King told the congregation, "There is a power in love that our world has not discovered yet." The unintended irony peculiar to any young preacher is that of bespeaking a truth that must be learned in experience. Love's power in the world is a truth that most often evades the lecture halls and graduate seminars.

During his studies at Boston University, King had organized a monthly gathering of black seminarians that met in his apartment on Massachusetts Avenue under the banner of the Dialectical Society. The society took its name from classical Greek metaphysical inquiry, but the participants were also familiar with the radical theological movement called dialectical theology, inspired by Karl Barth and Emil Brunner and currently fashionable, if not simply controversial, in the American academy. Dialectical theology represented a protest against nineteenth-century Protestant liberalism, its naïve confidence in human potential and its equivocations on original sin. Yet while Barth had ministered to the miners and industrial workers in his working-class parish in Switzerland, the discussions among King and his fellow theology students rarely strayed beyond current trends in philosophical and systematic theology. When social and political matters were addressed, they were shrouded in the garments of academic debate, loathe to their activist applications. (Indeed several black members lost interest in the Society when they discovered how little race and politics were taken seriously.[25]) King's grad-student ruminations on justice drifted toward fashionable criticisms of American capitalism, denunciations of the "the unequal distribution of wealth," and the unfairness of a system in which "a small percentage of the population could control all of the wealth."[26]

Yet King distinguished himself at Boston University not by a passion for social justice but by his silken manners and aspirations for academic respectability. "He was always very quiet, cooperative, gentlemanly, always very thoughtful of the other fellow," one of his advisors remarked.[27] Nice words, though they harbinger not a hint of the coming storm. Social engagement for King still meant driving a new green Chevrolet on a Saturday night and dating attractive women from local colleges. He had not yet heard the call that would change his life.

When the Kings moved to Montgomery, the population of the capital city was 120,000. Montgomery was racially segregated in the typical southern fashion, with blacks and whites inhabiting separate neighborhoods, schools, and churches, and the daily monuments of Jim Crow everywhere visible—separate drinking fountains, restaurants, ambulances, taxis, cemeteries, parks, and seating sections on city buses. Not a single black person sat on any municipal board or commission. Forty percent of the population was African American.

Dexter Avenue's middle class parishioners were clearly an exception to black Montgomery's more familiar social patterns. Most African Americans, especially those who had migrated to the city from the rural black belt, worked service jobs as unskilled or day laborers, or took menial positions on one of the military bases. Unlike the industrial hubs of Birmingham and Gadsden or the port of Mobile, the Alabama capital city was short on good opportunities and long on dead-end jobs and humiliating wages. The annual income for a black family in Montgomery was $908, dramatically lower than Birmingham's $1,609 or Gadsden's $1,480. The coastal city of Mobile and its annual black family income of $1,173 mirrored the gap between unionized industrial cites and nonunionized maritime labor. In Montgomery, the disproportionately high number of service-oriented jobs helped create a social environment in which insulting personal exchanges between white employers and black employees were part of the daily grind, making conditions ripe for protest.[28]

Still, Montgomery showed some signs of racial progress unfamiliar in most of the Deep South. Two weeks after the *Brown vs. Board* decision of May 17, 1954, Montgomery's professional baseball team drafted three Negro players, and the city made plans to hire its first black police officers.[29] A man widely regarded as a racial liberal was elected as one of the three city commissioners and launched a campaign against the "ringmasters" at city hall, accusing white officials of giving tax breaks to the rich and ignoring the plight of the city's poor.[30] Across the piazza from Dexter Avenue Baptist, "Big Jim" Folsom had taken office as the new governor of Alabama. Folsom would soon be known as one of the South's most colorful progressives, the six-foot-eight "friend of the little man." When the state legislature tried to implement a voucher system that would have crippled public schools and further eroded educational funding for Negroes, Folsom defiantly blocked the bill. "I never did get all excited about our colored brothers," he explained. "We have had them here for three-hundred years and we will have them for another three-hundred years. I have found them to be good citizens and if they had been making a living for me like they have for the Black Belt, I'd be proud of them instead of kicking them and cursing them all the time."[31]

Like most good Baptist preachers, King understood that ministerial success depended on polish in the pulpit and people in the pews. In addition to keeping track of the ambitious slate of new programs, as well as completing his doctoral dissertation and going about the business of the church, King preached forty-six sermons his first year at Dexter, seven guest sermons at other churches, and thirteen sermons and lectures at various colleges around the country. He quickly earned a reputation for homiletical refinement and panache. His father, observing his son's spreading fame—and having been provoked by a colleague who told Daddy that young Martin "could preach rings around you any day you ascend the pulpit"—warned his son that too much popularity at an early age was a dangerous combination. "Persons like yourself are the ones the devil turns all of his forces aloose to destroy."[32] But King's typical response to his father's frequent and bombastic intrusions was to placate him with an obsequious nod and then to proceed with his own plans.[33]

King spent his first year in Montgomery proving to the membership that he deserved their trust. He had been given an earful about the embarrassment and vexations that his predecessor, Vernon Johns, had heaped upon the congregation. Johns confronted the tweedy Dexter parishioners with their distrust of emotion and enthusiasm; and, in a manner sometimes feckless and manic, he challenged and often mocked their complacency on race relations and their aspirations to middle-class respectability. His high-pitched yelps and hollers were meant as a not-so-gentle reminder that most black Baptists in the South intoned a different spiritual scale than the stodgy Dexter crowd. "If you ever see a good fight, get into it" was his motto, learned from his mother.[34]

A summa cum laude graduate of Oberlin College and a classics scholar, the Virginia-born Johns was a man fully at home with his intellectual powers, and as a result, constitutionally impatient with pretense. Near the end of his stormy tenure, he told the congregation one Sunday of having recently taken a seat in the white section of a city bus and ignoring the driver's orders to move. When the driver finally shouted, "Nigger, didn't you hear me tell you to get the hell out of that seat?" Johns shocked the white man—and the Negro congregation—by replying, "And didn't you hear me tell you that I'm going to sit right goddamned here?" Johns's story was a veritable minefield of cultural transgressions: he disregarded segregation laws, talked disrespectfully to a white man, and took the Lord's name in vain. After the Klan killed a black man in a rural assault, Johns advertised the title of his upcoming sermon on a banner draped across the front of the church: "It's Safe to Murder Negroes in Alabama."[35] Johns quit his position five times in frustration, swearing never to return, and he came back four times at the request of the deacons. But when he quit in anger the fifth time, the congregation let him go. Most parishioners had had enough of the Latin-quoting preacher whose pajamas sometimes stuck out of his Sunday suit, who dug up the well-manicured lawn of the Dexter parsonage for a vegetable garden and then sold the vegetables on the front steps of the sanctuary like a field hand, and who had mocked middle-class black pretenses throughout his cantankerous year-and-a-half tenure. The Dexter Avenue leadership sought a minister who would stick to building budgets, saving souls, and preaching the Gospel in a manner appropriate to the congregation's tastes.

Suffice it to say, King's entrance into the civil rights movement lacked the existential intensity that would become almost formulaic a decade later. His congregational letter of October 27, 1955, less than six weeks away from the start of the bus boycott, is a testament of discretion. "We solicit your cooperation and prayers that our work for Kingdom building will reach new heights in the 1955–56 church year," King wrote. He might have been any southern Baptist preacher working the crowd with affecting platitudes—not a word about the kind of Kingdom building that involved social protest. Asking the members for "prayerful consideration" of the pledge card while reminding them of the Dexter heritage, his letter struck a familiar chord for Baptist ministers of his generation. He said, "As we have worked so nobly in the past for this great church which is so near and dear to our hearts, and whose efforts God has so richly crowned with success, so let us work in the future; let each of us go out at this moment with grim and bold determination to extend the horizons of Dexter to new boundaries, and lift the spire of her influence to new heights, so that we will be able to inject new spiritual blood into the veins of this community, transforming its jangling discords into meaningful symphonies of spiritual harmony." Translated, the message reads: Don't rock the boat. King's entrance into civil rights life happened so quickly that he didn't have time to think it through. He later recalled, "It is probable that if I had, I would have declined the nominations."[36]

On December 1, 1955, Rosa Parks was arrested for violating Alabama segregation laws when she refused to move to the rear of the bus and yield her seat in the front to a white man. Parks had been preparing most of her life for this day. Along with a handful of local dissidents—which included Jo Ann Robinson, as well as E. D. Nixon, a former president and cofounder of the Alabama NAACP and cofounder of the Brotherhood of Sleeping Car Porters and Maids, and the white liberal lawyer, Clifford Durr and his wife Virginia—Parks had monitored the bus situation for years, waiting for the right moment to seize as a test case. Three months earlier, she had attended interracial workshops on democracy at the Highlander Folk School, the training center for social reformers nestled in the mountains of eastern Tennessee, and visited with legendary organizers Septima Clark and Myles Horton.[37] Parks's arrest in December 1955 was not even her first. According to historian Aldon Morris, the same driver who kicked Parks off the bus in 1955 also forced her to leave in 1944, when she had also been arrested.[38]

Not to be forgotten is that, six months before the bus boycott, a fifteen-year-old high school student named Claudette Colvin refused to surrender her seat to a white passenger as required by law. Police officers charged Colvin with failure to obey local segregation laws and with assault and battery—she had swung her arms and kicked her legs as she was forcibly removed from the bus. Following Colvin's arrest, Parks and her colleagues moved quickly toward plans for a boycott, thinking the test case had finally arrived. But when organizers learned that the teenage girl was pregnant, they postponed the protest until a better opportunity for all parties arose, sparing Colvin, and themselves, the inevitable embarrassment. The Montgomery dissidents would not have to wait long.

On the cold, overcast afternoon of December 1, Rosa Parks had worked an exhausting day tailoring garments at the Montgomery Fair department store. Christmas rush was in full swing, and Parks's workload was unusually heavy.

She was in no mood to stand in the crowded back aisle when there were empty seats in the white section. "I had been pushed as far as I could stand to be pushed," she said, "and decided that I would have to know once and for all what rights I had as a human being and a citizen."[39] In the days following Parks's arrest, the core group of Montgomery activists became convinced that their time had arrived. "*This is the case,*" E. D. Nixon exclaimed.[40]

On Sunday, December 4, 1955, an above-the-fold article on the front page of the *Montgomery Advertiser* read, "Negro Groups Ready Boycott of City Lines." The one-day boycott would be held the next day, on Monday, December 5, the article indicated.

In fact there was only one group, but the team built around the likes of Parks, Nixon, and Robinson packed a solid punch. Expecting that negotiations with city officials would follow the Monday boycott, the group of organizers put together a list of all the ministers who should be enlisted in the organization—ministers having the greater gifts of persuasion and negotiation, it was assumed. Phone calls were made to influential churches with some success. Ralph Abernathy, the exuberant pastor of the colored First Baptist Church, was especially interested in the plan. Martin Luther King however let it be known that he had more pressing matters before him. Aside from the dissertation, he felt pressed in by preparations for the church's annual planning conference, coming up in a couple of weeks. He was expected to present his congregation with a detailed program for the year ahead, complete with a schedule of events and a new budget.[41] King told Abernathy that organizers could use the meeting space on the bottom floor of the Dexter sanctuary. "The people will be gone from the capital by nightfall," King said, "and the whole square will be lit up. You can all gather in the basement."[42] But King turned down the nomination to serve as president of the Montgomery Improvement Association (as the boycott organization would be called) when it unexpectedly came his way during the session.

The result was that Abernathy took upon himself the task of recruiting the young preacher for the job, and he worked his friend hard. On the Monday of the boycott, in an afternoon meeting of eighteen pastors at the Mount Zion AME Church, King accepted the nomination. "If you think I can render some service, I will," he said. Still, King fully expected the boycott to be resolved quickly and without much difficulty.[43] "Negotiations between people of good will" will be resolved within a matter of days, he reasoned.[44]

That night, December 5, 1955, the newly elected president of the Montgomery Improvement Association gave his first public address at Holt

Street Baptist Church. Sitting in his office in hurried preparation of his remarks, King cobbled together notes from a variety of sources, which he hoped would offer some perspective on the moment at hand. The words of the Holt Street address are those of a minister who has had less than an hour alone in his study to put together the evening sermon. His address and the thunderous response from the congregation reveal a man awakening to a call. But it is not King's spiritual genius or existential resolve that pulls him into the movement that changed America, but the spirit of the people.

> *King*: The Almighty God himself is . . . not the God just standing out saying through Hosea, "I love you, Israel." He's also the God that stands up before the nations and said: "Be still and know that I'm God."
>
> *Congregation*: Yeah.
>
> *King*: "That if you don't obey me I will break the backbone of your power."
>
> *Congregation*: Yeah.
>
> *King*: "And slap you out of the orbits of your international and national relationships."
>
> *Congregation*: That's right. . . .
>
> *King*: If we are wrong, God almighty is wrong.
>
> *Congregation*: That's right. [Applause]
>
> *King*: If we are wrong, Jesus of Nazareth was merely a utopian dreamer that never came down to earth.
>
> *Congregation*: Yes. [Applause]
>
> *King*: If we are wrong, justice is a lie.
>
> *Congregation*: Yes.
>
> *King*: Love has no meaning. [Applause]
>
> *King*: And we are determined here in Montgomery to work and fight until justice runs down like water.
>
> *Congregation*: Yes. [Applause]
>
> *King*: And righteousness like a mighty stream.
>
> *Congregation*: Keep talking. [Applause][45]

In the Holt Street address, a basic theological conviction comes to light, which in turn illuminates King's perception of these awakening days of the struggle: "We are guiding and channeling our emotions to the extent that we feel that God shall give us the victory."[46] The beautiful chaos that America would see daily on the streets of Montgomery—the tens of thousands of African Americans walking beneath a winter sky, the empty buses rolling through the capital city, the mass meetings overflowing the black churches—bear evidence of God's presence and promise. In passages that evoke a host of powerful biblical images—the disinherited of the land, the long night of captivity, the glimmering promise of deliverance, each image as alive with meaning for the sufferings and hopes of African Americans as it had been for Israel in the long years of exile—King describes the moment as the beginning of a larger and complicated theological drama.[47]

King made many inspiring remarks in his talk. "Standing up to the truth of God is the greatest thing in the world," the veritable "end of life." Jesus was not merely a utopian dreamer but the incarnate truth of God enabling the church and its people "to work and fight" and to "keep talking." "We, the disinherited of this land," King continued, "we who have been oppressed so long, are tired of going through the long night of captivity." But it is the congregation that gave these words their power; the congregation that sang, "Onward Christian soldiers, marching as to war, with the cross of Jesus, going on before"; and "What a fellowship, what a joy divine; what a blessedness, what a peace is mine, leaning on the everlasting arms"; and the sweet song of beloved fellowship, "Blest be the tie that binds, our hearts in Christian love, our fears, our hopes, our aims are one, our comforts and our cares." It is the congregation that amens the words of the thirty-fourth Psalm, read melodiously by Pastor Uriah Fields of the Bell Street Baptist Church: "The righteous cry, and the Lord heareth, and delivereth them out of all their troubles." The singing, worshipping, and amening church seems more eager to move into action than the young preacher with his unfinished dissertation and his ambitious plans for the church budget.[48]

King concluded his remarks with a gentle admonition, "Now let us go out to stick together and stay with this thing until the end," and he then stepped down from the pulpit and walked slowly through the sanctuary and out the front doors, many people reaching out their hands to touch him as he passed.[49] "It was like a revival meeting. The church was so full, there were so many people," recalled one participant, "and King prayed so that night, I'm telling you the goddam truth, you had to hold people to keep them from gettin' to him."[50] No doubt, the Montgomery protest grew out of a particular tradition of activism and organizing. The seeds of dissent had been planted by faithful laborers throughout the years of preparation. Yet the people gathering strong at Holt Street got a glimpse of a new world ahead, and it felt like a divine gift.[51] The Holt Street address of December 5, 1955, marks but the beginning of a theological education at once chastened and empowered by the living church.

To call King's initial demands forceful is an overstatement. Even to call them demands is a stretch. In his public letter of December 8, 1955, to the national office of the National City Buslines in Chicago, King called for fair access to public accommodations and proposed three changes:

1. Courteous treatment by bus drivers.
2. Seating of Negro passengers from rear to front of bus, and white passengers from front to rear on first-come-first-serve basis with no seats reserved for any race.
3. Employment of Negro bus operators in predominantly Negro residential sections.[52]

King shocked both blacks and whites when he noted that these requests were not intended to challenge state segregation laws but were consistent with these segregation laws. No one apparently had asked King about his intentions. In his mind, the boycott was about minor adjustments in seating policies for Negroes using city buses—policies that made little difference to Dexter Avenue members anyway since they mostly traversed city streets in their own automobiles. Contesting segregation was a separate matter "for the legislature and the courts," King said.[53] "All we are seeking is justice and fair treatment in riding the buses."[54]

Not surprisingly, the core group of activists considered King's modest proposal a slap in the face of their own steady assault on Jim Crow. For its part, the national NAACP voiced concern that the Montgomery organizers—as represented by King—were settling for something far short of integration. What was the purpose of Parks's act of civil disobedience if not to defy segregation laws?

But, King refused to go any farther. To the Baptist preacher with the downtown parish, segregation seemed too entrenched a tradition to call into question.[55] The gradualism King would lament in his 1963 "Letter from the Birmingham City Jail" was the gradualism he embraced in the first days of the Montgomery protest.

King's position was appreciated by many white residents, even though the appreciation hardly turned sentiment into shifts in public policy. The editors of the *Montgomery Advertiser* expressed sympathy for King's proposal, especially since black ridership had dropped 75 percent in the few days following the December 5 boycott. "If the grievance is confined to that, then attention should be given to it promptly."[56] Letters to the editors were overwhelmingly sympathetic to the black cause as rendered by King's requests. A white man writing from the hamlet of Geraldine praised King's "plausible and sensible plan"; after all, he added, the Negro would "continue to accept and occupy the seats in the rear of the bus," aside from the stated exceptions.[57] A white woman wrote, "I have yet to find one person who feels that it is right that a Negro be made to stand that a white person may sit."[58] One reader said that she was a regular on city buses and it made her sick to see the discourteous treatment often shown to Negro riders. "In a city where so many Christian churches flourish and where one constantly hears that the right way of life for the South is to be found in the 'separate but equal' doctrine, I find it difficult to understand how so many people can knowingly condone the injustices of the present system, which I know from experience is not equal even in courtesy."[59] A few whites went even further than King by calling the whole framework of southern segregation into question.[60]

Then there was the heartbreaking case of Juliette Morgan, a white librarian and member of a prominent family in Montgomery society, whose dissent led to tragic consequences. In a letter to the editor on December 12, Morgan wrote, "It is hard to imagine a soul so dead, a heart so hard, a vision so blinded and provincial as not to be moved with admiration at the quiet dignity, discipline and dedication with which the Negroes have conducted their boycott." She expressed profound sadness for the white Montgomerians who met King's requests with a pharisaical zeal and with an attitude of "Ye rebels! Disperse!" The Negroes of Montgomery, Morgan said, "have filled me with great sympathy, pride, humility and envy." Their "willingness to suffer for great Christian and democratic principles should inspire deep admiration among decent whites." She continued, "Instead of acting like sullen adolescents whose attitude is 'Make me,' we ought to be working out plans to span the gap between segregation and integration to extend public services—schools, libraries, parks—and transportation to Negro citizens."[61] The next year, after frequent harassment, Juliette Morgan lost her job, fell into despair, and committed suicide.[62]

King's strategy of moderation was not greeted with the same enthusiasm by white city officials. Police Commissioner Clyde Sellers promptly announced that bus service would be cancelled in most Negro districts at 6:00 P.M. on December 9. Sellers promised to enforce the city's boycott ordinances—once he had a chance to dust them off—and to arrest black cab drivers if they failed to require the minimum rate of forty-five cents. Many black cabbies had agreed to offer free or cheap rides to the protesters.

As the boycott slowly unfolded, King began to glimpse a longer road ahead and to reckon, publicly and privately, with the greater demands of the enlarging protest. King would not be able to get back to his church plans by the end of the week as hoped, and his dissertation would consist largely in unoriginal, cribbed, and plagiarized material. "No end to the racial boycott of Montgomery City Lines was in sight yesterday as it entered its seventh day," the *Montgomery Advertiser* announced on December 13.[63] Each step forward, however unforeseen or hesitant, brought him closer to a sober acceptance of an uncertain and tumultuous future. King announced that day that the boycott could last a year.

In the Holt Street address, the congregation had heard King speak of his confidence in the teachings of Jesus applied to the social order, but also of his appeal to the "weapon of protest," the "tools of persuasion," the "tools of coercion." They heard in the sermon a certain kind of restraint and feeling around for a theological anchor. King had come to Montgomery convinced that the theologian Reinhold Niebuhr offered the most compelling account of an ethics of dissent. Niebuhr's analysis of the social situation is "profound indeed," King had said, "and with it I would find very little to disagree."[64] Niebuhr, the most influential Protestant theologian in mid-century America, had argued that coercion was a practical necessity in view of the collective selfishness of groups. "Equality is a higher social goal than peace," he had written in his landmark 1932 book, *Moral Man in Immoral Society*. Niebuhr would not recommend violent measures to the social reformers and activists who looked to him for counsel primarily; for violence was strategically nonsensical in the case of a minority population lacking political power. Still, he was to quick to emphasize that "a war for the emancipation of a nation, a race or a class" belongs in a "different moral category" than the use of force for the perpetuation of class domination or imperial rule.[65] Once in a blue moon, love might inspire a bigot to change his life, but most of the time love lacked the potency to transform oppressive systems of power. Had African slaves softened the hearts of their oppressors by their loyalty and "pure obedience"? No, one cannot live in history without sinning, and sometimes, one has to sin boldly. As King put it, "Since man is sinful, there must be some coercion to keep one man from injuring his fellows."[66] Niebuhr was right to insist that Christians face social existence with maximum realism and acknowledge the harsh and undeniable realities of human sin, the transactions of aggression and power, self-interest, and pride.

In the early days of the bus boycott, King continued to keep a loaded gun in his home. Glenn Smiley, a white minister from Texas with the Quaker Fellowship of Reconciliation, may have been exaggerating when he claimed to have discovered "an arsenal" in the parsonage during his visit; but King was no pacifist when he arrived in Montgomery.[67] "When I was in graduate school," he later explained, "I thought the only way we could solve our problem . . . was an armed revolt."[68] But as the boycott stretched into the year 1956, King's basic convictions about his life and work were beginning to change. He was also on the eve of a momentous personal experience, an experience reminiscent of his namesake, Martin Luther, whose mystical encounter with St. Anne on the stormy road to Erfurt crystallized the Protestant reformer's vision and strengthened his resolve, and King would soon drop the language of coercion. By the time a Chicago professor by the name of John Gibbs St. Clair Drake praised King's "prophetic . . . fight for justice with *weapons of the Spirit*" in a letter of March 21, 1956, his theological journey to nonviolence was well underway.[69]

By the end of January 1956, the boycott appeared to be floundering. White city leaders had been working hard to crack the movement's fragile unity. One scheme to undermine the black protest centered on the city official's fraudulent announcement that three black ministers representing the MIA had reached a settlement. The *Montgomery Advertiser* lent its support to the hoax, reporting in a front-page story in the Sunday edition that "prominent Negro ministers" had called an end to the boycott and that Negroes would resume city service the next morning. City officials hoped to create mass confusion in the black churches just as the worship day was commencing.[70]

The hoax would have very likely proved successful had not the tenacious journalist Carl Rowan read the article coming across the wire. The first of Rowan's articles on the boycott, "Dixie Divided," was scheduled to appear in the *Minneapolis Tribune* the next morning, and his editor had called to give him a heads up and to ask whether the piece should be killed to allow for revisions.[71] Rowan had just returned to Minneapolis from an assignment in the South and the Associated Press story didn't square with his research. The article claimed that no commitments to hire black drivers, no change in the whites-in-the-front, blacks-in-the-back policy were included in the settlement. "That sounds phony to me," Rowan said. The MIA's request may have been modest, but it was not frivolous.

Rowan called King in Montgomery. Alerted to the report, King immediately placed disclaimers into MIA's network of community leaders and church people. Since it was still Saturday night, and not all of the black population was home preparing their hearts and minds for the Lord's day, King got in his car and personally canvassed the town's taverns, juke joints, poolrooms, and nightclubs to dispel the rumor.[72] As the MIA's disclaimer spread through the neighborhoods, King pondered the identity of the "prominent Negro ministers." The only information Carl Rowan could get from the mayor was the minister's denominational affiliations—Baptist, Presbyterian, and Holiness. At least this gave King the certainty that the men were not MIA members: There were no "prominent" Holiness preachers in Montgomery.[73]

When King finally located the men in question—Benjamin F. Mosely, William K. Kind, and D. C. Rice—and listened to their accounts, he knew for certain that they had been hoodwinked by city officials. Kind told King that he had been invited to the mayor's office to talk about a group insurance policy for the city and was only then presented with the settlement document—and that too without explanation.[74] Mosely and Rice offered similar accounts of the report. The most compelling evidence of the three ministers' credibility (as King and other MIA leaders discussed the matter among themselves) was their willingness to dispute the official report and "challenge the veracity of the city fathers."[75] On Sunday afternoon, King issued a statement accepting the ministers' public explanations and affirming the MIA's determination to continue the boycotts "until our proposals [are] given sympathetic treatment."[76] King and his colleagues had managed to defuse the rumors of a boycott settlement and, as a result, the boycott continued Monday morning in full force as empty buses rolled once again through the streets.[77]

Nevertheless, Mayor Gayle and his colleagues were hardly feeling chastened. William "Tacky" Gayle, who had always kept his office open to Negroes in the years before the boycott, now announced that all negotiations with black organizers would be terminated for as long as the protest remained active. "We have pussyfooted around on this boycott long enough," he told reporters.[78] Calling the MIA "a group of Negro radicals," Gayle dismissed the boycott as a strategic and moral failure that had done nothing to unloose white Montgomerians' hold on segregation. "It is not important to whites that the Negroes ride the buses," he said bluntly.[79]

Gayle now intended to pursue a more forceful means to defeat the boycotters. He told white housewives that they should stop driving their maids home after work and supplying them with spare change for fares, no more "blackmail transportation money." More than half of all employed African American women worked as domestics in white homes.[80] But Gayle was not worried in the least about the prospects of unwashed dishes, unwaxed floors, and unburnished furniture. As he saw it, the maids and cooks of Montgomery were "fighting to destroy our social fabric just as much as the Negro radicals who are leading them," and the white ladies were selfishly putting their own needs over the southern way of life.[81]

To enforce his new resolve, Gayle announced that he was joining the Citizens' Council, the white supremacy organization formed in Mississippi two months after *Brown vs. Board* to protect southern segregation. "What [the Negroes] are after is the destruction of our social fabric," he explained.[82] Gayle took comfort in the familiar complaint among white Montgomerians that Negro organizers were beating the Citizens' Councilors at their own game, using "economic warfare as a matter of enlightened self-interest." It was time for all concerned white people to take stock of the situation and organize in massive resistance to black demands. "I wouldn't trade my southern birthright for a hundred Negro votes," he said.[83] Even so, membership in the Citizens' Council seemed but a reasonable gesture toward balancing the scales of powers, evidence that white acquiescence in the face of racial aggressions could not be tolerated. Whites had best put aside their pre–1954 gestures of biracial munificence and patrician equanimity and face the facts of the new day.

Police commissioner Sellers—already a Councilor himself—was dispatched into action in accordance with the mayor's plan, ordering officers to disperse Negroes who waited on street corners for cabs. Police officers were especially encouraged to crack down on cab drivers and boycott organizers. Enforcement also took the form of tailgating and dispensing traffic tickets for trivial or trumped-up offenses.[84] Police officers questioned cabbies about their automobiles, their financial records, their insurance policies, their unpaid bills, and their personal lives. Citations and arrests were issued for loud talking, walking on lawns, and congregating in white neighborhoods (as in the case of maids waiting for cabs on street corners).

The major's resolve proved successful. Fault lines began appearing in the voluntary transportation system, which had worked so well since the beginning of the protest, providing 15,000–20,000 rides each day.[85] Black drivers grew agitated, and many decided they were tired of losing money. "The voluntary pick-up system began to weaken," said one MIA member, and "for a moment the protest movement seemed to be wavering."[86] In response to housewives who ignored Mayor Gayle's warning, an unsigned memorandum appeared in the mail box of white Montgomerians, grave evidence of the vanishing line between law and terror: "Dear friend, listed below are a few of the white people who are still hauling their Negro maids. This must be stopped. These people would appreciate a call from you, day or night. Let's let them know how we feel about them hauling Negroes."[87]

The *Montgomery Advertiser*, which had been a voice of moderation in the years before the boycott, cast its support soundly behind Gayle's zero-tolerance policy. The Negro protest was destined for failure, the editors promised. The white man's "economic artillery is far superior, better emplaced, and commanded by more experienced gunners," and whites hold all government offices and will continue to do so. "There will be white rule as far as the eye can see," the editorial read. "Are those not the facts of life?"[88] The

Advertiser seemed now convinced that any change in the existing seating arrangements on city buses would open up a Pandora's box of racial chaos. The *Montgomery Advertiser* did not need to remind whites about their superiority in real firepower. For those people who continued hauling their Negro maids to work, a little old-fashioned artillery would suffice as fair warning, and indeed word spread that the Ku Klux Klan was studying the situation and preparing to march on the city. The time had come for a greater show of force.

The pressures of the recent arrests, city crackdowns, and mounting fears had started taking their toll. In an organizational meeting on January 23, a despondent King offered his resignation as MIA president. None of the other MIA board members seriously considered accepting the resignation, but King's self-doubts had been registered loud and clear. He even planned to publish an advertisement in the *Montgomery Advertiser* reminding townspeople that the boycott was not seeking to challenge segregation laws. The protest was approaching its third month with no end in sight.

The season of police harassments reached a dramatic climax on Thursday, January 26, when King was stopped by two police officers on motorcycles after having chauffeured several Negro workers to their drop-off spot. In a confusing roadside arrest, King was charged with driving thirty miles an hour in a twenty-five-mile-per-hour zone and placed into a police cruiser, which had presently arrived on the scene. As King sat alone in the back seat, he quickly realized that the police car was moving in the opposite direction of downtown. The car then turned into an unfamiliar street, and through a wooded area and over an unfamiliar bridge, and King's hands began to shake. "These men were carrying me to some faraway spot to dump me off," he thought. "Silently, I asked God to give me the strength to endure whatever came."[89]

The neon sign that appeared on a building in full view of the car indicating their arrival at the Montgomery City jail must have seemed an unlikely answer to prayer, though appreciated in its own way. Inside, King was fingerprinted and locked into a crowded holding cell. "Strange gusts of emotion swept through me like cold winds on an open prairie," he recalled.[90] As he slowly adjusted to the shock of the new surroundings, he found himself the center of attention. A crowd of black inmates gathered excitedly around him, and King was surprised to find two acquaintances, who offered their hearty greetings, locked up with the rest of them. King spent the evening listening to stories of thieves and drunks and drifters, and in exchange he gave the men a vivid account of his afternoon. Several asked if King could help get them out of jail. "Fellows, before I can assist in getting any of you out," he said, "I've got to get my own self out," and the cell was filled with laughter.[91]

King had crossed the first threshold of fear and there discovered that presence of mind could still be summoned. In the spirited company of these unlikely allies—movement people, "vagrants," and "serious criminals"—he realized that even jail could be endured for the sake of doing the right thing. "From that night on, my commitment to the struggle for freedom was stronger than ever before," he said. "Yes, the night of injustice was dark; the 'get-tough' policy was taking its toll. But in the darkness I could see a radiant star of unity."[92]

King's release later the same night no doubt made the radiant star even easier to behold. Dozens of church members and friends in the protest had steadily gathered in the parking lot throughout the evening and waited for their pastor.

But whatever momentary relief King felt was gone the next evening when he returned to his parsonage, exhausted after another long day of organizational meetings. Coretta and their two-month old daughter, Yolanda, were already asleep, and King was eager to join them. He would not be so lucky. The phone rang out in the midnight silence, and when King lifted the receiver, a drawl released a torrent of obscene words and then the death threat: "Listen, nigger, we've taken all we want from you; before next week you'll be sorry you ever came to Montgomery."[93] King hung up without comment, as had become his custom. Threatening phone calls had become a daily routine in the weeks of the protests, and King had tried to brush them off at first. In recent days, however, the threatening phone calls had started to take a toll, increasing in number to thirty or forty a day and growing in their menacing intent.[94]

Unwelcome thoughts prey on the mind in the late hours, and King was overcome with fear. "I got out of bed and began to walk the floor. I had heard these things before, but for some reason that night it got to me.[95] Stirred into wakefulness, King made a pot of coffee and sat down at the kitchen table. "I felt myself faltering," he said.[96] It was as though the violent undercurrents of the protest rushed in upon him with heightened force, and he surveyed the turbulent waters for a way of escape, searching for an exit point between courage and convenience—"a way to move out of the picture without appearing a coward"—and he found none.[97] "I was ready to give up," he said.[98]

King thought of baby Yoki sleeping in her crib, of her "little gentle smile," and of Coretta, who had sacrificed her music career, according to the milieu of the Baptist pastor's wife, to follow her husband south. For the first time, he grasped the seriousness of his situation and with it the inescapable fact that his family could be taken away from him any minute, or more likely he from them.[99] He felt himself reeling within, as the Psalmist had said, his soul "melted because of trouble, at wit's end."[100] "I felt myself . . . growing in fear," said King.[101]

Sitting at his kitchen table sipping the coffee, King's thoughts were interrupted by a sudden notion that at once intensified his desperation and clarified his options. "Something said to me, 'You can't call on Daddy now, you can't call on Mama. You've got to call on that something in that person that your daddy used to tell you about, that power that can make a way out of no way.'"[102] With his head now buried in his hands, King bowed over the kitchen table and prayed aloud. He said:

> Lord, I'm down here trying to do what's right. I still think I'm right. I am here taking a stand for what I believe is right. But Lord, I must confess that I'm weak now, I'm faltering. I'm losing my courage. Now, I am afraid. And I can't let the people see me like this because if they see me weak and losing my courage, they will begin to get weak. The people are looking to me for leadership, and if I stand before them without strength and courage, they too will falter. I am at the end of my powers. I have nothing left. I've come to the point where I can't face it alone.[103]

As he prayed alone in the silent kitchen, King heard a voice saying, "Martin Luther, stand up for righteousness. Stand up for justice. Stand up for truth. And lo, I will be with you. Even until the end of the world."[104] Then King heard the voice of Jesus. "I heard the voice of Jesus saying still to fight on. He promised never to leave me, never to leave me alone. No never alone. No never alone. He promised never to leave me, never to leave me alone." And as the voice washed over the stains of the wretched caller, King reached a spiritual shore beyond fear and apprehension. "I experienced the presence of the Divine as I had never experienced Him before," he said. "Almost at once my fears began to go," King said of the midnight flash of illumination and resolve. "My uncertainty disappeared. I was ready to face anything."[105]

Five years earlier, in the fall of 1950, in his Crozer seminary class "The Religious Development of Personality," King had written an autobiographical essay on his own religious formation. The paper is distinguished not only by its intellectual posturing, the sort you might expect of a brilliant young graduate student, but by its complete lack of moral and spiritual intensity. King described his "early environment" as "very congenial," in which he was always able to think of God as a benevolent being presiding over a friendly universe.[106] "Conversion for me was never an abrupt something," King wrote. "I have never experienced the so-called 'crisis moment.' Religion has just been something that I grew up in." Conversion he regarded as the "gradual intaking" of the noble ideals promoted by his family and his environment, an intaking which had been for him "largely unconscious." He described his call to the ministry as an "inner urge to serve humanity." King did recall one disturbing incident in his childhood when a white playmate, whose father owned a store in the neighborhood, told King they could not play together any longer. But King reassured his professor that any "anti White feeling" the incident provoked had long been resolved as a result of his own college involvement in interracial organizations and of his positive frame of mind.[107]

King aimed to please his white professors at Crozer, boasting even of his early hermeneutical suspicion toward the Sunday school lessons of the Baptist church. "I guess I accepted the Biblical studies uncritically until I was about twelve years old," he wrote. "But this uncritical attitude could not last long, for it was contrary to the very nature of my being. . . . [I] came to see that behind the legends and myths of the Book were many profound truths, which one could not escape."[108] George Washington Davis, the philosophical theologian who had assigned the paper, scribbled in the margins, "Correct!" "Right!" "Good!" and remarked of King's boyhood doubts, "This is early." All in all, King's paper exudes the sort of self-sufficient finitude that the theologian Paul Tillich once derided in the overly confident piety of nineteenth-century bourgeois Protestantism. "On coming to the seminary," King writes, "I found it quite easy to fall in line with the liberal tradition I found there, mainly because I had been prepared for it before coming. At present I still feel the affects of the noble moral and ethical ideals that I grew up under."[109]

In his Montgomery kitchen in January 1956, King experienced the crisis moment, and it burned away pretension even as it fortified courage. Faced with the possibility of death, he could not turn to Daddy for consolation (besides, Daddy, who thinks he knows best, wants his son out of Montgomery at the earliest opportunity). And faced with the intransigence of white resistance, liberal platitudes failed him; notions of essential human goodness and perfectibility were not what the moment required. To be sure, the kitchen experience was part of a theological pilgrimage underway since early childhood, and it should not be cast as the all-determining moment in King's civil rights life. Nevertheless, as every Baptist girl and boy knows, such single transformative events matter, as when the individual soul reckons with the question of salvation. "That experience gave King a new strength and resolve," writes historian David Garrow. "He went back to bed no longer worried about the threats of bombing. The next morning he went down to the Montgomery courthouse and was convicted of the Thursday speeding charge."[110] Such a claim as Garrow's is altogether consistent with King's abiding habitation in the black church.

In the black church tradition in the South, preaching does not always require the benefits of formal theological education, and thus a distinction is often made between preachers who are "schooled" and those who are "called."[111] (The same is sometimes true in the white evangelical tradition.) A man might be dirt-poor, and he might be illiterate, but if God has called him to preach, which means that he senses in his heart this compulsion and conviction, then his pastoral vocation is secured: God's call is sufficient. Many black ministers "based their right to interpret the earthly and heavenly affairs of humanity on having been 'called' rather than schooled," explains historian Aldon D. Morris in his book, *The Origins of the Civil Rights Movement: Black Communities Organizing for Change*. Martin Luther King had been schooled at Morehouse, Crozer, and Boston, and that privilege gave him a pedigree and put him in a class of ministers in every conventional way superior to the others. But in Montgomery, King was called, and the calling propelled him into the crisis that would shape his life and legacy.[112]

Here is another way of describing the call: The Baptist minister's son pursues a doctorate in philosophical theology as a means of settling a private conflict. In the child's spiritual formation, through repetition and duty, the language of the church has become tedious and uninspiring. "The lessons which I was taught in Sunday school were quite in the fundamentalist line. None of my teachers ever doubted the infallibility of the Scriptures. Most of them were unlettered and had never heard of Biblical criticism."[113] And yet this disenchantment with the church bothers the son, because he knows the church's power, the way it can ignite feeling and imagination. He has felt the power, a raw but arousing energy moving him to praise and wonder. Though the son may be loathe to admit it now, he does not want to live his life without that power and the language it crafts. As he casts around for new sources of inspiration, graduate school holds out a promise. "I had been brought up in the church and knew about religion, but I wondered whether it could serve as a vehicle to modern thinking, whether religion could be intellectually respectable as well as emotionally satisfying."[114]

Then reality sets in. There is no fire in the lecture halls: in redaction and critique, in Yankee acquiescence to prudence and objectivity. The invocations of ultimacy are as cold as a city sidewalk. It is never entirely clear to the son of the preacher why the academic theologians talk in terms "practically un-known to us in our experience," as King said. Perhaps the theologians are working through some private drama of their own (so many of them are preachers' kids too), though in a different frame of reference, drawn from dif-ferent repositories of memory and feeling, Germanic, melancholy, austere. In time, under the greater influence of his heart and in response to an anxious world, the son turns the theologians over to their diversions as he discovers anew the God of his fathers, grandfathers, great-grandfathers. He puts aside "these little gods that are here today and gone tomorrow," for the God "who is the same yesterday, today and forever."[115] The "ground of being," "being-itself," "the source of human good" proved to be "conceptions of divinity un-worthy of worship," as historian Clayborne Carson writes in an essay on King's student years.[116] In the end, the son of the Baptist preacher, the grand-son of the Baptist preacher, and the great-grandson of the Baptist preacher needs much more than "a metaphysical category." He needs a "living reality," "a personal God"—a God who is "responsive to the deepest yearnings of the human heart," who "both evokes and answers prayer."[117] So the preacher's son takes from his doctoral studies a scholarly discourse, some potent metaphors and categories of thought, which he will sometimes stir into the tried-and-true language of the church to appreciative audiences. He develops as well an appreciation for diverse understandings of truth—of the self's social, psycho-logical, and historical formation—and he learns to interpret the world judi-ciously and with an open mind. While he will not have much time for reading books in the busy years ahead, his interpretive skills will serve him well as he traverses the rough terrain. Through it all, he becomes more generous of heart and head, and he relearns the church's language while also becoming more open to new possibilities of human experience. He understands that in the inner recesses of his heart he is, above all else, a minister of the Gospel.

In his biography of King, historian Taylor Branch attributes to King a kind of Jamesian apperception of the numinous, an excitement at the "habit-ual center of his personal energy." The moment lacked "the splendor of a vi-sion or a voice speaking out loud," even as it marked King's first "transcen-dent religious experience," inspiring him with the "limitless potential" to face his fears, "to think anything, and therefore to be anything." "He spoke the name of no deity," Branch writes, "but his doubts spilled out as a prayer."[118] Branch appreciates the power of the kitchen epiphany to strengthen resolve and courage, to remind King that "the essence of religion was not a grand metaphysical idea but something personal, grounded in ex-perience."[119] But, too eager to cast King as a man for all faiths, Branch ap-pears to miss King's grounding in the tradition of radical Christianity. King's kitchen epiphany is not the product of his interior genius, or the whispered hush of an unnamed Other. Jesus speaks intimately to the fearful pastor. The "quiet assurance of the inner voice" as well as the "voice of Jesus saying still to fight on" came to King as a gift, after the felt impoverishment of his own spiritual resources, in a kind of rededication of his faith.[120] King's experience in Montgomery—not just the single experience of the kitchen, but the kitchen as metaphor of the protest year—pressed upon him a sober counting of the costs of his Christian calling. As Marcus Garvey Wood, the pastor of the Providence Baptist Church in Baltimore, would say to his friend the next month, "You have thrown Crozer aside and you have found the real God and you can tell the world now that he is a God who moves in mysterious ways."[121] The God of William James is not the God worshiped at Dexter Avenue Baptist, not the God preached and professed by King.

Importantly, King's organizing strategies as head of the MIA become more confrontational. Three days after the kitchen visit, he authorized attorney, Fred Gray, to challenge segregation laws. "My uncertainty disappeared," King said, making clear that he supported "immediate integration" of the buses. "Segregation is evil, and I cannot, as a minister, condone evil."[122] King told reporters that his decision against calling segregation itself into question had been a mistake and needed to be reversed.

The same day, January 30, 1956, King addressed a standing-room only audience from the pulpit of the First Baptist Church when word reached him that his home had been bombed. King had been talking to the congregation about two recent developments in the boycott that he found distressing: the city's new get-tough policy and the discontent among certain members of the black community with the church-based leadership. He knew that some members of the black community had begun complaining about the slow pace of negotiations and were unhappy with the organizers' commitment to "the Christian Way," as the MIA had described its motivation in newspaper advertisements. The Christian Way was the "only way of reaching a satisfactory solution to the problem."[123]

In his sermon at First Baptist Church, King had offered a simple and eloquent rendering of the protesters' collective soul. "We are a chain," he said. "We are linked together, and I cannot be what I ought to unless you are what you ought to be."[124] He appealed to the beloved community, although not yet by name. His words echoed Jesus' sunset meditations in the Garden of Gethsemane, spoken on the eve of the crucifixion, his prayer for his disciples that the world would see the oneness of their love, "I in them, and thou in me, that they may be made perfect in one." The movement community, King told the audience, is linked with a force greater than moral resolve, strategic goals, or sentiment; the movement is an echo, a distant but truthful repetition, of the overflowing love of God. King encouraged the congregation to recommit themselves to nonviolence and to keep their trust in God.[125]

King received the news of the parsonage bombing like a man inwardly prepared for battle, surprising many in the congregation when they later learned the details from Ralph Abernathy. "My religious experience a few nights before had given me the strength to face it," King said.[126] By the time he arrived home, a crowd had already begun forming in the street and front yard. Memories of the size of the crowd vary greatly; some say hundreds, others thousands. But everyone recalls the anger and insult incited by police officers who pushed and threatened bystanders in an effort to clear the streets. As King made his way through the crowd to the house, he overheard one man saying, "I ain't gonna move nowhere. That's the trouble now; you white folks is always pushin' us around. Now you got your .38 and I got mine; so let's battle it out."[127]

King felt the undercurrents of rage that had run strong for years in the black community swelling into the immediate threat of violence. He felt the drifting of sentiment away from peaceful protest to militant conflict. The weeks of nonviolent protest seemed on the verge of turning suddenly violent.

Inside the house, with the front window shattered and a hole blasted into the porch, King was relieved to find Coretta and Yoki safe and in good spirits. Mayor Gayle, along with police commissioner Sellers, the fire chief, and newspaper reporters, had assembled in the dining room and were making official declarations of regret to anyone who would listen. Gayle offered promises to bring the perpetrators to justice.

Meanwhile, the crowd outside, still collecting newcomers from all corners of the neighborhood, continued to press forward against the police barricade. King knew he needed to address the people, and he walked onto the porch and called for order. He offered the reassurances that Coretta and Yoki were unharmed. Then he told the crowd from the damaged front porch, "Let's not become panicky. If you have weapons, take them home; if you do not have them, please do not seek to get them. We cannot solve this problem through retaliatory violence. We must meet violence with nonviolence. Remember the words of Jesus: 'He who lives by the sword will perish by the sword.' Remember that is what God said."[128]

"We must love our white brothers," King continued, "no matter what they do to us. We must make them know that we love them. Jesus still cries out in words that echo across the centuries: 'Love your enemies; bless them that curse you; pray for them that despitefully use you.' This is what we must live by. We must meet hate with love.

"Remember, if I am stopped, this movement will not stop, because God is with the movement. Go home with this glowing faith and this radiant assurance. Go home and sleep calm. Go home and don't worry. Be calm as I and my family are. We are not hurt, and remember that if anything happens to me, there will be others to take my place."

Jo Ann Robinson recalled that as King spoke a "respectful hush" settled over the crowd. Even the police grew still and listened to the pastor's words.[129] A scattering of gentle "Amen's," "God bless you's," and "We are with you all the way, Reverend's" created a new momentum. Tears rolled down the faces of many people in the crowd, as some hummed church songs. King's words and the congregation's response drew together the parsonage and the street and wrapped the expanse of the Montgomery night into a unifying evocation of peace.

Police Commissioner Sellers then took the porch and stated his regrets and good intentions. When some "bless you's" and "Amen's" slurred into "boos" and hisses, King finally interrupted Sellers and held up his hand for silence. "Remember what I just said. Let us hear the commissioner."

King knew all too well that the gathering could have turned into the "darkest night in Montgomery's history." But "something happened" to avert the disaster, King said. "The spirit of God was in our hearts, and a night that seemed destined to end in unleashed chaos came to a close in a majestic group demonstration of nonviolence."[130] Church happened, and the reluctant man who had been called to "stand up" for God's righteousness, justice, and truth saw the evidence of their rarely tested power.

African Americans around the South saw the evidence too. "Be assured," wrote Mrs. Pinkie Franklin from Birmingham in a letter the next day, "that day and night without ceasing I shall be praying for your safety and that of your family's. The Arm of God is everlastingly strong and Sufficient to keep you. . . There shall no harm come to you, and the Comforting Spirit of God shall guide you."[131] Pastor Wood from Baltimore addressed his young colleague as the "Lion King" and told him to keep on "preaching like mad," for God is sending his angels to camp around him.[132] Letters, cards, and telegrams with prayers and spiritual admonitions poured in from around the country.

King emerged from the Montgomery bombing with a single-minded theme, the transformative power of love. He began now to speak forthrightly of the "weapon of love," of "compassion and understanding for those who hate us," of "the truth of the real God".[133]

By the end of the boycott year, he would dispose of the gun. "I was much more afraid in Montgomery when I had a gun in my house," he said.[134] The gun was an emblem and an incubator of fear, and its removal, he believed, cleared a wider space for God's purposes in the world. There was also too much in the gun's machinery that obscured the basic require-ment of the disciple to go the distance for peace. If Christians cannot serve God and Mammon, as they are told by prophets and preachers, then how can they serve God and Mars?[135] Removing the gun did not remove King's fears or uncertainties about the future—and he was in the end a victim of gun violence—but it gave him a greater sense of freedom, forced him to reckon soberly with death and "to deal with it."[136] King emerged, out of the "cradle of the confederacy" and the gun-slinging South as one of his-tory's most eloquent proponents of nonviolence, and he delivered his prophetic message to whites and blacks alike.[137]

Importantly, King had come to Montgomery convinced that Reinhold Niebuhr was the most reliable theological guide in negotiating complex so-cial realities. King has often been called a Niebuhrian for his sober recog-nition of human sinfulness and the need to confront unjust institutions and structures with tough and effective organizing. King's Holt Street address, as we have seen, had commended the tools of coercion and sounded the notes of political realism. Yet the Niebuhrian resonances fade from King's speeches as the bus boycott unfolds, and for good reason. At the moment the black church in Montgomery began to put its faith to the test and con-test the unjust social order, Niebuhr admonished patience, and equivocated in his support of King and the Montgomery protest.[138]

By the year of the boycott, Niebuhr had become widely known in both religious and political circles as America's public theologian and as an in-tellectual architect of Cold War liberalism. He had been a leader in the Committee for Cultural Freedom, an organization established by the CIA to support anti-communist efforts in Europe, and he had helped organize the Americans for Democratic Action, which co-founder Arthur Schlesinger had described as "a group of pragmatic liberals opposed to all dogmatisms, conservative, socialist, or communist, and dedicated to piece-meal and gradual reform."[139] Niebuhr had even approved of the execution of Julius and Ethel Rosenberg, the Communist Party members who had been found guilty in 1953 of transmitting atomic military secrets to a So-viet spy.[140] As the bus boycott unfolded in Montgomery, Niebuhr was serv-ing as an advisor to Adlai Stevenson in the 1956 Democratic primary.[141]

He counseled Stevenson on civil rights and race and encouraged him to pursue a moderate course in response to the emerging black church struggle. Niebuhr advised Stevenson against federal support of desegregation on the grounds that it would "arrest the promising organic growths of racial amity" and fortify white southern resistance; it would also cost Stevenson the Dixiecrat vote.[142] Niebuhr even refused to endorse a letter to Eisenhower in support of the bus boycott, which King had drafted. Never mind that the agents of black dissent were seeking federal support of their courageous actions—even the most token gesture would have been appreciated and helpful.

When the Supreme Court handed down the *Brown vs. Board of Education* decision on May 17, 1954, making segregation illegal in public schools, Niebuhr had praised the Court for its "boldness and concern for the political realities" of the decision, but he had also expressed hope that the nation would give the white southerner some time to accept the decision in a rational manner. The "slow erosion of racial prejudice" was underway, Niebuhr explained (in a curious departure from his much-heralded realism), because there exists a "general tendency of increasing social intelligence to withdraw its support from the claims of social privilege" and to give it to the downtrodden and disinherited.[143] He might have shared this with the founders of the Citizen's Council for a good laugh, who in two short years since *Brown vs. Board* had grown to an influential organization with branches in most southern towns. "Surely one might expect something a little more forthright—a little more moral—from the foremost exponent in the United States of the Protestant 'crisis theology,'" wrote Irving Howe in his magazine, *Dissent*.[144] King could not have missed these troubling equivocations on black protest, which must have taken him by surprise even as they reminded him of persisting concerns.[145]

As early as his presentation to the Dialectical Society as a graduate student, King had worried about Niebuhr's Christology, the absence of a living relationship with the worldly Jesus. Niebuhr's Jesus is "pure abstraction," King had said, not "the Jesus of history who walked in Jerusalem.[146] Of course there was no way that King could understand the implications of his Boston presentation for the events that lay ahead, his exceedingly prescient concern that an abstract Christ could not offer meaningful instruction to the black church on its social mission in the world. King would risk his life on the proposition that "the immanence of *agape*" can be "concretely conceived in human nature and history," and that "the availability of the divine Agape is an essential affirmation of the Christian religion," convictions Niebuhr regarded as dangerous.[147] The only moral precept the Christian knows is the one incarnate in Jesus Christ; and that precept fashions a life devoted to incarnate love—"an overflowing love which seeks nothing in return."[148] This was the theological realism that King would embrace. Turgid discussions about "the general tendency of increasing social intelligence" ultimately proved unhelpful—and increasingly un-Christian—to a young Baptist preacher struggling to take the Bible seriously in Montgomery, Alabama. (No wonder King stopped reading theology.) Abstractions cannot empower acts of compassion and self-sacrifice, or sustain the courage to speak against the day. Niebuhr's much-heralded Christian realism was about working out ethical problems within the framework of options provided by Western liberalism.[149] It was not about having a dream. "I am convinced that God lives," King wrote in a letter to Lillian Smith, the writer and social progressive from Georgia, and the movement came to life because of that conviction.[150]

By the end of February, a Montgomery grand jury began handing down indictments against MIA members under state boycott law. "We are committed to segregation by custom and by law," read the report, and "we intend to maintain it."[151] King had left the state for a few days on speaking engagements, but hearing the news, promised to return to stand trial. His father, not having been graced with a midnight visit from Jesus, demanded that his son not now or ever return to Montgomery. But King was unmoved. "I would rather go back and spend ten years in jail than not go back," he said.[152]

On the first day of the trial, Monday, March 19, 1956, King and his fellow organizers entered the courtroom in solemn procession as Negro spectators sat quietly with cloth crosses on their lapels that read, "Father Forgive Them." After four days of deliberations, Judge Eugene Carter brought the trial to a close on March 22. King was found guilt of conducting illegal activities against Montgomery City Lines, and he was given a choice between a $500 fine plus court costs or 386 days in jail. Posting $1,000 bail and released on appeal, King was greeted later that afternoon by several hundred supporters as he exited the courthouse. He told the crowd that the "more than forty thousand Negro citizens of Montgomery" were more than ever determined to use the weapon of love, and that violence always proves self-defeating, for, as Jesus taught, "he who lives by the sword will perish by the sword."[153]

That evening, at another mass meeting at Holt Street Baptist, three thousand people overflowed the church onto the front steps and sidewalk. With the court's guilty verdict fresh in hand, and following the congregational singing of the hymns, "We Shall Not Be Moved," "Go, Send Me,

Oh Lord," and "Walk Together, Children," King called the Montgomery protest a "spiritual movement" and a "Christian movement."[154] Beyond the season of the boycott and whatever strategic gains it would bring, the spiritual struggle must be fought with "moral and spiritual forces," for these are "the only weapon we have." King acknowledged that he and his fellow church people "may not get to see the promised land"; but they could rest assured that God was true to his word. "So don't worry about some of the things we have to go through," he said. "They are just a necessary part of the great movement that we are making toward freedom."[155]

In naming the Montgomery struggle a spiritual and a Christian movement, King's intention was surely not to exclude non-Christians from participation (even though interfaith coalitions were not part of the Montgomery story); rather he was naming the protest in reference to its specific source, the church and its faith. Everything the Montgomery movement sought to accomplish came "from what we have prayed over."[156] In calling the protest a spiritual and a Christian movement, King was not laying claim to an ecclesial monopoly over racial progress in America. Who is served by a monopoly on righteousness but the elites and institutions that would wave the yellow flag at black church people stirring into protest? In fact, that specificity would make King more rather than less open to fellow travelers from other confessions in the work of justice; that specificity gave the church struggle a humility and a generous reach. At its best, the "civil rights movement" (as it would soon be called) embodied this generosity, and King would expand his circle of black church people to include Jews and humanists. "I feel that there will be a victory and it will be greater than any particular race," he said to *Montgomery Advertiser* reporter Joe Azbel. "It will be for the improvement of the whole of Montgomery, and I think that is so because this is a spiritual movement depending on moral and spiritual forces."[157] King understood that a public disciple has no need to say that only a Christian may suffer for the sake of a just cause.

By April, King was showing signs of physical exhaustion. His old seminary friend, J. Pious Barbour, was shocked by King's appearance when the two men visited in Ohio. "He is not the King I knew," Barbour said. "He has grown twenty years in about five. He is almost to a fault exceedingly retiring; he wanders around in a daze asking himself: Why has God seen fit to catapult me into such a situation?"[158]

Then on April 23, while King was out of state, the news broke that the United States Supreme Court had affirmed a federal appellate court decision striking down segregated seating on the municipal buses of Columbia, South Carolina. Fearing more legal complexities, the management of the

Montgomery City Lines announced its decision to comply with the federal court order. City bus drivers were ordered to immediately stop enforcing separate seating policies. The vice president of the bus company even resolved that all drivers prosecuted by the city for carrying black riders would receive the full legal support of the company.[159]

However, Mayor Gayle, however, working under a different set of expectations, showed little sign of conceding defeat. Reacting with the fury of a man betrayed, Gayle promised white Montgomerians that city commissioners would stand their ground. It did not matter to him at all that the Montgomery City Lines had thrown in the towel or that the U.S. Supreme Court had ruled against segregated seating in South Carolina.

City commissioners hurriedly filed suit in the state court, hoping to receive a temporary restriction against the local bus company's decision to desegregate its services. But the momentum of the protest had decidedly shifted. At a five-hour hearing in the U.S. District Court in Montgomery on May 11, the city's suit was rejected in a two-to-one vote.

The court's decision to strike down the city's segregated seating policies introduced the Montgomery protest and the nation to an unlikely ally in the black struggle—a white Republican, Alabama native, and Southern Baptist churchman named Frank M. Johnson whose great-grandfather had served as a captain in the Confederate army.[160] Johnson had already helped abolish the Alabama poll tax. He would later order the state to reapportion its election districts and integrate its school districts and he would preside over the 1966 trial that brought convictions to the killers of Viola Liuzzo, the white civil rights volunteer murdered in March 1965 near Selma.[161] Judge Johnson, in whose court the appeal had been filed, had argued that segregation in public facilities violated the equal protection clause of the Fourteenth Amendment.[162] Defying enormous social pressures at a time when local courtrooms throughout the South were closing ranks to protect the status quo, Johnson had affirmed the central legal claim of the Montgomery Improvement Association, and thus acted in accordance with his high republican standard of placing law and country over equivocation and prejudice. [163] "The [court] will not tolerate discrimination on the basis of race," he wrote.

Many white Alabamians were fit to be tied. "I would have had my right arm cut off. . . before I [reacted] as you did," a man wrote to Judge Johnson from Union Spring. "I trust that you get on your knees and pray to God All Mighty to forgive you for the mistakes you have made."[164] Judge Richard Rives, who had cast the other affirmative vote, would not escape the condemnation of segregationists either. One Alabama newspaper complained that the judge had betrayed his southern heritage and "forfeited the right to be buried in Confederate soil."[165]

With deep gratitude for the District Court's decision but uncertain about its implementation, King and the Montgomery organizers agreed nonetheless to continue the boycott. For nothing seemed likely to change in the short run, as there would be no immediate implementation of the decision. The same city commissioners whose resistance to change had not been softened by the bus company's change of policy were also unbowed by federal court's ruling. Determined to fight the battle to the end, Mayor Gayle pledged to appeal the ruling of the Fifth Circuit Court to the U.S. Supreme Court.

King spent much of the summer on the road. The work had become overwhelming. Numerous movement ministers' homes in Montgomery were bombed; insurance policies had been cancelled for property and automobiles; and outside contributions declined even as weekly expenses of the protest exceeded five thousand dollars.

King felt guilty about the time away from his parish and the chaos of his personal life. "I have often lagged behind in my pastoral duties," he said.[166] Yet precisely because King's service depended on the daily sacrifices of the black protesters, he found it difficult to decline the invitations to take the Montgomery story to churches, arenas, meeting halls, and convention centers around the country. Though he would decline a few at the insistence of his doctor, King stuck to the demanding schedule, patiently discussing with audiences outside the South the movement that had "ignited ordinary black people and brought them for the first time into the struggle for equality." King reaffirmed on every occasion the power and dignity of resisting injustice nonviolently, "with love and unrelenting courage," and in anticipation of "the coming of a new world in which men will live together as brothers." And despite (or perhaps because of) his exhaustion, King fell back on the language he knew best, the language of the church.

In a speech to the American Baptist Assembly and American Home Mission Agencies Conference in July, King acknowledged the conviction that stands at "the center of our faith" as the "great event" of Good Friday and Easter.[167] He made more explicit the meaning of the Montgomery story as a Christian movement, weaving the protest into the cosmic events of the cross and resurrection. He believed that the great event of the cross and resurrection injected the movement with its inner meaning and power. "There is a great *event* that stands at the center of our faith," he said, "which *reveals* to us that God is on the side of truth and love and justice."[168]

King understood the fading of the "old order" and the emergence of a "new age" as a pervasively theological movement. "God is working in history to bring about this new age." The church, no less, is the animating center of humanity's redemption. "[The] church is the Body of Christ. So when the church is true to its nature it knows neither division nor disunity. I am disturbed about what you are doing to the Body of Christ."[169] Again, the movement is a divine gift, for only on the basis of the "great epic of the Cross" can we affirm the "broad universalism" discerned at "the center of the gospel." The brotherhood and sisterhood of humankind radiates outward from the fellowship of the camp meeting.[170]

King described the great epic of the cross as "the event" that *interprets* the non-violent direct action. The practice of nonviolence exemplifies the event of the cross in lived experience; in other words, "the method of nonviolent resistance" embodies the meaning of the cross in the human struggle for justice.[171] But there is more. The cross is also the event that *enables* resistance, the power of the "nonviolent resister [to] suffer and not retaliate"; and further, the cross *activates* the mission of the church, its comprehensive retelling of the human story, its pursuit of the peaceable kingdom. No longer is the church solely in the business of saving individual souls from damnation, but it embodies the "great event" of the cross by making free space for redemptive community. If "[s]egregation is a blatant denial of the unity which we all have in Jesus Christ," King said, then the reconciling church demonstrates to the world that "it is still true that in Christ there is neither Jew nor Gentile (Negro nor white) and that out of one blood God made all men to dwell upon the face of the earth."[172] The "forces of darkness, the iron feet of oppression," "the dark chambers of pessimism," "the tranquilizing drug of gradualism," "the dark and desolate valleys of despair," "the sagging walls of bus segregation"—have been defeated once and for all. The good news is that the same divine power that has defeated the "forces of darkness" in the "great epoch of the Cross" fuels the spirit of the "black church people in Montgomery."[173]

In this context, King understood Gandhi's astonishing sacrifices to humanity as gifts to the Montgomery movement, parables of justice standing beside and complimenting the "long tradition of our Christian faith."[174] Christ furnished the spirit and motivation while Gandhi furnished the method," King would later write in his "Experiment in Love."[175] Gandhi's witness supplied the Christian doctrine of love with a strategy of social protest, just as Negro spirituals sometimes nourished the soul of the Indian peace movement.[176] In his "Six Talks in Outline," written in 1949 at Crozer, King had included Gandhi among those individuals who "reveal the working of the Spirit of God," along with David Livingstone, Albert Schweitzer, and Jesus Christ.[177] "AS [sic] the circle is narrowed from the world to the Church and from the Church to the individual, the work of the Holy Spirit becomes more specific and intense," King explained.[178] Yet King had not at that time been convinced by Gandhi of either the strategy or morality of nonviolent protest, and apparently he had also not given much attention to Gandhi's writings. When Glenn Smiley visited King in February of 1956 after his home was bombed—the same Smiley who had earlier remarked on the arsenal in the parsonage—King allowed that he had never seriously engaged Gandhi's thought, though he had always admired him. "I have read some statements by him, and so on, but I will have to truthfully say . . . that I know very little about the man."[179] But as King now lived more deeply into the truth of the Sermon on the Mount, he more deeply engaged the "little brown saint of India" and his "doctrine of passive resistance" as a fellow traveler in the spirit, whose witness inspired the work of local black churches throughout the boycott year.[180] His copies of Gandhi's books grew worn and tattered.

In late October, during a speaking visit to Boston, Harold DeWolf pleaded with King to take a restorative retreat before returning to the South. De-Wolf offered to make the arrangements and to find him an appropriate sanctuary, where King could be alone for "spiritual renewal and writing." King's friend and Boston classmate Roland Emerson Haynes worried too about King's health. "One wonders how one can effectively play the role of Pastor, Husband, Father, and Public Leader when every role demands so much from the individual."[181] But King begged off on the plan. The time was not right for reflection; the work was unfinished, and there were too many details that needed attention.

In October, the city officials once again targeted the car pools, seeking another injunction against the volunteer and professional drivers who carried Negro protesters to and from work. Attorneys for the city hoped that by going after the car pools they could force the Negro protesters to walk and thus bring the boycott to a halt. King once again succumbed to despair about his leadership. He felt he had let people down, people who had trusted him and put faith in nonviolent solutions, risking jobs and welfare. "It was a desolate moment," King later recalled. "Was the boycott going to fail?[182]

On November 13, King was back in court, listening as the city demanded $15,000 in damages for the boycott and that the car pool be shut down. But at the noon recess, a reporter from the Associate Press approached King excitedly with a clipping from the news wire. "Here is the decision you have been waiting for," the journalist exclaimed.[183] King read the article with a grateful sigh. The United States Supreme Court had just affirmed Judge Johnson's and the U.S. District Court's decision in declaring illegal Alabama's bus segregation laws. The church struggle had achieved its victory, and black Montgomery was ecstatic.

Later the same evening, forty carloads of Klansmen rolled through the black neighborhoods of the capital city, but instead of barricading themselves inside and keeping clear of windows, black residents now swung open their front doors and gathered on lighted porches watching and waving as the hooded men rode by. "They acted as though they were watching a circus parade," King exclaimed.[184]

In the first week of December 1956, the MIA held a weeklong Institute on Nonviolence and Social Change at the Holt Street Baptist Church. King's opening address, "Facing the Challenge of a New Age," was delivered nearly one year to the date after his first public speech and the beginning of the boycott. The address revealed a broadened theological perspective on the year that had passed. King paused on this jubilant evening to reflect on the achievements of the preceding months. The legal decision brought needed changes in public policy, and no doubt more difficult work lay ahead. But as importantly, the boycott year had renewed the mission of the church. The boycott showed the world a church whose power stemmed from its deliberate discipline, whose moral authority was the hard-earned result of its suffering and willingness to love the enemy—religious passions, it should be noted, that Niebuhr's thin ecclesiology could never embrace. The struggle required, and in turn fostered, the kind of discipline needed both for the large tasks of defying unjust laws and institutions and for the mundane tasks as well: mimeographing fliers, stapling papers, sitting in pews for hours in order to get a seat for the evening meetings, waiting, and walking. "Our church is becoming more militant," he said.[185]

King was not sanguine on the matter. The "new order" in which all people live together as sisters and brothers has not arrived in its promised fullness. One only had to look around at the mass meetings to know this: Aside from Robert Graetz, the white Ohioan who pastored a local black Lutheran Church, not a single white minister in Montgomery had accepted King's invitation to attend the Holt Street service. In the early months of the boycott, King had held out hope that white ministers, when approached by their Negro brethren, would reciprocate the hand of friendship. He had even handwritten letters to white pastors inviting them to participate in the programs and events. But on this evening King laid claim to an ecclesiology born of the hard lessons of the boycott year, affirming reconciliation with whites but with chastened hopes and expectations.[186]

Still, Montgomery had been an encouraging experiment in love, an exemplification of the untested power of the Sermon on the Mount. Then King said:

> It is true that as we struggle for freedom in America we will have to boycott at times. But we remember that as we boycott that the boycott is not an end within itself. . . . [The] end is reconciliation; the end is redemption; the end is the creation of the beloved community.

He implored the militant church in Montgomery to commit itself to the mission of reconciliation with a passion at least equal to its commitment to legal reform. "It is this type of spirit and this type of love that can transform opposers into friends. . . . It is this love which will bring about miracles in the hearts of men."[187]

Mayor Gayle promised to appeal the case to the U.S. Supreme Court, and he did, but the signs of the end were everywhere evident. White officials survived a few more rounds of missed chances and legal jabs; but on December 17, 1956, the knockout punch came. To a city trying its best to get into the spirit of the Christmas season, despite the unseasonably warm temperature, the news arrived that the Supreme Court had rejected the Montgomery city commissioner's final appeal. Three days later, on December 20, the U.S. Supreme Court's decision took effect.

In the final two mass meetings before returning to the buses—held concurrently at Holt Street Baptist and First Baptist Church—the black Montgomerians declared an end to the 382-day boycott. King reminded the congregations to follow the "Integrated Bus Suggestions" distributed earlier in the evening.[188] He encouraged a civil and forgiving transition to the new arrangements and a spirit of forgiveness and reconciliation. "Pray for guidance and commit yourself to complete non-violence in word and action as you enter the bus," he said. "In sitting down by a person, white or colored, say, 'May I' or 'Pardon me' as you sit. This is a common courtesy."[189] Sensing a popular sentiment of vindication, King cautioned against smugness. The black church's victory in Montgomery dare not be used as an occasion for "wild" emotions or aggressive celebration. Negroes in Montgomery should rather board the buses as if they were proceeding into their church sanctuaries on Sunday morning, with respect for the moment. King then fortified the practical advice of the "Suggestions" practical advice with a final theological hope: "We must now move from protest to reconciliation."[190]

The next morning, the young Baptist pastor was the first Negro to board the bus at the corner of South Jackson and Key Street, a few blocks from his home. "Is this the reverend?" asked the white driver politely. "That's right," answered King, visibly nervous as reporters and photographers looked on. "We are glad to have you this morning," the driver said. "Thank you," said King, who then stepped on the bus and took a seat on the third row. Glenn Smiley, the peaceworker from Texas, sat alongside King, and Ralph Abernathy sat in the next row in front of them. "I rode the first integrated bus in Montgomery with a white minister and a native Southerner as my seatmate," King said.[191]

In Montgomery, Martin Luther King Jr. came to a new understanding of redemptive social relation: the beloved community. In a "confluence of optimisms," where the kingdom of God met the American dream, Christian hope would serve the cause not so much as an opiate but as a stimulant.[192] When the U.S. Supreme Court ruled in favor of the Montgomery Improvement Association and in opposition to segregated transportation in Montgomery, a church person was heard saying, "God Almighty has spoken from Washington, D.C."[193] Although it would not be correct to say that the emerging "new world" of God was but the theological rendering of a political achievement, the federal government nonetheless delivered the goods on civil rights and made it tempting to regard the democratic process as an extension of the divine will fulfilling the promissory notes and prayers of black America. King did not so much strike a balance between prophetic religion and the American dream as he imagined democratic possibilities from the perspective of Biblical hope.

In using the term "beloved community," King borrowed from a discourse which had been fashionable in American philosophical and theological circles throughout the early and middle twentieth century.[194] Most of these formulations, however, had the effect of reducing transcendence to some mode or modulation of human experience, or of describing beloved community as an inevitable historical achievement. The influential philosopher Josiah Royce spoke of beloved community as "a perfectly lived unity of individual men joined in one divine chorus," and gave voice to the essence of Protestant ethical religion; the beloved community shimmers with liberal hopes of human progress and perfectibility. Most of what one needs to know of God is discovered in ethical religion, slightly adjusted for churchgoers in capitalist economies.[195]

But in King's hands, the idea of beloved community was invigorated with theological vitality and moral urgency, so that the prospects of social progress came to look less like an evolutionary development and more like a divine gift: "God is using Montgomery as his proving ground."[196] God remains from beginning to end the ultimate agent of human liberation, not only in America but throughout all the nations and in creation. The fading of the "old order" and the emergence of a "new age" is not written into the genetic code of American history as its manifest destiny; rather, beloved community depends on a theological, one might say ecclesiological, *event*. In other words, the brotherhood and sisterhood of humankind radiates out from the fellowship of the faithful. If "segregation is a blatant denial of the unity which we all have in Jesus Christ," as King said, then reconciliation demonstrates to the world the truth that "in Christ there is neither Jew nor Gentile (Negro nor white) and that out of one blood God made all men to dwell upon the face of the earth."[197] Thus, the beloved community is the new social space of reconciliation introduced into history by the Church, empowered by the "triumph and beat of the drums of Easter." The beloved community is not shaped finally by a "religion of loyalty" (Royce), "the good life of personality lived in the Beloved Community" (Randolph Bourne), or even by the "social egalitarianism" of Jesus Christ (Rauschen-busch);[198] rather, the beloved community is established by the "great *event* on Calvary," "the great *event* that stands at the center of our faith which *reveals* to us that God is on the side of truth and love and justice," as King explained in his Dexter sermon, "Paul's Letter to American Christians."[199]

Over the course of King's lifetime, the deep wounds wrought by the "sinfulness of man" in American society intensified the idea of the beloved community theologically. "Life is a continual story of shattered dreams," King told his Ebenezer congregation in March of 1968. A few weeks later, on the eve of his assassination, King lamented to the Memphis crowd, which had gathered in support of the sanitation workers' strike, "The world is all messed up. The nation is sick. Trouble is in the land. Confusion all around."[200] The righteousness of God would not transmogrify the human frame from the inside out like some inexorable and innate force. The long arch of the universe bending toward justice extends beyond finite horizons into the eschaton. The beloved community remains broken and scattered, an eschatological hope, yet precisely a hope that intensifies rather than absolves us from responsibilities in the here and now.[201]

CHAPTER 2

~

In the Fields of the Lord:
The God Movement in South Georgia

In August of 1956, in the ninth month of the bus boycott, King, received a letter from a white supporter named Ernest Morgan, who wanted him to know of the recent assaults on Koinonia Farm, an intentional community near Americus, Georgia. Intentional or experimental communities had flourished in the South for at least two decades, though none had attracted as much hostility from local residents as the spread near Americus.[1] At Koinonia, Christian radicals in pursuit of racial reconciliation lived in total community, taking vows of poverty and practicing the common purse. Morgan was not a resident of Koinonia. He was a successful book publisher and a patron of the religious left. He had once served as the chairman of the Ohio Socialist Party and worked for a Quaker organization administering relief for Palestinian refugees in the Gaza Strip.[2] His interests now lay in racial reform.

Morgan informed King that workers at Koinonia, with profits from their vegetable markets and roadside stands, had chipped in an hour's pay earlier in the year to help support the Montgomery Improvement Association. But now, Morgan added, white people in Sumter County had begun applying the same strategies against the residents of the interracial farm, boycotting an institution they considered to be an offense against the southern way of life. Retail merchants, seed salesmen, the fertilizer company, and auto dealers all had begun closing their doors to these strange Christians working the red-clay fields of south Georgia and dreaming of reconciled community; and to make matters worse, the farm's insurance providers had begun canceling policies one by one until not even the tractors were covered, until even the crop duster crew joined the protest and refused their services.

Morgan's plea to King for help in assisting the victims of the Sumter County boycott offers a fascinating glimpse into an experiment in radical Christian community which has remained largely ignored by civil rights scholars and yet plays a prominent role in the consideration of the civil rights movement as theological drama.[3] The story of Koinonia Farm introduces us to the search for beloved community shaped solely by the promise of Christian faith to create alternative social structures and practices. That the story also introduces us to an experiment in faith-based socialism indicates the extent to which our contemporary discussion of the more recent faith-based movement has not fully appreciated its own radical origins. Morgan wrote to King:

> You have probably heard of Koinonia Farm, Route 2, Americus, Georgia. Founded [fourteen] years ago by a southern white Baptist minister who was expelled from his church for preaching racial equality. [This] farm applies Christianity directly in the form of racial equality and common ownership, and, like your movement, is dedicated to non-violence. It has grown now to include 1100 acres and about 50 men, women and children. It is an efficient outfit, well equipped with houses, barns, trucks, tractors, and modern irrigation. It has, also, of course, a nice big mortgage.
>
> As its strength and influence grew and its interracial habits became better known, Koinonia has come under severe attack by southern reactionaries. To have an operation like this carried on in the deep south, by white southerners, would badly undermine their position. Not only has Koinonia run an inter-racial children's camp and accepted a Negro family in membership, but lately one of the leaders, a graduate of the University of Georgia, sponsored a Negro candidate for that institution. . . .
>
> One of the most dangerous threats is the gradually tightening boycott against the farm products. While Koinonia has many friends and enjoys a good business reputation, its enemies are slowly but surely cutting off its markets. It is at this point that your organization might help. Your members [would] buy food. Might it not be possible for a special committee to be formed to work out some arrangement with Koinonia? Perhaps wholesale connections might be found, or possible [sic] a weekly food market could be set up. That would have to be worked out. It would mean a lot to the spirit of your members to extend fellowship and aid to a group of hardpressed white southerners who are fighting the same battle. And it would strengthen them, both financially and morally. I might mention that my

younger son has spent the summer at Koinonia without pay, driving tractors and doing other farm work, to help pull them through.[4]

A few days later, King replied to Morgan and expressed his admiration
for "the noble work that is being done there."[5] King assured Morgan that
he would do everything possible to assist the farm during their crisis. Over
the next two years, the "Koinonians" (as members of the community called
themselves) would be received warmly by Dexter parishioners on their numerous visits to Montgomery lending support to the protest, and members
of King's congregation—including Martin and Coretta—would provide
hospitality and modest financial assistance for their spiritual kin in south
Georgia. King would write directly to Clarence Jordan, the white Southern
Baptist preacher who founded Koinonia, offering his sympathies for the
"indignities and injustices that you are now confronting" and his generous
hope that "you will gain consolation from the fact that in your struggle for
freedom and a true Christian community you have cosmic companion-
ship."[6] Periodically a group of Dexter parishioners would make the two-
hour drive to Koinonia to share a meal and offer encouragement of their
own. It is unknown whether a special committee was formed at Dexter.[7]

Two years later, in April of 1958, King invited Clarence Jordan to give a series of lectures on the "Church and the Kingdom of God." "We have not
recently had any real discussion on the church," King wrote.[8] King's hope
was that his white preacher colleague would help the people in Montgomery "take new courage and be inspired to do [even] greater work."[9]
The converging paths of these uncommonly intense Baptist preachers for
a few evenings in the spring of 1958 illuminate a broadened field of
church-based racial reform in the South.
   Jordan and King had never met in person. But having visited with other
Koinonians in the Montgomery parsonage and in the coffee hour after
church, King had come to admire the Jordans' pioneering work in Baptist
racial reform. He may well have counted them among those "fearless
souls" helping to create the atmosphere for the movement emerging in the
South.[10] In fact, King's dream of beloved community, rendered immemori-
ally in his 1963 address at the March on Washington, may have evoked the
Koinonia story, the image of white and black people sitting down at a picnic table in south Georgia acting like kin. For their part, Jordan and the
Koinonians had prayed regularly for the Negro church people during
the year of the bus protest, grateful for their bold demonstration of Christian pacifism, and, as Morgan mentioned in his letter, providing occasional

financial assistance. The two pastors born and raised in Georgia shared not only a common commitment to racial reconciliation but also the conviction that the South as a region of deep faith offered unique resources for building beloved community. They shared a common hope in Christian faith's power to redeem the social order.

Jordan focused his lectures on the themes of the "Church and the Kingdom," the "Church as a Revolutionary World Order," and the "Church in God's Plan for the Ages."[11] Like King, Jordan had been influenced by the theology of the social Gospel as taught by Walter Rauschenbusch (1861–1918), an American theologian who had revived the doctrine of the kingdom of God in his enterprise of mobilizing Protestants for social justice. Rauschenbusch believed that without a vital conception of the kingdom of God, Christians were forever inclined to retreat into private virtuousness and otherworldly piety.[12] But with a renewed kingdom-theology, faith would become socially engaged and transformative; for indeed the kingdom of God "is the energy of God realizing itself in human life."[13] As Rauschenbusch explained in his influential book, *A Theology for the Social Gospel*, a Kingdom theology involves "the redemption of social life from the cramping influence of religious bigotry, from the repression of self-assertion in the relation of upper and lower classes, and from forms of slavery in which human beings are treated as mere means to serve the ends of others . . . the redemption of society from political autocracies and economic oligarchies; the substitution of redemptive for vindictive penology; the abolition of constraint through hunger as part of the industrial system; and the abolition of war as the supreme expression of hate and the completest cessation of freedom."[14]

On the first night of the series, Jordan described the kingdom of God as a living, moving reality, dynamic and unsettling.[15] Jesus never gave an easy definition of the kingdom, but instead used parables to describe it as a new way of life, a fellowship, a family, a movement. "The Kingdom of heaven is like yeast that a woman took and mixed into a large amount of flour until it worked all through the dough."[16] Jordan took pains to distinguish the kingdom of God from the "sanctuary," or the institutional church, which bore little resemblance to the new order proclaimed in the Gospels.

Rauschenbusch had talked about the false and tragic identification of the kingdom and the church, wherein people began to think that they were serving the kingdom by "cementing a strong church organization." But Jordan went even further, saying that the "Christ of the fields and the marketplaces" has been "entombed in cathedrals and holy places" and "rendered innocuous by making him Lord of the lips and the hymnbooks."[17] It was the responsibility of Christian radicals like the Koinonians and the Montgomery church people to free Christ from his institutional shackles. Martin King must have offered a hearty "amen" to Jordan's refrain that Jesus had not come to start a religion but a revolution.

The spring lecture series was a success. The next week King wrote Jordan enthusiastically, "Words are inadequate to express my appreciation to you for the great contribution you made, not only to the Dexter Avenue Baptist Church, but to the Montgomery community, during our spring lecture series." King called the messages "profound and inspiring," the "finest series we have had in our pastorate here at Dexter." He encouraged Jordan and the other Koinonians to call on him anytime and passed along the greetings and blessings of Coretta. "You are always in my prayers," he wrote.[18]

Sadly the exchange produced no lasting friendship. There would be no interracial speaking tours or evangelistic campaigns modeled on Billy Graham's successful crusades, at the time attracting enormous audiences in the cities of the South. The next year King left his one and only tenure as a parish pastor, to work full-time for the Southern Christian Leadership Conference, while Clarence Jordan, despite his harsh and exceedingly prescient judgments on the white evangelical church, came to a notion of Christian community so extreme in its rigor and discipline that it risked becoming as insular and obsessed with purity as the segregated churches he loathed. The differences between the two ministers then intensified. From King's perspective, Koinonia Farm simply became irrelevant to racial reform in the South, to the massive legal changes necessary for a more just nation. From Jordan's perspective, King became a parody of his former self, a man of nonviolence who relied on the men of great violence for his well being, a politician (and not a very good one), whose pastoral energies were long spent.[19]

No doubt, as the new civil rights leader, King had little choice but to broaden his scope, fortify his leadership, and forge ahead into complex political terrain. But as a professional organizer with a staff position in his father's church in Atlanta, King was no longer accountable to the Dexter deacons of the world, proud church people who kept his feet to the fire on moral rectitude. (One of King's successors at Dexter would tell the story of how his own wrinkled shirts became a source of anguish to the Robert Nesbitt family in the first weeks of his pastorate. Rebecca Nesbitt, the deacon's wife, became so distraught one night that, unable to sleep, she drove to the parsonage early Sunday morning, woke up the new pastor, and insisted on pressing his shirt and pants—and she had brought along her own iron and ironing board.) King's new freedom to operate must have no doubt felt liberating after years of negotiating the scrupulous Dexter crowd; but in Jordan's estimation it was a freedom purchased with a moral cost. "*Hectic* activity," a pastor-friend had written to King, "i[s] not necessarily an indication that the cause of the Kingdom is being promoted."[20]

Jordan believed that the only way authentic change could transpire in southern race relations was through "incarnational evangelism," and that meant making Christian truth concrete in community and in shared life with the excluded and the oppressed. Evangelism at its highest, Jordan said, is "based not upon a sermon, not upon a theory, not upon an abstraction, but upon the word of God become flesh and dealing with us, and restoring us to our right minds." "Taking out one bunch of politicians and putting in another will not bring about the Kingdom of God," he said. "That would be kind of like exchanging a mule that's blind in his right eye for one that's blind in his left eye.[21] A revolution based on bread is also incomplete. "If we abolish all slums and all poverty, and provide free medical care and social security for all, we still won't have the kingdom."[22] In short, soul-regeneration—and having that born again experience transform the whole self—was the key to the transformation of race relations in the South and the nation.

Having been nourished as a seminarian on social Gospel hopes, Jordan was not suggesting that slums and poverty not be abolished, or that federal agencies not play a role in their abolition. Rather he believed himself to be retrieving a more radical faith, one exemplified in the socialism of early Christian communities, one which revealed humanity's true history, a history without violence, competitive assaults on human dignity, and the principle of "what is mine is mine." Still, for Jordan, socialism as a political achievement could never yield the kingdom of God. Socialism might serve as an allegory of the kingdom or as a reflection of the kingdom in history, but the socialist movement could not produce God's new order. Jordan was not speaking disingenuously when, under investigation by anticommunist agencies, he denied socialist or communist intentions in the experiment of Koinonia; he believed that the kingdom of God finally exploded the hard shell of politics from the inside out. Over against socialism as an ideological system, the ultimate meaning of history flowed from the "deep, rich fellowship" of God's love; and only this fellowship could enable real social change, heal the wounds of injustice, overcome oppression, and renew the earth.

Early in his ministry, in a small Baptist church, Jordan preached a sermon on the white southerner's responsibility to the Negro. He had taken as his proof text a passage from Paul's Epistle to the Galatians. "For ye are all the children of God by faith in Christ Jesus. For as many of you as have been baptized into Christ have put on Christ. There is neither Jew nor Greek, there is neither bond nor free, there is neither male nor female: for ye are all one in Christ Jesus."[23] At the conclusion of the service, an elderly woman made her way down the aisle, "as crisp with pride as a dead honeysuckle vine," Jordan recalled. The woman was furious with Jordan for his harsh words for the South and his irreverence towards its time-honored customs. "I want you to know that my grandfather fought in the Civil War," she told him, "and I will never believe a word you say." But Jordan had seen it coming and was ready with an answer. "Well ma'm, I guess you've got to decide whether to follow your granddaddy or Jesus."[24] Jordan was a man who understood the deep loyalty of his region to a cluttered pantheon of cultural gods.

It is not at all clear why certain white children form early impressions of racial inequities and feel moved to correct them. Perhaps their sensitivity is the result of feeling different themselves, or of an event, momentous or small, brutal or seemingly insignificant, that enables compassion, broadens vision, and sharpens awareness of injury. In her 1943 memoir, *Killers of the Dream*, the Georgia writer and racial progressive Lillian Smith described her southern childhood as one woven of "dissonant strands" like "threads tangled into a terrifying mess." Sometimes "a design was left broken while another was completed with minute care"; quite often archaic and startling designs appeared in the weaving. The mother who taught her child all that she knew of kindness also instructed her in the rituals of keeping black people in their place. The father who chastised the child for her superior air toward her poor classmates also explained in careful detail that courtesy titles should never be given to black adults. "I do not remember how or when," Smith wrote, "but by the time I had learned that God is love, that Jesus is His Son and came to give us more abundant life, that all men are brothers with a common Father, I also knew that I was better than a Negro, [and] that white southerners are a hospitable, courteous, tactful people who treat those of their own group with consideration and who as carefully segregate from all the richness of life 'for their own good and welfare' thirteen million people whose skin is colored a little differently from my own."[25]

Jordan's was a slow turning composed of a series of numerous early impressions of race framed by high standards of holiness and a sensitivity to the maternal face of poverty.

Born in Talbotton, Georgia, on July 29, 1912, Clarence Leonard Jordan was the middle child of seven in a prosperous home. His father, J. W.

Jordan, was a hard-working if humorless Baptist who in addition to own-
ing the local bank also ran a general store. His mother, Maude Josey Jordan, was born in Talbotton but was raised in the Pacific Northwest and
never felt at home as an adult in the South. Jordan was a likable though
solitary child who could often be impatient with others, earning him the
nickname "Grump." Though he lacked natural abilities as an athlete, he
was dogged in his determination to excel in basketball and made the varsity
team. Jordan was encouraged by his parents to think independently and to
aim his sights high.

Like his friend Lillian Smith, Jordan had been perplexed as a child by the
strange chemistry of race relations in the South. He once even called his father's manners into question when he observed him scolding a delivery man
for knocking at the front door instead of the side door where Negroes were
expected.[26] Jordan wondered how his favorite hymn, "Jesus Loves the Little
Children," squared with the harsh conditions of black life in Talbotton. The
song said that God loved all people the same—"red and yellow black and
white, they are precious in his sight." So why then were the Negro children
always "so ragged, so dirty and hungry?" As a boy, Jordan wrote in his journal, "Did God have favorite children? The question arose in my mind:
Were the little black children precious in God's sight just like the little white
children?" Jordan couldn't answer the question, but he knew something was
wrong with the world. "A little light came when I began to realize that perhaps it wasn't God's doings, but man's. God didn't turn them away from our
churches—we did. God didn't pay them low wages—we did. God didn't
make them live in another section of town and in miserable huts—we did.
God didn't make ragged, hungry little boys pick rotten oranges and fruit out
of the garbage can and eat them—we did."[27]

The occasion of Jordan's conversion at the age of twelve was an outdoor
revival on an August night. During the service, a choir from the nearby jail
had sung the old-time hymn, "Love Lifted Me." Jordan was captivated by
the performance, especially by the sight of the burly warden singing bass
on the dramatic chorus. Together the white warden and the black inmates
had blended their styles and voices in a moving rendition of the Baptist
standard, stirring the congregation with the wonderful news that the love
of Jesus was stronger than even the most despairing cry, or the deepest sins:
"When nothing else could help, love lifted me."

Jordan had always been fascinated by the Talbot County jail. The brick
building lay just a hundred yards from his home, and in the afternoons on
his way back from school he often walked through the jail yard and greeted
the inmates working on the chain gang. Jordan knew many by name.

Sometimes the cook gave the boy a piece of cornbread and slice of fatback, and he ate the snack in the yard.

The night after the revival service, Jordan was awakened by an agonizing sound coming from the direction of the jail. He snuck out of the house to investigate and was horrified to see in the chain gang camp an inmate named Ed Russell laid out on the device called "the stretcher." Operating the lever that controlled the tension of the device was the white warden. "That nearly tore me to pieces," Jordan said. "I identified totally with that man in the stretcher. . . . I really got mad at God. If He was love and the warden was an example of it, I didn't want anything to do with Him." Having gone to bed refreshed by the revival, Jordan was awakened into the grim reality of the Jim Crow South.

As an adolescent, Jordan exhibited an independent mind, strength of character, and conviction. By the time he graduated from high school at the age of sixteen, he was committed to the Christian life and a high standard of personal holiness. Although the seeds of racial empathy planted by his childhood experiences had not yet come to full expression, Jordan's decision to study agriculture at the state university was motivated by a concern for poor farmers and an eagerness to use his academic skills in service to the less fortunate.[28] His father was not convinced, however. "If you want to be a farmer," he said, "why go to school? I'll buy you a mule and you can start right now."[29]

With their low church sensibilities and distrust of ornamentation, Southern Baptists do not regard the Eucharist as an essential part of Christian faith—celebrating the Lord's Supper infrequently and only then with grape juice and soda crackers. Instead Baptists look for the presence of Christ in shared worship and in the fellowship of the congregation. Their sacrament is community—though Baptists would not call community a sacrament— the weekly feasts of chicken and trimmings, the periods of Bible study and intercessory prayer, soulful laughter over coffee and pie, the season of revival. These are the elements of deep communion, and experiences that are often more formative than participation in the sacraments, which may be theologically potent but leave one hungry for experiential vitality.

Young men and women of Clarence Jordan's generation were also nurtured in their spiritual formation by denominational youth camps and retreats, where they learned the practices of Christian devotion—Bible study, prayer, sharing the faith, and discerning the will of God for their lives. A midsummer retreat in North Carolina following his sophomore year in college initiated Jordan into the soul-benefits of shared fellowship and retreat. He related the experience in a letter to his mother:

I wish there were words with which I could describe my stay at Ridgecrest. I
don't need to though, because you've seen and been in the mountains yourself and know how beautiful the scenery is, how cold the water, how exhilarating and cool the air, and how close to God it makes you feel. But even
greater than all this were the wonderful messages brought by men such as Dr.
Louie Newton, William Russell Owen, Kyle Yates, Fred Brown, John L. Hill
and Frank Leavell. To me the most impressive service was the one each night
just before bedtime when everybody would gather around the campfire down
by the lake, sing a song or two, and then listen to a short soul-stirring message by Dr. Roy Angell (very fittingly named). After his talk, everyone would
join hands and pray first for the one on your left and then on your right, as
the soft tones of a lone violin floated over the calm lake. As it ended a bugle
would blow "taps" softly from the other side of the lake. Then we would go
quietly to our rooms, thus bringing to a perfect close a perfect day. [30]

Jordan accepted the call to the ministry as a senior at the University of
Georgia. The decision brought him a sense of peace about his life and vocation. "No mortal has ever known the joy that floods my soul," he told his
mother. "It seems that God has smiled his sweetest on me, because he has
given me the privilege of serving in His vineyard by entering the ministry."[31] Jordan had no clear road map of what lay ahead; the important
thing, he felt, was that he had said "yes" to the call and was trusting God to
"take care of the rest." "It is my sincere judgment that he has made a complete surrender after fighting the desire—or call—for some time," Jordan's
advisor wrote in a letter to his parents. But in fact Jordan's surrender to
God was a quiet yielding to an inner conviction. "No battle was fought," he
said. "My heart and soul were not torn by doubt." The voice of God was
tender and motherly: "My child, I want you to preach for me." And Jordan
answered with the trust of a child. "Yes, Lord, whatever you say, just
promise me that you'll go with me."[32]

A few weeks after graduating from college, Jordan attended a weeklong
ROTC camp to receive his commission into military service. He had never
questioned his involvement in the training program, at least until late in the
spring of his senior year, when he had begun studying the Sermon on the
Mount in his daily devotionals. He had been proud of his military
accomplishments and on days of exercises wore his riding boots and spurs
with the same confidence he brought to his leadership in the Baptist Student
Union and the YMCA.[33] But ROTC camp brought to a crisis the growing
uneasiness he had felt in trying to reconcile his military training with his
Christian commitments. Jordan had been memorizing the Sermon on the

Mount in the few minutes he had to himself in the early mornings and was struck by the clarity of Jesus's words. The Sermon on the Mount seemed unambiguous as far as ethical teachings were concerned. Dedicated to the example of the New Testament community, Baptists were a people that regarded the Bible as the final authority in matters of belief and practice. Loving your enemies and nonviolence as a way of life suddenly seemed to Jordan like moral certitudes compared to some of the other Baptist principles.

One afternoon during exercises, Jordan was positioning himself to shoot a life-size target when the words of the sermon rushed to his mind. Drawing a bead, he pressed the trigger of his pistol and a white spot appeared in the black circle of the target's head." Then Jordan heard the words, "I say to you, LOVE YOUR ENEMIES." Jordan tried to fight off the conviction. This is not my enemy, but a dummy, he thought. I'm only practicing. Yet he also knew that the target would someday be a real person; one must be prepared to defend his country against the enemy. Then Jordan encountered another dummy, but he noticed his hands were trembling. "When I arrived on the other side there was only one empty cartridge in my pistol," he recalled. "I was shaking as though I were having chills. And it was crystal clear that this Jesus was going one way and I another. Yet I called myself his follower."[34]

Jordan refused his commission, explaining to the commanding officer that he could not serve two masters, the Prince of peace and the god of war. The colonel in charge listened to Jordan's account, and then rose from his chair, put a hand on the young man's shoulder, and said, "God bless you, lad. I hope that someday you will make my job impossible.[35]

In 1933, Jordan left Georgia to attend the Southern Baptist Theological Seminary in Louisville, Kentucky, the largest Protestant seminary in the world and the most academically respected in the Southern Baptist Convention. Having spent the remainder of the summer after ROTC camp at home, he departed for Kentucky in late July with much excitement about the adventure ahead. "I shall like this place very much," he wrote to his mother on his first night in Louisville. Jordan was impressed with everything in his new surroundings: the metal dresser and bed, the mahogany desk and book-stand, the steam heat, the cold drink dispenser in the hallway, the tile in the bathrooms, and the classes. "What classes!" he said, "Hebrew, Greek, Bible, etc., etc., etc."[36]

Jordan had long regarded his mother as the finest expression of God in maternal form. In college, he wrote her every week on Sunday evening. He spoke of her as an "Angel" and "one of the truest evidences of the divinity of God," the "noblest, purest, finest, sweetest angel." "It seems to me," he said, "that the terms 'God' and 'Mother' are closely allied. One is not complete without the other. I believe that Mother is only God come to earth and that in Heaven God will be Mother gone to Heaven. Whether this be so or not God has certainly created a lot of himself into our mothers."[37] His mother taught him spiritual virtues which he would seek to cultivate all his life: the gifts of holy sharing, reciprocity, and generosity, and the qualities of duty, beneficence, and "graceful submission," all of which stood in sharp contrast to more familiar conceptions of an avenging and acquisitorial deity demanding human approval.

Jordan's ritual of a Sunday evening letter to his mother, maintained faithfully throughout his college years, would soon be replaced by his responsibilities in the pulpit. Training Union, a Bible study hour, followed by a Sunday evening service were part of the weekly routine in Southern Baptist churches. Toward the end of the fall semester of 1933, he informed his mother that he would not be coming home to Talbotton for the summer; his church duties required him to stay in Louisville over Thanksgiving and Christmas. She responded by congratulating him on his first pastorate, though her letter registers a sense of regret, if not finality. The next week Jordan received word of his mother's collapse. "She has fallen off to just skin and bones and weaker than I have ever seen her," the father wrote.

Months later he embarked on his first journey to the slums of Louisville to worship in a congregation composed of "a handful of ragged, dirty, hungry, yes starving humanity."[38] He had begun to discover that he preferred these places of need and desolation—the "Children's Homes, tuberculosis sanatoriums, Missions and hospitals"—over the sanctuaries. These excluded places allow him to "rejoice that I have a place in the service of suffering humanity."[39] Jordan was not able to visit his mother in Talbotton, where she died in the spring of 1935, but in his widening embrace of a suffering world he would see her in the faces of the poor and oppressed. "I am seeing that the gospel of Jesus Christ has had its greatest growth when men have been dedicated enough to Him and His principles to quietly live them in the midst of dying and distressed humanity," he wrote. "Right now, I'm inclined to revert to the simple but vital expression which Christianity had [in] its period of beginnings."[40]

In May of 1936, Clarence Jordan married Florence Kroeger in Louisville, a tall, blue-eyed, independent-minded daughter of an immigrant liquor dealer who shared his distrust of "a normal life" and his passion for the poor.[41]

During Jordan's student years, the Southern Baptist Theological Seminary in Louisville was not at all the anti-intellectual backwater it has become in recent decades. There were certainly qualities of the place that would come to feel oppressive to Jordan: a narrowness of vision, the blithe acceptance of white supremacy, and a pervasive militaristic sensibility. The seminary president, J. R. Sampey, described by one historian as "a tall, straight, rigorous, military-looking man with long, hairy fingers," liked to speak of Robert E. Lee as the "greatest Christian since Paul."[42] But while the founding fathers of the school had uncritically accepted the practices of racial separation in their antebellum South Carolina (where the seminary was established in 1859), courses on race relations had been part of the curriculum for more than fifteen years.

First came the remarkable Charles Spurgeon Gardner, who taught the "brotherhood of humanity" as the basis of Christian morality, and then Jesse B. Weatherspoon, William Hershey Davis and Edward McDowell. Weatherspoon, whose course "Christianity and Race Relations" provoked intense debate among the seminarians, became a leader in race reform at Southern Seminary, presiding over the 1954 annual Southern Baptist convention when delegates voted to support the recently enacted *Brown vs. Board* decision. Not only did Weatherspoon espouse a biblical ethic of racial equality in the tradition of his predecessor, Gardner, but he also encouraged his students to think about the church's involvement in the social order and advocated full voting rights for blacks, equally distributed educational funding, fair economic policies, and the elimination of discriminatory laws.[43] Edward McDowell may have lacked Weatherspoon's commanding baritone and eloquence, but he no less resolutely encouraged a generation of Baptists preachers to make "the Word . . . come alive in currents of history and social change." McDowell introduced Jordan to the progressive minds who ran the Southern Interracial Commission and to opportunities for social ministry and interracial fellowship in Louisville, including an inner-city mission program working in black churches.[44]

The 1930s was a period of innovation in race relations among Southern Baptist progressives. Although the defense of racial caste and white supremacy was given popular expression throughout Southern Baptist life and in publications and periodicals, there also existed an emergent discourse of dissent in the convention. While the racial dissidents did not always challenge segregation laws, they questioned inherited attitudes and ideas, and chipped away at the religious underpinnings of racial separation. Most seminaries featured courses in Christian ethics that discussed Southern Baptist attitudes on race. At denominational colleges from Mississippi to Maryland, men and women could be found working to improve race relations and challenge prejudice; agencies like the Social Service Commission and the Negro Ministerial Education were formed to respond to pressing social concerns; and denominational publications featured commentary on race relations. Southern Baptist progressives in North Carolina even managed to adopt a report recommending that every college and school, public and private, offer a course on race relations and that every minister in the state be encouraged to preach an annual sermon on the Bible and racial unity. Throughout the twenties and thirties, the Women's Missionary Union (WMU) of the Southern Baptist Convention supported the work of the Commission on Interracial Cooperation, an initiative in interracial understanding established by the Department of Women's Work, and campaigned actively against lynching. Four of the original members of the Association of Southern Women for the Prevention of Lynching were Southern Baptists and leaders in the WMU.[45] Despite their sometimes patronizing tone—or perhaps because of it—Southern Baptists progressives intended to accept their "missionary task" in race relations as "vital to our civilization and the Kingdom of God as any task found anywhere on the face of the earth."[46]

When Jordan began his doctoral studies in New Testament Greek, he began working part-time at a mission in a black neighborhood in Louisville. By the time he completed his dissertation four years later on the concepts of *thanatos* and *nekros* in Paul's letters, he was directing the missions' center of the Long Run Baptist Association, in charge of Baptist social ministries in the Louisville area. Jordan could appear patronizing in his concern for Negro uplift, as he sometimes presented himself as an authority on Negro life, once going so far as to correct a minister on his use of the term "negro" in written correspondence. "They prefer that it be spelled with a capital N," he explained to a colleague.[47] Jordan also disapproved of the incendiary rhetoric and "revolutionary spirit" of Negro leaders who "fan the fires of race prejudice and hatred into a white hot flame."[48] Nonetheless, he quite deliberately trampled on southern racial etiquette in his covered-dish suppers and worship services with black church people and by staring down the disapproving gaze of white clergymen who objected.[49] He also proposed an initiative called the "Lord's Storehouse," an urban cooperative that sold new and used goods to the poor at cut-rate prices, and sometimes gave them away.

In Louisville, Jordan came to believe that the only way the South could rid itself of its notion of "the inherent superiority and inferiority of the races" was by raising up a generation of young people "courageously and fearlessly" on authentic Christianity.[50] This involved giving southern Christians something other than their own warmed-over culture as the content of their faith, and it meant changing the South from the inside out. Jordan sought a new level of Christian service to the poor beyond the familiar parameters of charity, as his proposals for programs and policies showed sensitivity to the limitations of traditional social ministries, the need for building leadership at the grassroots and for living in community with the poor. "Frankly, I see no reason for not moving into a Negro community," Jordan wrote, "but I see little point in doing it if care is taken not to sleep or eat with Negroes." When he became the director of the Baptist mission in a low-income black neighborhood in Louisville, he promptly changed its name from the Sunshine Center to the Baptist Fellowship Center, hoping to convey a greater sense of gravitas to the work. "His goal was to make black churches, rather than missions led by whites, the centers of ministry in black communities," writes biographer Ann Coble.[51] Jordan believed that black Christian experience offered white Christians a potent and untapped source of spiritual vitality. In the early decades of the century, white southerners had stolen reconstruction from the Negro and given him Jesus in return. Now the white southerner needed the Negro to help him get Jesus back. The Negro Christian, Jordan said, "has an interpretation of Christ that the rest of the world needs."[52]

In time, a group of seminarians gathered around Jordan that called itself Koinonia. The purpose of the group was to develop Christian community as a means of fostering racial reconciliation in the church. Jordan believed that the spirit of fellowship and shared resources stood "in radical proximity" to the Biblical community's practice of bearing witness to the resurrection. "Never did Paul or Peter or Stephen point to an empty tomb as evidence of the resurrection," Jordan said. "The evidence was the spirit-filled fellowship." As would be the case in south Georgia, Louisville Koinonia established a common purse, from which members drew according to their needs and into which they deposited personal funds not required for living expenses. Jordan never expected black people to join the group. Rather, he encouraged the seminarians to attend black churches and to join them if they felt led.

There were nearly sixty Negro churches in Louisville in 1941. The Koinonia fellowship sought to deepen white missionary and philanthropic work in the neighborhoods of these churches by creating opportunities of interracial fellowship and cooperation that lay beyond philanthropic endeavors. The work included launching Baptist Training Unions, Boy Scout troops, a toy library, study courses, vacation Bible schools, training seminars for black pastors, and ministering to Negroes "in any way possible," which sometimes involved raising money among white philanthropists for black churches and community organizations. Many of the members of

Louisville Koinonia followed Jordan in moving into low-income neighborhoods in the city. Any doubt that he was reaching for an expression of Christian discipleship beyond traditional racial improvement was put to rest after he eventually joined a black Baptist church in the city and rebuked a disapproving white minister who accused him of violating Christian principles of racial separation. "I guess it is also a Christian principle," Jordan replied, "to tear out of the New Testament all those pages which proclaim the universality of the Christian brotherhood and which so terribly upset our complacent social traditions."[53]

If Jordan was right in his interpretation of scripture, that the "closeness of sharing" had been used to communicate "the spirit of Jesus" alive in New Testament times, then "why not now?"[54] Why not in Louisville? Because, as it happens, students are a transient lot, who are most often not able to make the kinds of life commitments needed for sustaining common life together.[55] Koinonia Lousiville never moved beyond the experimental stage.

Jordan was beginning to feel restless in Louisville. He was a country boy with a degree in agriculture, and his commitments to the city were shaped by an interest in farming. It was but a natural progression of his calling to begin thinking about the dynamic interactions between the slums and the fields and the extent to which instability in rural areas encouraged steady migration to the inner cities. The thousands of black southerners moving to the urban centers of the North were evidence of the far-ranging implications of rural blight and oppression. Jordan understood that an important dimension of renewing inner cities involved reform of rural areas.

As he was considering his vocational options in the fall of 1941, Jordan met a missionary named Martin England, who shared his hopes for racial reconciliation in the South. At the time, England and his wife, Mabel, were living in an experimental farming cooperative in Wakefield, Kentucky. War had broken out in Burma, where they had been assigned, making a return to their mission posts impossible. Jordan had read a letter published in the magazine *The Next Step in the Churches*, in which England outlined his ideas of an interracial community organized along the lines of small communal experiments described in Acts of the Apostles. "[If] the barriers that divide man, and cause wars, race conflict, economic competition, class struggle, labor disputes, are ever to be broken down," England had written, "they must be broken down in small groups of people living side by side."[56] Jordan read with excitement as he recognized many of his own hopes and convictions in England's remarks. He asked England to meet him at a meeting of the Fellowship of Reconciliation in Louisville. "We've got to talk," England replied.[57] The two ministers quickly discovered that they shared other interests beyond racial reconciliation and intentional community, namely, beliefs about Christian pacificism and the dignity of land.[58]

Less than a year later, Jordan and England set off in search of some land of their own. They were on the verge of purchasing a property in Alabama, when Clarence's oldest brother persuaded them to look at a farm in southwest Georgia. According to Frank Jordan, the three men were inspecting a forlorn spread near Americus—440 acres of dusty red soil, bearing the scars of erosion, treeless but for a single seedling pecan tree—when Jordan announced, "This is it!" The families purchased the property for $7,500, with the financial assistance of a Baptist philanthropist named Arthur Steilberg, and there amidst briars and dusty fields and withering heat, in a dirt-poor county, Jordan and England set about turning their vision of New Testament community into a reality, a "demonstration plot for the Kingdom of God."[59]

The Koinonia Farm experiment, like its trial run in the Louisville Koinonia group, emerged as a result of certain exegetical decisions regarding the interpretation of the fourth chapter of Acts, the book in the New Testament that described the birth of the earliest Christian communities. The question Jordan had pondered as a graduate student was whether the verb tenses of verses 32–37, indicating the holding of all things in common by the disciples, was a "once-and-for-all" action, or an occasional action recommended as the need arose. His seminary professor W. O. Carver argued that the sense of the passage favored an occasional action. "To surrender all of their goods once and for all would be to neglect the duty of responsible stewardship and to lose the discipline of administration," Carver said.[60] Jordan heartily disagreed: the sense favors complete dispossession, not the continuing right to determine one's own actions and loyalties. Only complete dispossession is consistent with other similar purposes in the New Testament, as when Jesus instructs the rich young ruler, "If thou will be perfect, go *and* sell that thou hast, and give to the poor, and thou shalt have treasure in heaven." Koinonia Farm was thus built on a hermeneutical decision.

Jordan's consideration of community was also influenced by Paul's first letter to the Corinthians, the description of the "cup of blessing" shared by believers in the Eucharistic meal. "Praying us with much entreaty that we would receive the gift, and take up on us the fellowship of the ministering to the saints," Paul wrote. Jordan discovered in his studies that the drinking of the cup and the eating of the bread offered a *koinonia*, or fellowship, with the sacrifice of Jesus; and that all Christians share in the one body of Christ. Jordan concluded further that Paul had also used the same term in talking about both the collection for the poor and the practice of the common purse, the sharing of all worldly possessions: Such giving, sharing, and finally relinquishment of wealth brought with it a koinonia with Christ, real participation in his body. Jordan would come to think of deliberate powerlessness as the standard of Christian discipleship and authentic community.

In the early days, building Koinonia in Sumter County, Georgia, must have seemed a lot easier than teasing a harvest of apples, pecans, pears, figs, turnips, plums, cabbage, and persimmons from red-clay fields. With neither oxen nor mules, Jordan and England took turns hitching each other to the plow, turning over the hard ground and watering the fields one bucket at a time, a comic rehearsal of the strange drama unfolding.[61] "We believed we had a call," England said. "We believed that it was the will of God that somebody make a demonstration of these applications of the teachings of Jesus, not only to the life in the church and on Sunday morning, but to all of life."[62] Sumter County was surely fertile ground for the ministers' seeds. Sixty percent of the county's 24,000 residents were black; and most of these people rented shacks on farms and worked as sharecroppers, or lived in dense clusters of shanties in town.

In 1944, after war subsided and the mission posts reopened, the Englands returned to Burma, though they would come back to the States ten years later. Martin England performed his missionary duties overseas with a growing sense of urgency about his involvement in Christian racial reform back home. After 1954, he worked under the auspices of the American Baptist Ministers and Missionaries Benefit Board as a point man for the civil rights movement, marching at Selma, keeping a friendship with Dr. King, raising money for the Southern Christian Leadership Conference, and availing himself of movement activists and organizers in need of pastoral care.

In the plains of southwest Georgia, credentialed as a farmer and a preacher, Jordan settled in for the long haul. "Tall, high-hipped, hands jammed into blue-jean pockets, floppy stray hat shading a grin—dusty from the peanut rows, greasy from the tractor shop, bespectacled from persistent study," writes his first biographer Dallas Lee, "Clarence Jordan was a gentle man who thundered."[63] Jordan launched a soil conservation program by terracing the land to create greater water retention and preserve the topsoil. He experimented successfully with the technique of using ground-up peanut vines as fertilizer for the next season's crops. He established a "cow library" that enabled poor families to check out a milch without charge and to keep her until she was dry. He organized an egg and a seed cooperative, and hosted informal gatherings when neighboring farmers shared farming tips and stories. He offered seminars on chicken coops, fertilizers, soil conservation, hybrid seeds, and new farm machinery, and these seminars were attended by blacks and whites alike. Although most of the white farmers stopped coming after a while, they didn't seem to mind that Jordan offered instruction for their black neighbors.

Jordan never intended for Koinonia Farm to be a center of civil rights organizing, and it never really was. But he also never thought of the farm as an experiment to promote integration, even though the Jordans were intentional in their commitment to interracialism. Jordan rather imagined Koinonia Farm as a place of Christian fellowship whose members sought to practice "the Way of Jesus" in their daily life and work.[64] Jordan repeatedly asserted Koinonia's "family principle" that there "be no favorite children, whether they are blondes or brunettes, white or black."[65] Certainly the application of the teachings of Jesus Christ to southern society would have unsettling consequences for the status quo; but the means by which Jordan hoped to achieve reconciliation (a term he always preferred to integration) would be wholly theological. Reconciliation was first and foremost a quality of life in the body of Christ, a requirement of citizenship in the kingdom of God. And, as he saw it, life in the body of Christ from the perspective of Sumter County, Georgia, involved three interconnected passions: the practice of nonviolence as the moral disposition of the Gospel; the preservation, cultivation, and protection of the soil, "God's holy earth"; and the proclamation and provision of hope to "those who suffer and are oppressed."[66]

The community evolved without clear design or direction. In the next few years, only a dozen or so men and women moved to the farm; most were like-minded Christians from Southern Baptist or Anabaptist traditions. Other people came for short visits—college students, volunteers from the Mennonite Central Committee, and a handful of Baptist radicals like Will Campbell and Foy Valentine. Still, as far as racial reconciliation was concerned, Koinonia was all dressed up with no place to go. And as the Jordans discovered when they moved into their dilapidated farmhouse, it wasn't even dressed up. All the residents of Koinonia Farm were white—unless the black family who stayed on the property to work for the new owners could be counted as part of the interracial experiment.

But Jordan was not discouraged. The undoing of three centuries of white supremacy would take some time. Meaningful and uncoerced interracialism would have to be built relationship by relationship with the patience of a farmer working a barren land. Jordan introduced himself to a local black farmer named Carranza Morgan; and a few days later Morgan appeared at Koinonia in his pickup truck asking to borrow some farm equipment. Focused on the work at hand, Jordan and Carranza Morgan talked about their work and frustrations, their families and their faith. They gave each other advice and offered a helping hand. These informal partnerships increased over time and gave the farm the feeling of friendly and casual interracialism focused on the tasks of agricultural life and the practical concerns of working Christians. As historian Tracy K'Meyer writes in her study of the farm, "The members believed that bringing whites and blacks together in wholesome activities would allow them a chance to get to know each other in an informal situation where fellowship would come naturally."[67] The Koinonians spent the rest of the forties creating opportunities for economic development among rural blacks as well as interracial exchanges in the everyday operations. An organic approach to racial healing seemed the best way to proceed.

Jordan and the Koinonians tried to keep theological matters simple, hoping their straightforward emphasis on loving Jesus, building community, and being reconciled would keep doctrinal controversies at bay. Theological doctrine too often contributed to the separation between black and white, and Clarence Jordan thought that the Bible was all the Christian really needed anyway. Still, after a decade of steady growth and the arrival of women and men influenced by the Bruderhof tradition, the Koinonians agreed that an official process of membership and a more clearly defined administrative structure were in order.[68] As a result, a community pledge was drafted in 1951 formalizing the practice of total community. The Koinonian's pledge may have been ecumenically generous, but the practical application obligated members to the practice of a common purse and proved to be a greater obstacle to racial unity than theological doctrine. With the pledge, the demonstration plot for the kingdom was fixed in a rigid formula of inclusion. The document read:

> We desire to make known our total, unconditional commitment to seek, express, and expand the Kingdom of God as revealed in Jesus Christ. Being convinced that the community of believers who make a like commitment is the continuing body of Christ in earth, I joyfully enter into a love union with the Koinonia and gladly submit myself to it, looking to it to guide me in the knowledge of God's will and to strengthen me in the pursuit of it."[69]

Under the terms of the pledge, a novice first put his possessions in trust outside the community or gave them to Koinonia to hold pending further decisions. At the "provisional level" of membership, that person's assets were given to the community but could be returned if he decided to leave.

A full member, however, surrendered all possessions to the group with the understanding that these possessions would not be returned. Thereafter the living expenses of community members, along with food, shelter, medical care, individual needs (shoes, clothes, books), and whatever else the community regarded as a basic necessity, were provided by the farm's common purse. Membership in Koinonia Farm was thus linked to the obligation to give up all one's personal possessions and share completely in the community. "I think our duty is to make Koinonia as nearly the body of Christ as we are able," Jordan said, "that is our task."[70]

Besides Clarence and Florence Jordan, six couples signed the covenant when it was drafted in 1952. Only nineteen people would sign it by the end of the decade, and all were white. The Koinonia Farm enjoyed friendships with numerous black farmers and church friends, but black members would prove considerably more difficult to find. (Imagine the response the request for complete dispossession would receive from the parishioners at Dexter Avenue driving to church in their late-model sedans.)

Yet the pledge should not be dismissed as white privilege posing as a dramatic exercise in religious devotion. The discussion of the common purse and its requirement arose during an especially difficult period of Koinonia's history, some understanding of which helps make more meaningful the community's decision. Jordan's home church, the Rehobeth Baptist Church in Americus, had voted to excommunicate the Koinonians after Jordan had brought a guest to church one Sunday morning who parishioners mistakenly believed to be a black man. The visitor was an Indian exchange student in agriculture who was spending the year at Florida State University, yet the mistake masked a deeper concern: Most parishioners had long grown tired of the Koinonians's presence in the congregation. In 1948, a Koinonian had invited the black chauffeur of a church member to attend his Sunday school class, and the resulting outrage of parishioners left the white progressives stripped of the privilege to hold leadership positions.[71] The visit of the Indian scholar brought the tensions to a crisis. After a formal vote was taken, the Koinonians were asked to leave the church and their names were removed from the membership. The minister of Rehobeth Baptist informed the Koinonians that "because of our differences in opinion on the race question . . . and the proper relationship to the church, it seems to be the consensus of opinion that members of the 'Koina' Farms cannot be retained in the fellowship."[72]

The desire to formalize the policy of the common purse arose in response to the sanctuary's rejection of the Christ of the fields. Jordan and the Koinonians had become Christians without a church; the fellowship of the farm was all the church they would ever have. Thus, as a means of bearing witness against domesticated religion, the practice of the common purse marked Koinonia as a Christian community set apart from the political world. "Our witness is no longer divided," Jordan said. "We are now whole-heartedly committed to complete brotherhood across all barriers with no other commitments to compromise our witness."[73] After 1951, Jordan referred to himself as "Ex-Baptist," and with his fellow Koinonians entered a sixteen-hundred-year tradition of Christian asceticism and countercultural living.[74]

In fact, the situation of white southern religion bore striking analogies to fourth-century Christianity after the Edict of Milan in 313 brought an end to Christian persecution and Theodosius I in 380 made the Roman Empire an orthodox Christian state. The sanctuaries of the Protestant South and its segregationist piety had become something akin to an official state religion. As in the period of the emerging Constantinian church, men and women were needed who could offer their lives as testimonies to the crucial difference between loyalty to God and loyalty to nation. In the fourth century, the desert fathers had left their homes in the towns and cities of Christendom to live in loosely organized communes, making dramatic demonstration to this difference through their ascetic disciplines of self-denial and contemplative prayer. Simon Stylites, the desert anchorite and holy man (and subject of Luis Buñuel's 1965 film, *Simon of the Desert*), climbed atop a ninety-foot column, naked and filthy, there to remain for forty years. His body's accumulation of dirt and excrement, which rained daily to the ground from his perch, was seized upon by devotees as souvenirs of a militant faith. St. Anthony battled demons within and without, gave away his inheritance, and lived in poverty in caves and on rocks to exemplify the difference between genuine devotion and civic piety. In time, a movement emerged from the desert experiments that challenged the official Christian religion of the emperor, giving birth to the first monasteries, where beloved community took ritual form, its practices codified in the Rules of Benedict and St. Francis.

Jordan understood that at such times as when the church becomes but a mirror of the dominant culture, communities like Koinonia Farm were desperately needed as reminders of the difference between the Christian Gospel of reconciliation and the closed society of Jim Crow. The farms of Sumter County would be the desert places in this cotton-patch rendering of the *ars moriendi*. Jordan explained,

> Maybe, as far as the world is concerned . . . maybe, even as far as Christian-ity is concerned, maybe we are too Christian. Maybe we take the Gospel too

seriously, maybe we do believe too much in the vision of the Old Testament Prophets and the words of the NT messiah. Maybe we do try too hard to work toward that day when the Lion and the Lamb will all lie down together peaceably, and swords and spears are beaten into hammers and saws, and when unto others is done as we'd like to have done to us. Maybe we try too hard to be in the world but not of the world in order to make a difference in this blooming world. Yes, maybe Jesus Christ is too real for us."[75]

Christian discipleship amidst the conformist demands of the Constantinian or the southern way of life required the rekindling of that certain abrasive quality that the apostle Paul had described as the willingness to appear freakish and peculiar. Like the early monastic community, it would not be Koinonia's mission to change the culture through campaigns of organized action or political force, but rather to embody an alternative social order shaped by countercultural habits and practices.

Jordan deplored the way southern Christendom had domesticated the meaning of *metanoia*, or "conversion," turning the transformative decision of commitment into a cultural rite of passage. He would later extend that analysis to the whole church in North America. Jordan wanted churchgoers to know that *metanoia* did not mean becoming a better person, a better citizen, more wholesome and virtuous. Jordan explained that Matthew 18:3—"Except ye be converted and become as little children, you shall not enter the Kingdom of Heaven"—meant literally "Unless you change your mind." To be sure, the conversion experience still carried significance to the child who walked the aisle during the invitational hymn in public profession of his faith in Jesus Christ, followed by baptism by immersion. Jordan had been that child, and he knew firsthand the great emotional cost of the "moment of decision." But he also knew that the sanctuary had failed the child by muting the social scope of salvation. If abstinence from drink, billiards, and dance was essential to "growing in Christ," as Baptists believed, certainly transformed attitudes on race should be part of the church's instruction as well. But instead, sometimes intentionally and sometimes through force of habit, the racial meanings of conversion were governed by southern tradition and its legacy of white supremacy.

Thus, the decision to formalize the community's membership in the pledge represented a full-scale assault on southern Christendom. Jesus as the living presence of God in history overflows the sanctuary and resists the intention of institutions and denominations to bring him under the management of the wholesome and the friendly. As a result, the difference between "being in Adam" and "being in Christ" should not then be represented as a continuum, but as an abyss, the taking-on of an altogether new moral identity. God revealed himself in Jesus Christ, Jordan said, "not to evoke inspiration but perspiration."[76]

The pledge may have indicated a collective desire to build rather than organize community; nevertheless, most members understood the decision not as a withdrawal from the social order but as a way of demonstrating that racial reconciliation and beloved community emerged out of engagement in a common life in a particular place. And it is worth emphasizing that the decision *to be* a Christian community hardly spared Koinonians persecution. During the eight-year period that followed, Koinonia would pass through its most trying season of violence and harassment—a time of "very fiery trials," Jordan said. Attempting to be a reconciled community, even one with all the rough edges, unfulfilled promises, and naïve hopes of Koinonia Farm, was—in the minds of most white southerners—an exercise equally as subversive as bus boycotts, demonstrations, and voter registration programs. The families that left Koinonia complaining that the turn inward to total community diminished "the social aspects of Christ's teaching" (as one member said) might have stuck around long enough to see what a nuisance intentional Christian community could make of itself. Jordan was certainly not giving up on the race issue; he was rather attacking it from a different angle.

By 1956, the farm had grown to its largest number of Koinonians—sixty, including two black members and several black novices. Many other informal friendships with local black families figured into the daily life of the community. Koinonia was also enjoying a period of financial stability as its vegetable markets, roadside stands, egg business, and truck crops flourished.[77] With black and white, children and adults, coming and going freely, the farm operated in clear violation of southern racial customs. Although the 1954 Supreme Court *Brown vs. Board* decision had declared the end of segregation in public schools, nothing in southern society changed overnight as a result of the decision. No doubt the foundations were being laid for wider protest, and there were isolated testings of the new laws throughout the South. But it was not until 1956 that the nation and the residents of Sumter County got a good look at what to expect over the next decade. King assumed leadership of the MIA's year-long challenge on discriminatory policies in public transportation, and, in a lesser story, Clarence Jordan became known as Georgia's second most famous racial subversive.

Two black students, Thelma Boone and Edward Clemons, had applied for admission to the state business college in Atlanta, and after running up against a defiant board of regents, both sought Jordan's support. Although

Jordan had always gone to great lengths to define the mission of Koinonia as evangelistic rather than political, his endorsement of the black applicants—given only after being convinced that they were sincere in their desire to study and not simply testing the admissions policies—put him squarely in the ranks of the racial agitators. No matter that he failed to convince the state board of regents that the black students should be admitted. As far as white locals were concerned, the demonstration plot for the kingdom had finally revealed its true colors.[78] The day after his support was made public, the headlines of the *Americus Times-Recorder* announced, "Negroes Fail in Attempt to Enroll at Ga. College; Endorsed by Americus Man." From the perspective of local white people, Jordan had crossed over to the "world-wide integrationist movement" and "the conspiracy to mongrelize America."[79] "There was no boycott so long as they stayed in their own backyard," one local official said, "We didn't like it, but we put up with it."[80] But after 1956, they weren't putting up with it any longer. Whatever theological message Jordan had hoped to convey by distinguishing between racial reconciliation in Christian community and integrating the South was lost on his white neighbors. To them, Koinonia Farm was as much a part of the civil rights movement as the Montgomery Bus Boycott, and about that they were right.

The nights were electric with fear: Shots rained on the farm from speeding cars and Koinonians were attacked and beaten on the streets of Americus and in other nearby towns. Terrorists bombed buildings on the property, burned crosses, and vandalized and destroyed the roadside markets. Koinonia children were ostracized by their classmates at school when they weren't being bullied; some had to be sent away to live with friends and relatives in safer places. The front gate of the Farm, beneath the defaced Koinonia sign, which bore the image of a black and white hand clasped in friendship, became a depository for hostile letters and notes. One item, retrieved by a small child, announced in large letters penciled on the blank side of an Easter bulletin, "GET OUT YOU MONGRELS."[81] And since no southern terrorist campaign would be complete without the KKK, seventy cars of Klansmen arrived in caravan one night to tell the Koinonians they needed to sell the farm and move elsewhere. Meanwhile, in the light of day, business owners (including Jordan's dentist) and shopkeepers refused the patronage of Koinonians, and the farm moved front and center in a slate of official and unofficial investigations of subversive and un-American activities in the state. Atlanta Cotton States Mutual cancelled its insurance coverage of the farm, and Jordan found himself, the son of a banker, unable to find a bank that was willing to issue loans, extend credit, or retain accounts. In time, the members of the Chamber of Commerce piled in their cars for a visit of their own and urged the Koinonians to sell the farm and leave the area. To Citizens Councilors concerned about Koinonia's leftward leanings, Jordan tried explaining the difference between Jesus and Marx, hoping to reassure the group that he was a follower of the former not the latter; but, as Jordan would later explain, it was clear they didn't know much about either.[82]

In May of 1958, the governor of Georgia signed a bill authorizing a formal investigation of the farm and a series of hearings. The state representative from the south Georgia town of Dublin called Koinonia a threat to "our whole stand on segregation," and said that "something ought to be done about it."[83] The only local support for the embattled Christian community came when a ministerial association drafted a declaration against violence and called for respect of differences and protection of lives and property.[84] Jordan appreciated the declaration, however belated it was in coming, but at the same time he accepted the growing opposition to his work as an affirmation that he was doing the right thing. A mark of the Christian was being persecuted for righteousness sake.

Word of Koinonia's travails eventually reached religious and human rights organizations and publications outside the south—articles appeared in *Christian Century*, *The Nation*, *New York Times*—and petitions for prayer, expressions of solidarity, and assistance in fundraising made their way into an expanded network of pastors and peace workers. Groups calling themselves "Friends of Koinonia" sprung up around the nation organizing vigils and raising money. Some even came to Georgia to help during the season of boycott and terror. Dorothy Day, the founder of the Catholic Worker Movement, paid Koinonia a visit during her 1957 tour of the South and stood guard one night, barely escaping with her life after being fired at in a drive-by shooting. "I will not be afraid for the terror by night nor for the arrow that flieth by day," she wrote prayerfully from Koinonia in her journal.[85] The result was that national support of the farm and its products increased dramatically, especially the new mail-order pecan business advertised under the banner, "get the nuts out of Georgia."

Jordan spoke now of the need for a "wide-awake Christian," whose honest reckoning with the state of things could not be ignored. (The season of violence and its rituals of around-the-clock lookouts encouraged a wakeful faith.) The wide-awake Christian confronts the world "with an entirely different way of life," illuminating a "new kind of thinking." "They face you with the Kingdom of God on earth," Jordan said—now pointing to his besieged experiment in Christian community.[86] But the farm's scars attested to a stunning paradox, that the most Christian region in the most Christian nation on earth had grown afraid of a "real live child of God." Jordan's translation of the Sermon on the Mount in his *Cotton Patch Gospel* tells the story: "You are all God's people when others call you names, and harass you and tell all kinds of false tales on you just because you follow me. Be cheerful and good-humored, because your spiritual advantage is great. For that's the way they treated men of conscience in the past."[87]

Jordan reminded southern churchgoers, not only white but black, of the inescapable mission of "suffering for God." The apostle Paul had spoken of "the power of [Jesus's] resurrection and the fellowship of sharing in his sufferings," illuminating the way in which Christians shared in a koinonia of Christ's suffering. While Southern Baptists preferred sermons decrying the evils of godless communism and praising those who endured persecution for the gospel, beyond receiving a few polite digs about their teetotaling ways, whites were not interested in suffering for God in their own neck of the woods. Jordan, however, believed that suffering remained a necessary condition of the Christian life. If not in physical suffering, or in its extreme form of martyrdom, Christian radicals (or "Kingdom men" as he sometimes said) must pay the price in exclusion, ridicule, and persecution. The kingdom of spirit and truth is the mortal enemy of all worldly systems of power, and the two worlds will never be reconciled. To be sure, the American civil religion, with its jingoistic pieties and idolatrous constructions of nation, may offer successful formulas for filling the pews and offering plates, or for achieving personal success through thrift, wholesomeness, and love of country; but it does so by cheapening the life of the faith. "Persecution is a terrible thing," says Jordan, "but faithlessness is far worse."[88] In fact, in Jordan's estimation the condition of America's proud reputation as the most Christian nation in the world is the church's cowardly refusal to lift up "a mighty 'Thus saith the Lord'" against the controlling elites. "The biggest lie being told in America today is, 'Jesus is Lord.'"[89]

Jordan pressed the simple question: Is the word of God true, the word that became flesh and lived among us, the word of scripture? If the word is true, then a new world is shaped by its truthfulness. "If the Father knows their needs, as he obviously does," Jordan asks, "and has promised to meet them, why not trust him completely?"[90] If the word of God is true, then Christians must learn to live in this new world before choosing their sides and loyalties on the basis of the old world: the old world as defined by nationhood, the free market, white supremacy, and violence. It is one thing to enter the "narrow way" in anticipation of a wonderful and expansive adventure, Jordan said, but it is quite another "to keep on climbing this upward trail." "Jesus wanted people to understand that he wasn't taking them on a picnic," he said.[91] Trust in the Lord is the hardest yet the most freeing of human activities.

These difficult convictions shaped Jordan's thoughts as he considered proposals by some of the Koinonians to relocate the community to safer regions. A concession to the terror perhaps; but certain residents of the farm believed that the integrity of their life together was more valuable than maintaining civil courage on the race issue. Some property in southern New Jersey was explored with real interest. In fact, more than half of the sixty members would be gone by decade's end. Many of the programs that had given Koinonia its uniqueness as an experiment in Christian interracialism had disappeared—the weekly agricultural classes, the vacation Bible schools, the summer camps.[92] As the violence and terror faded to indifference and harassment by quieter means, Jordan awakened to a community in ruins and with diminished purpose. Still, he said "no" to the offers of refuge outside the South almost as if he were resisting the temptation to renounce his calling.

Jordan described his decision to stay put in a moving 1958 sermon:

Fifteen years ago we went there and bought that old run down eroded piece of land. It was sick. There were gashes in it. It was sore and bleeding. I don't know whether you've ever walked over a piece of ground that could almost cry out to you and say "Heal me, Heal me." I don't know if you feel the closeness to the soil that I do. But when you fill in those old gullies and terrace the fields and you begin to feel the springiness of the sod beneath your feet and you begin to feel that old land come to life and when you walk through a little old pine forest that you set out in little seedlings and now you see them reaching for the sky and you hear the wind through them; when you walk a little further over a bit of ground . . . and you go on over a hill where your children and all the many visitors have held picnics and you walk across a creek that you've bathed [in] the heat of the summer, and men say to you "Why don't you sell it and move away?" they might as well ask, "Why don't you sell your mother." Somehow God has made us out of this old soil and we go back to it and we never lose its claim on us. It isn't a simple matter to leave it.[93]

Having survived the boycotts, the harassments and the investigations, the Koinonians began the new decade of the sixties uncertain of the future and of what their mission in the changing South would be. Jordan never intended Koinonia Farm to be anything more than a "demonstration plot of the Kingdom of God," a living parable of reconciliation, although he never had a clear picture of how a Christian community of total sharing and racial equality would transform the social order. The question was: Where should Koinonia Farm go from here?

The Psalmist had spoken of "waiting on God," of dwelling in the house of the Lord and gazing quietly upon the beauty of the Lord. As it turned out, in the period of uncertainty following the years of boycotts and violence, Koinonia Farm was given the grace to do nothing. One of Jordan's theological influences was the nineteenth-century Swiss pastor and social reformer Christoph Blumhardt, who liked to say that in times of uncertainty, God teaches his children lessons in waiting and abiding in the truth. Blumhardt was a man of enormous energy fully engaged in the social challenges of his day; yet he always made clear that the kind of moral action most energizing to the kingdom of God was the kind that emerges from a disciplined waiting. "Get busy and wait," he said. There is "action in waiting."[94]

How then could Koinonia bring to unity its two basic commitments, which so often felt like conflicts: *being* a Christian community and *acting* in the world for the sake of the kingdom? Out of the long season of attacks and harassment, and despite the attrition and confusion that followed, Jordan and the remaining Koinonians were to be surprised by an infusion of new energy.

In 1961 a young black pastor from Petersburg, Virginia, named Charles Sherrod moved into a poor neighborhood in nearby Albany, Georgia. Sherrod had come as an organizer with the newly formed Student Nonviolent Coordinating Committee (SNCC), and he had come with the purpose of getting to know his neighbors and learning the needs of the community. Jordan was impressed with Sherrod, especially by his respect for place, his attention to the grassroots and his commitment to living among the people he served. Sherrod, like most SNCC activists, was full of admiration for Martin Luther King and came to the movement as a result of his leadership. But, also like most SNCC workers, Sherrod had become uneasy with SCLC's top-down approach to civil rights organizing. Decisions about local protests tended increasingly to be made by a small circle of advisors. In Sherrod and other young activists moving into southwest Georgia, Jordan rediscovered many of the same beliefs and convictions that had animated Koinonia's mission in the early days: the respect for particular communities, living with the poor, concern for economic development, and attunement to the local story.

A remarkable thing happened. From 1962 to 1965, Koinonia Farm found itself reborn as a place of hospitality for movement activists, peacemakers, and southern dissidents. SNCC workers in southwest Georgia came for Bible studies and prayer meetings with Jordan and the Koinonians, but also held organizing and training sessions on the farm, seminars on nonviolence, voter registration meetings, literacy schools, and citizenship workshops; scores of "ministers, priests, rabbis and lawyers" stopped by as well for a meal, a shower, and a night's sleep, and sometimes stayed longer.[95] "On Sundays I used to go out there and talk to Clarence and meditate," recalled Sherrod, "and it was just nice to be on a farm and be quiet."[96] Some years as many as a thousand men and women came to the farm for retreat and fellowship. Among them were CORE staff members who found friends in the Koinonians and helped tend the vineyard; as well as pacifists of all stripes who offered each other help filing their applications for conscientious objector status or mustering up the courage to face jail; and back-to-nature-types who came for the simple life. In all of this, Koinonia Farm's contribution to the movement was essential, if not easily discerned. A young activist said, "Koinonia was my haven because if it hadn't have been for Clarence, I don't know whether I would have been able to exist."[97]

Burnout is the activist's occupational hazard, yet little attention has been given to the role of retreat in the study of the movement.[98] The Koinonia story has been ignored because of the difficulty of appreciating the importance of contemplative and moral discipline in social protest. Koinonia makes nothing happen in terms of a familiar statistical-legal measure. Yet the movement in the South, like Bonhoeffer's resistance movement in Germany and Gandhi's *satyagraha* in India, depended on intentional communities dedicated to work, study, and contemplation.[99] "A life of hospitality is much less about dramatic gestures than it is about steady work," the theologian Christine Pohl has written, about "faithful labor that is undergirded by prayer and sustained by grace."[100] Koinonia might be best described as a vital part of the health of the movement, where weary men and women found refreshment and restorative fellowship between the major campaigns.[101]

During these years of intensified civil rights organizing in the South, the nation experienced dramatic changes. As a result of SNCC's work in southwest Georgia and Mississippi, Martin Luther King's campaigns and marches, the martyrs of Birmingham and Neshoba County, and a maelstrom of other related activities and efforts, the Voting Rights Act of 1964 and the Civil Rights Act of 1965 were enacted and forever changed race relations in the United States. And yet by the end of 1965, the movement began to experience its own dramatic changes as black nationalism emerged in the Student Nonviolent Coordinating Committee, a generation of student activists moved on to causes other than civil rights, and war escalated in Vietnam. On the homefront, an SCLC organizing initiative in Americus under the leadership of megalomaniacal Hosea Williams proved disastrous, and Jordan's soulmate Charles Sherrod left Albany. In light of these shifting realities, Jordan discerned the need to restate a nearly forgotten truth: The civil rights movement at its best was a spiritual movement, and all of its later troubles and misdirections were the result of forgetting its origins.[102] "From where I sit," Jordan said, "it seems the intense, bitter phase of the racial revolution . . . is largely behind us. The stage into which we are entering will be the slow tedious one of mopping up, or rebuilding bridges, of learning to live together in the new order."[103] Jordan had been willing to accept the fact that morally ambiguous strategies might sometimes be necessary or pragmatically useful in achieving racial progress, though he had not pursued these himself. The time had come now for the movement to reclaim the vision of redemption, reconciliation, and the creation of beloved community.

Jordan proclaimed the message of the "God Movement." "There must be a greater and deeper movement than the civil rights movement," he said, "the God Movement, the stirring of His mighty Spirit of love, peace, humility, forgiveness, joy and reconciliation in the hearts of all of us. Maybe it's just a dream . . . but the only alternative that I can see to the dream is a nightmare."[104] Jordan began translating the Greek New Testament term *basilia* as "movement" rather than "kingdom," as "something that gets underway spontaneously"—a "New Order," "Spiritual Order," "Kingdom Movement," "Spiritual Movement," and "Spiritual Family." "The God Movement is not something you enter into and flop down and say, 'God, I made it.'" The God movement is rather like the day of the Sabbath, not in a sense of rest or withdrawal from action but in the sense of harmony and tremendous activity concentrated in the task at hand, "activity coordinated with God's purposes." In short, Jordan's God movement was the new social order that bursts into being in the life and teachings of Jesus. Jesus had founded the most revolutionary movement in human history: a movement built on the unconditional love of God for the world and the mandate to live in that love. Jordan wrote to peaceworker Craig Peters: "I am increasingly convinced that Jesus thought of his messages as not dead-ending in a static institution but as a mighty flow of spirit which would penetrate every nook and cranny of man's personal and social life . . . I really don't think we can ever renew the church until we stop thinking of it as an institution and start thinking of it as a movement." [105]

Preaching the God movement circa 1965 carried with it inevitable criticisms of the civil rights movement. Jordan asked the questions: Has the civil rights movement mistaken its demand for equal rights as the fulfillment of the search for beloved community? Has the movement lost sight of the fact that the Christian always passes through the mortal world as so-journer, pilgrim and "stranger to the well-ordered communities of this earth."[106] Have movement leaders and participants failed to acknowledge that the affirmation they seek can only be conferred by God? Abiding by a different logic and motivation, and thus "set apart by God's spirit," the Christian, said Jordan, must remain a stranger amidst the violent and de-humanizing structures of the world. Jordan explained in a sermon:

> [The Christian] is a stranger because his ideas are strange and foreign. He's a stranger because he's a new creature. His life is on new foundations. He's got new motivations, new valuations, a new outlook. He's a stranger in the council halls of the wicked. . . . He isn't at home there. He has caught a vi-sion of a world of sharing and he isn't at home in the halls of finance and big business. That's not his land. . . . The real home of the Christian is this earth, under the spirit and guidance and influence of Jesus Christ.[107]

In other words, the civil rights movement might have succeeded in changing the laws of the South and the nation, but if it secured these changes by compromising its redemptive mission, it was a failure.

What would Jordan have King do? King would do his own body and soul good and also further nourish the movement by going to the wilderness and making retreat, regathering his spiritual and moral energies, rekindling his affection and loyalty to Coretta, and rebuilding his relationship with his daughter, Yokie, and his two sons, Dexter and Martin, living now in an At-lanta netherworld of nannies and tutors like fatherless children. He should seek to live single-mindedly in a community and demonstrate in a local en-vironment the truth and meaning of his preaching and prophesying. King should not consider himself exempt from the ordinary demands of the Christian life: walking humbly, "rooted and built up in him," in the words of the New Testament, "clothed with humility," "sober," "vigilant," "subject one to another."[108]

Perhaps, but King had led the Montgomery movement on the founda-tions of the black resistance church. With so secure a foundation, King, unlike the Southern Baptist Jordan, felt no ambivalence in engaging and reforming the civic and political realm. As a result, the "spiritual struggle" in Montgomery had included both the church and the world in its scope; the church's politics demanded action in both fields. Any affirmation of racial unity that did not require material change was cheap, and it was not an appropriate Christian response. One need only observe the Gnostic arrangements of white evangelical Christendom, its preference for the spirit over the harsh judgments of the body, especially when the black body was on its feet in social protest. But the black church was everywhere in Montgomery, on the streets, in the cars, overflowing onto the sidewalk, and as a result there was no need to worry about politicizing the parish. Legal and social reform were essential to the movement.

Still, Jordan's criticism that the civil rights movement had failed to stay the course on redemption and reconciliation in the South paled in comparison to his unforgiving judgments on southern evangelicalism, the heartbreaking calumny, indeed the heresy, of the white church. Jordan's denunciation of the southern sanctuary in his final sermons is harder than any King's had ever been. (It would not be until the late 1960s and the writings of radical black theologians such as Vincent Harding and James Cone, that denunciations of the white church appeared with similar fury and power.)[109]

In his "Letter from Birmingham City Jail," King had assumed the role of spiritual counselor to an erring white church, which stood in need of instruction. He described his "deep disappointment" with the white church. "I have wept over the laxity of the church," he said, "Yes, I see the church as the Body of Christ. But, oh! How we have blemished and scarred that body through social neglect and fear of being nonconformists."[110] The judgment of God was upon the church as never before, he allowed, but as the forfeiture of the church's authenticity and relevance. His tears were "tears of love."

But Clarence Jordan asserted with prophetic wrath that the southern church had been overtaken by "false prophets" who would be "chopped down and thrown into the fire."[111] The righteous man sheds no tears for the apostate church. Jordan read scripture with the passion of an old-school fundamentalist, except he refused to demythologize reconciliation so as to save his hide.[112] Jordan believed that born-again faith, if followed through to the end, if genuine, could not but transform white supremacy from the inside out. The process of transformation is set in motion, "when we receive Jesus, when we open our hearts to him and let him come in, bringing with him all his queer ideas about loving everybody, even one's enemies, about racial equality, about complete economic sharing, about humility."[113] Racial reconciliation, economic redistribution, and prophetic pacifism are fruits of the spirit, the gifts of Pentecost. Jordan's born-again social radicalism stood as evidence that when the fruits were absent, so was salvation. The southern sanctuary was the construction of apostates and atheists.[114]

"Here is what I am trying to say," Jordan told an interviewer toward the end. "If the barriers that divide man, and cause wars, race conflict, economic competition, class struggles, labor disputes are ever to be broken down, they must be broken down in small groups of people living side by side, who plan consciously and deliberately to find a way wherein they can all contribute to the kingdom according to their respective abilities."[115]

Koinonia Farm is best remembered as an exercise in repentance, reconciliation, and costly discipleship—not as a solution to the race problem. To be sure, Jordan's lessons were not lost on a younger generation of civil rights workers, including Charles Sherrod, who understood that "much of the spade work" of SNCC's organizing in southwest Georgia "has already been done by the Koinonia farm people . . . even if it is emblazoned with bullet fringes," and even if the community "could have gone a lot farther than it did."[116] Still, in another sense, Koinonia went further than SNCC, for while the civil rights movement defeated segregation and forever changed American society, the nation has experienced precious little of repentance, reconciliation, and costly discipleship. Jordan's alternative theological vision of the South required a quieter and yet deeper revolution.

In the end, the civil rights movement and the God movement illuminate two trajectories of building beloved community, which diverge and sometimes turn against the other: the church as the agent of social empowerment and the Christian community as a distinctive social reality that repudiates secular power. These two visions are not mutually exclusive; they overlap at times and coexist in complex ways relative to the social situation. Yet as these trajectories form an arch from Montgomery through Sumter County into subsequent decades of congregational activism, they forge differing visions and hopes of beloved community. Charles Sherrod summarized one of the basic differences: "The Koinonians didn't believe in anybody suing people. We were nonviolent but we believed in suing the hell of somebody if we could, especially when they left us without jobs."[117] Although there was a small degree of white involvement in Montgomery, as there was some degree of black involvement in Koinonia, the work of reconciliation did not offer the satisfactions of political organizing. Reconciliation's success was difficult to measure, and there seemed to be no end to the complexity of its conditions and demands. Reconciliation and beloved community would always be experienced as broken and incomplete, as an eschatological reality. Jordan explained in a 1966 letter to one of his sons, "This is what always baffles me—Koinonia is forever dying and forever living. We should have conked out long ago, but somehow others came in the nick of time. This half-born condition is agonizing, and I could wish it otherwise, but there it is."[118]

Jordan died suddenly on a cold and clear afternoon in late October of 1969. He had been working in his one-room writing shack in the cornfield, where he had recently completed his *Cotton Patch Gospel of Matthew*. The county coroner refused to come to the farm to issue a death certificate; so the dead body of the preacher was driven into Americus in the back of a station wagon. Jordan was buried the next afternoon in a cedar coffin, wearing blue jeans. The service bore the familiar evidence of a prophet never honored in his home as white clergy and churchgoers from Americus ignored the occasion. But when the coffin was lowered into the red ground, the two-year-old daughter of Millard and Linda Fuller, a couple who had recently joined the Koinonia community and would soon establish Habitat for Humanity, began singing the only song she knew by heart:

Happy birthday to you,
Happy birthday to you,
Happy birthday, dear Clarence,
Happy birthday, to you.[119]

~~

CHAPTER 3

A Theology for Radicals:
The Rise and Fall of SNCC

In a report on his work in southeast Georgia from 1961 until 1965, Charles Sherrod, the young SNCC field secretary from Petersburg, Virginia, and friend of Clarence Jordan, wrote:

> But let me bear witness before you that I have seen the earth, moving, surging, and falling, struggling to breathe, eager to learn the truth; I have seen it in stinking jail cells packed with people, singing and sweating people, brought before the Pilates of this day; I have seen the church under the stars praying and singing in the ashes of a burned down church building, in the winter shivering under a tent in the open country, in a home where people cried together without speech but with a common understanding; I have seen the church in a pool room. I have seen with my eyes whites protecting blacks with their bodies and blacks bleeding to shield whites from whites.
>
> I have seen ministers lead their congregation from Sunday service to the City Hall to condemn the state. I have heard ministers with three grades of education put Ph.D.'s to shame. I have seen men share their bread till the last was gone. I have seen a band of rugged brothers willing to risk death for each other if need be. I have seen the strength of fellowship among those who formally refuse the fellowship of the church. Somehow I think this life must be shared for it to be comprehended; we do have something to offer but there is probably much to receive. This is an experiment in truth to find truth.[1]

SNCC's "experiment in truth to find truth," as Charles Sherrod's luminous testimony makes clear, far from being a matter of mere intellectual interest, was grounded in the concrete struggles and stories of poor and excluded communities in small southern towns.

The student-based movement, represented by SNCC, grew out of the 1960s sit-ins, which began on the afternoon of February 1, 1960, when four black freshmen at North Carolina Agricultural and Technical College walked into a Woolworth's store, purchased some school supplies, sat down at the lunch counter and ordered a cup of coffee. Within three months of the Greensboro incident, more than fifty cities had served as theatres for the sit-ins, and as many as fifty thousand students had joined in.[2] National news services often described a group of "well-dressed Negro college students" sitting together contemplatively, often concluding their protest with their hands joined together in prayer.[3]

At a conference on Easter weekend, organized by the brilliant movement strategist Ella Baker, a mission statement was drafted. "Peace dominates war; faith reconciles doubt," read the document, written by James Lawson, the Vanderbilt seminarian expelled earlier in the year for his work as the principal organizer of the Nashville sit-ins. The members of the new organization resolved their commitment to "a social order permeated by love and to the spirituality of nonviolence as it grows from the Christian tradition." Love was affirmed as "the central motif of nonviolence," the "force by which God binds man to himself and man to man," which goes to "extremes" in radical acts of compassion and forgiveness, "even in the midst of hostility." The student movement would bear witness to divine love by its dedication to nonviolence and to organizing in poor communities for political power and expressive focus. Only "redemptive community" could supersede "systems of gross social immorality" and nurture an "atmosphere in which reconciliation and justice becomes actual possibilities."[4] "Our goal was to reconcile," organizer Diane Nash said, "to create a "community recovered or fulfilled," rather than " simply gain power over the opposition." Nash regarded the mission of SNCC as "applied religion."[5] "To redeem means to rehabilitate, to heal, to reconcile rather than gain power," she said.[6]

If Martin Luther King Jr.'s sartorial flair hinted at the usefulness of mainline respectability and the preeminence of the professional male clergy, SNCC's uniforms of denim, T-shirts, and work boots reinforced the claim of earnest solidarity with poor blacks, the holy garb of a "free-floating monastic order" (in the words of one activist pastor).[7] Martin Luther King left plenty of room for middle-class comforts in his dream, although his spiritual discipline of bearing witness to nonviolence was the antithesis of bourgeois religion. Nevertheless, it would be SNCC's mission to protest middle-class values in a more vivid social form and to seek satisfying alternatives to the American way of life.[8] And while the Student Nonviolent Coordinating Committee practiced an altogether different spirituality than SCLC's Sunday-go-to-meeting solemnity, so that sometimes historians even speak of the younger civil rights organization as the secularizing wave of the civil rights movement—Stokely Carmichael's avenging fantasies set against Dr. King's prayerful pacifism—in fact the distinctive radicalism of SNCC was theological to the core.[9] Victoria Gray, a business woman and civil rights leader from Hattiesburg, Mississippi, liked to think of the SNCC as the "enfleshened church."[10]

SNCC's founding mothers and fathers were very often radical Christians, exuberantly faithful people motivated by diverse theological sources mixed in unusual, sometimes exotic, combinations according to the demands of the situation. Theological existentialism, holiness fervor, contemplative asceticism, social gospel idealism, Protestant liberal hope, and even some good old-fashioned otherworldliness were all part of the mix. Fannie Lou Hamer, the SNCC leader from Ruleville, Mississippi, imagined the civil rights movement as a welcome table, the kind that might be found beside a rural Baptist church, where on special Sundays and dinners-on-the-ground, the abundant riches of southern cooking would be spread out for everyone to enjoy, even Governor Ross Barnett and Senator James O. Eastland, though they would need to learn some manners.[11] "Christ was a revolutionary person, out there where it's happening," Mrs. Hamer said. "That's what God is all about, and that's where I get my strength."[12] Her Christianity, like that of the other mothers and fathers, was unapologetically Christian in its singing and testifying, and yet equally generous to non-Christian fellow travelers. The work of organizing and building communities was about celebrating the common grace of women and men, black and white, the privileged and the poor, who found themselves together, miraculously, in the South, working in common cause for a more just and human social order. "You could see the young people from all over the South," Howard Zinn described the situation with SNCC in 1963, "black college students, a few white friends joining them, getting together, forming SNCC and then going out into the small towns of the South talking to the ministers, talking to the local people, getting a place to live in local homes and then creating the kind of commotion which is necessary to create in order to bring about change."[13] The enfleshened church pursued a form of Christian discipleship that was life affirming, socially transformative, and existentially demanding: a theology for radicals.[14]

SNCC's collapse can best understood as the retreat from this theological experiment. The other important factors involved in the organization's demise, none more pressing that the dispute over interracialism, nonviolence and organizing styles, are part and parcel of this shift.[15] SNCC's fragile unity of form and freedom, sustained for a while by spiritual convictions and passions, finally collapsed on the side of freedom; and freedom unfettered from sacrificial love produced an unforgiving legalism. Compassionate action can never drift too far from its sources without forgetting purpose and mission.

By the end of the decisive year 1964, SNCC had moved away from Christian formulations of nonviolence and beloved community. The "circle of trust" began to forget its lineage as a child of the church. Some members even sought to obliterate this identity. By the end of 1964, the social disciplines that had once been focused on particular organizing goals gave way to a broader and yet deracinated therapeutic field. "Some people want to experiment with personal freedom and go where they want to go," SNCC's John Lewis said in late 1965.[16] By the spring of 1966, SNCC's pursuit of the beloved community was a distant memory. "We should never again seek to involve the church in actions of SNCC," Stanley Wise would say in a staff meeting that year.[17] The goal of "redeemed society," it was duly noted, remained only "the minority position" of Sherrod and a few other believers lacking credibility in the new SNCC vanguard. What began with SNCC organizer Fannie Lou Hamer's exuberant affirmation, "I've got the light of freedom," concluded with Wise's arrogant claim that Hamer is "no longer relevant," no longer at "our level of development." "We have closed ourselves in a haven and the movement has passed us by," a dejected staff member said.[18] Without a spiritual vision, there would be no more summer projects, no more coalitions between local organizers and white students, no more innovations in community action.

By the end of 1964, many in SNCC had given up their former dreams and abandoned nonviolence, community-based social reform, and the vision of beloved community.[19] Still, the tragedy of SNCC's collapse is not the inevitable disillusionment and anger that followed an intense season of organizing, but its lack of spiritual resources for turning that disillusionment and anger into realistic appraisals of beloved community.

In the beginning, SNCC brought to the movement a broad cast of characters representing uncommon cultural and economic diversity. Bob Moses was a Harvard-trained philosopher whose signature overalls and tattered Camus paperbacks gained an iconographic status for student progressives in the South. Moses explained SNCC's sought-after balance between the global and the particular as the "unique position of combining the vision of the long range need with roots in the local communities."[20] Mrs. Hamer was "a lady in homespun dress with a bandanna to keep the sun away," who left the cotton fields of Sunflower County, Mississippi, in 1962, to "work for Jesus" in civil rights.[21] Victoria Gray was a black middle-class landowner and business woman, who took her first step into movement life during a church service one night in her hometown of Hattiesburg, speaking the decisive words, "Here am I, Lord, send me, I'll go."[22] Gray saw the civil rights movement as "a journey toward the establishment of the kingdom of God," and as a journey she felt called to make. John Lewis, a student at the Baptist seminary in Nashville, said that "faith in God was at the heart of all I did." As a teenager in south Alabama, Lewis had heard a radio broadcast of Martin Luther King's sermon "St. Paul's Address to American Christians," and was struck by the contrast between the Pike County preachers of his childhood, who talked about the pearly gates of heaven and the streets paved with gold, and Dr. King, who spoke of Jesus alive and active on the highways and byways of America. Lewis soon thereafter resolved "to enter the struggle and to turn myself over and follow, and somehow believe that it was all going to be taken care of; it was all going to work out."[23] White activists like Bob Zellner and Jane Stembridge entered the struggle out of a sense of spiritual incompleteness, out of the recognition of their own enslavement to white supremacy. Stembridge was a student at Union Theological Seminary in New York and the daughter of a Southern Baptist minister, who understood her commitment in terms of a "great need" for freedom.[24] "I came here because I, too, needed to be free, respected, a person, understood," she said. "You see, this is my movement, too."[25] Zellner grew up in south Alabama, the son of a former Klansman and Methodist minister, and he crossed over to the movement while writing a term paper at a local Methodist college on the Montgomery Improvement Association. "I left the old world and went into another one," Zellner said. "White shackles needed to be broken too."[26]

If SCLC assumed a professional and preacherly role in mobilizing people for power, SNCC sought to embody what might be called an incarnational ethic in its preference for grassroots organizing among the poor. "Local people—local leadership—was at the center of everything we did," said Moses. "Local folk might not be paying us, but we were working for them."[27] Mary King emphasized SNCC's "stern insistence" in its conceptualization and strategy that "our thinking, our framework" should grow "from engagement with the people that we were working with rather than any doctrine or any ready-made philosophy."[28] Incarnational organizing should not, of course, be misunderstood as the saving of souls from eternal damnation. Mississippi segregation, like its historical master, slavery, was hellfire enough for the souls of black people. Nor should SNCC's incarnational organizing be confused with incarnational evangelism, as in Clarence Jordan's evangelical experiment, the explicit proclamation of the Christian Gospel in social practice and community identity. Rather, for SNCC, incarnational meant organizing shaped by the discernment and trust of local people, by the commitment to live with those one serves and by the release of the tyrannical desire to manipulate others. "Whenever you want to really do something with somebody else," Moses said, "then the first thing you have to do is make this personal connection, you have to find out who it is you're really working with. You have to be interested in that person to work with them."[29] This was the credo of SNCC's relentlessly public faith.

To be sure, the desire to control the organizing situation ran fierce in the moral convictions of many crusading white student volunteers, who sometimes behaved as if their bookish knowledge of social movements of the past translated into necessary wisdom for the civil rights movement of the present. Jane Stembridge acknowledged the "very subtle ways" in which the "danger of 'playing God' and planning the movement" operated among white participants. "I have constantly had to stop short and remember my 'outsider' status," she said.[30] "The surest ways to kill the movement are for adults and white students to get in with the determination to organize, etc."[31]

Nonetheless, the incarnational ethic also encouraged student volunteers and SNCC staff members simply to be present with each other and with the poor. Being a "revolutionary," somebody once said during a staff meeting, meant learning how to act out of the deepest silence. As an enfleshened church, SNCC displayed a remarkable capacity to anchor itself in particular neighborhoods and accommodate its disciplines to local needs. Yet as a "free-floating monastic community," SNCC also made time for reverie and solitude and for rituals that were refreshingly unproductive.[32] A certain kind of contemplative discipline was an important predisposition in building community and enabling trust.

This is an important but often overlooked point. It is easy to forget that so much of a civil rights life involved sitting around freedom houses, community centers, and front porches with no immediate plan of action. The discipline of waiting required uncommon patience even as it sustained humility and perspective, resisting the cultural paradigm of efficiency. SNCC's genius was its ability to demonstrate to black southerners the strategies available to social progress within an unhurried and sometimes languorous emotional environment. As such, a condition for achieving beloved community was a certain kind of stillness in a nation of frenetic activity and noisy distractions, learning to move at a different pace. Certainly there were more than a few volunteers who left the south out of boredom. Yet most who pursued a movement life understood the quality of their life together as an attempt to live into a new and distinct kind of time. Jane Stembridge described waiting as a discipline, as a spiritual and aesthetic attunement to the "lonely center of the spinning earth."[33] And in her opinion, the movement could have used a lot more frivolity, beauty, and stillness. She wrote in one of her remarkable Mississippi poems:

When we loved, we didn't love right.
The mornings weren't funny, and we lost too much sleep.
I wish we could do it all again with clown hats on.[34]

Even so, the unhurried pace of incarnational organizing and the spirit of play evoked in the freedom community could not dispel the ever-present prospect of death. Death as a likely consequence of participation in the movement encouraged some activists to shift the emotional weight from the defensive to the offensive, even as it encouraged others to reckon with the prospects of civil rights martyrdom. Either way, however, the possibility of death was the condition of the mental environment that intensified every situation. "It was an axiom that you would probably die," said Tom Hayden. "So you had to have something around you strong enough to take the fear of death and dissipate it, and that was this community."[35] "We had expected violence, even death," said Joyce Ladner.[36] One volunteer from the northeast told a *New York Times* reporter, "We know there is a chance of being hurt, of being jailed, or being killed, but we still believe in the cause so strongly that we must go."[37] John Lewis borrowed Dr. King's theme of "redemptive suffering" to describe his willingness to sacrifice life and well-being for the sake of justice, a deliberated suffering that "opens us and those around us to a force beyond ourselves, a force that is right and moral, the force of righteous truth that is at the basis of human conscience."[38]

t with the vertiginous sense of mortality, the youth movement's discipline forged an intensely felt solidarity. "In Mississippi, I have felt more love, more sympathy and warmth, more community than I have known in my life," a student wrote.[39] Charles Sherrod recalled the vanishing of social privilege that took place in the jails as a result of the "bond of togetherness" shared by doctors and lawyers, teachers and domestics.[40] Solidarity linked by sacrifice, acceptance of death, and the shared "desire to be free" made possible a new perspective on the old social order. "You find people walking together, people talking together. People who would never think they would speak to this person, or that person."[41]

SNCC's renunciation of middle-class values differed in other ways as well from Clarence Jordan's experiment in Christian community. For Jordan, organizing was about creating the theological conditions for being the community of Christ. For SNCC, incarnational organizing was about creating the moral conditions of effective social change. Organizing for power meant listening with humility to the concerns of local people but not in order to make poverty normative. "Being powerless is part of not knowing how to use organization for power," wrote national staff member Mike Miller; and for this reason, organizing communities for power was part of the modus operandi of participatory democracy.[42] More concretely, organizing for power meant protecting and advancing the interests of poor people by creating networks to focus on urgent social needs; it meant transforming the material conditions of minority communities. "In relation to local protest areas, SNCC's role is suggestive rather than directive," read one of the convictions of an early SNCC source document.[43] To be sure, SNCC's organizing vision was not indifferent to national and global concerns, for as Miller explained, "we seek change not only in Mississippi but in the nation."[44] Yet the point of entry was always local and particular. "Our work must . . . be in the black communities," John Lewis said, "in the rural areas, the farms and hamlets [and] the slums and ghettos of the city."[45] The revolution waited patiently at the front porch for the handshake of assent.

SNCC's model of community organizing also gave rise to a distinctive form of intellectual engagement.[46] Marion Barry claimed that the movement was engendering a different kind of people, people who had been "jerked from the complacency of the ivory tower and thrown up against the barriers that separate men from men and thus, men from themselves."[47] As a counterpoint to a dominant culture that had made a virtue of the shallow and the superficial, SNCC probed every angle of the organizing situation and exemplified a communicative ethics of unflinching honesty in its meetings, seminars and everyday exchanges. "[There] is nothing that we were afraid to discuss," said Mary King.[48]

The enfleshened church was built then on the trinity of social disciplines comprising incarnational organizing, nonviolence, and interracialism. At the Conference on Human Rights in 1960, a young organizer from Mississippi named Chuck McDew described the practice of nonviolence emerging in the movement as evidence of spiritual renewal among a generation of black students in the South. "Students are more sincere about the Christian faith than they have ever been before," McDew said.[49] In a region marked by a zeal for guns and God, the movement introduced a new method of social protest and an unfamiliar moral claim on Christian social practice. Chuck McDew called this method "the philosophy of love overcoming hate, of nonviolence conquering violence, of offering oneself as a sacrifice for a valuable cause."[50] At a demonstration in Orangeburg, South Carolina, he noted, several hundred students had quit the march and reconvened in a nearby church for prayer, so frightened had they become of fighting back on provocation.[51]

Casey Hayden spoke of nonviolence as a liberating way of life in which the individual is "broken open, released from old and lesser definitions . . . into the large self of the Beloved Community."[52] Marion Barry spoke of nonviolence as a dynamic affirmation of the other—a Yes to the individual, "be he friend or foe." "The potential of the movement is fantastic," he said, as it seeks to realize "through a belief in Something greater, the community of persons."[53] Diane Nash spoke of nonviolence as "both the creation and the activity of the redemptive community."[54] No doubt, SNCC's acceptance of guns in the mid-sixties "affirmed the legitimacy of a long-standing tradition of armed self-defense among blacks in the rural deep South," as historian Clayborne Carson points out.[55] But these facts simply underscore the rather uninformative observation that SNCC's eventual endorsement of racial reform by "any means necessary" was conditioned by a gun-slinging culture. Rather, what was truly remarkable was that out of that culture, a movement emerged that rescued the nonviolent teachings of Christianity from a piety saturated with militaristic passion. Thomas Merton once said that the civil rights movement offered church people in the United States the opportunity to recommit themselves to the difficult truth that "non-violence comes very close to the heart of the Gospel ethic, and is perhaps essential to it."[56]

SNCC's commitment to nonviolence, then, quite aside from internal disagreements about its sources and aims, offered students (in McDew's words) "a chance for the word to become flesh" and further committed them to a set of spiritual disciplines that could only be sustained by the energies and convictions of the church.[57] McDew went so far as to imagine the sit-ins as a sacramental reenactment of Jesus's sitting-in with the Samaritan woman, recorded in the Gospel of John. Like the sit-ins in the South, Jesus's simple request, "please give me a drink of water," defied the established wisdom of the day and transgressed widely-accepted ethnic boundaries. "How is it that you, being a Jew, and a man, say to me, who am a Samaritan and a woman, 'Give me a drink'? Don't you know that Jews and Samaritans have no dealings?" As Jesus' request for a drink of water had provoked "all the old antagonisms of the centuries," so now the black students' request for a cup of coffee at a drug store unsettled "the entire fabric of our Southern civilization."[58] Jesus was simply saying that there is enough water in this well for the two of us, and that God "blesses us with gifts "which would enrich us both if we shared them."[59] But Jesus' simple words were revolutionary to the core; and not only that, they were a "gift of God" to an excluded woman in second-century Palestine and also to the youth movement today. (For his part, McDew had seen the most compelling example of real religion when a rabbi invited him to temple after the white Protestant ministers in Orangeburg had closed their doors, and McDew converted to Judaism later in the year.[60])

Advocates of nonviolence and reconciliation would certainly emerge from different faith traditions as well as from solely humanistic motives. Still, the movement pressed men and women with ultimate questions that gave the experience itself an unmistakable spiritual intensity; and the energies and convictions of the church transformed the perceptions of volunteers and staff members who were otherwise unmoved by religion and religious sentiment (sometimes unexpectedly and against their better judgment). Consider the testimonies of surprise and wonder:

Sunday I went to a real whoop and holler church, with people shouting, screaming and stomping. The sermon began as a talk and ended up as a song. The preacher jumped up and down and had tears running down his face. He finally was overcome by the sheer power of his word and started to sing 'This Little Light of Mine' in the middle of the sentence. We joined him, and people came up to grab his hands. I was one of them. This was the only House of God I had ever run into in my life. Amen! It was real, powerful and glorious.[61]

This is something really big—yes, a revolution—a New Way of Living and Being . . . There is hope here that does not exist in the North.[62]

I do not want to spend my life in the pursuit and enjoyment of comfort and security. I want to pursue my spiritual growth. . . . I sense somehow that I am at a crucial moment in my life and that to return home where everything is secure and made for me would be to choose a kind of death.[63]

Indeed the non-Christian fellow travelers in the movement quite often understood the peculiar manners and speech of the enfleshened church as the best articulation of their civil courage in the south; the entry point for universal affirmations.

For each of us "We shall overcome" held a different meaning, a more personal hope or prayer, yet, from it we discovered a common bond.[64]

In other instances, too, the living faith of local black people challenged the presuppositions of secular activists, a point well illustrated in a letter written by a Harvard student to his roommate in Cambridge:

I went to church today, the third time since I've been here. . . . It's just like the scene in Go Tell It On the Mountain—but it's real—there's a direct tie between every person in that church and God, and every person with me and I with them.

Or by other students to their family:

Tonight was different from the first time. . . . I left the church wondering the eternal question of God, which we so easily answer with terms of science and evolution and theories of the Beginning . . . *We* think more or less in the context which we were brought up—Aye, liberal and thought-provoking though it is, it is still enslaving us.[65]

For many local citizens our coming was a religious event. I found it difficult to be cynical.[66]

At the same time, the incarnational model played havoc on traditional southern notions of cultural stability as SNCC volunteers living in black neighborhoods elicited the hostile stares and reactions of local whites. Howard Zinn described SNCC as "a recapturing from some time and place long forgotten," an approach to life that aimed beyond politics toward the removal of barriers preventing authentic relation with other people.[67] "The cause of the Movement was to live the kind of life we wanted for the world in the midst of the struggle to change the world—for civil rights or anything else," said Ed King, the organizer and white chaplain at Tougaloo College.[68] Most movement activists wanted more for black people than the reversal of power or the truculent assertion of ontological blackness. As Fannie Lou Hamer said, "If I knew today, [that] Mississippi would be taken over by all the black folk, nothing but Negroes, I'd fight that just as hard as I'm fighting this white power."[69] There had to be more at stake in the struggle than political power, and interracialism, however undesirable it might have been to some, attested dramatically to that alternative order. Dr. King had spoken of the unleashing of the power of love, of a redeeming, reconciling, redemptive love that reached beyond the divisions toward the compassionate center of being itself.[70] In this manner, the movement anthem, "We Shall Overcome," was about a coming over from the old to the new—a closing of the distance between human beings—not only about an overpowering of segregation or the segregationist.[71] Blacks and whites who gathered together in tension-filled COFO offices, in mass meetings in black churches, in smoky debates in cafes and freedom houses, and in whatever other places where chaos broke out in the pursuit of justice, must then not only *act* in specific emancipatory ways, but even more must seek to live in the present time that kind of reality that they hoped the movement would bring about later. When Bob Zellner spoke of SNCC as "the greatest thing that ever happened in my life," he was not talking about a march or a demonstration but *a way of life*.[72]

In October 1961, Charles Sherrod opened up a SNCC office near the campus of Albany State University. From 1961 until he left for seminary in 1965, Sherrod worked tirelessly in southwest Georgia with an organizing skill and devotion in every way equal to that of Moses in Mississippi—and with a more clearly defined theological perspective on the local story. In his seminal study, *In Struggle: SNCC and the Black Awakening of the 1960s*, Clayborne Carson claimed that "Sherrod infused his work with the religious zeal of a southern black preacher and with the idealism of SNCC's early years, whereas Moses, the northern intellectual, evinced a patient pragmatism and an overriding commitment to humanist values." But these differences, most sharply observed in Moses's focus on voter registration and Sherrod's on civil disobedience, were not as significant as the two men's shared commitment to the integrity of the organizing situation. In Albany, Sherrod and his fellow Virginian Cordell Reagon moved into the community to begin the process of discerning the mood and needs of the people, acting like "neighborhood boys." They talked to people "in churches, social meetings, on the streets, in the pool halls, lunch rooms and night clubs."[73] "We must forever be under the judgment of the community in which we live," Sherrod explained. "Whatever we do or propose must be executed after careful consideration of the people."[74]

Like Bob Moses in the Mississippi theatre, Sherrod understood that "common people" needed to be encouraged and included as leaders and participants in the local movement, but Sherrod showed greater interest than Moses for enlisting ministers and other middle-class blacks in the struggle. Such persons—however reluctant and afraid, however unwilling "to think further than a new car, a bulging refrigerator and an insatiable lust for more than enough of everything we call leisure"—were indispensable to the movement's progress. Sherrod believed that "even the hypocrisy" of the church bore the "seeds of the ultimate victory of Truth."[75] Moreover, as a Christian pacifist in the tradition of King, Sherrod also believed that a vital part of the theology of nonviolence involved accepting people where they are.

The Albany movement may not have brought great strategic success. It certainly did not bring the same level of national attention to the movement that the Freedom Summer Project would attract in 1964. Nonetheless, Sherrod's work in southeast Georgia left an indelible mark on the shape of the black freedom struggle. Sherrod helped convince SNCC activists that organizing among the grassroots was effective, respectful, and appropriate. Through a ministry of discernment and shared struggle, Sherrod identified the social needs with a clear head and with sober expectations. He befriended Negro factory workers in a region hostile to unions, insisting that the absence of labor unions adversely affected the work of civil rights organizing in southwest Georgia. "Without economic guarantees people are limited in participation in direct action," he said. He befriended black farmers in rural areas and helped develop partnerships with Koinonia Farm in pecan growing and sales. "We believe that the solution may be cooperatives and [we] have been working in that direction," he noted. Sherrod understood the interconnection between identifying and addressing local social needs and the progress of the civil rights movement in the south. "If we can guarantee food and clothing to people," Sherrod said, echoing his friend Clarence Jordan— to the "people without money"—"they won't move north in search of support and we can organize them to act politically to force the kind of changes that must come."[76]

Sherrod's interests almost always steered clear of insular or abstract debate—such as "what does it mean to be a revolutionary?" a fashionable question at the time—focusing instead on the urgent matters of "union type organizing among the maids" and selective buying campaigns in southern towns. To be sure, some SNCC members complained of Sherrod's preoccupation with the particular—"talking about a pecan factory to employ a few hundred [when in] the meantime there are 77 million people in poverty," as one disgruntled activist put it. But Sherrod understood that there was no place surer than local soil on which to build beloved community. Julian Bond would observe in a 1962 meeting that when SNCC activists left an area, it left behind a "community movement with local leadership, not a new branch of SNCC."[77]

The story of Bob Moses's journey into Pike County in the summer of 1961 has taken on mythic proportions in the literature of the civil rights movement: the unlikely philosopher-activist who sails solo into the threatening waters of Pike County, Mississippi. Moses had gone to the Delta the previous fall at the invitation of Amzie Moore, a World War II veteran and president of the NAACP in the Delta town of Cleveland, Mississippi. Moore taught Moses that local leadership can be trusted as a reliable guide to the appropriate course of action and appreciated as a source of wisdom. With only 22,000 of the state's 500,000 blacks registered to vote, Moore explained to Moses that he wasn't interested in sit-ins, freedom rides, and boycotts. (In Pike, Amite, and Walthall Counties in the southwest corner, the numbers were more depressing, with only 200 of the region's 16,000 black citizens registered to vote.) What good was it, Moore asked, for a poor black family to gain the right to eat in a white restaurant or stay in a white-owned hotel when they didn't have any money? Gaining access to a cleaner bathroom was nice, but it would not give a sharecropper greater control over his economic circumstances. Moore argued that only voter registration could break the grip of Jim Crow and achieve for blacks the political power they needed for greater self-determination. Moses heard him loud and clear.[78] Late in the summer of 1961, Moses, with Moore as his advisor on local matters, established a voter registration project in McComb, Mississippi, and he would remain in Mississippi until 1966.

Although Bob Moses is often described in civil rights literature as a kind of solitary mystic, his mystical insights were social and his cell was a corner in the crowded freedom house. Contemplative and retiring, Moses chose his words carefully with maximum attention to the situation. "All the talk about long-and-short-range goals," he said, "makes us forget some very simple goals. Basically, what we are after is some kind of change for the betterment of people, primarily Negroes."[79] While making life better for Negroes clearly involved economic empowerment, social progress was not tantamount to a training in capitalism, enslavement to the "great god" of the "profit motive." As a prophet of the particular, Moses imagined a Mississippi where blacks (and sympathetic whites) would show the nation something better and more human: communities of simplicity and justice, where women, men, and children shared resources, tended the earth, read books, and attuned their lives quietly to the rhythms of beloved community. Moses's manner was to respond to grandiose plans—such as Frank Smith's proposal to "take all the Negroes from the rural areas into the cities and force the revolution"—by returning the discussion to the task at hand, and until late 1964 he epitomized SNCC's incarnational focus: "We don't know what terms such as 'revolution' and 'revamp the economy' mean. . . . We need to work further on specific things such as simple homes that people can build and national boycotts used effectively." Moore would come to call Moses an "apostle," "who makes his circles, and he goes to this mission and that mission and the other mission, to straighten them out on anything that they might be confused about. And then he makes the circuit. But they have the responsibility of carrying out . . . their particular mission."[80] (Moses would in turn liken Moore to "a brick wall in a brick house, dug into this country like a tree beside the water."[81])

Still, if Moses was the student movement's Jesus, as one volunteer claimed, he was a Christ of the fields and the crossroads, not of the sanctuary, steeple, and pew. [82] Moses shared little in common with the buffed and shined clergymen who filled the ranks of the Southern Christian Leadership Conference, and his worn overalls, Sartrean eyewear, and left-bank aesthetic offered gentle rebuke to SCLC's preacherly demeanor. Yet Moses was no secular intellectual. Though often described by historians and journalists as a humanist visionary, his humanism had spiritual roots. "He talked a great deal about religion and was always against violence and war," observed a Justice Department investigator filing a report on Moses's 1962 request for conscientious objector status.[83] Moses's grandfather had been a Baptist preacher in the South, and while Moses's father may have tried to put some distance between himself and his own preacher-dad, haunted by unfulfilled promise and stuck in a janitorial job in New York City, he made sure his children attended a Baptist church near their apartment in Harlem. Bob Moses was himself a child of the church, and he would attend worship services during his years in the South—though like most former enthusiasts, he remained on his guard against dogmatic claims and otherworldly consolations, content to stay on the outskirts of the orthodox.

But, Moses had once considered the ministry. As an undergraduate at Hamilton College, he experienced a spiritual renewal through the influence of an evangelical student group and became known as a campus apologist for the Christian faith. Using his considerable intellectual talents in service to the Gospel, he could often be found in the student center arguing the existence of God with athiests and cynics. He took day trips to New York City with an evangelistic team, passed out tracts in Times Square and tried his hand at street preaching. Although soft-spoken by nature, Moses learned a few things about timing and the well-paced thought, about how to turn heads on a busy street and how to work an emotional curve. Moses's eventual turn to Quakerism seemed better suited to his quieter conviction; and later his discovery of Camus, the patron saint of Jesus-haunted dissent, inspired his passion for the concrete situation. When he told his father he was considering the ministry, he was reminded that the ministry was a "calling . . . not just an occupation."[84] But Moses had no interest in the ministry occupation; he sought, rather, an experience of God somehow linked to the street but freed from the pulpit, faith lived on the borderlines. Moses found that faith, and he lived it with humility, power, and persuasion for several years in the civil rights movement.

His first step into the movement came during the spring of 1960. He had taken a leave of absence from his graduate studies in philosophy at Harvard and was teaching mathematics for the year at the Horace Mann School in New York. While visiting an uncle in Virginia over break, Moses felt a sudden calling, an unexpected sense of "release," when he observed a sit-in at a coffee shop in Newport News.[85] "I knew this had something to do with my own life," he said, impressed by the courage of the student participants his own age.[86] Moses accepted the call and turned his sights towards Atlanta, where he imagined an apprenticeship for himself in the civil rights pantheon of the Southern Christian Leadership Conference. However, the professional clergy there showed little interest in mentoring the young philosopher from New York City, who had the habit of disappearing inside himself like a Zen Buddhist monk. Dejected, he spent his days stuffing fund-raising packets in the corner of the one-room office on Auburn Avenue.

Jane Stembridge had also recently arrived from New York to work in the Atlanta office with a Virginia connection of her own. Stembridge had been recruited by Ella Baker to run the SNCC office until a permanent administrator could be found, and she left her own studies at Union Theological Seminary.[87] Her suggestion that Moses move over to the new student organization sharing space in the SCLC office marked the beginning of SNCC's presence in the South.

Moses discovered in Stembridge a mutual admirer of mysticism, Christian theology, and the French avant-garde, and they spent long hours together in conversation.[88] His early letters to Jane from the field offer up this rich gumbo by the spoonfuls. St. Paul meets Celiene on the highways of a Deep South on the threshold of enormous change. Moses wrote of his week on the road:

> There is neither Jew nor Gentile in Christ: there is neither salt nor pepper in this salad! Please pass the salt. Don't you like the pepper? A person puts on the spirit of Christ like a loaf of baking bread puts on a crust! No, it's more like putting on an old fashioned girdle. Won't the new one's do? [sic] Well, the squirming and twisting is important here. Is it also like putting on a sock? NO, that isn't helpful at all. . . . Well I can't imagine it's much like putting on a girdle! Reality is wrapped up in being like a command is wrapped up. Something wrongs here. How is a command wrapped up? Come here!.. . . Did you hear what I said! . . . well!.. . . Do the dots represent becoming. Procrastination is to the command as becoming is to reality. OH? Identity is being in the body of Christ. Is that like swimming at night? There is neither black nor white in the body of Christ. . . . I guess it is like swimming at night . . . a little.[89]

Stembridge played the precocious preacher's daughter, the theologian and poet, who could match Moses's wit while hinting even at a different complexity:

> Identity is being in the body of men the which there is no whicher [sic]. By "men" we mean the general run of the mill kind of fellowship born of need and nourished by the nonviolent approach [to] the whole question of me-ness? I believe it. And undoubtedly, we shall overcome. The question is when? When persons like Robert Q. Moses are willing to suffer the slings and arrows of misunderstanding and narrowmindedness and still and yet and always continue to work asking no reward but to be allowed to be Robert Q. Moses from NYC and Atlanta and everywhere there is hurt and hope and waiting and searching and a little gin on the side to break forth from the slightly shy self. I like you.[90]

Whether as a result "of some old forgotten Bible or Sys. Theology Book," or her own sentimental nature, Stembridge could not resist the thought of Bob as the Moses of old, rescuing the people from the "land of bondage." "I may be getting a Messiah complex about you and you are my hero."[91]

From his first journey into the magnolia jungle until he left the South, Moses worked in small Mississippi towns organizing for power among the poor and excluded. With a heart for the individual man and woman thrown into oppressive social situations struggling passionately for dignity and authenticity, Moses tried to be a catalyst—without being the determining force—of the other person's decision to act. He understood that as an outsider he could never badger the reluctant participant.[92] Whatever organizing style emerged out of SNCC's participation in local struggles should be the result of unscripted transactions and exchanges in a concrete social context. Moses worked patiently to foster an emotional space in which people would feel freely "called forth by the movement" and in turn, feel free to accept, or reject, the call. Moses believed that an oppressed people—if affirmed in their created dignity through participation in a supportive community—could find the power to voice their goals and to determine the steps necessary to realize them.

SNCC's vision of social reform through incarnational organizing came to its fullest expression in the Freedom Summer Project of 1964. The summer began with training sessions, prayer meetings, and the martyrdom of three civil rights workers, and it unfolded as a series of events circumscribed by the singing, testifying, and burning church. (Throughout the spring and summer of 1964 black churches, especially those that had opened their doors to activists, burned at a rate of one every week and would continue to do so for the next year.[93]) Through activities that kept one's hands to the plow—voter registration, freedom schools, and political organizing—the Summer Project habituated staff members and volunteers to the rhythms and textures of black life in the rural south. Voter registration required organizers to get into the neighborhoods and discover the people's needs—"which cannot be done from the outside," as Moses said.[94] Freedom schools bound northern students to the rural poor in relationships based on love and trust.[95] The formation of a political party of the poor, the Mississippi Freedom Democratic Party (MFDP), meant building relationships and nurturing hope in people humiliated by southern apartheid.

The winter of 1963 had been unusually harsh. Cotton pickers in the Delta whose ranks were already stretched thin as a result of automation and machinery had an especially difficult time finding work.[96] By summer 1963, the voter registration drive in Mississippi had reached an impasse. In Greenwood, only three hundred African American voters were registered in a county of 10,000 white voters, a county that was two-thirds black.[97] Although there was more local leadership in SNCC-targeted areas at the end of the year—or precisely because of this fact—beatings and jailings and death threats, church burnings and bombings of freedom houses, had become part of the daily grind.[98] The White Knights of the Ku Klux Klan waged a campaign of terror against civil rights activists and any of the other "forces of Satan on earth" who sought to defile their sacred south.[99] No doubt, the violent assaults on white volunteers and local black organizers could have been much worse; but the prevailing atmosphere of terror made every insult, threat, and assault feel like details of a well-scripted plan. "We were at a point where we didn't know what to do," recalled the pastor-activist Ed King.[100]

In certain Delta counties, local officials eliminated the federal commodities program in response to voter registration initiatives, blocking the supply of rice, sugar, cheese, and flour that was distributed to the state's poor.[101] The Citizens' Council filled its ranks with business owners and civic leaders, and with the assistance of the Sovereignty Commission and other state officials, they were able to keep tabs on local people involved in the movement and to hand out punishments when necessary. "Almost all the Negroes who are known to support the civil rights movement in Ruleville have lost their jobs," the student volunteer Leonard Edwards wrote in his affidavit on harassment in Sunflower County.[102] Further compounding the difficulties facing organizers was the discovery that the federal government had little interest in protecting civil rights workers from southern terrorists. Reprisals from extremists and moderates alike largely went unchecked by Justice Department officials. One cartoon in SNCC's newsletter, *The Student Voice*, featured the burly character J. Edgar Standby, gazing indifferently into the distance, his left hand stuck deep in his coat pocket. "We were learning," said Moses, "that we weren't just up against the Klan, or a mob of ignorant whites, but political arrangements and expediencies that went all the way to Washington, D.C."[103]

The strategy of the Summer Project was to focus on Mississippi, the core of the iceberg of southern segregation, in hopes that the rest of the South would crumble in its wake. Mississippi was "a qualitatively different problem," Howard Zinn wrote in a report in late 1963.[104] A detailed report filed by the SNCC Atlanta office entitled, "The General Condition of the Negro in Mississippi," offered harrowing statistics of high infant mortality and death rates; widespread adult illiteracy and inadequate educational opportunities; job discrimination; shrinking populations of Negroes in most counties as a result of migration north; and an average annual income of $606 (compared to $2,023 for whites, even though a higher proportion of black family members were in the labor force).[105] Black Mississippians over the age of twenty-five had completed only six years of school on average. Only four percent of the 500,000 Negroes employed in the state worked in manufacturing and construction, jobs that often included health benefits and federal protections. Most worked on farms and plantations. More than 150,000 of the 200,000 homes rented or owned by African Americans were classified as deteriorating or dilapidated. Over 90 percent of rural homes lacked flush toilets, bathtubs, or showers.[106]

Yet Moses insisted that the new project not be conceived primarily as an awareness-raising measure—claiming the notice of a nation with a short moral attention span—but as "a larger unifying force" that would enable "people in Ruleville to see themselves connected to people in Liberty or Tylertown."[107] In October of 1963, the Council of Federated Organizations (COFO) launched the "Freedom Ballot Campaign," a mock election aimed at empowering black voters and showcasing their determination to go to the polls. Mississippi "nigras" were not content after all, as white politicians had been hyperactively telling the media, their constituents, and themselves. At its freedom convention at the Masonic Temple in Jackson, COFO nominated Aaron Henry, the Clarksdale pharmacist and state NAACP representative, as its gubernatorial candidate, and Ed King as lieutenant governor.

In the first week of November, 83,000 blacks and some whites cast their ballots for the two men. Most people voted at church, before or after Sunday services, but some cast their votes at cafes, grocery stores, pool halls, or beauty parlors, wherever ballot boxes were available.[108] Although the number fell short of the organizers' goal of 200,000, the turnout was strong enough to give substance to the claim that African Americans were ready to move in impressive numbers to the polls. It also showed the Negro population that "politics is not just a 'white folks' business," as SNCC's Ivanhoe Donaldson said.[109] The strong turnout was just the thing the languishing Mississippi movement needed in the fall of 1963. Grassroots organizing in key sections of the state had proven effective in mobilizing black citizens to vote in this experiment in "parallel institutional-ism."[110] The question was raised (as Howard Zinn put it), "Why not by-pass the white Mississippi machinery and set up a new party, open to all, with no rigmarole?"[111]

In light of the success of the Freedom Vote, Moses began to sketch the contours of a more ambitious voter registration initiative that would con-nect local activists with a larger group of student volunteers in a compre-hensive civil rights campaign. In partnership with activist lawyer and edu-cator Allard Lowenstein, at the time a freshman dean at Yale, Moses considered the details of a project that would provoke some kind of delib-erate confrontation and create "a platform, an opening wedge for future pressure."[112] The plan bore the imprimatur of Lowenstein's organizing style, especially his recognition of the pragmatic value of white participa-tion and "his magnetic appeal to the young," as biographer William Chafe wrote.[113] (Lowenstein had brought a group of white students from New Haven in October to help organize the successful Freedom Vote.) The twenty Freedom schools, each staffed with fifteen teachers, would supple-ment the notoriously substandard public education of the state by offering summer programs in black history and culture, American social move-ments, and the arts. SNCC would also develop thirty community centers, with ten workers in each center, and in addition would assign four volun-teers to each of the eighty-two counties to coordinate voter registration. To fill these ranks, SNCC planned to recruit men and women from progres-sive ministerial associations, teachers unions, legal and medical associations (including the Medical Committee for Human Rights), and universities and colleges to assist the summer organizers. "Folk singers are being re-cruited [too]," a staff memo noted.[114] (The SNCC leadership also planned to reassign many of its staff members and veterans from other cities in the South to Mississippi.[115])

But Moses had concerns about white involvement. Unlike Sherrod, who, convinced that "the reconciliation that occurs within the Christian community is the deepest and most permanent of reconciliations," had in-troduced interracial ideals from the start in his work in southwest Georgia, Moses and the Mississippi organizers had not initially considered white participation a desirable or necessary part of the plan.[116] What would hap-pen to indigenous black activism when white college students with their fi-nancial and educational privilege inundated the state? Would grassroots leadership be "drowned in a tidal wave of white volunteers"?[117] Would local organizers be able to maintain the fragile balance of the various black coalitions with "a bunch of Yalies running around in their Triumphs"?[118]

Some SNCC organizers argued—and with good reason—that white college students would be reluctant to take orders from local black men and women. Did not the invitation to northern white students perpetuate the debilitating notion that blacks needed whites to solve their problems? Moses worried further that "many undisciplined and unorganized people will just wander into the state and confuse the situation"—though this was not so much a concern about white involvement as about the role of outsiders in general.

But these reservations were offset by the reality of the situation and the scope of the problem. Blacks could use some help from whites. The white students from Yale had performed a useful service in assisting local organizers; and a few of them had even gotten arrested, which made for good publicity. The white volunteers brought with them "channels of publicity and communication."[119] John Lewis, who worked with SNCC in Greenwood, believed that the time had come "to take Mississippi to the nation" and that "the best way to do this was not only to organize black people, but to bring a large number of young whites to the state, and let people live alongside each other, and in the process, educate not only ourselves and the volunteers, but, perhaps more importantly, the whole nation."[120] Anecdotal evidence further suggested that local black people were deeply moved by the sight of white volunteers coming to their assistance. Fannie Lou Hamer considered the summer volunteers "the result of all our faith—all we had always hoped for. Our prayers and all we had lived for started to be translated into action."[121]

The Freedom Vote had also educated black Mississippians on two important matters; namely, that an African American could run for governor in Mississippi and that an interracial political party could exist with legitimacy.[122] At first skeptical of white student involvement, proposing a limit of a hundred white volunteers in Mississippi, Moses was soon heard making the case not only for the strategic benefits of interracialism but for its morality as well. "Can you make integration a goal and not live it?" he asked.[123] His response was decisive. "I am concerned that we do integrate, because otherwise we'll grow up and have a racist movement. And if the white people don't stand with the Negroes as they go out now, then there will be a danger that after the Negroes get something they'll say, 'Okay, we got this by ourselves.' And the only way you can break that down is to have white people working alongside of you—so then it changes the whole complexion of what you're doing, so it isn't any longer Negro fighting white, it's a question of rational people against irrational people."[124]

Although for SNCC as an organization, the controversy regarding white involvement was anything but resolved, with the recruiting drive fast approaching, organizers agreed to move ahead with plans for an interracial initiative, and Fannie Lou Hamer's axiom became the rule of thumb. "If we're trying to break down this barrier of segregation, we can't segregate ourselves."[125] By April of 1964, SNCC had drafted a proposal—a manifesto of sorts—that was posted on campus kiosks and bulletin boards throughout the nation. The document announced a program "planned for this summer" and solicited "the massive participation of Americans dedicated to the elimination of racial oppression."[126] The invitation to white student volunteers was no failure of nerve on the part of local blacks, but a cooperative effort appealing to "the country as a whole, backed by the power and authority of the federal government."[127]

On the first day of the Summer Project, civil rights workers Michael Schwerner, James Chaney, and Andrew Goodman were murdered by Klansmen in Neshoba County. Cleveland Sellers, who had come to Mississippi as a student volunteer and had accompanied one of the search parties dispatched after the disappearance, described the summer as his "longest nightmare," a constant state of being "stretched like a tight steel wire between the pit of the stomach and the center of the brain."[128]

But the summer was also a strategic success and an encouraging lesson in political organizing. The Freedom schools exceeded everyone's expectations, drawing more than two thousand students in the course of the summer, twice as many as anticipated, and the number of schools expanded to fifty by the end of the summer.[129] Joyce Ladner, a native of Hattiesburg and a Tougaloo College student active in the 1963 Jackson campaign, described her surprise at the changes she observed after returning in August of 1964. "Persons who in the past had been threatened with every kind of punishment, from loss of job to loss of life; who had accepted fear as a way of life; who had acquiesced to power, now had overcome their fear. I saw men and women stand up in meetings and say, 'I'm afraid, but I know I must do what is right, even if it costs me my life. None of us could have predicted the degree of success the project was to enjoy," said Ladner.[130] In July, President Johnson signed the Civil Rights Act, outlawing discrimination and segregation in public accommodations.

Still, the summer's undeniable successes seemed to many organizers overshadowed by the defeat of the Mississippi Freedom Democrats at the National Democratic Convention in Atlantic City, where Freedom Democrats had hoped to challenge the legitimacy of the all-white Mississippi Democratic delegation. This political party of the poor had hoped not only to challenge the limits of southern democracy, but to claim their well-deserved place at the table of the National Democratic Party as well. Indeed the Freedom Democrats would test the limits of liberal democracy, taking to the highest level of political life people who had fallen through the cracks of the system as it had operated until now. Their mission was to eventually unseat the Mississippi "regulars," the white Democratic delegation that would cast their vote for Republican presidential nominee Barry Goldwater. In the end, the Freedom Democrats were unsuccessful in their challenge, as the ragtag delegation proved no match for professional politicians with their eyes on the White House. The Mississippians were offered two honorary seats in the convention with no voting privileges. Worried about the southern vote, Lyndon Johnson had successfully dispatched his politicos to quell the storm, and the convention had proceeded without further disturbance.

Outraged and feeling betrayed, the delegation of domestic workers, sharecroppers, small-town beauticians, schoolteachers, janitors, and activists began to cast about for a way to understand the defeat. The Mississippians lamented the fact that the Democratic Party—faced with the perfect opportunity—had failed to bring morality into politics and to accept meaningful representation to the poor.[131] The poor and the excluded might find a place in the political establishment as recipients of government largesse but not as power-sharers. Many of the student activists were ready to wash their hands of the political establishment. "Atlantic City undermined my faith in the democratic process," said one summer volunteer.[132] "My hopes and dreams of being part of the National Democratic Party were dead," said Willie Peacock.[133] "We assumed that this country is really a democracy, which just isn't working," a staff member said. "We had no concept of how brutal it could be."[134] Some Freedom Democrats went so far as to cast the defeat in Manichean terms, a battle between the forces of good and evil. "The world was now defined between us and them," Ed Brown said, "in the way a religious person defines the world between believers and nonbelievers. We were pure and good; all the others were corrupt, even those middle-class blacks who wanted to compromise at the convention."[135] Cleveland Sellers gave voice to an anger that propelled many younger African American activists towards a more militant agenda in the months to follow. Sellers said, "Never again were we lulled into believing that our task was exposing injustices so that the 'good' people of America would eliminate them. We left Atlantic City with the knowledge that the movement had turned into something else. After Atlantic City, our struggle was not for civil rights, but for liberation."[136]

With the long hot summer giving way to the cooler days of fall, questions about mission, identity, leadership, discipline, and interracialism came now again to the surface, nowhere more dramatically than the staff retreat in November held at the Gulfside Methodist Assembly in Waveland, Mississippi. The transcripts of the meeting offer a glimpse into an organization facing irresolvable conflicts on the cusp of enormous change; they also remind us that often the most revealing insights and discoveries are those born of extreme uncertainty. No doubt, the Waveland meeting marks the beginning of the end; but it also documents SNCC as a "volatile and kaleidoscopic movement" of uncommon energy and imagination.[137] Even more, the meeting attests vividly to SNCC as an alternative social space that made room for the personal transformation of individuals.

Conflicts came to the surface that had long remained half-spoken; between college-educated staffers and those with little formal education; between outside activists and local people; disputes over administrative decisions, policy and strategy, gender inequities, and of course white involvement.[138] Many of the questions were addressed in a series of position papers, drafted in smaller sessions, which tried to make sense of the organization's new priorities and responsibilities. Should SNCC rededicate itself to building local leadership or promote a more radical agenda? "Where does SNCC fit in politically, ideologically, and religiously in America?" Bob Zellner asked.[139] "This summer we worked for LBJ. We were a tool of the Democratic Party. What does it mean to be a revolutionary?"[140] Members agreed that the organization intended to do more than "just distribute food and clothing," but they could not reach an agreement on what they were trying to do in the community, much less what it meant to be a revolutionary.

Although Zellner insisted that "we have got to be a band of brothers and stay together from now on," the Waveland meeting made clear that SNCC's survival as an interracial, loosely-knit organization depended on whether its emerging recognition of disagreement could find some unifying center or ground, a unity that included difference. For what it meant to be a revolutionary was complex and multilayered, even if the context of revolutionary activity was specific to a single county in the state of Mississippi. To be sure, all the staffers were generally committed to participatory democracy, the notion that local people should work together in the democratic process to develop the power to control the significant events that affect their lives.[141] But participatory democracy, like the idea of the revolutionary, was not a method so much as an after-the-fact description of the organizing process.

Moses believed that SNCC's genius was its iconoclastic impulse, its resistance to structures and hierarchy. Being a revolutionary meant learning how to act out of the deepest silence. Charles McLaurin agreed with James Forman that SNCC "should not dwell so much on theoretical queries but rather do what we know needs doing." McLaurin posted the revolutionary banner in the simple act of "people going to courthouse for the first time, then telling their friends to go down."[142] Jean Wheeler reminded the staff that not all members were revolutionaries, even though they all shared common goals, and she offered the hardest insight of all: "We're really not going to make any major changes in our lifetime."[143] Nonetheless, the spirit of the youth movement was drifting toward a different end than attunement to poor black communities, and, in any case, everyone was exhausted, irritable, and (some would say) sexually unsettled. In the end, the position papers circulated at the Waveland retreat raised more questions than SNCC could answer. No longer did it seem enough to focus on organizing initiatives in poor and excluded communities. Philosophical matters needed to be resolved, and yet exhaustion mixed with resentment produced confused notions about where the movement should go from here. The effect of the Waveland retreat, despite whatever urgency the papers held, was to diffuse the organization's focus on programs: No coherent plan was developed and the retreat felt like the cruelest letdown after the intense summer.[144]

The assumptions enumerated in meetings after Freedom Summer often seemed like those of men and women awakening from a naïve slumber. "We assumed that we had a monopoly on truth." [145] "We assumed that the government will act to accommodate us." "We assumed that poor people were good and could do no wrong ('mystique of poor people')." "We assumed that since we were pure, then that which we organized would be equally good; pure, incorruptible and durable." "We assumed that [it] was our responsibility to show morality to America."[146] Bob Moses lamented the fact that the Democratic establishment had passed on a rare opportunity to demonstrate more than a rhetorical commitment to the poor and the socially excluded.[147] Although Moses returned to Mississippi after the National Democratic Convention, his distrust of the political system became acute in the wake of the MFDP defeat in Atlantic City. He resigned as COFO director in late 1964, and then after the summer of 1966, having received his draft notice for service in Vietnam, left Mississippi for Canada and eventually Tanzania, where he lived in exile until 1977.[148] But the lesson of the National Democratic Convention was that the moral witness of a political party of the poor and excluded was no match for the men in high places. "A deeply brooding anger and resentment began to generate within SNCC," writes historian Wesley Hogan in her excellent study of the New Left, "setting the stage for a permanent redefinition of the internal social relations of a movement that, only two years earlier, had been characterized as the beloved community."[149]

Clayborne Carson noted that staff members began to work more deliberately in directions that mirrored class, gender, and racial identities—and that is true as a historical observation. Still, we should keep in mind that differing identities could very well have contributed to the health of the organization had not a more insidious problem arisen.[150] Lacking the ecclesial anchor of its earlier years, SNCC went cosmic. SNCC abandoned its commitment to incarnational organizing and the integrity of the particular and unveiled a new slate of world-epochal aspirations. "We should hook up with movements in the Caribbean." "In the new colonies we will have to define our own laws." "There should be no more news issued to any publications, except to Negro and foreign publications from Africa, Latin America and the Caribbean." SNCC resolved to become a "Third World Coalition of revolutionaries who were anticapitalist, antiimperialist, and antiracist."[151] Global coalitions were formed, or at least proposed, between revolutionaries in SNCC and in the Soviet Union, the Dominican Republic, Puerto Rico, Israel, and Japan.

SNCC would promote, vocally, "an awareness of blackness" and "true humanity," and it would do this by radicalizing the black college campuses, the sharecroppers in the South, and the "ghetto dwellers" in the North, controlling all the institutions in black communities, teaching Swahili in the schools, "reading nothing but books by black people and reading about themselves," and destroying the "mad octopus" of the American capitalistic system "with all its life-sucking tentacles of exploitation and racism that choke the people of Africa, Asia and Latin America."[152] Let the "hunkies" sit under their own vine, it was resolved; SNCC should now advance a "hard line philosophy that will guide our action in the future."[153] SNCC's new cosmopolitanism shifted inevitably toward grandiose estimations of its global mission. "We are, without a doubt, vocally the most militant organization in the Civil Rights Movement."[154] SNCC's cosmic take on its historic mission further inspired a perception of the United States as malevolent and beyond redemption, even as all things black and African emerged as the only safe haven in a hostile world of enormous powers. The goal would no longer be that of identifying social and economic ills that could be improved upon through political organizing and social reform; the problem was that the nation has assumed "facistic [sic] control of the lives of all people."[155] The new goals were rather more elusive: "End racism in America"; "develop black consciousness"; "change [the] political and economic system that exploits black people"; "develop [the] concept of humanism."[156] These goals indicated a striking change from the days when voter registration, political organizing, and educational reform were the measure of success. Sadly, but inevitably, global ambitions disconnected from local commitments in organizing created strategic confusions.

To be sure, the cosmic appeal had never been absent from the speech and actions of the civil rights movement. But in its church-based forms the movement had rendered the cosmic struggle in theologically specific language, avoiding the Manichean turn more often than not. Sin and its social stains were the root cause of human oppression, not the vast and undelineated powers of whiteness. Thus, a Christian radical like John Lewis could say that America was "a racist country" with a "master-slave mentality" not as a way of washing his hands of responsible action but as a sober appraisal of the social dimension of sin. Lewis believed that the "deep disorder . . . eating away the inner substance of our society" could be healed by men and women fortifying themselves with the ultimate hope of redemption.[157] Fannie Lou Hamer appealed to Paul's admonition in his Epistle to the Ephesians "to put on the whole armour of God," for "we wrestle not against flesh and blood, but against principalities, against powers, against the rulers of the darkness of this world, against spiritual wickedness in high places."[158] Yet again these powers were framed in a historical narrative with the church commissioned with the necessary resources to combat and defeat them.[159]

An immediate result of SNCC's global mission was indifference to organizing projects in poor communities and a breakdown of personal and organizational discipline. In his study, Carson noted an increase in marijuana use and the collapse of accountability within the organizational staff.[160] Staff cars would disappear in Atlanta only to resurface in Arkansas or Mississippi; a staff member would leave his desk unannounced in Greenwood to party with friends in New Orleans. In short, the new SNCC vanguard was unable to offer black southerners programs that tapped into their awakening political energies. The philosophers, anarchists, and floaters turned away from the concrete situation in their desire to get "high of freedom."[161] Cleveland Sellers complained,

If a confrontation developed in Jackson, Mississippi, and a group of Free-dom-High Floaters was working in southwest Georgia, they would pile into cars and head for Jackson. They might return to Georgia when the Jackson confrontation was over—and they might not. No one ever knew for certain what they were going to do or where they might turn up next. They were great talkers, who generally ended up dominating those meet-ings and conferences they saw fit to attend. Holding forth with long, in-volved existential arguments, they would take as long as three days of non-stop talking to win a single inconsequential point; but they didn't mind. They loved to bring meetings to a screeching halt with open-ended, theo-retical questions.[162]

Sellers's diagnosis, however, fails to capture the more basic conflict at play; namely, that the line of division in SNCC was not finally drawn be-tween the hardliners and floaters, but between the localists, who were most often church people and open if not hospitable to white partner-ships, and the globalists, who saw the movement as a world historical event that should be determined by black people alone. As long as SNCC had remained committed to an incarnational ethic, its commitment to nonviolence and interracialism had been nourished, despite the organiza-tion's precarious unity. Yet equally important, SNCC's theological com-mitments had sustained its focus on organizing for power in poor and ex-cluded communities; and for this reason, the conflict or set of conflicts that would eventually bring the organization to crisis was not even finally about race or nonviolence or about the clashing organizing styles of the "floaters" and the "hardliners." The basic conflict was between movement activists based in local churches and poor communities and movement ac-tivists gone cosmic; between incarnational reformers and Gnostic revolu-tionaries. "Be careful how we use such terms as 'revolution' and 'overturn government,'" organizer Jim Mansonis had cautioned. "Be concrete, spe-cific."[163] The conflict lay in the irresolvable disagreement between staff members working out of black churches and communities, who under-stood the urgency of place and the integrity of particular locales, and staff members, floater and hardliner alike, who summoned the student soldiers to battle on a field of metaphysical struggle; between members who re-garded the movement as part of the mission of the church and those who saw it as a reversal of fortune, an opportunity for satisfaction or revenge, or a utopia for the "wretched."

When SNCC's incarnational ethic faded after 1964, it became easy for self-appointed organizing experts to claim unilateral control and orchestrate people and events according to a privileged script. The disciplines of incarnational organizing, nonviolence, and interracialism, and the spirit of wonder, openness, and love, gave way to hardened attitudes and judgments. In time, SNCC members came to deride SNCC's respectful, sometimes worshipful, attitude toward the poor and to seek a cure from the plague of "localpeoplitis." The shifts in Moses's own vision from Christian humanism to secular apocalypticism in late 1964 were further symptomatic of the youth movement's washing its hands of the black church. Ambivalence and increasing hostility toward the church finally produced conspiratorial evasions on the sources of racial oppression, evasions that demonized whiteness while making concrete reform undesirable and irrelevant. SNCC's talk about the "negro ghettoes" and the "northern cities" became abstractions no less deracinated than "the system" and "the people." Removed from its home in the church, the work of building beloved community withered and died.

In December of 1964, a rally was held at the Williams Institutional CME Church in Harlem to support the Mississippi Freedom Democratic Party, which had reorganized after Atlantic City on a smaller scale but with a determination to help elect local African Americans to political office. Fannie Lou Hamer was the main speaker, but Malcolm X had also been invited to say a few words. The Harlem rally was part of the Freedom Democrats' fund-raising tour of northern cities and a modest turnout was disappointing to the sponsors. Yet the stakes were high. Civil rights organizers were seeking national support to block the seating of Mississippi's five U.S. representatives when Congress reconvened in January of 1965. In Mrs. Hamer's opinion, nothing less than the right to vote hung in the balance for black southerners.

Hamer's speech was part testimonial and part educational. She sang the "song of nonviolence," as one member of the audience recalled her eloquent remarks, and she discussed the importance of the Voting Rights Act under consideration in Congress and its implications for racial progress in the South. Following her talk, Malcolm X took the podium. At first he appeared ready to offer a conciliatory word to those few whites in the audience aligning themselves with the struggle. "I'm for anybody who's for freedom," he said. Yet Malcolm soon made clear that freedom would not come through nonviolence, patience, or love. Freedom would not come through Jesus or the peaceable reign of God. "We *need* a Mau Mau," he declared. "We need a Mau Mau in Mississippi," a reverse campaign of terror against the Klan. Malcolm called on the movement to learn the language of the oppressor, the language of the shotgun, rifle, and rope.[164]

By the end of 1964 much had changed on the racial landscape of the country. The Civil Rights Act had been passed and the Freedom Democrats' challenge, despite the defeat, had inspired black southerners toward political representation in a way that had not been experienced since Reconstruction.[165] Yet "the weary warriors of SNCC" were dazed and confused. "They no longer had the will nor the strength to plan new strategies," Ed King writes. "They could no longer listen patiently to the people of the communities or even assist their friends, the new leaders that they had helped find in the black communities of Mississippi."[166] SNCC had been forced to reckon with the scope of the problem, with the fact that ending Jim Crow laws could not solve racism in America. The struggle for beloved community would take longer than anyone had ever imagined. "We were asked to sacrifice so much more than we thought possible," Ed King said.[167]

SNCC's attraction to the fire and brimstone message brought with it a new ostensible measure of purity and loyalty, and yet at the same time signaled a decisive break with "the over-thirty generation of fearful, church-loving Southern Negroes," as Jack Newfield unfairly described the local women and men who filled the ranks of the civil rights movement.[168] Yet even before the showdown on the role of whites in the organization, the new SNCC vanguard shocked many friends and supporters by ousting John Lewis as chairman. This was a decisive moment in SNCC's turn to the hard line.

John Lewis represented the SNCC of the freedom rides, the sit-ins, and nonviolent direct action. Lewis was of a generation of black southerners who came to civil rights life seeking not only social justice but their own—and their church's—spiritual renewal. He had joined the movement while studying theology in Nashville and been jailed more than forty times. Although Lewis embraced many of the liberationist themes in black power, he continued to preach a truly interracial democracy, the heart of which was his belief that "the movement was based on the simple truth of the Great Teacher: love thy neighbor as thyself."[169] But Lewis's Christian pacifism and commitment to building beloved community were not what the times required.

After his dismissal, SNCC leaders spent much time deflecting criticisms and denunciations from white liberal and black supporters as well as from national media. James Peck, who had been both an SNCC member and freedom rider, called black power a racist ideology. "Black power is no more insurance against social injustice than white power," Peck said.[170] The NAACP's Roy Wilkins—never a SNCC fan to begin with—called black power an "anti-white power," "a reverse Hitler," and "a reverse Ku Klux Klan," which "can only mean black death."[171] Ralph McGill, a journalist regarded by most readers of the *Atlanta Constitution* as a liberal-minded southerner, claimed that SNCC had been "taken over by what amounts to a secret Klan-type group which openly states its racial hatreds and its objective to foment disaster and chaos in order to destroy Western civilization."[172] John Lewis himself, in an interview published in the *Los Angeles Times*, described his dismissal as the final rejection of Dr. King's Christian conviction in the civil rights movement. Ever the integrationist, Lewis understood that meaningful social reform required the continued commitment to the moral witness of beloved community. Yet Lewis's most damning criticism was that black power shirked the discipline and focus that the commitment to nonviolence engendered and sustained. Most Negroes, he explained, "will never identify with black nationalists and other black reactionaries who talk loud and use cutting words like 'Black Power,' but also never engage in confrontation to bring about change."[173] If racism is finally a matter of whiteness fully embodied in national identity, there is no longer any good reason to organize in poor communities. Even the moral potency of rage is squandered. Newfield described the new scene, "The prophetic band that had provided the rest of the freedom movement with so many new ideas, grew stale, repeating old formulas."[174]

As field operations deteriorated, the "brilliant, glib, complex, twenty-five year old" Stokely Carmichael took to the speaking circuit and insisted on traveling first class on airplanes and getting a thousand dollars for a public appearance.[175] His popularity in leftist circles and his appearance as a gadfly in public debates about civil rights soon earned him the nickname "Starmichael" by both friends and foes. From late 1964 until the winter of 1966, the number of SNCC organizers in the field decreased from 200 to 120.[176]

In the end, the construction of a rigid racial orthodoxy—no doubt a symptom of what activists Spencer Perkins and Chris Rice would later call "race fatigue"—led to the formulation of a new policy in which all white members were excluded from SNCC as a matter of principle.[177] In a decisive staff meeting in New Orleans in May of 1967, in response to the request of Bob and Dottie Zellner to organize a SNCC project in a white working-class neighborhood of New Orleans, the new central committee resolved that "the remaining five Caucasians or people considered to be Caucasians" be fired.[178]

Bob Zellner had argued before the central committee that in order "to get rid of racism and get people's minds straightened out, some amount of inter-racial cooperation" had to be accepted. His caveat, "although it may be repugnant to us," is no doubt a sharp indication of where things stood as far as the beloved community was concerned; nevertheless, Zellner reminded his comrades of their higher calling to embody on a small scale what they wanted America to be as a whole. The Zellners were excited about their new project in New Orleans. The Grass Roots Organizing Work, or GROW (sometimes referred to as "Get Rid of Wallace"), sought to build coalitions and alliances between poor blacks and whites. GROW seemed the perfect example of the kind of project that SNCC should be pursuing: the expansions of community organizing activities into sustained community building. White organizers needed to work hand in hand with black activists, and this meant forging a solidarity deeper than coalitions or alliances; whites and blacks must bear witness to new patterns of human relationship and to new interracial possibilities. Zellner's argument showed how far many in SNCC had come in redressing white racism and white paternalism. He was not telling blacks they needed whites; he was telling blacks that whites needed them. SNCC must hold itself to a higher standard, aspiring not only to "redeem the soul of America," but to build beloved community.

The central committee was not interested. As Zellner sat smoking cigarettes in an adjacent room, the muted voices of the debate penetrated the walls of the dingy SNCC offices. Staff members encouraged each other to "rise above the personal friendship level and as a group . . . strive to be objective as much as possible." The Zellners might be retained as useful idiots in possession of "vital information that SNCC can use"— like those "many women who gave up their bodies during the second World War" in order to get information. But "they are for *your* movement." "We must learn how to utilize people." SNCC must "make a cold decision . . . a cold political decision." "When we talk to Zellner, we are not talking to him as Bob Zellner; we are talking from a decision that we made about the group."[179]

Zellner was eventually summoned back to the meeting. Rap Brown delivered the verdict: "Bob Zellner's relationship, or any official relationship that Zellner has with this organization [must] be severed, and any resources that he needs, he [must] request through the Program Secretary."

"I think it is a mistake," Zellner replied, "but that is among us." Zellner kept his anger, and his sorrow, to himself as he and Dorothy returned to their house on Napoleon Street in New Orleans to resume work on the Poor People's Project. He promised to say nothing to the press.

"My anguish was extreme after getting kicked out of SNCC; my discontent was immense," Zellner explained years later. "But I fully understood the issue at stake. My reaction was so very different from Abby Hoffmann who complained in the *Village Voice* that after all he'd done for SNCC, it was outrageous to see what had happened. Actually Hoffman overstated his involvement with SNCC. Dottie wouldn't allow him to go to Mississippi, she found him so flaky. Anyway, there was some rhetoric at the end of the meeting about coalition building with white projects; but that was never pursued. We were exhausted and burned out."[180]

The problem with denouncing America as a "racist country," of summoning the inner cities to rise up as colonies in rebellion, of hooking up with liberation movements in Johannesburg and Latin America, of "starting a new history of Man," of admonishing one's fellow travelers "to go forward all the time, night and day, in the company of Man," was its inability to answer the basic question, how shall we attend to the pressing demands of the concrete social world? How shall we live? Still, black power's tragic flaw was not finally its racial separatism but its capitulation to consumer society and the American culture of death. Violence *was* as American as apple pie, and everybody wanted a big piece for himself. Rap Brown's "Letter from Prison" read like the boast of a steroidal black Rambo, the ideological grandfather of modern urban violence. "We must move from resistance to aggression, from revolt to revolution. . . . For every Orangeburg there must be 10 Detroits. For every Max Stanford and Huey Newton, there must be 10 dead racist cops . . . an eye for an eye, a tooth for a tooth, a life for a life." [181]

On September 11, 1968, the *Washington Post* released the following dispatch from the civil rights front:

> The office of the Student Nonviolent Coordinating Committee (SNCC), which was located at 2208 14th Street, N.W., Washington, D.C., was closed and padlocked due to the internal differences between several factions within the Washington, D.C. (WDC) group, one loyal to Lester McKinnie, Head of WDC, SNCC, and the other loyal to Stokely Carmichael.

Throughout the late summer, the SNCC offices in Washington had been hit repeatedly by gunfire. Lester McKinnie claimed they were under attack by the Black Panthers, and after the first attack he enlisted the services of Colonel Hassan Juru-Ahmed Bey and his Black Man's Volunteer Army of Liberation, a paramilitary group distinguished by their black trousers, green tunics, black berets, and tricolor shoulder patches.[182] When the building was again hit by bullets and bombs, the Army opened fire on an apartment building across the street. Bey, who had never considered himself a friend of SNCC or Stokely, despised the Black Panthers even more. The potent Panthers, he believed, were embarked on a nationwide campaign to create a single black militant organization and thus determine unilaterally the future of urban America.

From his headquarters in Oakland, California, the Black Panther minister of information, Eldridge Cleaver, denied allegations of a takeover and wondered why anyone would think he cared about a dilapidated office and a few washed-up militants. Investigators agreed with Cleaver, concluding that the shots were more likely fired by disgruntled SNCC members who regarded Lester McKinnie as an incompetent leader.

When reached at a hotel in Dakar, Senegal, Stokely Carmichael denied any prior knowledge of the attack and regretted that the movement had come down to black men fighting black men. One week later, however, Carmichael surprised many when he announced from the African continent that he was now the new prime minister of the Black Panther Party. But this announcement prompted Lester McKinnie along with Julius Lester, who had recently finished his book, *Look Out, Whitey: Black Power's Gon' Get Your Mama*, to say there was no way Carmichael could have quit his post with SNCC because SNCC had fired him first.[183]

"Coalitions and new alliances in the Black movement are occurring like many games of ideological musical chairs all over the nation," wrote Robert Maynard in the *Washington Post*.[184] The black Maoists, black nationalists, black liberators, black hippies, black Egyptians—the smallest variation in the pursuit of a "Third World Coalition of revolutionaries who were anticapitalist, anti-imperialist, and antiracist" was enough to start a street fight. The decade that began with the Albany nonviolent movement ended with the formation of the National Negro Rifle Association.

The German theologian Helmut Thielicke, in a seminar on the church and integration at Harvard Divinity School during his visit to the United States in the sixties, was asked after his presentation to respond to the observation that most of the changes in race relations resulting from the civil rights movement had been merely "symbolic solutions." "At most the door has only been opened a crack," the student said. Thielicke's remark was not what students had expected of the German dissident and radical pastor. "So what?" he said, "What do you have against 'symbolic solutions'?"

Thielicke told the students that if the "symbolic acts" of the movement revealed the fact "that one is secretly aware of the remote goal," then symbolic solutions have greater power than we might imagine. A symbolic act properly executed might even be better than having proceeded in a haphazard way to open the doors for all to flock in as they please. "I believe that we must always think in terms of developments and not of instant radical solutions which would only provoke dangerous reactions," he said.[185]

Thielicke reminded the students of Jesus' admonition that we not be anxious about tomorrow. Jesus had not meant the coming week or year or indefinite future, but the day that follows the present one. The word of God is "intended to be a lamp for our feet that lights only the next step in the darkness." The "big programmatic searchlights" that seek to illuminate all present and future actions do not count much in the kingdom of God. In fact, the first, small symbolic steps can themselves produce decisive transformations. "We practice living together in small homeopathic doses," Thielicke explained. "We learn to know each other, we can or are compelled to discuss things with each other, we learn at firsthand the other persons's feeling about existence, and his understanding of the situation.[186] The world begins to look completely different when we face each other eye to eye. Thielicke had more in mind with this idea of "living together in small homeopathic doses" than the discovery that we are all one human family. For Christians, being in a *status confessionis* means acting with humility and with the understanding that our best efforts will still not bring about the kingdom.[187]

SNCC became impatient with the small steps, but failed to illuminate a meaningful social alternative beyond the global appeal and the retreat to racial difference. For this reason, the risk of inviting white northern students to the South may have been less that of whites intruding into black spaces than about an invitation to grandiosity—an invitation to white volunteers to impose their expertise and design on the southern struggle. For this reason, black power was an inevitable and necessary moment in the developing interracial movement; a moment of breaking away from collective identity that promised growth and guarded against sameness. Black power was a sober reminder that the piety of global togetherness had become forced, that there could be no beloved community until there was individual affirmation and no reconciliation until there was differentiation and individuation, and that racial reconciliation was of no practical use to most black Americans. It was one thing for whites to appreciate the thrill of the soul shake and the narcosis of black spaces, but it was quite another for whites to take those energies and experiences back home to their own neighborhoods, enduring ridicule without the consolation of their Negro pals. "One of the most disturbing things about almost all white supporters of the movement has been that they are afraid to go back into their own communities—and work to get rid of it," Stokely Carmichael said.[188] White liberals should take responsibility for their own moral evasions and sizable contributions to the civil rights movement's collapse. "They want to run from Berkeley to tell us what to do in Mississippi," Carmichael added, "Let them look instead at Berkeley."[189]

As we will see in the next chapter, the emerging counterculture was no better prepared than the black power regime to see beyond the recognition of difference towards strategies for rebuilding relationships and for reconnecting with the sources of redemption, reconciliation, and beloved community. A new objectivity was not much help here, for difference made absolute yielded aspirations to purity impervious to grace, otherwise known as fanaticism. Carl Oglesby, the president of SDS, who had written in the early sixties, "We want to create a world in which love is more possible," would later say, "Revolutions do not take place in velvet boxes . . . Nuns will be raped, and bureaucrats will be disemboweled."[190]

In his October 23, 1964, memo to the national staff, the Berkeley-based SNCC organizer Mike Miller had acknowledged the emerging shift among a number of staff members toward black nationalism. Miller had discerned hints of the new impulse in the recent SNCC proposals to staff only black field secretaries, and he had questioned the usefulness and morality of such proposals. "[If] we are building in our own movement that beloved community," he said, "then race cannot be used to automatically disqualify the argument of a white field secretary when policy matters are being discussed amongst ourselves." Miller concluded that it would be better if SNCC as an organization were honest about the issue and admitted that "it doesn't want whites working in the movement"; that it no longer wants to serve as "frontiersmen for the 'beloved community.'" Miller appreciated the cultural agenda of black nationalism, its attention to the importance of black leadership, the affirmation of blackness, the study of African history, and the value of black role models for the inner city.[191] "All these things seem so apparent that there should be little need to discuss them."[192] However, Miller explained that "problems begin to get tough" when trying to translate a cultural agenda into social programs and strategies. Cultural shifts do not produce programs for relieving poverty, create decent schools in the South, or end discrimination.[193]

But by 1968, the obstacles to African American progress came to be understood as some kind of ontological whiteness that infected the very being of the country itself, no longer the result of unjust laws and discriminatory social practices that could be corrected, or improved upon, through social reform and organizing. But when the problem is ontological whiteness, there is no real solution. Preferring an emotional catharsis over the discipline of achieving progress by ordinary means, SNCC abandoned the theological framework within which it had once affirmed human dignity, and it was left with a vision of community narrowed to the whims of self-authentication alone.

PART TWO

CHAPTER 4

The Burdens of Perpetual Freedom:
The Dream as Hallucination

The story of the civil rights movement that runs from Montgomery to Memphis, from Albany to New Orleans, concludes amidst shattered dreams and moral torpor. By 1968, the vision of beloved community lies in ruins. A movement that once seemed content to organize for power in excluded communities, animated by the moral energies of the black church, changed the subject. For many, the new engagement was more about feeling things and being aware than jumping into the tedious work of social reform and racial reconciliation. The psychological field of an expanded self eclipsed the prosaic miseries of the poor and the oppressed. "The dream is over," John Lennon said. "I'm not just talking about the Beatles, I'm talking about the generation thing. It's over, and we gotta—I have personally gotta—get down to so-called reality."[1] But the utopian dream of the 1960s counterculture offered little to hold on to in a universe of disenchanting options. Reality is the lion devouring the lamb.

Martin Luther King did not abandon the hope of the lion lying down with the lamb, but his hope endured an eschatological intensification that unsettled his worldly confidences and left him finally at wit's end. King knew that it was only the love of God that would illuminate the ugly and unjust spaces of this transitory world as a groaning after redemption. His own tired and tormented self surely could not do the work. But with the young generation now emptied of the dream of God, the search for beloved community gave way to the dark comedy of yodeling into the abyss. The assassinations "finally confirmed all the apprehensions," said Thomas Merton, "the feeling that 1968 is a beast of a year. That things are finally, inexorably, spelling themselves out."[2]

The notion that King moved from identification with mainstream values to rage against "the system" may be too easy. He never identified the beloved community with the American dream, and his furious demands for justice were always chastened by the qualitative theological distinction between the city of God and the city of man. We dare not forget that "I Have a Dream" was delivered just weeks before "Eulogy for the Martyred Children," delivered after the Klan bombing of the Sixteenth Street Baptist Church in Birmingham. Considered together, the two speeches offer the most sober reckoning with the dream's earthly prospects. For the hope that "my four little children will one day live in a nation where they will not be judged by the color of their skin but the content of their character" is wagered amidst a nation where four little girls are killed in their Sunday School rooms in one of "the most vicious, heinous crimes ever perpetrated against humanity."[3] Let us not forget too that cashing the "check that will give us upon demand the riches of freedom and the security of justice" is a gesture in defiance of an America that "has given the Negro people a bad check," a check which has come back with "insufficient funds."[4]

King understood that "black religion is constantly in tension with all political systems, even those favored by the church's prophetic brigade," Michael Eric Dyson writes. "But the radical remnant tirelessly works to make politics reflect the justice that prevails in God's kingdom."[5] The kingdom of God illuminates and enables human potential. Yet as the daybreak of freedom gave way to "midnight in our world" and "a darkness so deep . . . that we can hardly see which way to turn," as the shouts of "amen" and "tell it" and "come on, now" turned into jeers and catcalls from many who had once called him brother, King began to understand even more clearly that those who labor under the burden of the cross, who dwell in the radical remnant, cannot rely on the vicarious actions of the state. "To be a Christian," he explained, "one must take up his cross, with all of its difficulties and agonizing and tension-packed content and carry it until that very cross leaves its mark upon us and redeems us to that more excellent way which comes only through suffering."[6] If King is a prophet it is not because he called America to its better self, but because he risked everything on the premise that the word of God is true when it names Jesus as the peace of the world.

What happens to faith when worldly achievement grows distant; when the partnership of hope and progress dissolves into the brutal ambiguities of history? In King's civil rights ministry, the eschatological dimension intensified. In his rage-heavy 1967 sermon at Riverside Church in New York, delivered one year to the day of his death, King showed us the fault lines in his chastened vision of history. While renewing his "commitment to the ministry of Jesus Christ" and standing in the "fierce urgency of now," King spoke out of the searing clarity of holy despair. He told the congregation that just a few years earlier, during America's "shining moment" of compassion, there was "a real promise" for black and white alike; "there were experiments, hopes, new beginnings." Then came the escalation of war, and King watched in sorrow as the experiments were abandoned as if they were "some idle political plaything of a society gone mad on war," and as Vietnam proceeded to ravage our soul "like some demonic destructive suction tube." "A nation that continues year after year to spend more money on military defense than on programs of social uplift is approaching spiritual death."[7] A nation that has fashioned the god it trusts from its own violent needs could never be redeemed.

SCLC had sought to redeem the soul of America, but now King worried that America's soul has become "totally poisoned." He worried that the American dream was revealing itself as a narcissistic force as brutal in its expansive drive as it was aggressively irresistible to those it seduced. Certainly white liberals had performed many noble deeds in their commitment to racial justice, but one thing they could not do was stand under the judgment of God. King pleaded with America to be a servant among nations for the poor. King resolved that America's only hope lay in a spirit of repentance, in a broken and contrite heart, which must take the form of servanthood among the nations of the world. "Our only hope today lies in our ability to recapture the revolutionary spirit and go out into a sometimes hostile world declaring eternal hostility to poverty, racism, and militarism."[8] But the hour was late and not many were listening. "After the Riverside sermon, King was treated by the white press like a second class citizen," says historian Taylor Branch.[9]

In any case, Noam Chomsky was right to say that most Americans never really cared for Martin Luther King anyway.[10] At the time of his murder in Memphis, even most of King's liberal supporters had long found him hard to take. His ungrateful notion, pondered late, that the problem of American racism had not been solved by eliminating southern segregation, cast doubt on the nation's big-heartedness as far as the civil rights cause was concerned. The intensity of most Americans' interest in racial matters, their thumbs-up to the black freedom struggle, was inversely proportionate to the miles that separated them from Montgomery and Jackson. "Northern liberals might admire black dignity at a distance," Thomas Merton wrote in 1968, "but they still did not want all that nobility right next door: it might affect property value."[11] The dispatches from ground zero of the struggle had inspired white people living outside the South to outrage, even as it reassured them that the evils of racism lay elsewhere. (This was a point that Lyndon Johnson never failed to bring to Humphrey's attention when the Minnesotan waxed high-minded about southern prejudice.)

This chapter offers a break from the story that begins in the pulpits and pews of the black churches, although its diverse and perhaps somewhat unexpected characters provide important lessons for understanding the causes of the movement's demise and the prospects for reclaiming its convictions and energies for the present time. What happens in the search for beloved community when the dream of a just society becomes abstracted from the lives and struggles of real people in real communities? Observing the cultural effects of morals cut like flowers from their roots enables a fuller appreciation of the spiritual conditions required for building beloved community and the challenges of renewing social hope in the uncertain years ahead. The search for authenticity and freedom deracinated from concrete engagement spirals finally into chaos.

"The center was not holding," Joan Didion writes in her 1968 book, *Slouching Towards Bethlehem*. "All that seemed clear was that at some point we had aborted ourselves and butchered the job, and because nothing else seemed so relevant, I decided to go to San Francisco."[12] Joan Didion's eulogy for the counterculture offers a harrowing description of the mental chaos and shocking banalities of those who unwittingly mocked the dream and its source—the chaos that the pop-theologians, now arriving on the scene with their dead gods and unknotted libidos, would simply not permit either. Friedrich Nietzsche had tried to explain to an uninterested nineteenth-century bourgeoisie that the death of God meant the death of moral purpose and of all things, good and evil, related to God. "At last," he said, "the sea, *our* sea, lies open before us. Perhaps there has never been so open a sea."[13] To those who spoke of the death of God as the occasion of psychic and erotic expansion, Didion's honesty, like Nietzsche's, is unflinching and born as well of the tremulous clarity of a soul in torment. She writes, "As it happens, I am comfortable with . . . those who live outside rather than in, those in whom the sense of dread is so acute that they turn to extreme and doomed commitments . . . I know something about dread myself, and appreciate the elaborate systems with which some people manage to fill the void, appreciate the opiates of the people, whether they are as accessible as alcohol and heroin and promiscuity or as hard to come by as faith in God or History."[14]

Didion documents "the proof that things fall apart" in ways that are measured and honest, "neither villainous nor glamorous," but "alive and botched and often mournfully beautiful" (as journalist Dan Wakefield noted).[15] San Francisco had become a leper colony of lost hopes, the final stop on the road west, where adolescents who "drifted from city to torn city, sloughing off both the past and the future as snakes shed their skins" gathered in pursuit of something real, or at least real fun. "It was a country of bankruptcy notices and public-auction announcements and commonplace reports of casual killings and misplaced children and abandoned homes and vandals who misspelled even the four-letter words they scrawled."[16] In a profound sense, Didion reveals the bitter ends of beloved community unanchored from biblical traditions of compassion and mercy, and from sources of the self more sustaining than the dreams and desires of individuals. The past had exhausted its possibilities, though these children had as little interest in the past as they had in God; and now all things had to be made new.[17]

Didion's flower children come and go like the ephemera of summer. "If everybody chanted, there wouldn't be any problem with the police or anybody," says a hippie living in a public park. "We're just gonna let it all happen," says another. "Everything's in the future, you can't pre-plan it. First we get jobs, then a place to live. Then, I dunno." Joan Baez appears shimmering in sunlight. "My life is a crystal teardrop. There are snowflakes falling in the teardrop and little figures trudging around in slow motion."[18] Baez has established an Institute for the Study of Nonviolence, where she meets with students four days a week to discuss C. Wright Mills, Marshall McLuhan, Thoreau, and Gandhi, and to dance ballet to Beatles recordings. The child of a Quaker educator, granddaughter of two ministers, Baez has sought to build beloved community without creed or conviction, "a place where everyone can be warm and loving and share confidences."[19] "These sessions are way over my head, but I go floating on air," says one matron of the activist-chic.[20]

The "inchoate happenings" of Didion's book conjure the mood of a movement etherealized, the peaceful, uneasy feeling that things better work out here on the West Coast "because there's no more continent left." The end of the dream is an apocalypse burning slowly "to unhappiness, to restrictiveness, to entrapment in the mechanics of living;" a rough beast slouching towards San Bernadino.[21] "All that seemed clear was that at some point we had aborted ourselves and butchered the job."[22]

If the center does not hold—and Didion convinces us that it can't—then her final exhortations to a sense of "one's intrinsic worth" are the sweat of a mausoleum.[23] Any disgruntled generation lacking self-respect will run away to find itself and there find no one home. Thus, to lack self-respect is to be trapped inside the discovery that there *is* no one home, that the emptiness without is the same as the emptiness within.[24] Character is the source of self-respect, she says ever more desperately, "the willingness to accept responsibility for one's life." Yet with the self, as Didion describes it, now stripped free of its delusions, the "unhappy analysand" will not find self-respect in social movements, drugs, or shared confidences. Didion points us beyond the unsuccessful therapy of social dissent to some private psychic terrain, "a separate peace, a private reconciliation," where real battles are fought.[25] Therein she may chant self-affirmations in the manner of a contemplative whispering prayers on the hour. But she cannot promote a private discovery as a social achievement. Her capabilities to thrive, ascertained somewhere off page, may inspire narratives that clear the head, but they do not contribute to the renewal of social hope or inspire action on behalf of others.

In the opening scene of the 1970 film *Zabriskie Point*, a contentious debate between black and white student activists is underway on a California campus; as the camera surveys the scene in a documentary fashion, the students speak in tired revolutionary cliches. The film, even with its amateur actors and tedious plot, offers insight into the causes of a movement unraveling. Furious black men in Che Guevara berets and army fatigues punctuate their violent mantras with seething street wisdom. "Molotov cocktails are a mixture of gasoline and kerosene. White radicalism is a mixture of bullshit and jive." A concerned woman protests that "a lot of white people" are potential revolutionaries, even as a goateed Marxist complains that the coffee's run out. "Can't a man make a cup of coffee," the woman replies in disgust. Black radical Kathleen Cleaver, playing herself, threatens to close down the school "because we haven't gotten what we need." Meanwhile, Mark, the film's protagonist, appears agitated and annoyed. When someone asks the young radicals if they're really willing to die for the cause, Mark rises to his feet and replies, "I'm willing to die. But not from boredom." He then leaves the room with a shrug. The debate continues briefly in the protagonist's absence but there is not much more to learn: these young activists have grown to hate each other as much as the system against which they wage inchoate struggle.

What became of these student radicals holding forth on the revolution, and, more importantly, what became of the summer soldiers, beatnik

"Jesus still cries out in words that echo across the centuries: 'Love your enemies; bless them that curse you; pray for them that despitefully use you.' This is what we must live by. We must meet hate with love." Martin Luther King Jr. speaks from the porch of his bombed parsonage in Montgomery, Alabama, on the evening of February 4, 1956. (Corbis)

A member of the
Montgomery Improvement
Association reads scripture
at a mass meeting at the
First Baptist Church of
Montgomery, Alabama.
Dr. King sits behind her
holding his notes. (Corbis)

Dr. King rides a Montgomery bus next to Reverend Glenn Smiley and directly behind Reverend Ralph Abernathy the morning after calling an end to the bus boycott. "We must now move from protest to reconciliation," King said the night before at a mass meeting. (Corbis)

Karl Barth and Martin Luther King Jr. exchange greetings at Princeton Theological Seminary, 1962. Karl Barth and the "theologians of crisis," said King, were "calling us back to the depths of the Christian faith," warning us "that we too easily capitulated to modern culture." (H. Martin Rumscheidt Collection, Princeton Theological Seminary)

The Preacher King, April 1964 (Flip Schulke, Corbis)

Clarence Jordan works the cotton fields of Koinonia Farm. "Somehow God has made us out of this old soil and we go back to it and it never loses its claim on us. It isn't a simple matter to leave it." (Koinonia Partners)

The Koinonia sign marks an inauspicious entrance to the "demonstration plot of the Kingdom." (Koinonia Partners)

"[If] the barriers that divide man, and cause wars, race conflict, economic competition, class struggle, labor disputes, are ever to be broken down," Martin England wrote, "they must be broken down in small groups of people living side by side." Black and white men shared tasks in this experiment in intentional Christian community. (Koinonia Partners)

Christian radicals in Bible study with Clarence Jordan. (Koinonia Partners)

Clarence Jordan and Millard Fuller, the Koinonian and founder of Habitat for Humanity, walking down a dirt road in Sumter County, Georgia. "Clarence introduced me to 'the God Movement'," Fuller said, "to the concept of being God's partner and partners with one another to do God's work in the world." (Habitat for Humanity International)

Church people sing "We Shall Overcome" in a mass meeting at True Light Baptist Church, in Hattiesburg, Mississippi. (The Herbert Randall Collection, University of Southern Mississippi)

A day in the life of the COFO-Hattiesburg Project office. (The Herbert Randall Collection, University of Southern Mississippi)

Although Bob Moses is often described in civil rights literature as a solitary mystic, his mystical insights were social and his cell was a corner of a crowded room. Bob Moses at a SNCC conference in 1964. (Danny Lyon, Magnum Photos)

SNCC field secretary Charles Sherrod and Randy Battle visit a family in rural southwest Georgia. "We must forever be under the judgment of the community in which we live," Sherrod said. "Whatever we do or propose must be executed after careful consideration of the people." (Danny Lyon, Magnum Photos)

SNCC's Cordell Reagon gives instruction in nonviolent self-defense. "We were asked to sacrifice so much more than we thought possible," one activist explained. (The Herbert Randall Collection, University of Southern Mississippi)

View of a porch, where voter registration activists canvass a local resident in south Mississippi. (The Herbert Randall Collection, University of Southern Mississippi)

The Freedom Schools exceeded everyone's expectations, drawing more than two thousand students in the course of the summer, twice as many as anticipated, and the number of schools expanded to fifty by the end of the summer. A boy stands by the road reading after class. (The Herbert Randall Collection, University of Southern Mississippi)

"We were spirit people," said Victoria Gray, one of the saints of the "enfleshened church" of the civil rights movement. "We were planted for a rich harvest." (The Herbert Randall Collection, University of Southern Mississippi)

Street Apocalypse. National Guard patrols the streets of Washington, D.C., in the wake of the riots following Dr. King's assassination. (Burt Glinn, Magnum)

The search for authenticity and freedom deracinated from concrete engagement with the poor and excluded spiraled into absurdity. Hippies dance in a circle in Berkeley, California. (Corbis)

Christian intellectual and social critic Os Guinness lectures to a group of students in the Swiss commune called L'abri. "There had been no lack of human thought, action and effort," Guinness wrote of the secular counter-culture, "but underneath the efforts of a generation lay dust." (Sylvester Jacobs, courtesy of the photographer)

Francis Schaeffer, the father of the evangelical counter-culture, celebrates a Communion service at L'abri in 1969. (Sylvester Jacobs, courtesy of the photographer)

"[There] are heavy social implications to the equality expressed in God's spiritual activity in creation," said John M. Perkins, civil rights activist, pastor, and founder of the faith-based community development movement. "Perhaps the heaviest is Christ's identification with the poor. . . He calls the poor person his brother: 'Whatever you did for the humblest of my brothers you did for me' (Matt. 25:40). (Billy Graham Center Archives)

John Perkins lectures on the Three R's of Christian community development: redistribution, reconciliation, and relocation. (Billy Graham Center Archives)

"Living involvement," John Perkins said, "turns poor people from statistics into our friends." (John M. Perkins Foundation)

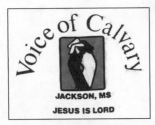

Reconciliation may indeed produce handshakes and hugs and the tears of reunion, but without confrontation and corrective action it is an empty gesture. Voice of Calvary T-Shirt. (Billy Graham Center Archives)

Members of the Voice of Calvary community stand outside the educational center in Mendenhall, Mississippi, in the late 1970's. (John M. Perkins Foundation)

The Christian Thrift Store, Mendenhall, Mississippi, (Billy Graham Center Archives)

"Poverty is a constant assault upon dignity and humanity," writes Mark Gornik. "But Jesus says, 'you count'. So you count. Now, let's create a community where that can be embodied." Reverend Gornik leads prayer during a park dedication in the Sandtown neighborhood of Baltimore. (Courtesy of Sandtown-Winchester Habitat for Humanity)

Russell Jeung and his neighbors build community in Oakland, California. "We've come with the intent to care for the poor," said Jeung, "but what we've learned is far deeper." (Courtesy of Russell Jeung)

There is a resurgence of moral energy in many of the universities of North America inspired by religious conviction and the social movements of the past. Students and former civil rights activists march for racial unity in Oxford, Mississippi, 1999. (Institute for Racial Reconciliation and Civic Renewal, University of Mississippi)

Prayer Meeting for Peace and Reconciliation, University of Virginia, 2003. (Ambrose Faturoti)

Christs, and young idealists who traveled South with their hopes of building the beloved community? And why did their goals become so deracinated and self-referential?

The philosopher Richard Rorty pondered these questions in his provocative book *Achieving Our Country: Leftist Thought in Twentieth-Century America*.[26] In particular, Rorty wonders how it came to be that an activist tradition committed to piecemeal social reform gave way to a culture of theoretical and self-indulgent spectatorism. He wonders how the generation of intellectuals and activists concerned about citizenship schools and voter registration came to embrace the cultural politics of the contemporary Left.

In *Achieving Our Country*, Rorty introduces us to two varieties of leftist thought in twentieth-century America: the old Left and its reformist children of the civil rights movement and the new Left and its academic children of the postmodern university. As Rorty tells the story, the moral vocabulary of the reformist-activist Left shaped such progressive movements as the labor and civil right movements, the courageous work of those who struggled between 1900 and 1964 "within the framework of constitutional democracy to protect the weak from the strong." But it is the new Left one hears at the end of the Summer Project when SNCC goes cosmic, in the rhetorical pyrotechnics of black power and the student militants, and in the claim increasingly heard among the activist ranks that America itself is inherently corrupt and white; and it is the new Left's children that one hears in the trendy sobriquets of contemporary culture studies and postmodern theory. Rorty argues that since 1964, the Left has increasingly operated as a "spectatorial, disgusted, mocking Left rather than a Left that dreams of achieving our country," a fashionably cynical rather than a responsibly hopeful Left.[27] Demonizing whites, or males, or "Amerika," made it all too easy to stop thinking of oneself as a citizen with responsibilities to community and civic life and to begin thinking that one lives in an evil empire, and thus one has no responsibility to the community or nation.[28] By contrast, the old, reformist Left sought to achieve its country by taking responsibility for social progress, which required a love of nation that remained honest about its faults.

Readers of Rorty's work will know that he is hardly a conservative pundit dismissing the sixties as a period of unrestrained hedonism. Had these passionate young men and women restrained their anger, he believes, America might still be sending its young people off to kill Vietnamese.[29] "It is even possible that the Defense Department might lie to the public more frequently and fluently than at present (although that is difficult to imagine)," he adds.[30] The counterculture reminded America that there can be beauty in dissent and that resistance leaves room for pleasure. Still, the reformist Left accepted the inevitability of compromising principles and the necessity of sacrifice, and it accomplished much, while the new Left believes it needs to remain pure—never sell out to the system—and it has accomplished very little. In other words, the old Left inspired social hope and civic participation, while the new Left inspires cynicism—cynicism that manifests itself in a preoccupation with theoretical description and the crafting of exotic vocabularies.

Consequently, the Whitmanesque hope of democracy as the most beautiful poem which lifted the hearts of the American Left before the 1960s was seen to have been a symptom of naïve humanism, if not a conspiracy to impose dominant values on so many helpless others.[31] The left began to worry more about such matters as the psychosexual motivations of cruelty than straightforward avarice and corruption; the study of political economy was replaced by the study of "apocalyptic French and German philosophy." Sadism and cultural marginality were recognized as having deeper roots and more insidious social effects than economic and political factors. Basic discussions about resurgent activism and community organizing were rendered quaint.[32] In short, the contemporary Left exchanged its reformist commitments for ethereal delights and Gothic horrors and became incapable of national pride and meaningful engagement in political life.[33] Beloved community is a liberal guilt trip.

Rorty's book reads like a sermon preached with missionary conviction. He calls the contemporary Left down from its ethereal perch, to reckon with everyday misery and social despair and to set forth clear proposals for social progress. The problem with theory is not its complexity, he explains. The problem is rather more prosaic and mundane, namely the difficulty of clambering back to earth from a high level of abstraction to a level on which one might meaningfully discuss tax laws, organizing initiatives, housing policies, or a political candidate.[34]

In turn, Rorty ponders how the Left can ever again be mobilized in support of policies that help achieve our country, or more directly, in a manner that attends soberly with social misery and its political solutions—and he offers two suggestions. First, the Left should put a moratorium on theory. "Disengagement from practice produces theoretical hallucinations," he writes marvelously.[35] Second, the Left should make it a matter of great urgency to ask how the country of Lincoln, Rauschenbusch, Dewey, Whitman, and Baldwin might still be achieved—an America, one might add, that does not derive its meaning through war and conquest. Rorty thinks it might even be a good idea to convene a series of meetings around the country for the purpose of drafting a "People's Charter." These revival meetings of the Left would produce a confession of sorts, a concrete political platform that would serve as the standard for new directions of research and writing and help inspire alliances with people outside academe.[36] But the intent of the "People's Charter" would not be to underwrite a retrieval of an exclusively grassroots approach to political problems as in participatory democracy, or to construct a politics of "the people" in the sense of "the people" as a "redemptive preternatural force . . . whose demonic counterpart is named 'power' or 'the system.'"[37] A "People's Charter" would rather signal the cultural Left's reorientation to real political concerns, and it would indicate that the left had finally learned that its insouciant use of terms like "system," "late capitalism," and "the people" serves to evade talk of specific social practices and specific changes in dehumanizing social practices.[38]

Rorty's helpful analysis of the Left's retreat from the working of mercy and justice runs aground, however, in his blithe indifference to the rich history of faith-based social reform. For one thing, Rorty's secularized narrative of American social reform and his hopes for the renewal of the reformist Left willfully ignore the religious convictions that mobilized large numbers of clergymen and church people in support of labor in the early twentieth century. With the longing of a fundamentalist for the return of Jesus, Rorty longs for a day when humanity will produce "a document" that offers a "this-worldly utopia without assuring us that this utopia will emerge full-blown."[39] He longs for the day when a generous hope will captivate our hearts and minds without the reassurances of a divine savior; when humanity is able to engage the world, as in Freud's *Future of an Illusion*, with reason stripped of its tutelage to transcendence. But in ignoring the religious motivations of social activism in twentieth-century America, Rorty undermines even his own best pragmatic case for renewing social hopes. Rorty gives us so little to imagine. Atheists have been with us for a long time—long enough to notice that they have not in fact given us much evidence to suppose that the godless heart is capable of a more generous hope than the religious. In reality, liberal ironists, sullen postmoderns, and Nietzschean self-creators do not create soup kitchens, tutorial programs, AIDS hospices, health clinics, or hunger coalitions.

It is true that in the closing decade of the nineteenth century there were frequent complaints within the ranks of the labor movement about the church's lack of involvement. In 1892, for example, Terence Powderly, a member of the Knights of Labor, said, "You can count on the ends of your fingers all the clergymen who take any interest in the labor problem."[40] But that same year, Walter Rauschenbusch (who was Rorty's maternal grand-father) led a group of Protestant ministers and theologians to commit themselves to the "practical realization in the world" of the kingdom of God, which they understood to include "the marching hosts of labor."[41]

By the 1930s social activism in America, and especially the progressive experiments in agricultural cooperatives and labor organizing in the South, were saturated with religious conviction, as Anthony Dunbar has shown in his important book *Against the Grain: Southern Radicals and Prophets, 1929–1959*. The radical Christians who made up such organizations as the Southern Tenants Farmworkers Union, the Fellowship of Southern Churchmen, the Southern Conference for Human Welfare, the High-lander Folk School, and the Fellowship of Reconciliation, people like Howard and Alice Kester, Sherwood Eddy, Claude Welch, James Dom-broski, Myles and Zilphia Mae Horton, and Septima Clark, spoke passion-ately of social progress and reform, of "land for the landless," "full and de-cent employment," the holding in common of "all natural resources and all scientific processes," and "the liberation of all workers from enslavement to the machine."[42] These radical Christians cared for the poor and oppressed through a broad range of initiatives in community and union organizing and in educational reform, and they used the power of testimonial and nar-rative to educate the nation about poverty; presenting heartbreaking por-traits of day-laborers who "swelled the ranks of the dispossessed," squeezed out by the large plantations, insurance companies, and banks; of homeless families combing the South for a decent living and a decent landlord, "on the rivers in flat boats, in the coves, swamps and on the barren hillsides, a great mass of wanderers, without homes, food or work, half clothed, sick of body and soul, unwanted and unloved in the Kingdom of King Cotton"; of the manipulation of racial fears by well-to-do planters who played black against white in their cynical game of material acquisition.

"We were trying to call attention to the implications of the Christian faith for all humanity," Howard Kester said. "Nothing made any difference to us but human need, that was the measure, and you went because people were in need, it didn't matter who they were, or where or how they lived."[43] These men and women were carried by a river of spiritual passion into lifetimes of social activism and reform. Such accounts offered a vivid and synoptic realism about social existence precisely because these radicals saw Jesus in the disenfranchised.[44]

Rorty dispenses with sin and redemption, however, and leaves us with little understanding of why we should care about the poor and the ex-cluded. He regards sin as an "un-representational" notion, which like any theological concept may be useful to some in their private quests for perfection but is a nuisance when trying to decide what concrete tasks need to be done. Yet the problem with such claims from the ground level is that most women and men who work with the poor and on behalf of the excluded believe, at a minimum, that these people, like the rest of humanity, are created in the image of God and endowed with divine purpose. Catholic activists, liberation theologians, and radical evangelicals believe that God has "a preferential option for the poor"; that all life, including that of a malnourished or unborn baby or an incarcerated man, is inherently valuable. These beliefs may not get one speaking invitations in plush conference settings, as they remain theological convictions about the dignity of life. Still, academic secularists should be interested to discover—as they will discover when they leave the university campuses and engage their towns and inner-cities—that transcendence empowers rather than diminishes the love of life, animates the protest against cruelty, and focuses the moral energies of compassion and mercy.

Rorty's "solidarity" wanders aimlessly for a real social referent. It is not the poor or the excluded with whom readers are asked to stand in alliance against the oppressive powers and dehumanizing patters of fallen creation. Rorty's solidarity is an affirmation of individual mental resources, which in certain cases may be sustained long enough to inspire action; nevertheless, imaginative solidarity is fickle and fleeting and will likely be laid aside as quickly as a book whose novelty has been exhausted.

So here we are waiting for Rorty's reformist Left to make a comeback, and wondering what became of the search for beloved community. But having dispensed with God as an annoying distraction, having dispensed with the self as a residue of sacred reality, having dispensed with truth in favor of irony, where does Rorty think the sources of our moral and civic passions will be found? The search for beloved community, unfettered from its theological origins, produced first spiritual frenzy and then a certain torpor of spirit resembling malaise. In the end, Rorty turns out to be as much of a purist as those socialists he castigates for their ideological rigidity or the postmodern theorists seeking to live beyond history. The cultural Left is purged of those who offend Rorty's cultural sensibilities, whether these are Catholic Workers feeding the poor, evangelicals building community in housing projects, or social gospelers lending their hand to living wage campaigns. Rorty's aspirations to a nonreligious purity of heart even preclude the use of the term "movement," because movements, in his view, emerge against a backdrop of providential expectations and are better suited to onto-theological Platonists, or to hopes for the coming om of God. By relegating religious conviction to the individual's private psychic garden, Rorty may have gotten rid of the marauding fundamentalists and religious know-nothings, but he has also asked Martin Luther King and Fannie Lou Hamer to leave the table, and thus unwittingly promoted the same kind of retreat from action that he loathes in the postmodern academy.

What then sustains a vital affirmation of the human, the protest against avarice and greed, and a lived commitment to social progress and redemptive community? Before we return to the southern theatre and the final part of the story, we should take note of one influential Christian critique of the secular counterculture and its constructive response to the demise of social hope. In his influential 1973 book, *The Dust of Death*, the Christian social critic Os Guinness surveyed the ideas and practices of the secular counterculture in a sympathetic effort to reshape these ideas and practices theologically as constructive elements of a renewed Christian witness. Guinness argued that authentic Christian community provides the sole context for a fully realized and multidimensional humanism, a fulfillment of the basic longings of secular humanism and the counterculture, a humanism returned to its origins.[45] The day the secular radical falters is the day the Christian radical must demonstrate his staying power, Guiness insists.[46] Christians must then seek to reform or rebuild the broken world as an expression of obedience to God.[47]

The Dust of Death remains the most compelling work of cultural interpretation to emerge from the evangelical counterculture. Guinness's polemic is "gentle and urbane," as James Gaffney noted in his *America* review, uncommon traits of an evangelical Protestant writing about secular humanism.[48] The book offers a rich compendium of intellectual life in America and Britain in the sixties and a probing analysis of the counterculture's philosophical failure. Guinness situates the story of student protest against the background of Western humanism in the twentieth century; and he sees the youth movement as a courageous defiance against the ethos of technique and control. Western humanism, shaped by classical civilization, the Renaissance, and the Enlightenment, was built on the four optimistic beliefs of reason, progress, science, and human autonomy. Toward the end of the nineteenth century, the philosopher Ludwig Feuerbach and the sociologist Auguste Comte were speaking confidently of human self-sufficiency as a fully realizable achievement. Feuerbach described the idea of God and the theological attributes as the self-projection of humanity's own infinite value into a transcendent other. Comte was confident that a universal religion of humanity lay in the not-so-distant future, awaiting the intellectual coming of age of our species. But the outbreak of the First World War, followed by the Russian Revolution, brought an end to the happy conceit that humanity was moving toward perpetual peace. "The buttresses of human existence are collapsing," wrote Franz Kafka after World War I. Postwar society in America and Great Britain may have sought to revive the social optimism of better days, but it was only an Indian Summer.[49] For Nietzsche had been correct to say that the meaning of humanism lay in its passionate assertion of the will to power. The choirs of historical progress sang a little too loudly; and what followed this assertion would not be perpetual freedom but a period of decadence whose logic was nihilism.[50] "I started out with the idea of unrestricted freedom," says the revolutionary Shigalov in Dostoevsky's novel *The Possessed*, "and I have arrived at unrestricted despotism."[51]

Guinness charted the counterculture's explorations of alternative realities and visions of social order, admiring its protests against technological society and impoverishing humanism, while noting that the new Left's "great refusal" of the values, principles, ideals, and goals of bureaucratic society was actually based on the same "humanist premises" that it presumed to reject. The members of the counterculture were thus doomed to replicate the same dehumanizing habits of technique and managerial control.[52] "Without a basis and balance for a true alternative," Guinness writes, "they oscillate between the logic of Marxism which achieves too much and the logic of mysticism which achieves nothing."[53] The counterculture was unable to create and sustain communities that were not flattened by technological reality and, as a result, it too became one-dimensional.[54]

Guinness was a gracious reader and was not in a hurry to insert Christianity into the scene as some kind of *deus ex machina*. Guinness pandered to no one in those early years of his involvement in the L'Abri Fellowship, not even his own constituency. He acknowledged the huge failure of contemporary Christians to rise to the intellectual and moral challenges of the modern world. He insisted that orthodox Christians put aside their antediluvian opposition to novelty and dissent, their shallow denunciatory judgments against intellectual culture, and begin to appreciate the youth movements and their creations. At the same time, he insisted correctly that the shallowness of much contemporary Christian testimony does not falsify its message.

Guinness's pastoral influence was Francis A. Schaeffer, the Presbyterian minister and popular writer with whom Guinness worked in the L'Abri community in Switzerland. Schaeffer was the intellectual de rigueur of

American evangelicals; he had founded the Christian commune in the Swiss Alps with his wife, Edith, and authored numerous popular books that engaged reformed orthodoxy with modern culture. Schaeffer's basic claim, hammered home in nearly every lecture, book, and conversation, was that divorced from the foundations of historic Christianity, humanity was left with two options: escape into an unreality that produces mysticism or descent into a nihilism that reduces humans to machines.[55] Thousands traveled to the village of Huemoz to attend Schaeffer's lectures and to be part of the community; even more attended his seminars in the United States. Schaeffer sounded a rare note in the intellectually guarded circles of American evangelicalism, calling Christians to think critically, to read widely, and to understand the modern world in all its diversity. At the same time, he spoke passionately against nationalism, racism, materialism, and religious complacency, and he applauded the counterculture's spirit of nonconformity and adventure. "The older generation hasn't given them anything to care about," he said. "And [they] are smart enough to know that they have been given no answers, and they are opting out." Schaeffer encouraged Christians to learn the language of modern culture in order to explain to atheists and agnostics the devastating consequences of these basic options, and thus to pave the way for a bold retrieval of historic Christianity.

In Guinness's account—which added weight and detail to Schaeffer's slim volumes—the ecological and urban crisis, the arms race, the population explosion, the exposure of Western racism and its effects, and the war in Vietnam revealed "the striptease of humanism," the step-by-step unlayering of the naïve optimism that liberal sentiment tries hard to obscure.[56] Learning the language of the modern world made possible a clearer diagnosis of the problem: The counterculture lacked the resources to create alternatives that sustained moral focus and spiritual vitality. The ideals that first inspired resistance and dissent had grown so distant that they became "barely distinguishable from illusions."[57] As Guinness writes, "There had been no lack of human thought, action, and effort—even blood—all given in generous quantities. But underneath the effort of a generation lay dust."[58]

Guinness proposed a theological alternative, a "third race." Shaped by revealed Christianity and its historic reformed convictions, the third race would represent a theological counterculture that fosters meaningful protest against dehumanizing forces and institutions and sustains genuine community. The third race was not American evangelicalism—not even its more edgy forms. Guinness had little sympathy for the Jesus movement, currently at the height of its fifteen minutes of fame when *The Dust of Death* appeared in 1973. Jesus shirts, bumper stickers, posters, buttons, badges, watches, cheers, rock festivals, and slogans—"Jesus is just the best trip, man"[59]—all these examples of mass-marketed piety seemed to Guinness nothing but "another California-born neophiliac fashion."[60] Rather, Guinness built his description of the "Third Race" on the foundations of "Reformation and Revival"; only through commitment to revealed truth can the "rigorous practice of truth and love" be nourished and sustained.

Guinness had no illusions that the Christian alternative would be easy, nor was he at all certain that its "constructive Christian radicalism" would not taper off into rhetoric or degenerate into bitterness and anger. Much is demanded of Christians by virtue of the truth they hold; indeed the Christian's commitment to the sacredness of life and the purposefulness of history require an even more uncompromising stand against the cultural stream than that of the secular counterculture. Unlike the shtick of recent conservative Christian leaders, who build their personal franchises through the mockery and vilification of liberals, Guinness understood that the Christian community's first priority is putting its own house in order, struggling to restore integrity, discipline, conviction, compassion, and courage to its proclamation and mission.

Above all else, however, inhabiting the third race means learning to "practice truth and love." It means learning to see that the created world groans under the weight of injustice and inhumanity; to expose those habits, patterns, and forms that have choked off God's original purposes; and to work steadfastly for the healing and flourishing of creation. Revealed truth and the attendant practice of truth in the world enable Christian radicalism to develop "adequate criteria for radical critique and a basis for a genuine revolutionary alternative." In this way, the Christian perceives anew all reality from the double perspective of creation *imago dei* and the redemption of the world in Jesus Christ; and this perception enables compassionate and responsible engagement in the world, as well as the deepest affirmation of dignity, depth, and purpose. Christian radicalism, in Guinness's words, is radicalism "beaten out by the hammer of transcendent truth on the anvil of empirical reality," and for this reason the Christian radical will not shirk the harsh existential realities of technological society but will concretely engage these realities from a theological perspective.[61] Indeed, it was not Rousseau, Hegel, Marx, or Kafka who first defined the essential condition of human alienation but St. Paul, Augustine, Luther, and Calvin.

Christians must then build humane environments in cities and towns that support and sustain proper human aspirations and their fulfillment. Christians must demonstrate and defend the created dignity of the human in every area of life, from integrity in advertising to morality and justice in national defense. No doubt, this task requires great discipline, for the dark side of optimistic humanism, configured by alienation, mystification, and romanticism, has yielded habits of survival and expansion for the nation and the Church in North America. But the church has the resources to re-sist the mystification of reality (defined as "the conscious or unconscious masking of the true nature of things") and to extricate itself from the man-ufacture of propaganda.[62]

Nevertheless, despite its promise to affirm "personal significance and to forge solidarity with those who suffer," Guinness's description of Christian counterculture and the practice of truth remains singularly abstract. A re-viewer in the *Times Literary Supplement* questioned the intent of Guinness's critique inasmuch as his was a crusade "launched from a mountain eyrie in Switzerland ironically named L'Abri."[63] Having dressed his Christian radi-cal up in the fashionable garb of resistance and rebellion, Guinness seemed reluctant to let his radical loose in the world. Or more precisely, Guinness's radical is distinguished more by the books he reads and the clothes he wears than by his social commitments; his Christian radical does not take any special interest in the poor and the excluded. In this manner, Guin-ness's appeals to scripture as the Christian radical's "script of truth" re-mained singularly uninvolved with the social teachings of Jesus.[64] The teachings of Jesus are politically relevant as a criterion of humanness, but they do not appear to shape a distinctive way of life.

Guinness moved from Switzerland to Washington, D.C., in the early 1980s. By the time *The Dust of Death* was released in a revised edition in 1994, the L'Abri Fellowships had emerged—whether they liked it or not—as ethical-theological think tanks for the Moral Majority.[65] The new edi-tion was published by Crossway Books, the leading book publisher of the religious right, with the original subtitle, "A Critique of the Countercul-ture," replaced by the more politically potent "The Sixties Counterculture and How It Changed America Forever." In his 1973 edition, Guinness de-scribed the civil rights movement as an organic protest against humanism's myopic cultural inheritance, rather than as an expression of generational optimism. However, the afterward of the new edition, entitled "The Seis-mic Sixties," evoked the shrill tone of the decade's conservative despisers, as Guinness now described the civil rights movement as a "moral spasm" lacking "any genuine philosophical and ethical rigor."[66] While the original version of *The Dust of Death* was aimed at the reformation of the church in North America, the revised edition sought the reformation of America. While the original version took inspiration from the secular counterculture's spirit of dissent and protest and spoke directly to the church's complicity in militarism, environmental ruin, racism, intellectual dishonesty, and theological shallowness, the revised edition was pitched as a morality tale about unrestrained hedonism and moral bankruptcy.

What happened between the first and the revised editions was *Roe vs. Wade*, the Supreme Court decision of January 1973 handed down a few months after *The Dust of Death* had gone to press. *Roe vs. Wade* unified the conservative evangelical movement in ways that civil rights and antiwar activism had fractured it.[67] Christian intellectuals and writers living and working in study centers dependent on charitable contributions also discovered that conservative Christians could be effectively mobilized by fearful prognostications of eugenics and the genocide of the unborn; whereas images of impoverished and disenfranchised African Americans had left most conservative white Christians largely unmoved. Martin Luther King Jr. had spoken in judgment of the liberal establishment in his denunciations of Vietnam and the American culture of violence. His comprehensive devotion to the sacredness of life would have surely included the unborn, or risked grave inconsistency. After hearing of the Supreme Court decision, Fannie Lou Hamer, who had been forcibly sterilized in her twenties, had remarked, "Now they're starting to kill black babies."[68] The disproportionate number of aborted black babies to white in the South could be claimed by white liberals as a demonstration of social compassion only by mocking the civil rights movement's protection of society's most excluded and vulnerable. Reverend Ed King of the Mississippi Freedom Democratic Party had taken the Supreme Court decision as an expression of the "anti-poor policies of the Republican president, Richard Nixon," an insidious and now legal way of achieving massive cuts in welfare spending by "cutting down on black welfare babies."[69]

But white conservative Christians could not share the civil rights movement's outrage at *Roe vs. Wade* because most white Christians had really never cared about black babies to begin with. Lacking a commitment to the poor and the excluded, conservative white opposition to abortion produced nothing so much as a generation of pious patriots; and, as it turned out, any action would be justified in waging war against abortion except support of precisely those social policies for the poor that would make abortion less

desirable. Schaeffer and Guinness's inability to reckon with the racism of
the conservative Christian establishment undermined all that had once
been so promising in their pursuit of a theological counterculture. The
Third Race had nothing to do with the reconciled races; the Third Way
veered toward the Christian right, and the right's campaign against abortion became a cynical posturing for a political edge that obscured its deep
complicity in killing by other means. Campaigns against abortion deracinated from the poor and the excluded produced a collective delusion of
righteousness and the presumption of morality, and once again enabled
white Christians to ignore their greatest historical burden, slavery and its
legacy in legal and social segregation.

CHAPTER 5

~~~

Between the Times

There has been little attention in studies of the civil rights movement to the years following the death of Dr. King, the dispersal and collapse of the Student Nonviolent Coordinating Committee and the dissemination of the movement into inchoate forms of protest and confrontation. It is true that by the end of the sixties, the white and black volunteers who had worked in the deep South had moved on to other concerns: women's liberation, free speech, the pursuit of an alternative consciousness, and above all, the war in Vietnam, which imposed vast demands on the activist energies of the counter-culture. Intensified warfare in Southeast Asia made the pace of southern racial progress tedious by contrast in what is often a zero-sum equation for the nation's moral attention. Racial peace in America was still a dream deferred, but the struggle (now "the black struggle") seemed a lot less urgent in view of the daily body counts in Vietnam.

No doubt, the 1969 Supreme Court decision in *Alexander vs. Holmes County* was a landmark case, and deserves greater attention in civil rights scholarship. The accompanying mandates of the Fifth U.S. Circuit Court of Appeals ordered immediate integration of sixteen school districts in Mississippi and effectively ended legal segregation in the South. Public school districts could no longer avoid compliance with the *Brown vs. Board* decision by seizing upon the phrase "all deliberate speed" as a means of deferring implementation indefinitely. Still, it was hard to keep America on the edge of its seat with discussions of a "unitary non-discriminatory school system" and the drafting of guidelines for redesigned school districts in rural jurisdictions.

To be sure, a decade of dramatic legal victories had changed forever the public face of the South. In 1970, not only were all remaining school districts finally integrated, but the Ku Klux Klan found itself persona non grata in its own playgrounds, as most of its wizards and henchmen began serving time in federal prisons. In southern towns and cities, black people could take their meals in white-owned restaurants, spend the night in motels and hotels, and borrow books from the public library. Even in Mississippi, the movement "had won significant victories" and a "degree of civility" finally arrived, as the historian John Dittmer wrote in his book, *Local People: The Struggle for Civil Rights in Mississippi*.[1] Dittmer's hopefulness is a cautious one, however, as the significant victories concealed the secret that little had really changed in the racial shape of daily life. Not even the University of Alabama's Bear Bryant— the head coach determined to win football games by any means necessary— had yet shown any interest in breaking the unlegislatible color line of college sports. That would have to wait until 1971, one year after a black halfback named Sam "the Bam" Cunningham at the University of Southern California ran for 135 yards and two touchdowns against the Crimson Tide defense and humiliated Bryant on national television. The color bar was broken over the objections of George Wallace.

White racism in America did not end with the collapse of legal segregation in the South, as many northern liberals had naïvely hoped; but southern segregation did not really end with the collapse of segregation either, if one wanted to press the point. When Lillian Smith wrote in her 1949 memoir, *Killers of a Dream*, of the tutelage of every white southern child in the triangulation of race, sex, and religion, she could not have foreseen how Jim Crow's inheritance would long survive its legal demise. Perhaps the prospects were simply too unbearable to entertain. Southern school children might become teammates on the playing fields or sit next to each other in classrooms—though they would not sit next to each other in church—but apart from dramatic moral transformations nowhere in sight, the new familiarity only called attention to the distressing fact that every bridging of the gap deepened the chasm between black and white. Somehow, too, in the course of the fourteen years since the Montgomery Bus Boycott and the two years since King's assassination, the popular impression had formed that the civil rights movement was more about rhetorical provocation, unleashed desire, and perpetual liberation than the difficult work of community building; more about high moral and sometimes highly scripted drama than legal justice and transforming the heart and soul of white people.

The new decade began with America's invasion of Cambodia, the killing of student protesters at Kent State University and at Jackson State University, George Wallace urging his fellow southern governors to defy federal integration orders, and hopes of racial peace deferred. The promised land glimpsed on that fateful April evening in Memphis had vanished into a pale horizon, and the moral reserves of a nation that had once applied its energies to racial equality and reconciliation were now extended elsewhere, and they were running on empty.

For years the civil rights preacher Will Campbell had complained about the civil rights movement's priorities: why had organizers been singularly concerned with access to public bathrooms, coffee shops, and waiting rooms in bus stations?[2] Why make these places the battlefield for racial equality? They were the last places you could expect to find the men who controlled the social arrangements. If white power was the real culprit, Campbell insisted, then stage sit-ins at the Rotary Club or during the midsummer debutante cotillion; then seek to reform the culture of the white church. Forcing a short-order cook at the five-and-dime lunch counter to remove the "colored-only" sign was too easy a target; and, in any case, it was not going to bring electricity and plumbing to needy families, alter the subterranean world of feeling and opinion, or halt a retreat of the sentiments and of white people to the suburbs.

The rise of the private "Christian" seg-academies was but one manifestation of an expanding range of creative options that fortified the walls of social segregation. The claim recently set forth by some African American intellectuals that the real winners of the civil rights movement were the white Republicans who came into power during the 1980 presidential election may be an exaggeration, but it is also a completely understandable response to the depressing fact that the shifting legal landscape of race left unchanged too many of the supporting structures of white supremacy. The movement had unsettled the world of working and middle-class whites even as the privileged classes continued their bridge games without interruption. "The ultimate solution to the problem of race," King had said, "lies in the willingness of men to obey the unenforceable."[3]

National conviction for racial peace languished. As something called a civil rights establishment emerged in response to diminished public concern for racial justice, the piecemeal work of social reform and renewal was largely abandoned. Activists seeking the hard-earned rewards for years of sacrifice and struggle abandoned the poor neighborhoods and communities that had once been at center stage of the civil rights story. One could not really blame these men and women for cashing in on their overdue promissory notes. Nonetheless, as members of a generation of creative and skilled black (and white) activists moved out of poor communities and into networks of political influence, non-profit work, cultural and academic leadership, and corporate boardrooms, no one took their place in the freedom houses and community centers.

"In America of the late 1960's, with its congested cities and streets, its high crime rates, its guns and knives, its instant communications that pipe reports of civil disturbances into every household, its divisions and strife, its overbearing technology, its mass culture, mass education, and mass government, history seems to cry out for a new tradition that would provide a nonviolent means for change and for expression and protest." This was the observation of *New York Times* reporter John Herbers in his essential book, *The Lost Priority: Whatever Happened to the Civil Rights Movement in America?*, published on the eve of the new decade of the 70's. Herbers continued, "Martin Luther King and his nonviolent armies seemed for a time to have implanted this kind of tradition. Anyone who followed the civil rights movement could not escape the feeling that here was a spirit that could enlighten the country. In those days they talked of saving not only themselves but the soul of America as well, and after some of the great movements they would talk about saving the world with nonviolence. But nonviolence as a national and mystical movement . . . died.[4]

No doubt, some of the missionary zeal needed to die. The presumption of a chosen few saving the nation and the world with nonviolence seemed but a progressive Protestant rendering of Billy Graham's saving the world for Jesus, minus the football stadiums and altar calls. The real hitch was that while redeeming the soul of America may have sounded like a good way to capture the nation's moral imagination, short of illuminating the spaces of repentance, forgiveness, and reconciliation, the call seemed increasingly to lead nowhere in particular.

Other banners flew in the chaotic winds. For a few humorless children of the movement, the emerging culture of sensitivity-training configured the zones of white redemption. In and out of the seminar room with tears shed and minds "conscietized," absolution had never been so easy. A few wasted hours and a declaration of white depravity was a small price to pay for the centuries of slavery and American apartheid. But not only was the new race therapy a lot easier than organizing in poor communities, it presupposed the utter naïveté of King's vision, as it coolly dismissed the vision of beloved community as an illusion of the unanalyzed soul, now considered—in the case of the white soul—racist all the way down. No one was quite sure where to go from here.

But one thing seems clear to us now. If America is ever to renew its search for beloved community, the nonviolent armies will have to return to those abandoned places of the nation and the heart where the "mystical" remains alive. The convictions and commitments that animated the movement will need to be rescued from ambiguity and equivocation. Dr. King's final eschatological intensities—"Now the judgment of God is upon us, and we must learn to live together as brothers or we are all going to perish together as fools"—confront us with a severe and chastened hope.

Yet the story will never be complete until we confront the difficult truth that King's final apocalyptic judgments also register a slight demurral on his own sinfulness and complicity in violence. Like the Bible prophets, King had called the nations to repentance; they shall see and be ashamed of all their acts of oppression, he said with unforgettable fury. But King kept the finger pointed on the dark powers around him while mostly avoiding the prophet's harder truth; that the sin outside remains always the co-conspirator of the sinner standing here. "There is none upright among men, they all lie in wait for blood," says the prophet Micah, who beckons us to "go up to the mountain of the Lord," so that the Lord might teach us "in his ways" and we may "walk in his paths." The prophet Amos lists the sins of Israel's neighbors and the terrible judgment awaiting them—"For three transgressions of the Ammonites, and for four, I will not revoke the punishment; because they have ripped up women with child in Gilead, that they might enlarge their border"—but he does not stop until he also lists Israel's own. "For three transgressions of Israel, and for four, I will not revoke the punishment; because they sell the righteous for silver, and the needy for a pair of shoes— they that trample the head of the poor into the dust of the earth, and turn aside the way of the afflicted." The same God who preaches the "good news to the poor" and "proclaims release to the captives," "recovery of sight to the blind," and "liberty to those who are oppressed," *also* "desireth truth in the inward being." It is not only the "great house" that is smitten into fragments but the "little house" as well. Let us not forget that Jesus did not call prophets but disciples, ordinary people willing to lay down their nets and journey through dust-ridden towns. The dream, unanchored in the disciplines of repentance, forgiveness, and reconciliation, becomes an evasion of love's duty in the everyday.

PART THREE

CHAPTER 6

Unfinished Business:
John Perkins and the Radical Roots of
Faith-Based Community Building

At sunset on the evening of February 7, 1970, state patrolmen outside the town of Plain, Mississippi, arrested nineteen students. Most of the nineteen had come from Tougaloo College, the historically black private college north of Jackson, though a few were white students from southern California. Earlier in the afternoon, the group had taken part in a protest against downtown businesses, the fourth installment in a month-long selective buying campaign launched two days before Christmas.

Throughout the demonstration, the students had handed out copies of a 15-point document called the "Demands of the Black Community." Drafted by a local activist named John Perkins, the "Demands" outlined a comprehensive restructuring of race relations in the central Mississippi town of Mendenhall. The "Demands" included calls for 30 percent black employment in all business establishments, desegregation of public spaces, a minimum-wage campaign for domestic workers, paved streets in black neighborhoods, removal of the police chief and his cohorts, and a thorough overhaul of arrest procedures. Not much had changed in Simpson County as a result of the civil rights movement. In addition to persisting segregation, the per capita income for a black person remained under a thousand dollars a year, and more than half the black families in the county lived below the poverty level.[1]

Earlier in the fall of 1969, after several months of unsuccessful boycotts against downtown businesses, Perkins stood on the steps of the courthouse and explained the situation to an audience of black townspeople:

> We've been patient. We've waited for them to change but they ain't gon' change until we stand up and be men and women. Stand up and look them straight in the eyes and demand our freedom. I don't know about ya'll, but me and these children done decided that we ain't going to take it any more. We ain't going to take being second class citizens. The United States Declaration of Independence says, "We hold these truths to be self-evident, that all men are created equal." Well I am a man and I'm ready to stand and be treated like one.
>
> How are we going to get what we want? They sure ain't going to give it to us just because we ask them—and they ain't going to ever give us anything out of the goodness of their hearts. Well, there are plenty of ways to make them listen, but ya'll all know me, and ya'll know I always try to do what's right. We don't need to sink to their level and return hate with hate and violence with violence. That's just what they want us to do. We've got to stick together! If it's just me by myself, they can kill me and that'll be the end of it. But if somebody's got to die, then I'm ready.
>
> I tell you how we can make them listen. We can make them listen with our money. We can stop giving it to them until they are ready to listen to us. Let's keep our money in our pockets. Let's boycott all of their businesses—then they'll be ready to listen to us. They treat us like niggers but they love our nigger money. Let's march up and down Main Street and let's picket all of their stores. Let's tell all of our friends to spend their money in some other town—in McGee or Jackson. Let's bring this town to its knees. Then they'll listen to us. Then they'll know that we mean business. Then they'll know important we really are.[2]

John's fourteen-year-old son Spencer, in his second year in an integrated school, stood beside his father with tears in his eyes, "feeling very proud that he was my daddy," and relieved that his father had finally come to the end of his patience.[3] For like King in Montgomery, John Perkins found himself in the middle of racial protest in spite of his own best efforts to avoid it.

The march had begun with a mass meeting at the Simpson County Cooperative Store. After a time of singing and praying and summoning courage for the day, the hundred-strong crowd proceeded in single file through the narrow streets of the black neighborhood, then along Main Street and around the court square and through the downtown streets, and then back to the co-op to begin the march again. Something new was in the air in this backwater town that had not seen such collective action since the civil rights movement swept through the state six years earlier. "The rhythm of our music and the words of our songs propelled us as a single organism," Spencer would write later of the afternoon, "a single organism instinctively seeking the justice and equality needed for its survival."[4] As they walked, the student volunteers and black residents of Mendenhall sang freedom songs, waved placards, and clapped their hands. "Do right, white man, do right," some chanted. Police officers stood on the roadside and observed the protest with nightsticks and shotguns, letting the marchers pass. "Do right, white man, do right, before we get mad, before we get mad."[5] Aside from a smattering of insults from white bystanders, the demonstration proceeded without incident.

But a few hours later on the side of Highway 49, policemen would not show the same restraint. The officer who had signaled the first van to a stop leaned into the driver's window and said to a long-haired student named Doug Huemmer, "Son, we're not going to take any more shit . . . we're not going to take any more of this civil rights."[6] The officer held the Californian's drivers license as he asked questions about the march, occasionally looking inside the van and studying the black and white faces as he spoke. Who was in charge? Where were the black students from? He then called for backups.[7]

At first, Huemmer was not intimidated by the questions. He even had some of his own. Were the students under arrest? What was the reason? How long were they going to be held up? The officer looked directly at Huemmer, shifted his belt, tapped his finger on the .38 in his holster, and told the student he would shoot him in the head if he didn't keep quiet.

Backups soon arrived, and the nineteen protesters were put in squad cars and taken to the Rankin County jail. Huemmer was placed in a separate police car, where he was beaten by policemen in two- or three-minute intervals over the next forty minutes, struck repeatedly in the head, face, abdomen, and groin.[8] Officers gave him nicknames—the "goddman Moscow man," the "damn Cuban," "the outside agitator"—before finally carrying him into the county jailhouse. Inside, the students were booked on charges of reckless driving, carrying a concealed deadly brick, and possession of a deadly weapon (a stainless steel fork lifted from a church picnic), and they were all placed into a cell. Huemmer was taken aside one last time and beaten with blackjacks and billy clubs.[9]

John Perkins experienced a wave of panic when he got the phone call earlier in the evening with news of the arrests. The march through

Mendenhall had seemed a bit too peaceful, the officers too passive. News that the students had been taken to the county jail in Brandon confirmed his worst fears. "We knew all about Brandon," he said. "Sheriff Jonathan Edwards there had beaten blacks just for registering to vote. Compared to Brandon, Mendenhall was a liberated place!"[10]

Perkins called two of his friends, Currie Brown and Archie Buckley, and the three black men, armed with their Bibles and their guns, departed Mendenhall for the forty-five-minute drive to Brandon. The two-lane highway was sparsely traveled on this Tuesday night in January; and as Perkins drove in silence, his thoughts flashed to a night more than two decades earlier, when he had traversed these roads with his older brother, Clyde, who lay dying of gunshot wounds in the backseat. On a summer day in 1946, Clyde Perkins, recently returned home from the Second World War, was shot twice in the stomach at point-blank range during a confrontation with a deputy marshall outside a movie theatre.

The Perkinses of New Hebron were one tough family. "They wouldn't taken nothing off nobody," people said.[11] And Clyde was the most fearless Perkins of all. He had earned a reputation as one of the few black men in town who would not tolerate the humiliating rituals of southern race relations. He'd look a white man in the eyes straightaway and drop the obligatory "yassuh" if he needed to make a point, and he comported himself in a manner that indirectly mocked the docile role assigned to black males. He had also received a Purple Heart in the War and survived extensive combat wounds. But his return to the South as a war hero only made him more of a nuisance in the eyes of most local white people. A decorated black soldier with an attitude was not what the local draft board had in mind when they had recruited Clyde Perkins for service and shipped him four thousand miles from home.[12]

After being shot, Clyde had not died immediately. When John and his uncle Bill came for him at the clinic, he was stretched out on an examining table, covered in blood, struggling to breathe. The deputy and his assistant guarded the front door, barely moving aside for the relatives. "If I had a gun right now, I'd shoot that marshal," John thought.[13]

The doctor said there was nothing he could do for Clyde. Their only hope was to take him to a hospital in Jackson, ninety miles away on poorly paved roads. The town of New Hebron had one ambulance and it refused service to blacks.

With two other men crowding into the front alongside Bill, sixteen-year-old John held his brother's head in his arms in the backseat and begged him to hold on, begging God for a miracle. Miles from nowhere, the headlights of another car flickered behind them in the distance, and then more appeared out of the darkness flashing their bright lights and turn signals, as dozens of friends from New Hebron caught up with the Perkinses and drove with them in a caravan to Jackson. The cars sped along the state highway—"past the white folks' houses, past the sharecroppers shacks, past the cotton fields, past the tall stands of pine out there in the blackness."[14] Clyde was received by attendants in the colored-only emergency room and fought hard until the end despite the fatal wounds in his chest. Shortly before sunrise the doctor appeared in the waiting room with the dreaded news.

Clyde's death left John in a state of shock, his mind frozen into a "numbing blankness."[15] "I don't remember ever leaving the hospital," he said. "I don't remember going home. I don't remember the wake or anything else until the funeral." At the funeral, John gazed into the blue coffin opened on the red soil at the swollen body of his dead brother. As he bid him farewell, Perkins felt his heart harden, and he swore never to forget, never to forgive. His brother had been murdered by a redneck deputy—"home safe from the white man's war" only to be shot and killed for no other reason than for being black.[16] Now Clyde was gone, like his sister who had been killed by her boyfriend, like his mother who had died from pellagra when Perkins was seven months old, and like his father, who one morning years ago had picked up and left. He was alone.[17] "They closed the coffin and lowered it, and the folks began heading back to their homes."[18]

On this night in the winter of 1970, eerily reminiscent of that fateful day in 1946, the air felt heavy with fear as Perkins pulled his car to a stop in front of the Rankin County courthouse. A highway patrolman standing on the sidewalk approached Perkins and his friends, and told them to wait by the car until the sheriff arrived. But the sheriff never came. Instead ten other officers exited the building and seized the three black men. John Perkins, Currie Brown, and Archie Buckley were charged on counts of inciting to riot and possession of a concealed deadly weapon.[19]

Inside the jailhouse, Sheriff Jonathan Edwards had been waiting for his chance to get the black preacher alone. For months he had been waiting. Sheriff Edwards regarded Perkins as the worst kind of troublemaker: a Mississippi Negro who had lived outside the South and had then come home to stay. "This is the smart nigger," Edwards told his men as Perkins entered the room. Then he turned directly to Perkins. "And this is a new ballgame," he said. "You are not in Simpson County now. You are in Brandon."

The sheriff took a quick step toward Perkins and struck him hard against the cheekbone. He followed the first strike with a flurry of blows to the face and head, and Perkins collapsed to the floor. Other officers quickly joined the sheriff, swinging baseball bats and nightsticks, landing blows in the abdomen, arms, face, and head, until pools of blood surrounded his body. The officers then dragged Perkins to his feet and put a mop in his hands.

Edwards shoved a copy of the "Demands" in Perkins's face and told him to read it aloud. Perkins eyes were swollen shut and his mouth and gums were bloody.

"Read nigger, read nigger louder," Edwards said. "I can't stand a nigger that can't read loud."[20] The officers exchanged swigs of moonshine whisky and roared with laughter as Perkins tried to read.

But the worst was far from over. Edwards ordered the policemen to take Perkins to the fingerprint room, out of the sight of the students.

"That's when the torture began," Perkins recalled.[21] "I couldn't even imagine that this was happening." One of the officers took a fork and shoved it into the minister's nose and after that twisted it down his throat. Then the men dragged Perkins into the middle of the room and attacked him again.[22]

"They were like savages, like some horror out of the night. And I can't forget their faces, so twisted with hate. It was like looking at white-faced demons."[23]

Once during the beating, an officer approached Perkins and pressed the barrel of a pistol against his forehead. "I think I'm gonna kill me a nigger," he said, before squeezing the trigger. A hollow click signaled an empty chamber and the punch line of the cruelest joke. After nearly four hours of torture, Perkins was taken into a jail cell and left alone.

Throughout the night, Perkins drifted in and out of consciousness. He was only vaguely aware that the torture had come to an end. He had been moved to a steel-frame bed in a cell where he lay motionless on a blood-stained sheet. His face and scalp were covered with blue-red lumps the size of golf balls, and his abdomen was bruised throughout.

In the cell, the black students nursed him as he lay groaning in agony on the bed. They soaked shirts and cloths in water to drape over his body and head. No one thought he would survive.

Perkins's wife, Vera Mae, feared the worst too. An anonymous caller had asked her late in the evening, "Have they hung 'em yet?"[24]

When Vera Mae learned shortly before sunrise that her husband was still alive, she thanked God aloud and then moved quickly into action, applying

her seasoned skills as a church leader and social worker to the task of organizing support for her husband and the protesters. Nathan Rubin, an
NAACP leader and owner of a stump removal business in Simpson County,
helped raise money for Perkins's bail, canvassing the county in search of
land-owning blacks willing to post property as bond. The black physician
Robert Smith, who had nursed many an ailing civil rights worker in his work
with the Medical Committee for Human Rights, examined and treated the
victims of the torture.[25] The barber, Lurvell Purvis quietly trimmed the hair
away from Perkins's wounds. People from the neighborhood brought fresh-
baked pies and plates of fried chicken to the community center. When the
money had been raised for bail, business owner Alfoncia Hill, along with
Vera Mae and Spencer Perkins, retrieved John from the jailhouse.[26]

Once outside the courthouse, surrounded by more than twenty friends
who had come to seek her husband's release, with the singing of "We Shall
Overcome" filling the square and Perkins slumped over in the front seat of
the car, Vera Mae let down her defenses and wept.

Spencer was a freshman at Mendenhall High School, one of the few
black students attending classes under the dispensation of the 1964 Freedom of Choice Plan.[27] The sight of his father that February night would
forever haunt the son, as he later recalled:

> [Daddy's] cell was unlocked and he came out to see us—I mean to see my
> mother. I'm not certain that he even saw me. In fact, even to this day, nei-
> ther he nor my mother remembers that I was even there. But the look of
> terror on his face is something that I will always remember. Was this my
> father? The man who in the mind of his teenage son was afraid of no one.
> His eyes, as big as silver dollars, seem to almost bulge out of his head. His
> clothes were torn and full of blood. The bloody lump on top of his head
> was as large as my fist and the expression on his face looked as if he had
> been visited by death itself.
>
> When my mother saw him she stopped in her tracks. She was trying
> hard to fight back the tears. After a brief look at each other, they spent
> most of the rest of the time in an embrace—mostly to comfort my father
> but partly to not be overheard by the guard. I could barely hear what they
> said. My mother kept whispering over and over, "Toop, what did they do
> to you, what did they do to you?" Not trying to get an answer from him,
> but with reality rushing in on her, she was trying in her own way to make
> herself understand how this could be happening. My father spoke in a very
> quiet but desperate voice. "Git me out of here, get me out of here. If you
> don't they gon' kill me tonight."[28]

Spencer kept his emotions in check while resolving to one day even the score.[29]

John Perkins was born in 1930, the sixth child to Maggie Perkins and the fifth to survive, and he was raised on cotton plantations in Simpson County.[30] Perkins's earliest memory is of a winter afternoon and a close gray sky and a small house on a dirt road. In the memory, his grandmother sits inside the house sewing a quilt to keep the children warm. Perkins stands in the front yard chopping wood for the fire, and carrying small bundles of sticks to the porch. He remembers the raw, cold air and the warmth of the stove inside and an ambient sadness.[31]

Unlike Vera Mae's family, who owned their own land and farm, the Perkins family farmed on halves, moving from plantation to plantation with the changing seasons, according to the shifting demands for cheap labor. Like most rural black children, John Perkins was put to work in the fields picking cotton, alongside his grandmother, aunts, cousins, and sisters, waking up before first light and returning home after sunset, from September through November, riding to and from work in large open-bodied trucks—"just like hogs and cattle," he said.[32]

The current of repression ran wide and deep during the "dark journey" of black Mississippians in the Jim Crow years.[33] Less than a decade before Perkins's birth, the state's demagogic governor and U.S. Senator Theodore Bilbo had made white supremacy a matter of public policy. "This is strictly a white man's country," he had said in 1919 at a political rally. Bilbo took an angry stand against anti-lynching laws and the repeal of the poll tax. During his 1946 campaign for the United States Senate—the first statewide contest in Mississippi since the U.S. Supreme Court had outlawed all-white primaries two years earlier—Bilbo had publicly threatened any Negro who attempted to vote, saying, "If you let a handful go to the polls in July there will be two handfuls in 1947, and from there on it will grow into a mighty surge."[34] For Bilbo, there was only one sure way to keep the racial fires from spreading. "You do it the night before the election. I don't have to tell you any more than that. Red-blooded men know what I mean."[35]

After Clyde's murder in 1947, Perkins's relatives begged him to leave New Hebron. They feared he would strike back at white authorities and end up another casualty of the nation's most repressive pigmentocracy. Perkins took their advice and moved to Jackson, and stayed there for a while with an aunt who ran a boarding house. But Jackson turned out to be no different, only a bigger version of the same. Perkins's only remaining option was to save enough money for a train ticket and join the great migration of blacks out of the South. He headed west for California. "Mississippi was behind me. Forever, I told myself."

He ended up in the coastal town of South Gate, California, and found work at the Union Pacific Foundry. Immediately the air felt clearer, free of ghosts. For the first time in his life, Perkins was spared the anxiety of negotiating the expectations of white southerners. His pay of ninety-eight cents an hour was a fortune compared to the twenty dollars a month a black laborer could expect to earn in the South. The good pay and the wider spaces did wonders for his confidence. The mornings were cool; the Pacific Ocean lay to the west and a vast desert to the east. "I could see glimpses of hope that were once blocked off to me," he said. "I could live now."[36]

In the spring of 1949, Perkins returned for a few weeks to Mississippi to visit his relatives. One Sunday morning after church, he met Vera Mae Buckley at the fellowship hour held in the side yard following the worship service. He had never had much interest in religion before—too much whooping and hollering, too little practical wisdom. "I did not see the black church as relevant to my needs," he said.[37] But church had other draws. For example, there were not many other places to go in New Hebron to meet pretty girls. Sporting a new suit and tie, Perkins fell in love with the self-assured lady who wore a colorful dress and stylish hat, and he said to her. "'Vera Mae, you're going to be my wife someday.'"[38]

But Vera Mae was not convinced. The Buckleys were loyal members of the Pleasant Hill Baptist Church, respected throughout the black community as landowners. And Perkins's own lineage of bootleggers, gamblers, and renegades did little to strengthen his case. She responded to his declaration by saying she'd be happy to write, and the two exchanged letters for the next year and a half.

In 1951, Perkins traveled again to New Hebron during a twenty-one-day furlough from basic training. He was stationed at Fort Ord in central California, having been drafted to serve in the Korean War. But he wanted to pay Vera Mae a visit before leaving for Okinawa. Once again Perkins declared his love, though this time he *asked* her to be his wife, and this time she agreed. The two were married in New Hebron and honeymooned during John's remaining days in Los Angeles.

After the war, John and Vera Mae settled in Monrovia, a town fifteen miles northeast of Los Angeles, and Perkins returned to the pursuit of his life's twin ambitions: making money and forgetting the "bad memories from down home."[39] He got a new job as a janitor with a supermarket chain called Shopping Bag, and he so impressed the company owner with his work ethic that he soon moved up to the welding shop and eventually to equipment design. (Shopping Bag manufactured much of its own equipment.) Settling into the comforts of the black middle class in a spacious new house, he tried not to think too much about Mississippi and the life he had escaped.

Perkins may have never become a man of faith had his son not begun attending Sunday school at a church around the corner. Spencer liked the songs and the flannel-board lessons and the friendly white teacher, and it was not long before the bright and inquisitive boy was winning prizes for his Bible knowledge and scripture memorization.[40] At home, Spencer insisted that the family begin and end the day with devotions, and he often recited verses for them at meals and family times. Sunday school had captivated his imagination, and it bothered him that his parents weren't sharing the experience.[41] He knew his mother would be an easy recruit, since she had grown up in church and had been active in New Hebron until she married. She enjoyed hearing about his classes and his new friends, and she kept meaning to come with him. When Spencer wouldn't take no for an answer, she accepted.

However, getting his father into Sunday school was a challenge. In Perkins's mind, getting religion meant blunting the edge that had kept his senses sharp in his steady fight from the segregated South. For it was not just the hypocrisy of white southerners that got under his skin; it was also the black church.[42] "I always looked at things economically, and it was hard to see how the shouting and turning over benches . . . was giving any kind of incentive to people to develop. In fact, I always looked at these black Christians as sort of inferior people whose religion was keeping them oppressed by making them submissive to an oppressive structure."[43] Over the years Perkins had tried out a few variations on the Christian religion—Jehovah's Witnesses, the Church of Christian Science, and the Science of Christ Mind—but he found them no more relevant than the Baptists. He had even read Father Divine, the spiritual guru who rose from poverty in Harlem and preached racial justice, but Perkins thought the man's claims to be divine were preposterous.[44] Religion was an opiate he did not need.

Still, Spencer kept telling his dad about the exciting news he was learning on Sunday mornings and Wednesday evenings. Standing straight and tall, one arm held upward and the other by his side, he recited his favorite verse, the admonition in *Joshua*: "Be strong and of good courage, be not afraid, neither be thou dismayed, for the Lord thy God is with thee, whither so ever thou goeth." The child was discovering in the church the same virtues of strength that the father sought elsewhere, and eventually the boy's persistence proved irresistible. "I loved him so much, I finally decided to go," Perkins said. "Besides, his life had become so radiant I wanted to go and find out what they were teaching him down there. I found they were teaching the Bible."[45]

Perkins began reading and studying the Bible himself and took the first steps in his new journey of faith. Soon the entire Perkins family—four children now—was going to church. John's one stipulation was that they pass on the mostly white congregation around the corner that Spencer had been attending and worship instead in a black Holiness church in Pasadena, the Bethlehem Church of Christ Holiness. Perkins began to meet men he admired and whose company he enjoyed: strong, humorous black men with steady jobs and good marriages who encouraged each other in their spiritual lives and spoke of Jesus as if he were a friend.

Perkins had never studied the Bible before or given it much thought. But as he read and studied the Bible now in the company of his new friends, he felt drawn into its power. The Bible spoke to his longings for dignity and respect and gave him a new perspective on his purpose in life. Although some of the passages left him confused, the book's obscurities seemed part of its intoxicating mystery. Before dawn and in the late evenings after the workday, Perkins sat at his kitchen table for study and devotions. He scribbled comments in the margins of the Bible and kept a notebook of his insights and questions. He was moved by the Bible characters and their stories of hope and overcoming, their fierce human passions. He was especially partial to the letters of Paul: the apostle's accounts of new life in Christ and his affirmations of freedom. In fact, Perkins felt he could live his life in Paul's amazing letters: "For freedom Christ has set us free." "Therefore being justified by faith, we have peace with God through out Lord Jesus Christ." "Nothing can separate us from the love of God." Paul had been enslaved to harsh laws and set free by the power of Christ's resurrection.

One night after his studies, Perkins was resting on his son's bed in the back room of his home when he experienced "the Spirit of God" speaking to him.[46] He had been reading in the Epistle to the Galatians, the passage in which Paul says, "I am crucified with Christ; nevertheless, I live; yet not I, but Christ livest in me." In his childhood forays into black churches in Mississippi, Perkins had never heard anything about being crucified with Christ. "I'd never heard that being a Christian was Christ living in me, and I living out my life in Christ," he said. "Well, I realized I didn't have that life."[47] He realized he desperately wanted that Christ-force in his life. He wanted to "live by the faith of the Son of God," to be filled with the spirit of God who comes not in weakness but in power.

Perkins threw himself into the life of faith with the same high-voltage energy he had given to his professional ambitions. He read Bible commentaries and study guides, religious biographies and missionary chronicles, devotional tracts, and books on church history. Eventually he signed up for Bible classes with the popular radio teacher Jack Macarthur, pastor of the Calvary Bible Church in Burbank, and with J. Vernon McGee, a Presbyterian minister in Pasadena and host of his own show, "Through the Bible," which offered listeners a chance to study each book of scripture over a five-year period.[48] Perkins learned not only to read the Bible and discern its meanings but to teach it to others, aided with his improved reading skills gained through the tutorials of a Christian bookstore owner, and with his new knowledge of dispensationalist theology, which the white pastors had imparted and which was the interpretative roadmap of most Christian fundamentalism. Dispensationalists believed in an absolute separation between the pure kingdom of Heaven and the impure and corrupt earthly kingdom—between the church and the world. The responsibility of God's faithful on earth was thus to prepare themselves for the heavenly reward promised in the second coming of Jesus, which meant pursuing personal holiness and repudiating the world.[49]

By 1958 Perkins was on his way to becoming a leader in southern California's Christian subculture. He was ordained as a Baptist pastor and busy running numerous evangelistic missions and Bible study programs. He had also developed friendships with white evangelicals in the area, worshipped and preached in their churches, prayed with them in their studies and homes, and shared meals.

With a firm hold on a new life, Perkins nonetheless began to have a disturbing thought. Every time the thought crossed his mind, he tried desperately to suppress it—it seemed that preposterous. Perkins began to sense that God wanted him back in Mississippi. As he prayed through his fears, quietly hoping that God had mistaken him for some other black man with a Jim Crow childhood, the sense grew to a conviction, and he started to understand something of the purpose of the unmistakable calling. God wanted him back in Mississippi "to identify with my people there, and to help break up the cycle of despair—not by encouraging them to leave, but by showing them new life right where they were."[50] His work with black inmates and juvenile delinquents in southern California had brought home the fact that the ghettos of Los Angeles and the desolate traces of the South were deeply interconnected. Nearly 70 percent of California's jail population was black, and it seemed to Perkins that most of these young men had southern roots. "I could hear Mississippi and Alabama in their voices," he said. "I had to go back home."[51]

In the summer of 1960, John and Vera Mae packed their children in the car and their belongings in a U-Haul trailer and returned to Simpson County, Mississippi. The family lived for the first few weeks with relatives and then in a beat-up trailer in the back yard of a cousin. This scion of the tough Perkins clan explained to old friends that he had come home to evangelize poor blacks.

The Mississippi to which the family returned seemed not a lot different than the one in which his brother's murder had been a matter of course, except that the state was now more visibly organized in opposition to black progress. Nonetheless, the stirrings of black dissent in the South and the guardians of segregation were of no real concern to Perkins. John and Vera Mae had returned to equip local people with the message that genuine racial progress came only from renewed life in Christ—"emancipation from Satan and sin."[52] Evangelism seemed the best solution to the problem of southern segregation.[53] "What my father and mother were going to do was pretty much working among their own, working with black people" Spencer later explained, "and they weren't looking to raise any kind of ruckus."[54] The Perkins's plan was to reach poor blacks and supply them with biblical literacy and sound doctrine in hopes that the spiritual changes would inspire the skills and disciplines they needed to be independent. In short, poor blacks should become less dependent on emotions, more on scripture.[55]

Perkins understood that the first order of business in any serious attempt to build community with the poor was to get involved in a local church. So the family joined the Oak Ridge Missionary Baptist Church, an independent Baptist church pastored by the lay minister Isaac Newsome. Newsome invited Perkins to teach Sunday school and weekday evening classes in "fundamental Christianity." By the end of the Perkinses' first summer in New Hebron, the church had become the center of a grassroots Bible ministry to local black children and the site of vacation Bible schools and high school outreach ministries. The small clapboard church became "the first base that allowed me to reach out, to try great things," Perkins recalled. When a parcel of land became available in the nearby town of Mendenhall, the Perkinses left the New Hebron operation in Pastor Newsome's reliable hands and joined the Nazareth Missionary Baptist Church, establishing another Bible mission in the Simpson County seat. The work of spiritual renewal among the poor was proceeding apace.

By the summer of 1964, Perkins had turned an abandoned tin-roof shack into the Mississippi branch of the Fisherman's Bible Mission and gathered around him a group of men captivated by his teaching. John and Vera Mae also focused on youth outreach, speaking to hundreds of black children in the public schools and in tent meetings throughout the southern and central part of the state. The public schools in the state often provided chapel services and religious education as part of the curriculum. Many of the young people who came to faith in these services later devoted themselves to full-time ministry; and some returned to work as staff members and leaders in the ministry in Mississippi: Herbert Jones, Jimmy Walker, Artis and Carolyn Fletcher, Dolphus and Rosie Weary, Alice Mae Smith, Juanita Moore, and Melvin Anderson. Perkins gave the name "Voice of Calvary" to the complex of ministries that included his new weekly radio show broadcast out of a storefront near his home. From the Bible mission eventually emerged a day-care center, a gym, a playground, a cooperative farming store, and a church.

Unlike most church leaders, the Perkinses refused to accept money from the poor. Instead they were given eggs, milk, watermelon, potatoes, all kinds of vegetables, and an occasional chicken—"everything we needed in those early days to keep the family alive."[56] "Our key was that we lived in community and we depended upon the people for our support," Perkins explained. "As we would go out into areas like 'Baptist bottom,' 'Sullivan's Holler,' and 'Rabbit Road,' as we would cut wood and farm with people and speak in the schools, we could not escape the desperate physical needs of many of our people. We began to discover that real evangelism brings a person face to face with all the needs of a person. We had to see people not just as souls but as whole people."[57]

John Perkins became known throughout Simpson County as a different kind of black preacher. He wore a goatee and wire-rim glasses and comported himself in a professorial manner, speaking in a gentle and melodious voice, divining the secrets of the Bible. He taught from flow charts and mimeographed handouts and quoted the Scofield Reference Bible, whose marginalia placed each passage in an elaborate dispensationalist framework.[58] "They don't expect me to make no kind of spectacle," he said.[59] Some local blacks thought he was teaching a different religion altogether, and in a sense he was. He was teaching them about a quieter devotion grounded in the "objective truth" of scripture, about relating to Jesus as lord, savior and friend, and to God as trustworthy father who never leaves.

A cadre of local black people gathered around Perkins, sharing his passion for scripture and commitment to the spiritual renewal of poor blacks.

"He stirred up the spirit in a lot of people, not only at Voice of Calvary, but out in these community classes," said Pastor Newsome, who often drove his pickup truck over from New Hebron to attend classes. "He laid his whole heart out to God and out of that come some good things," Newsome said. "He was puttin' out stuff I know'd was right—both the gospel and letting folks know what sort of shape and condition they was in," said Archie Buckley, a Mendenhall resident and early supporter of the Perkinses. "I got with him because I know'd he had it—but he was heavy. He was so heavy that he scared some of the pastors out in the churches."[60] Eugene Walker recalled, "I would say that the biggest thing was the setting up of the Bible classes, so we could know more about God, because you know we never did have any Bible too much. . . . He gave us something to go by."[61] All these people would play important roles in the boycotts and events that followed, but not until Perkins was forced by historical circumstances to reconsider his basic theological convictions and the focus of his ministry.

When he arrived back in Mississippi in 1960, Perkins thought of himself as a certain kind of fundamentalist Christian, a premillennial dispensationalist. With judgment day waiting in the wings, the dispensationalist view of history held the belief that (as historian Joel Carpenter writes) "the social application of the gospel was a waste of time."[62] God was coming soon to transport his children to heaven in the rapture, and no one save those who had clothed themselves in holiness would be spared eternal torment. But as the civil rights movement in Mississippi gained momentum, and as the forces of white resistance gathered new strength, Perkins began rethinking his practice of keeping an arm's length from social protest.

Over the course of the 1964 Summer Project and the months of intense preparation and civil rights organizing that followed, the Perkinses opened up their Mendenhall facilities to movement activists, inviting students to spend the night, share meals, and attend Bible classes. Perkins and his friends steadily expanded their evangelistic mission to include civil rights activism in Simpson County.[63] The same aging school bus that picked up adults in the early morning for classes at the Fisherman's Institute carried them to the county courthouse to attempt to register to vote. Vera Mae established a Headstart program after attending a training seminar at Tuskegee Institute, and she conducted house-to-house research and organizing efforts for the Child Development Group of Mississippi. Among the many distressing results of her surveys was the fact that 85 percent of the black residents in Simpson County had never been seen by a doctor.[64] The Perkinses invited civil rights leaders Aaron Henry and Charles Evers to speak at Voice of Calvary. Youth for Christ meetings in the Bible training center would spill over into heated debates about segregation and racial equality. "I did not come back to Mississippi with a 'wholistic' concept of the Gospel," Perkins acknowledged. "I think I found it after I got back there."[65] The atmosphere was electric with change as the Perkinses' focus on biblical education for poor blacks broadened rapidly to include a comprehensive ministry that applied "the love of God in Jesus Christ to the poverty that surrounded us." "Some thought we were civil-righters, others thought we were fanatical, others just thought we were 'some crazy niggers,'" said Perkins. [66]

Still, the Perkinses support of the civil rights movement was always guarded. Like many other local black people, the Perkinses cast a disapproving eye on the lifestyles of the summer volunteers. John admired their courage but he reproved them for their loose morals. If a chain-smoking boy from Connecticut was so afraid of southern bigots that he needed a bottle of gin in his pocket, Perkins thought he should just go on home. Perkins wore the label of Bible-believing Christian proudly. He didn't smoke, drink, dance, play cards, watch movies, or work on Sundays; and he carried a gun. (He would keep guns in his home until the middle 1970s.)[67] Perkins tried hard to convert every Unitarian, Jew, and atheist who sat down at his kitchen table. He never ceased reminding the summer workers that their activism would be sharper and their courage deeper if they pursued the Christian virtues of personal holiness, chastity, and devotion to scripture and church. "Some of the wildest people we ever met were the civil rights workers who came down to the South," Spencer Perkins said. "There were black babies popping up all over Simpson County."[68] Vera Mae once claimed that her husband would make a fine black Muslim, considering his deliberate discipline and strict devotion to the faith; he would have risen straight to the top of the Nation of Islam chain of command.

Nonetheless, the emerging civil rights movement in Mississippi nudged Perkins toward greater involvement in the social realm. "I think I was starting to see that just being merely a fundamentalist Bible-believing Christian, the 'Jesus-saves' only type, was not radical enough for the problems that we were dealing with, and that people did need training, they did need skills, they did need jobs"—and sometimes, Perkins would add, they even needed a good dose of righteous anger.[69] A transformed mind without transformed social practices was worthless.

By the late 1960s Perkins had altered the shape of his work with the poor, adding to soul winning the double punch of political protest: "New birth in Jesus" meant waging war against segregation just as much as it meant putting the honky-tonks and juke joints out of business.[70] He also became a leader in the southern cooperative movement, serving the Federation of Southern Cooperatives as the state representative in 1967 and helping establish the Simpson County Coop Grocery Store, the Greenwood Grocery Coop, and the Milestone Farmers Cooperative in Holmes County. The Bible was irrevocably social, he concluded, not by implication but by direct intention. "Social action fleshes out the Lordship of Christ," he said.[71] Perkins may have come late to the movement, but with most of the civil rights professionals long gone from the state by end of the sixties, the work of racial justice depended now on local people taking the baton and running with it.

The summer of 1970 was one of the hottest in memory. Perkins had begun taking naps, sometimes several times a day, excusing himself in the afternoons from meetings or from the neighborhood baseball games he had always enjoyed playing. He woke up tired in the morning and went to bed tired at night. At first he blamed his fatigue on the weather. The heat was so heavy that summer "it dripped from the trees," he recalled.[72] He had also been determined to prove to himself and everyone else that the beating in Brandon had not slowed him down. Just a few weeks after the ordeal, with his wounds still heavily bandaged and his body in pain, he had organized another demonstration through the streets of Mendenhall, which attracted several hundred local blacks and also the controversial black paramilitary group, the Deacons of Defense and Justice, whose members carried barely concealed guns and weren't turning their cheek for anybody. (It may be true, as some historians argue, that the Deacons received little black support in southern towns because their revolutionary rhetoric failed to connect with local people; but the black evangelical Perkins appreciated their presence.) If anything, the jailhouse torture had inspired Perkins to take on a more demanding organizing and travel schedule.

In mid-July, Perkins traveled into the Delta to visit some cooperative stores he had helped organize in the town of Mound Bayou. Mound Bayou existed as a living testament to black economic resilience. Founded in 1887, the all-black community had seen days of prosperity followed by financial decline, disfranchisement, and exile, while still retaining a proud sense of its achievements. Teddy Roosevelt had once called it "an object lesson of hope for colored people."[73] In 1957, civil rights workers Medgar Evers and Aaron Henry set up one of the South's first citizenship schools there.[74] Perkins's own vision of black economic autonomy had been influenced by the Mound Bayou story, and he looked forward to a riposte in Bolivar County.

On his first evening in town, Perkins went for supper to a friend's house. During the meal, he felt several painful tugs in his chest and back. Blaming the discomfort on the travel and his ulcers, he told his host he needed to lie down. But the pain intensified through the night. At first light, Perkins checked himself into the Tuft Medical Center, where he was attended by a doctor who discovered evidence of a mild heart attack. Perkins was placed in intensive care but was released after a few days when his doctor determined that surgery was not required. With chronically high blood pressure, though, he would need to make some serious changes in his lifestyle; after consulting with the staff at the clinic on his work habits and diet, Perkins packed his things and drove home to Mendenhall. But he would soon be back in the Delta.

Over the next six months, his life became a revolving door of medical care in Mound Bayou followed by frenetic activity in ministry. He was treated for heart disease as well as for numerous other medical problems related to the torture. Chronic pain made his nights uncomfortable, and he often rose around three or four in the morning to begin the day. The ulcers and migraine headaches would last a lifetime, and eventually he would have two-thirds of his stomach removed.

Even with his continued work with Voice of Calvary, the months of treatment in Mound Bayou forced Perkins to slow down his pace. In a period of rest and healing in this black hamlet, Perkins was also finally able to face his deepest fears.

One night as he lay on his back in his hospital bed, he felt overcome with anger as intense as any he had experienced since Clyde's murder. He had been taking stock of his life and his calling, sifting through the memories of his decade in ministry. Perkins had been dispatched to Mississippi with the mission to preach the Gospel to his people. Solid training in the word of God would revolutionize men and women in their inner being, as the obstacles in the way of black empowerment could be largely blamed on biblical illiteracy and theological shallowness. But that belief had been naïve. The truth he had come to recognize was that white evangelicals in the South didn't care at all about the salvation of black people, their physical welfare, or doing anything to relieve their sufferings. White people just wanted blacks to keep their distance and accept their inferior lot. Perkins explained, "It's hard to make all this clear or real to white people, but a lot of black people had come to this same point—feeling that there simply was no justice, no hope. All those radical anti-whites—Stokely Carmichael, Rap Brown, George Jackson, Eldridge Cleaver, and the others—you hear about in the news, didn't invent the injustices they talk about. They saw and felt oppression in a thousand ways. And not always open brutality either. It's the system, the whole structure of economic and social cages that have neatly boxed the black man in so that 'nice' people can join the oppression without getting their hands dirty—just by letting things run along."[75]

Perkins's experience in the Brandon jail carried the black pastor into a period of deep despair. He began thinking about white people—really for the first time in his life. Why were they so hateful? And what made these men act with such cruelty? Were they insane? Were they possessed by demons? Perkins had developed a few friendships with whites in California. But California was another world, and whatever hopeful feelings these relationships had brought him had long been replaced by a greater distrust—a distrust he tried to ignore in acting as if local whites were irrelevant to his ministry. Perkins tried to sort through his conflicted thoughts. Whites, too, had been made in the image of God. He knew this, or at least he knew the Bible taught this. He knew the Bible gave him no license to regard Caucasians as "a race of devils" and "the great arch deceivers," as did the Nation of Islam. As a Christian, Perkins had no choice but to believe the apostle Paul, even against all evidence to the contrary, that these men had been redeemed by the blood of Jesus and could be forgiven from their sins by a merciful God.

But Perkins also thought about the sons and daughters of these white men, the children who ridiculed and bullied his son and daughter at school; he thought about the contempt of white churchgoers toward blacks. And he thought about the churches where these white men worshipped on Sundays, which contributed generously for missionary efforts in Africa but would not raise a finger to save local blacks from suffering or even permit them to step foot in their sanctuaries—unless it was to cook or dust. It had not been godless communists or hedonistic pagans who had created the evil system of Jim Crow and had turned lynchings into sacraments, Klan rallies into revivals.[76] It had been Bible-believing Christians. The more he struggled through his thoughts, the more Perkins felt certain that whites deserved all the hatred he could muster. In any case, he was sure he did not have the power to forgive, to "do good to them that hate you," as Jesus had taught. What did Jesus know about being a black man in Brandon, Mississippi?

On his back in Mound Bayou, Perkins finally let himself feel all the hatred in his soul and the "pull to reject everything," and as he did an image took shape in his mind. "The image of the cross," he said, "Christ on the cross. It blotted out everything else in my mind." Jesus was a Savior who had been tortured and murdered by a lynch mob, "nailed to rough wooden planks," and "killed like a common criminal." Jesus had been born homeless in poverty and deserted by his father at the moment of his greatest need. The image of Christ's suffering for the world worked its way into the center of his thoughts, fears, and humiliations, and Perkins came to a new understanding of his life's work. Hereafter, all that he would believe about his life's purpose hung on the astonishing prayer of Jesus, "Father, forgive these people, for they know not what they do." Embraced in the black arms of Mound Bayou, Perkins felt the spirit of God working on his battered mind and body until he was able to speak the words, "I forgive them, too." He found a way out of the "horror of hate."[77]

"I began to see things a little more clearly," he said. "I was able to see the needs of white people and what racism was doing to them. You see, I had gotten set to the fact that the sickness of racism had affected the black community in a way that kept them from functioning as a healthy community. A lot of our people were sick—affected by generations of slavery, oppression and exploitation—psychologically destroyed. But I had never thought much before about how all that had affected whites; how they had been affected by racism, by attitudes of racial superiority, by unjust life styles and behavior."[78] Racism had twisted the hearts of men, mangled their perceptions with its disfiguring effects. Such white men as the Brandon torturers had exchanged the truth of God for a lie, and this made the predicament of the white racist even more serious than the social scientists or the historians had imagined. For neither the psychologist nor the historian could give an adequate account of how the racist had yielded his heart to sin and become enslaved to the devil. "Racism is satanic, and I knew it would take a supernatural force to defeat it," Perkins said.[79]

Still, in his Mound Bayou meditations Perkins was forced to reckon with an even more difficult truth. The hatred that fueled the despicable acts of the white men in the Brandon jail had become the framework of his own emotional makeup. His hatred for the redneck officers bound Perkins to the spiral of violence and kept him enslaved to the men he most loathed. When the apostle Paul had written of the universality of the fall, he had meant exactly that: all humanity, red, yellow, white and black, rich and poor. Not only the sins of evil men and oppressors, but his own as well. Not just the white landowners and the counterfeit practitioners of southern Christendom, but the sins of John Perkins. Not only of whites living in plantation spreads and spacious suburban tracts, but of black people staying in shanties and housing projects. Perkins was able to see for the first time that these spiteful men were not the only ones who stood in need of amazing grace. Perkins also needed the forgiveness that only Christ could bring; Perkins also stood before a righteous God. In this hard admission alone lay true freedom and the double edge of forgiveness. Perkins came to see that the one inescapable fact, which he must accept before proceeding to the work of mercy and justice, was that he remained a sinner in need of salvation. Every man and woman had sinned and fallen short of God's glory, and the path to new life began with that recognition.

Perkins discovered a power of forgiveness that reinvigorated the everyday world and forever changed his life. "I could not come back and live and again go forward in work with hate. I really had to get that hate out of me in order to go forward."[80] Forgiveness became for him the most liberating of all human activities, conditioned by a power that, once unleashed, enabled discernment and action. "When you can sense that you've been forgiven," Perkins said. "I think it gives you a new energy to go forward in life. And so I think that on that hospital bed, going through that period, that I needed the forgiveness of sin to enter back into the world."[81]

In his Mound Bayou introspections, Perkins would follow these hard thoughts in a free-form testimonial of personal and spiritual illumination:

> The Spirit of God helped me to really believe what I had so often professed, that only in the love of Christ is there any hope for me, or for those I had once worked so hard for.
>
> After that, God gave me the strength and motivation to rise up out of my bed and return to Mendenhall and spread a little more of His love around.
>
> Oh, I know man is bad—depraved. There's something built into him that makes him want to be superior. If the black man had the advantage, he'd be just as bad, just as bad. So I can't hate the white man.
>
> The problem is spiritual: black or white, we all need to be born again.
>
> It's a profound, mysterious truth—Jesus' concept of love overpowering hate. I may not see its victory in my lifetime. But I know it's true.
>
> I know it's true, because it happened to me. On that bed, full of bruises and stitches—God made it true in me. He washed my hatred away and replaced it with a love for the white man in rural Mississippi.
>
> I know it's true.
>
> Because it happened to me.[82]

He now felt "overwhelmed by the love of God," and as that love coursed through his "spirit and soul" he experienced a refreshing power that could not be contained.[83]

Perkins emerged from six months of treatment at Tuft Medical Center with a new conviction that Christian love could not rest content until it ace for the neighbor and the enemy. He would make his life a parable of forgiveness and reconciliation. "I might go so far as to say that I experienced a second conversion while I lay in that hospital bed. It was a conversion of love and forgiveness."[84]

Nothing changed in the short term as a result of the Mendenhall protests. None of the prejudicial laws were scrapped or revised; and the two trials of *Perkins v. Mississippi*, which crept through the courts until 1972, ended in disappointment.[85] Perkins was forced to drop his suit against the state in exchange for the state dropping its charges against him and his companions.[86] Several national publications, including *Time* magazine, reported the beating and subsequent trial.[87] Nevertheless, the fires of dissent had been ignited in the once forgotten town of Mendenhall. Herbert Jones, a local black merchant who joined Perkins in organizing the boycotts and demonstrations, explained his own involvement as an expression of his "witness for Jesus Christ." "I didn't have to be militant or angry," he said, "I could be me, a son of God."[88] "Brother and Sister Perkins started the race," said Artis Fletcher, one of the young leaders in town, "and then the baton was handed onto us to continue that race. It's a race of ministry to the total person."[89]

Perkins began thinking about the unfinished business of the civil rights movement. In his talks and seminars, he made frequent mention of the "three Rs" of community building, with the "R" gently drawn out to two syllables in the old afro-southern manner: relocation, redistribution, and reconciliation. These comprised the trinity of disciplines that became the core of his expanded ministry. While partly descriptive of the Mendenhall work since 1964, the three Rs also illuminated new directions for the Voice of Calvary.

Relocation meant "incarnational evangelism" of the kind Clarence Jordan taught, the lived expression of the great Pauline theme that Jesus Christ did not consider equality with God something to be grasped but took on "the very nature of a servant."[90] The activist and organizer ceases to patronize the poor only when he lives in community with them and approaches them in a spirit of compassion and with the willingness to serve. "Living involvement," Perkins said, "turns poor people from statistics into our friends."[91] Relocation was incarnational because it shaped a new way of seeing the world, a view from below. Relocation placed difficult demands on both white and black Christians, as blacks would need the strength to resist middle-class comforts and whites would need the humility to submit themselves to black leadership. But Voice of Calvary went places that Koinonia could only dream of reaching. Perkins explained in a source document that the VOC was intended to be a "black-run, Christian organization"—and if that wasn't clear enough, volunteers could read Ed McKinley's pamphlet, "Submitting to Black Leadership." But relocation was undoubtedly an equal opportunity discipline.[92] Stokely Carmichael had said once that "every cat's politics comes from what he sees when he gets up in the morning. The liberals see Central Park and we see sharecropper shacks."[93] Relocation was about where you get up in the morning.[94]

Redistribution meant sharing talents and resources with the poor, but it also meant observable changes in public policy. Although Perkins would later demur on the full force of the second R, there is no denying that part of his original intention was to support the redistribution of wealth as well as the specific form of national reparations for slavery. He explained, "To me, reparations is basically Christian. It might be possible that reparations may be the tool through which many of our white brothers and sisters can creatively express their awareness of the very basic mistakes made since the founding of the country, mistakes like slavery, that have never been dealt with adequately by the church." Reparations offer an affirmative "Yes" to history's accusations of guilt but "then [move] quickly and powerfully to deal with the problems" by making concrete restitution.[95] Yet reparations were surely not the full intent of "the second R." Public policy had to be accompanied by a willingness to offer one's skills and knowledge as gifts to others. Indeed—quite apart from specific policy recommendations—Perkins imagined the Christian community as a distinctive social order that models the redistribution of wealth in more demanding ways than any capitalist economy.[96]

Reconciliation meant embodying the message that "ye are all one in Christ Jesus" and that Christ has "destroyed the barrier, the dividing wall of hostility" between blacks and whites. Especially in the South, though not only in the South, there was no more visible sign of the church's authenticity than its commitment to racial reconciliation. The visible demonstration of "a brotherhood of intertwined lives" subverted the godforsaken spaces of southern segregation unlike any individual act of racial heroism.[97] However, the hard work of reconciliation was a different matter indeed than emotional catharsis or psychological affirmation: It required the material compensation of whites in the disciplines of relocation and redistribution, the restoration of justice. Reconciliation may indeed produce handshakes and hugs and the tears of reunion, but without confrontation and corrective action, it is empty. [98] Charles Sherrod had once remarked that reconciliation depends on the prior condition of the person who says "no" to injustice and is involved in "correcting the injustices."[99]

John Perkins may not have nailed his "Theses" to the door of the First Presbyterian Church of Jackson, as Martin Luther had posted his famous "95 Theses" on the door of the Castle Church in Wittenberg, Germany, but his reformer's call to relocation, reconciliation, and redistribution was intended to shake the foundations of the white church's melanin captivity. In their concrete application, Perkins's "three R's" add up to a social agenda more radical than any advanced by the civil rights movement, placing far greater demands on white financial resources and moral reserves than even the most ambitious policies circulated in the halcyon days of the Great Society. In Perkins's mind, this trinity of disciplines illuminates the areas where the civil rights movement failed to deliver on its most basic promises: solidarity with the poor, black economic power, and racial reconciliation.

Perkins charted a new course for building beloved community in America—one that defied conventional political categories. Leadership must be based in poor communities and eventually rise out of these communities, but at the same time outsiders would be invited to play a critical role in fostering indigenous leadership. In Perkins's view, civil rights organization such as SNCC and CORE too often racialized and politicized the role of the outsider at the expense of the well-being of people in poor communities. Patronization is a worry only when outsiders fail to discern the gifts of the poor, their loyalty, fragility, creativity, and holiness, and to accept the authority of black leadership—that is, when outsiders fail to appreciate the diverse gifts of the body of Christ and the mutuality ingredient in redemptive community. Without backing away from his support of integration, equal opportunity, affirmative action, and welfare— but recognizing their incompleteness—Perkins further concluded that government programs alone failed to address the deeper sources of hopelessness in black communities. Despair weighed heavily on the men and women John and Vera Mae Perkins served in the neighborhoods of Mendenhall, which signaled a longing and emptiness that only God could fill. The civil rights movement had focused its energies on legal injustice— as the times had required—but it failed to offer a compelling account of the spiritual energies and disciplines required to sustain beloved community, and thus failed to give detail and depth to a "wholistic Gospel." The civil rights movement failed to reckon with the truth that personal salvation is the most enduring source of social engagement, care for the poor, costly forgiveness, and reparations for slavery.

Perkins turned his attention to implementing this renewed theological vision of beloved community. There was one problem, however. Aside from a few volunteers who had come south to work with Voice of Calvary, there was not much that was interracial about the Mendenhall ministry. Freedom Summer had captured the nation's attention and brought hope and change to many southern communities. Perkins decided that a similar kind of event needed to be organized to attract white and black activists back to the South, who would work now with a more explicitly evangelical focus and demonstrate the Gospel's power to reconcile the races. Perkins thus launched, single-handedly, "Freedom Summer 1971," a three-month period of intensified community building, which would serve as a kind of historical bookend for the 1964 Freedom Summer Project, the spiritual complement of the political event, and enlarge the interracial cast of his Christian movement. On a national speaking tour, Perkins recruited volunteers for his ambitious plan: a group of white students from the congregation of an old dispensationalist mentor in California and a pack of militants from the black student association at the University of Michigan. He knew these represented extremes, but perhaps the extremes would better dramatize the miracle of faith-based reconciliation: Bible-believing whites and liberationist blacks bringing their skills and convictions to the unfinished work of racial healing in the South.

"This summer will be great," Perkins said. "We have black students coming from a major university and white students coming from a good, fundamental church. What a combination: black and white, socially oriented and spiritually oriented, all with skills and energy!"[100] Perkins would later call the initiative the "biggest failure in Voice of Calvary history."[101]

The white students, armed with the "Four Spiritual Laws" and the Scofield Reference Bible, saw the summer as an opportunity to save souls.[102] They had never paid any attention before to the social causes of oppression or to the complex forces of southern segregation, and they were not about to start now. "They didn't have the awareness, the sensitivity to the issues of race and justice," Perkins acknowledged.[103] For their part, the black students from Michigan had prepared for the Mississippi trip by reading Franz Fanon and Eldridge Cleaver and the literature of black power. With their heads full of revolutionary ideas, they declared war on white racists everywhere. Half the group ended the summer bunkered down in the Jackson headquarters of the Republic of New Africa, sparring with local police and the FBI in a gun battle. (The RNA's founder, Imari Obadele, and a cadre of black nationalists were arrested for their role in the melee that left one police officer dead.) The other militants turned against the tract-toting evangelicals from California, who had not strayed far from the community center in Mendenhall. Freedom Summer 1971 came to an inauspicious end.

Surveying the disaster, Perkins took note: "Here were the fragments of what we believed in coming together—the preaching of the gospel, the social action that met people's needs, blacks and whites working together. But they were coming together without any mediation. There was nothing to glue them together. The poles were just too far apart. It seemed there could be no reconciliation."[104] Perkins had learned a lesson about the humility of organizing.

In the fall of 1973, the Perkinses bought a house in a middle-class neighborhood of Jackson that had recently been hit hard by white flight. John and Vera Mae had prayed for years about the move, and they discerned the need to work for black economic empowerment and racial reconciliation in the transitional neighborhoods of the capital city. God's purpose of raising up a generation of poor black men and women trained with the skills of Bible-based community development had been accomplished in the twelve years of community work in Simpson County. A talented young black man named Dolphus Weary, mentored by Perkins, had taken over the Mendenhall operation and within a few years would help create a black-owned construction company, a housing coop, a counseling center, an economic development program, legal services with a staff of fifty, and an expanded health center.[105]

The Perkins's new house on St. Charles Street was a redbrick cottage built in the forties. Most of the homes in the surrounding streets were single-family bungalows and ranchers on quarter-acre lots. Some of the homes had swimming pools and tropical gardens in the back, remains of a day when west Jackson enjoyed the westward sprawl of middle-class whites. But by 1973 the neighborhood was showing the telltale signs of urban decline and shifting economic fortunes, as unpainted shacks, housing projects, and semi-abandoned strip malls filled the abandoned spaces created by white flight.

After the debacle of Freedom Summer 1971, Perkins realized that racial reconciliation could not be orchestrated. If reconciliation was to happen, it would happen because the Holy Spirit had taken care of the details. Perkins resolved that it was enough now to seek repentance, forgiveness, and reconciliation in the everyday life of Voice of Calvary. His mission would be to extend an invitation to whites and blacks to come live in community in west Jackson. Come with your talents, your ideas, and your willingness to serve the poor of Mississippi, not for a summer but for a lifetime. As he prayed with his family and partners, Perkins began to imagine the community in west Jackson as a place where white and black professionals would give up their privilege and live among the broken and the desolate in one of America's most race-embattled cities.

Not many people took him up on the offer. The few whites that came were almost all Mennonites, Brethren, or members of one of the historic peace churches, from small farming towns in the Midwest or Northeast. Driving along Buena Vista Boulevard in the early years of the experiment, one saw white girls dressed in the simple cape dress and head covering walking alongside the neighborhood kids in their colorful rag-tag clothing; Jacob, Caleb, and Rachel alongside Tyrone, Duquetta, and Reggie, all taking part in a strange but somehow promising juvenescence of beloved community. Eventually whites from other Christian traditions would come to west Jackson (though none from the southern churches in those years), buying or renting one of the many homes around the ministry compound, an unlikely assortment of musicians, seminarians, social workers, and college dropouts. Occasionally some of the remaining old-time residents in the neighborhood wandered over for evening programs or to ask one of the members for a hand with yard work.

By the summer of 1976, Christians living in community in west Jackson had formed a comprehensive slate of theological and social ministries: a study center, children's ministry, medical clinic, thrift shop, family health center, nonprofit housing cooperative, mortgage company for the poor, Bible school, communications and printing office, hospitality house for volunteers, clothing distribution center, and a second cooperative store called Thriftco, housed in an aluminum-sided building in the town of Edwards, which Perkins formed with the help of black leaders in Jackson. The business operations of Thriftco were for the most part managed and staffed by blacks, a rare achievement in a region where black land ownership had been lost by the hundreds of thousands each year, as the *Jackson Advocate* noted.[106] The VOC health center partnered with the Mendenhall clinic to create the first rural health program in the South, helping black families move from grease-laden diets to more nutritious preparations of vegetables and meats. An international study center operated as a kind of faith-based freedom school, featuring educational programs on black history, seminars on community development, and courses on Christian doctrine and church history taught by guest professors and lecturers. People came to west Jackson to study from all parts of the United States, and from Haiti, Puerto Rico, Uganda, Kenya, South Africa, England, and Australia.[107] An interracial church grew out of the work, housed in a small brick building next to a convenience store, whose members shared commitments to the three Rs and to the visible racial unity of Christian community.[108]

Interns and volunteers at Voice of Calvary were trained by staff members in what Perkins called a "felt-need concept," a policy that intended to keep the community open to the contributions of diverse gifts but which often meant that the interns and volunteers upon arrival were whisked off by a staff member to their new service positions with only the vaguest of instructions. Occasionally a white volunteer would arrive at Perkins's house ready to save the urban ghetto only to be handed a broom and told to sweep out his garage. Still, like SNCC's presence in Mississippi in the mid-sixties, VOC was the only interracial show in town.

The infusion of Mennonites, Brethren, and Quakers played a vital role in developing trust among local blacks. Perkins's relationships with Christians from the historic peace churches also helped bring closure to his fundamentalist leanings. "I like to think VOC is a lot like the Quakers," he said. "Quakers have put a lot of emphasis on the God-given value of all human beings, on combatting slavery, and on peacemaking. I think this influence shows up here at VOC."[109] Though he had years ago grown disenchanted with the otherworldliness of fundamentalism, the experience of observing these pacifists and service-oriented believers, with their vows of poverty, simple lifestyles and radical devotion to Jesus, transformed Perkins's evangelical views anew. "I reflected their hopes, as they reflected mine," he said.[110] Perkins reexamined his interpretation of the Sermon on the Mount and the twenty-fifth chapter of Matthew—passages that he had read but "dispensationalized to the kingdom age" and not applied to his own life and work.[111] He would later even wonder aloud why black Protestant Christians had not drifted toward some form of the Anabaptist and Peace Church tradition. "It's a mystery to me that we haven't," he said.[112]

Perkins began using the term "prophetic" to describe the counter-cultural practices of the Christian community (long before Cornel West took on the term to describe a faith imbued with "the sobriety of tragedy, the struggle for freedom and the spirit of hope"), and he thought hard for the first time about the connection between racism in the south and national military spending, nuclear stockpiling, and the political neglect of the poor. He questioned America, as his hero Fannie Lou Hamer had done in her haunting testimony at the 1964 Democratic National Convention about her experience as a black Mississippian: "*Is this America, the land of the free and the home of the brave?* Where we have to sleep with our telephones off the hooks because our lives be threatened daily because we want to live as decent human beings?"[113] Prophetic Christians must speak a concrete word against the perversions of American capitalism—"the economic order that has made America unfairly rich and is creating massive poverty . . . at the very height of its productivity."[114] They must speak against the idolatry of the church in North America, the religious institutions that have made white supremacy and economic exploitation as Christian as the stars and bars. "We have so organized and incorporated the church into our economic system," Perkins said, "that not only can't that system be disciplined, but if one does speak against it he or she is speaking against God and America and must be locked up." No doubt, God will discipline that system, Perkins wrote in *Sojourners* magazine in 1978, "if not by the prophet, then by the terrorist."[115]

He moved away from the old fundamentalist preoccupation with the fate of the individual soul and began asking questions of a directly social intent: "What is God's program on earth and how do I fit in?"[116] To be a public disciple means finding a place in the world where the Kingdom of God is taking shape and getting yourself there. Yet Perkins's new message was not a simple shift to social or liberation theology. An evangelical emphasis on personal relationship with Jesus remained at the center of his community development vision; his point was that individual transformation required a disciplined and impassioned commitment to the transformation and healing of the social order. In the creation of the world, God fashioned man and woman with the basic needs for food, shelter, clothing, clean air, and health. These needs signal a "certain haunting equality," he said, a bottom-line description of human dignity, which shapes the Christian's entire outlook on social existence and political community.

While conservative supporters of the Voice of Calvary experiment would praise Perkins's candid assessment of welfare's disincentives to work, he made clear in the mid-seventies that the Gospel involved "redemptive release" from all forms of physical and economic oppression, and that Jesus Christ—whose message was "explicitly economic"—identified with the poor "to the point of equating himself with the poor person."[117] The presumption throughout Perkins's theology of community is that a people transformed and mobilized "by Jesus Christ in [its] institutional behavior" will consistently support economic policies preferential to the poor, not out of obligation to law but as an expression of public discipleship. Perkins might be considered the father of the faith-based movement, but the faith-based movement in its historical origins was about reading the Bible as the comprehensive divine plan of human liberation with resources for counter-cultural action and community building.

In his 1976 book, *A Quiet Revolution: A Christian Response to Human Need*, he spoke directly of the economic implications of the Gospel. The redistribution of wealth, he claimed, should be construed as a faithful embodiment of agape: God's unconditional giving of himself to a broken world. Christians must formulate public policies out of repentance toward people harmed by oppression in a spirit of what might be called the principle of the wounded brother.[118] The credibility of any "family values" platform—as well as policy decisions about affirmative action, reparations, cultural memory, and economic justice—would then be judged against this principle. For example, when African American Christians in the South attest to the confederate flag as an abusive symbol of a hateful past, white Christians would, out of a spirit of repentance and reconciliation, defer to their testimony and desire for change, letting go of their own prideful hold on "the southern heritage." Further, if Bible-shaped convictions guided white Christian thinking on affirmative action, then, Perkins said, "out of love for their black brothers and sisters, whites would proudly carry the affirmative action banner."[119]

Certainly the principle has more a regulative than a determining function: It is not a single capitulation for the other's demands. But it must hasten responses to injustice based on self-serving loyalties. However, of even greater concern to Perkins than affirmative action and cultural memory was the matter of wealth and poverty. He explained, "[There] are heavy social implications to the equality expressed in God's spiritual activity in creation. Perhaps the heaviest is Christ's identification with the poor ... He calls the poor person his brother: 'Whatever you did for the humblest of my brothers you did for me' [Matt. 25:40]. But now for the punch line in God's plan: *God meant for equality to be expressed in terms of economics.*"[120] The fall of Adam and Eve resulted in the "pollution and distortion of the equality which he intended," nowhere more obvious than in economic brokenness; for this reason, the body of Christ must be marked as an alternative social order that "breaks the cycle of wealth and poverty."[121]

Against a Christian culture of moral and theological equivocation, Perkins claimed that nothing less than the credibility of the Gospel is at stake. The Christian life requires people to reevaluate their personal desires, prejudices, opinions, and economic policies in the light of God's moral demands. Christians in North America must be known far and wide first as people with "a burden for the poor and oppressed," who "plead the case of the poor, defending the weak, helping the helpless. . . . We must as

Christians seek justice by coming up with means of redistributing goods and wealth to those in need." Reading the Bible as a comprehensive divine plan of human liberation from the perspective of God's own welfare system may not translate to specific partisan loyalties (although sometimes it might), but it undoubtedly requires some degree of public advocacy for economic policies preferential to the poor.[122]

Importantly, Perkins's remark in 1976 that welfare was "one of the most wasteful and destructive institutions created in recent history" intended to convey a point obscured by conservative appropriations of his critique; namely, that welfare did not go far enough in bringing financial restitution to black Americans and in creating conditions favorable to their economic independence. Even more importantly, his criticisms of the American welfare system were always made in the context of his work and life in poor communities. While agreeing with much of the black power agenda—the critique of liberalism's system of dependency and the affirmation of economic empowerment as the condition of social and cultural flourishing—Perkins's trust in the transformative power of the Gospel led him to the conclusion that evangelical Christians possessed a more potent arsenal for social protest than white liberals or black militants. For to truly break free of the "system" one must experience "deep repentance," "a thoroughgoing transformation of his mind through the power of God," and "an openness to biblical strategies of human development."[123] At the same time, Perkins responded to conservative Christians who wanted the church to replace the federal welfare system by pointing out that if such a policy were enacted, Christians would be obligated to divide up among its membership all citizens currently on welfare and make financial and personal commitments to each individual's spiritual and economic flourishing, with appropriate changes in lifestyle and neighborhoods for the advantaged partners.[124]

Throughout the 1970s and 1980s Perkins became increasingly popular on the national evangelical stage, appearing at Billy Graham crusades and political prayer breakfasts and at the annual Urbana Youth Leadership conferences, befriended by such white Christian writers and leaders as Carl F. H. Henry, Frank Gabelein, Charles Colson, Tony Campolo, and Doug Coe.[125] He appeared as a frequent speaker at Christian colleges and seminaries, lectured to student organizations from Harvard to Howard, and was invited onto the boards of evangelical and human rights organizations, including Bread for the World, the National Black Evangelical Association, and Koinonia Partners.[126] The third-grade dropout also became a Ford Foundation Fellow and a consultant to Democratic and Republic presidents.

His writings on faith, racial reconciliation, and poverty appeared frequently in *Sojourners*, the left-leaning evangelical magazine founded by peace activist Jim Wallis, as well as in such mainline evangelical publications as *Christianity Today*, *Decision*, *Campus Life*, *Eternity*, *Family Life*, and *Moody Monthly*.[127] His memoir, *Let Justice Roll Down*, published in 1976, became a religious bestseller (ranking fourth in sales of religious paperbacks), an achievement no doubt influenced by the accolades of Oregon Senator Mark Hatfield, then at the height of his considerable influence in Christian circles, who called Perkins "a modern saint." At the same time, hundreds of high school and college students, lay people, and ministers began traveling to west Jackson and Mendenhall for week-long internships in urban ministry and building development. Some stayed for longer periods of time, learned the VOC model, and returned to their hometowns to set up new initiatives. The neighborhood experiment in building beloved community turned quietly into a movement.

Yet even as Perkins became nationally known as a church-based activist and organic Christian intellectual, most local congregations kept their distance from the racial intermingling in west Jackson. Perkins was selected as the Mississippi "Man of the Year" in 1980 by the state chamber of commerce, but white churchgoers were not ready to invite him to Sunday school. His efforts at creating Billy Graham–style events in Jackson like the "Amen Rally" and "VOC Jubilee," which intended to celebrate "Christian unity" and address "wholistic concerns," went largely unnoticed.[128] One local who made the trip over was a bearded seminarian named Ralph Mareno, who moved into the neighborhood to work for Perkins after becoming aware that his "prejudices against black people" were displeasing to God. Another was Bill Lowrey, a graduate of Reformed Presbyterian Seminary and son of a newspaper editor in Hattiesburg. After a period of service in west Jackson, Lowrey helped form an interracial church in Clinton before proceeding to the work of "structural reconciliation." Lowrey expanded his ministry to include labor organizing among workers in the state's booming catfish industry, and later by forming a global reconciliation institute in Washington. "If a person is being put down by a structure," Lowrey explained, "then that structure needs to be changed. That's one aspect of reconciliation."[129]

As a second generation of blacks and whites learned the skills and disciplines of community building, committed themselves to serving the poor, and established new initiatives around the country, Perkins realized that some kind of organizational network needed to be created. So, in 1989 he formed the Christian Community Development Association (CCDA), the organizational infrastructure of the faith-based community-building movement. In its first year, the CCDA comprised 200 individuals and 37 organizational members. At a recent CCDA conference, Perkins announced that the CCDA had grown to 8,000 individual members and 500 member organizations with sites in more than 100 cities, including Bethel New Life, a comprehensive community development initiative in Chicago, and Habitat for Humanity. "The most creative long-term solutions to the problems of the poor are coming from grassroots and church-based efforts," Perkins explained, "from people who see themselves as the replacements, the agents, for Jesus here on earth, in their own neighborhoods and communities."[130] Annual meetings of the Christian Community Development Association resemble a mix of mass meeting, Billy Graham crusade, and SNCC planning session circa 1963. Between worship services, prayer meetings, and Gospel sings are seminars on community organizing; tutorials on writing applications for public sector grants; support groups for partnering with corporations and affluent churches; and nuts-and-bolts instruction on starting public health centers, running after-school tutorial programs, transforming crack houses into "Kingdom houses," and managing volunteers and prison aftercare. Perkins has extended SCLC's model of community mobilizing and SNCC's preference for community organizing to a distinctive theological vision of community building—activism mindful of the three Rs of relocation, reconciliation, and redistribution, the ingredients of wholistic faith.

The situation on the home front has improved since the creation of the Christian Community Development Association in 1989. In recent years, many white congregations have begun partnering with Voice of Calvary, enlisting volunteers in impressive numbers to work in children's programs and housing rehabilitation. The downtown churches that once closed their doors to black Christians have created internships in the inner city and brother and sister fellowships with black congregations.[131] In 1997 the Junior League of Jackson joined in to refurbish a home in west Jackson. "The hardwood floors have been spit-shined. The French doors are charming," wrote one of the volunteers.[132] Perkins appreciates these efforts even as he quietly laments white Christians' continued unwillingness to challenge the enormous economic disparities between whites and blacks. Perkins also worries that his name is often used by white evangelicals as a convenient way of avoiding Martin Luther King and the lessons of the civil rights movement, which despite its failures bore powerful witness to the nonviolent and countercultural impulses of the Christian faith. He thinks that unless white churchgoers learn to accept the civil rights movement as a spirit-wind of renewal and reformation, which made forever untenable the practice of an otherworldly faith, they should keep his name out of their agendas.

Perkins has not made his peace with white evangelicals. There remain too many habits and ideas in the culture that offend black Christians. Why did such "brothers in Christ" as Jerry Falwell and Pat Robertson vehemently oppose a national holiday in honor of Martin Luther King Jr., the most influential pastor in American history, even as they heaped praise and financial support on Ronald Reagan, the only president in recent decades (other than George W. Bush) who did not go to church regularly?[133] Why do white conservatives remain standoffish around black church leaders active in politics while they regard in high esteem such men as Oliver North, Newt Gingrich, and Tom Delay? And closer to home, why did conservative white Christians in Mississippi throw their undying support behind Trent Lott, whose lengthy congressional records are almost completely bereft of concern for the state's poor—even after his slip-of-the-tongue nostalgia for the golden days of southern apartheid? It is no wonder black Christians look with suspicion on white Christians who say they want racial reconciliation. White evangelicals have trapped themselves into an "ideological box"—the suburban family values agenda and all its trappings—leaving them without a credible witness in the black community. In all this, Perkins has become much more sympathetic to the black church tradition.[134]

In the end, the Voice of Calvary experiment is about the power of love in lived experience and how that love creates "an alternative Kingdom" amidst the harsh and unforgiving structures of the dominant social order. The way to the beloved community is straight and narrow, comprising "that group of people who have come together under the reconciling grace of Jesus to care for the world," making "visible demonstration" of the new relationships of healing and restoration that can happen when the spirit of God enters.[135] "The Bible teaches nothing about the universal brotherhood of man," Perkins said. Only those who have "accepted Christ as their own personal Savior" take part in the new community that transcends race, creed, or color.[136] Still, if the community of Christ remains faithful to its origins, it will explode into the old dominant order with new energies and possibilities—which of course may be repudiated and mocked. The rich are welcome in the new community, though only insofar as they "divest themselves of their excess wealth, maintaining that which is necessary for production and sharing with the poor and oppressed."[137] Perkins's striking claim is that the only credible apologetic of the Christian faith is its capacity to heal the distressed earth and its broken communities.

The civil rights movement failed to inspire America to move beyond integration to reconciliation because it had no clear picture of what reconciliation looks like. But the Christian community offers an exceedingly rich way of imaging reconciliation, indeed a veritable "workshop of reconciliation."[138] Therein every gesture of compassion is at the same time an expression of gratitude for the gift of life, and for time, fleeting and precious. The apostle Paul had written in Galatians of the new identity of those "baptized into Christ"—who have "put on Christ"—as "neither Jew nor Greek, male nor female, slave nor free." "For ye are all one in Christ Jesus." Perkins read the decisive Galatians passage to mean that "an individual who accepts Christ joins the body of Christ through spiritual baptism, thereby losing all racial ties."[139] At the moment of his salvation, the Christian is taken up into the "family of God and the invisible church"; thus, the habits and practices that sustain beloved community are ways of making concrete the individual's spiritual rebirth into a new family in salvation. The worldly body of Christ remains the only real counterculture, precisely because it is the place where obedience, gratitude, and praise create free, complex, and multiracial spaces—the most enduring source of forgiveness and reconciliation in a violent and balkanized world.

On weeknights, Perkins can often be found in the VOC study center talking to a group of student volunteers, running over the three Rs with as much enthusiasm as he had done thirty years ago, an aging Amzie Moore with his eyes ever open for a young Bob Moses or Jane Stembridge—or, as we will see in the next chapter, for a Mark Gornik, Amy Sherman, or Russell Jeung. John and Vera Mae still live in a poor neighborhood of west Jackson. The summer soldiers of SNCC withdrew from distressed and excluded communities after experiencing more disappointments than they could bear, but the Perkinses never left. John, Vera Mae, the children who live in Jackson, and the members of the Voice of Calvary all understand that the work of building beloved community demands spiritual and moral disciplines that only faith can sustain; a defeat, or a series of defeats, ought never break a person's spirit. Stokely Carmichael spoke tirelessly of black self-determination, but Perkins gave the rhetoric flesh in mentoring grassroots leaders among the poor of Mississippi. "Blacks were saying self-determination and black power," Perkins explained, "but there was really no base for it. If I was going to be relevant, then I had to get involved in trying to create a base for that."[140] Sticking it out for the long haul, Perkins and the Voice of Calvary communities have kept the movement spirit alive into the new millennium.[141]

Still, while Perkins's life and work bespeak a shoe-leather faith, the story of Voice of Calvary remains more about ideals than results. The work of the ministry bears the imprimatur of a man whose vision often outpaces preparation and planning, and the surrounding neighborhood today is one of the most violent in the nation. Perkins is the first to admit he's no saint. His leadership style has often been a source of conflict, and he can sometimes seem arrogant in his demands; but his manner, which sometimes feels overbearing to colleagues, is more bark than bite. Perkins is a gracious gentleman who walks to an ancient beat, and in a lifetime spent in the everyday disciplines of building community, he has illuminated the unfinished business of the civil rights movement. He says:

I do a lot of speaking. And whenever I speak to students they always ask a question that gives away their feelings. It goes something like this: "Rev. Perkins, after living through and being active as a Christian in the struggle for equal rights, do you see another movement developing today?

To me this question says something very positive, that there are many students on college campuses who wish deep in their hearts that they could have participated in the civil rights movement and are regretful.

The civil rights movement is over. But I would rather be standing at no other place in history than right now . . . There are people moving toward developing church communities, not just for themselves, but for organizing their resources around areas of need. There are Christians seeking and searching for ways to develop the church as the Body of Christ and to equip the saints with the gifts of the Spirit for real service to people. With these trends, I believe that we are quickly moving to a position where we can begin to really preach the gospel in a way that makes reconciliation and love meaningful to all people.

The test will be to see if these trends are more than a movement. Don't hope for a movement! The civil rights movement died on the brink of some real human development. We must have some people who will keep moving after the movement dies, after it is no longer popular to do what is right.[142]

CHAPTER 7

Building Beloved Communities:
Dispatches from the Quiet Revolution

A man or woman gets a notion to love as God has loved the world. Everyday people, African American and Caucasian, Latino and Asian American, women and men, read the Gospels—

Blessed are the peacemakers: for they shall be called the children of God. (Matthew 5:9)

—or the Epistles—

And all things are of God, who hath reconciled us to himself by Jesus Christ, and hath given to us the ministry of reconciliation. (II Corinthians 5:18)

—or the Hebrew prophets—

O man, what is good; and what does the Lord require of you but to do justice, and to love kindness, and to walk humbly with your God?" (Micah 6:8)

—and they resolve to turn their lives into parables of divine mercy. It may happen in a sudden decision to change one's life, through some trick of grace, or in a slow turning. There is a call that no one but the called can discern, and there is in the acceptance a first step, which changes everything. Some hear the call in mass meetings, lecture halls, hikes in the mountains, watching the evening news, or sitting at the kitchen table at midnight. The call does not promise happiness, prosperity, or that your territory will increase. It may invite the greatest complications and cannot be successfully analyzed. The call comes with no formula or guidebook, but when one accepts it, the world will never again looks quite the same.

"We came here out of repentance, to learn from our neighborhoods and just be a part of the community," said Mark Gornik, a young Presbyterian minister who in 1986 moved with his best friend Allan Tibbels into a row house in the Baltimore neighborhood of Sandtown-Wincester. They were both motivated by John Perkins's theology of community development. "As white Christians, we believed it was vital that we turn from our complicity in a culture that is anti-black, anti-poor and anti-urban and turn to the biblical obligations of justice and reconciliation. We came to listen, to learn, to build friendships, and to live out our faith. When people would ask us, 'What are you doing here?' our answer was always the same: 'We are here to be neighbors.'"[1]

At the time Gornik and Tibbels relocated to Sandtown, unemployment soared above 50 percent in a neighborhood where Supreme Court Justice Thurgood Marshall had been educated in public schools and where jazz greats Fats Waller, Count Basie, Dizzy Gillespie, Duke Ellington, Ella Fitzgerald, Billie Holliday, and Louis Armstrong were once regular attractions at the Royal Theater.[2] In the wake of plant closures and deindustrialization in the late sixties and early seventies, the population of Sandtown dropped from 50,000 to 11,000, infant mortality and teenage pregnancy rates became the highest in the country, and hundreds of houses were abandoned and boarded up. The median income was $8,500 a household, and the community displayed the grim rituals of the postmodern ghetto: drug crews working the corners, Ford Explorers cruising slowly down littered alleys, and dirt bikes speeding through streets and across vacant lots. Sandtown was a warren of hopelessness in a city of 40,000 abandoned homes that lost a thousand people each month in suburban flight; and yet, as Gornik and Tibbels discovered, Sandtown was also a neighborhood that many people still called home.

The year before moving to the city, Gornik had interned at Voice of Calvary in Jackson. Although he assisted the construction crew and worked on staff at the community center, he didn't feel prepared to rehab entire buildings, nor was he convinced that the Mississippi model could be applied to the urban Northeast. Tibbels faced a different challenge. During a pick-up basketball game several years earlier he had suffered a broken neck after getting undercut on a drive to the basket. Yet Tibbels felt called to leave behind the suburban home where his new life as a quadriplegic had become technologically manageable. In Sandtown, he became a familiar sight to residents: the bearded white man spinning down the middle of the street in his motorized wheelchair, making himself available as a friend and neighbor.

"We held tightly to a commitment of God's *shalom*, but we had no plans or programs. Instead of imposing our own agendas, we sought to place our lives in service to the community. We wanted to do something to help the community resurrect hope, to fight nihilism. We would make the road by traveling it together," said Gornik.[3]

In time, Gornik's row house on Mount Street and Tibbels's on Stricker became the two bases of a twelve-block "focus area" called New Song Community. With strong neighborhood leadership and financial support from Baltimore churches and philanthropic organizations, a slate of holistic programs was created under the auspices of New Song Community Ministries: a health center, job-placement program, private Christian school, legal cooperative, youth services cooperative, community church, and a Habitat for Humanity project, which Jimmy Carter launched himself on a festive spring day in 1992. Establishing the church was a decisive step in anchoring the ministry in the community, since many of the community-building initiatives that survive the first blush of excitement are based in common worship. All these commitments have formed the context within which Gornik thinks theologically.

I found that Christian doctrine in its unreconstructed mystery has profound implications for social existence. Like the doctrine of justification by faith. You take that idea to poor people and they will be moved to new self-understandings: the idea that I am saved by a merciful God, not because I have been able to do anything to earn salvation, but as a result of God's goodness. Or take the idea of unconditional grace: the idea that God has saved humanity quite apart from anything we could do ourselves. So our social standing, our economic background, our education, our race—none of this matters to God because he looks at us as his dear children reconciled by the blood of Jesus.

I cannot escape my background as a white male born into a world of options and privileges. But I can and should struggle with my obligation as a Christian to view the city in all of its forms and conditions through the eyes of the stranger, the excluded, and the poor. Christian reflection on the inner city must emerge out of relationships: the bonds of commitment to Christ and his peace for the poor. In Christ's fellowship with the poor, in his identification with the depths of suffering through the cross, the cries from the depths of the inner city are also his, and the plea that all things might be made right becomes a yearning in the Spirit of God for God's reign of peace.

Poverty is a constant assault upon dignity and humanity. But Jesus says, "you count." So you count. Now, let's create a community where that can be embodied.[4]

In 1999 Mark and his wife, Rita Azalos, a family physician with training in addictions medicine, moved to New York City to give their support to the start of New Song Harlem. Under the leadership of Sandtown native Laverne Stokes, who had become coexecutive of Sandtown Habitat for Humanity, and Tibbels, the organization continued to flourish with 40–50 houses rehabbed each year and as many as 10,000 volunteers assisting in the work. In an intense urban landscape, Sandtown fulfills the civil rights movement's mission of developing grassroots leadership committed to economic empowerment and incarnational organizing.

"I grew up in an unjust system," Stokes says. "And yet we are all in trouble now because of it. So the key thing is how do we get out of it? It takes all of us working together. We've got to know that it's going to be a long term investment, it's got to be sharing resources, it's got to be educating everybody's child—everybody's child has the right to be educated. You're going to have to examine your hearts and be truthful. What New Song means to me is fleshing out the true gospel. You see, just loving people draws them into Christ."[5]

In 1996, a young Chinese American graduate student named Russell Jeung, who had read Perkins's memoir, *Let Justice Roll Down*, in an Intervarsity student group, moved into an Oakland housing project to build community with Cambodian and Bosnian refugees.

"If you enter Oak Park apartments," Jeung explains, "you'd immediately feel like you're in a developing country. The smells of Cambodian soups waft through the air. Latina women hang their laundry on lines hung between trees as cart vendors hawk tamales and ice cream. Families with three to nine kids live in one bedroom apartments which all border a dirt courtyard. There, dozens of barefoot brown kids, like flocks of little chicks, skirt to and fro. Actual chicks also wander the courtyard, as well as assorted little pets."

With two degrees in sociology from Stanford and a Ph.D. from Berkeley, Jeung declined numerous job offers at prestigious universities to "share the love of Jesus" and "organize for power" among the poor. In partnership with members of the community, Jeung and eight other college friends established a weekly tutoring program, ESL classes, and Bible study groups, and they also organized a tenants' association. Jeung says,

> All our neighbors are poor people of color who inhabit some of the worst housing in the Bay Area. The majority of adults don't have high school degrees and either lives off of welfare or occasional day labor. Our ceilings leak, our walls are poisoned with lead paint and asbestos, and our floorboards are infested with roaches and mice.
>
> We've come with the intent to care for the poor, but what we've learned is far deeper. God has shown us His heart and His kingdom values.[6]

In Oak Park the Cambodian refugees, survivors of the killing fields, find themselves locked out of many jobs because they cannot speak English. Seeking to insulate themselves from the violence and racial hatred around them, they retreat to fearful lives inside the apartment complex. Their children assimilate into the social patterns of the urban underclass—drugs, gangs, and street crime. Domestic abuse in Oak Park is not uncommon. Neither are drunkenness, gambling, and other manifestations of anger and resentment. And Jeung has become accustomed to thieves stealing computers, car break-ins, and the threats of drug dealers. "So I've come to understand," says Jeung, "how we who live in poor areas hunger and thirst for righteousness and justice, the marks of God's Kingdom. We fervently pray daily, 'Thy Kingdom come, Thy will be done' because we see Satan's work all around."[7]

In 1998, the Christians living in community with Muslims and Buddhists in Oak Park organized a tenant lawsuit involving 200 of the residents, in which they demanded repairs from a slumlord who had ignored frequent reports of mildewing apartments, crumbling staircases, sewage backups, deteriorating roofs, and vermin infestations.[8] After a four-year struggle, the Oak Park tenants won a million-dollar cash settlement that enabled them to convert the complex to permanent affordable housing and create an endowment fund for the residents; each of the families in the apartments also received payments of $20,000. Jeung and the Christians used their money to purchase a building next to the apartments where a preschool, daycare center, and after-school program were housed.

In addition, the Christians began reaching out to the neighbors beyond the Oak Park complex through neighborhood cleanup campaigns, door-to-door requests for prayer needs, and cross-cultural block parties. The lawsuit reminded Jeung that effective community building sometimes requires the courage to confront and contest. Still, as Dr. King had emphasized throughout the Montgomery bus boycott, the goal of social protest should never be to humiliate the other, but (as Jeung says) to bring glory to God and to embody the Kingdom of God on earth.

> The battle at Oak Park is never-ending. But one day at a time, we pick up our crosses, deny ourselves and follow Jesus. When I am merciful to others, I'm fulfilling the potential that God has granted to humans. He told us to be compassionate because God is compassionate. Our acts of mercy are the end products of His creation and re-creation of us.
>
> Although I want justice now, justice doesn't always come about. But God's been showing us at Oak Park that His Kingdom isn't about our success or failures; it's about God's movement in this world. We must learn to simply join in, wait, and hope.[9]

~

In 1979, Gene and Jackie Rivers moved with their two children into the Dorchester neighborhood of Boston and established the Azusa Christian Community, named after the street in Los Angeles where the Pentecostal movement in America got its start in the early twentieth century. The center of the Dorchester initiative was the Ella J. Baker House, a renovated Victorian home that had been the site of neighborhood drug activity. Gene and Jackie painted the house in bold reds, blacks, and greens and turned it into a church and organizing center.

As undergraduates at Harvard, the Riverses had organized a black Pentecostal student group called the Seymour Society in hopes of forging "a Christian activist-intelligentsia empowered by the Holy Spirit." Gene was well equipped for the task: Dressed in army fatigues and beret, he introduced himself as a Pentecostal communist, overwhelming class discussions with his erudition and charisma, a brainy, restless activist who was also "saved, sanctified," and "filled with a mighty burning fire."[10]

After college, Gene embarked on his life as an organic intellectual, discerning the needs of the day according to the ever-changing winds of the spirit, while Jacqueline worked with the staff of the Algebra Project, the middle-school tutorial program that Bob Moses had organized after returning to the States. Gene explained his motivation: "Bob Moses and SNCC, Fred Hampton in Chicago, these folk laid their lives down. My understanding is that those acts of heroism were very Christian acts, in the tradition of the martyrs. I live in Dorchester and have weathered what we've weathered because that's my understanding of radical discipleship. There is no crown without the cross. Most folk aren't ready to hear that."[11]

Rivers believes that one of the flaws of the civil rights movement was the withdrawal of black intellectuals and professionals from the lives of the poor and excluded. It was his hope that Asuza Christian Community would not only offer holistic ministry to the neighborhood but further illuminate the essential work of African American and Christian intellectuals in a violent culture.[12]

"With faith, one can see beyond discrimination and poverty to a future that has meaning. Secular agencies don't explain to you why human life is meaningful, why there is a moral difference between spitting on the ground and killing another black person. [But] the church has the moral language to resurrect hope in the face of insurmountable obstacles. The only thing that is going to keep the United States from going in the direction of resurrecting apartheid is the church. If the church doesn't do it, it's apartheid in the future."[13]

Without God, everything is permissible—this is not only the lesson of modern philosophical nihilism, Rivers points out, but of the urban ghetto as well. "The bottom line is that Shaniqua needs to be brought into a church, and her child needs to be taught the basic moral teachings of the Christian tradition, which begins in Sunday School."[14]

Rivers speaks with profound admiration of his forerunners in SNCC, COFO, and CORE, and he regards the Azusa Christian Community as a living expression of that admiration. Still, he believes that the movement abandoned its own best spiritual resources—resources that might have otherwise helped sustain the vision and the work over the longer haul. But it was not only the secularist impulses that led to the movement's languishing and its retreat from piecemeal social reform; Rivers laments the black church's failure to channel its own potent energies into intellectual resources for sustained critique and action. Turning elsewhere for authenticity and relevance, subsequent generations of black intellectuals and activists lost the theological and moral vocabulary that had sustained the social hopes of their parents and grandparents and engendered strategies and resources for constructive change. He says, "Our concern in the black church should have been for integrating biblically orthodox Christian theology, social theory, and policy analysis with some programmatic organizing on the ground, with the goal in mind of rebuilding a movement."[15]

In the early 1990s, the Azusa Christian Community became the sponsoring church for the "Ten Point Coalition," a group that organized for comprehensive community development in an area devastated by urban decline. The "ten point plan," drafted by Rivers and other coalition members, read like a polemic against Christian otherworldliness, though it was in fact a strategic manual for community reform. The plan commissioned teams of missionaries serving as ombudsmen in court with juveniles; groups dedicated to the ministry of "adopting a gang"; black "brotherhoods" and "sisterhoods" that modeled alternative lifestyles to tribal violence; evangelism crusades on drug corners; health centers as sites of healing; and partnerships with suburban black and white churches.[16] "We recognize," Rivers says, "that a community of faith that is willing to really follow the leading of the Holy Spirit can make a difference in the worst neighborhood. Dramatic change will always require dramatic sacrifice. Dramatic blessings have dramatic costs."[17]

In Charlottesville, Virginia, Rydell Payne, an African American raised in Fluvanna County and educated at James Madison University, moved with his wife, Hope, a real estate lawyer, and their three small children from a spacious modern home into a small duplex near a low-income housing complex. Payne directs a community development center called Abundant Life. "God called, and I needed to be in a place where Jesus would make himself real," he says. Payne's desire was to bear witness to "the love that cements itself to the conditions and fears of the oppressed."[18]

One mile from the stately grounds of the University of Virginia, beyond the medical center and the train tracks, is a neighborhood called Prospect Heights. Most of the community's residents live in the Blue Ridge Commons, a drab 1970s housing complex with wilted Cape Cod facades and tar-paper roofs. Seventy percent of the residents are "working poor"; the rest are unemployed.[19] Eighty-nine percent of the population is African America, 10 percent is Hispanic, and the remaining 1 percent is white and poor. Most of the households are headed by single mothers. Nightfall brings out the drugs dealers, who assume their positions at the apartment entrance and wait for business.

Prospect Heights is an unlikely place to call the inner city, since it lies near the center of "Mr. Jefferson's university" and adjacent to an upper-middle-class residential development. But when an urban renewal program was approved in a redevelopment referendum in 1965, the African American cultural center of Charlottesville called Vinegar Hill, once a vital district of black businesses, churches, and homes, was decimated in a series of buy-outs and forced relocations. The Vinegar Hill residents were dispersed throughout the city according to income and influence in new residential pockets, giving casual observers and intellectuals the mistaken impression of the town's racial homogeneity. In fact, Charlottesville boasts a sizeable and talented African American community. The public school system, which all but a few white families use, is 52 percent minority and renowned for its high academic achievement and a music program that has produced numerous recipients of college scholarships and professional musicians, including violinist Boyd Tinsley of the Dave Mathews Band. Abundant Life is located inside the Blue Ridge Commons, in a three-bedroom apartment adjacent to the playground. Payne says,

> The incarnational approach to organizing addresses issues of crime, poverty and deterioration by going to the community and asking how we—as outsiders—can be helpful; then using our resources and whatever influence we have in creating programs that help people vocationally, spiritually and materially. Building community requires developing personal relationships with others; but sometimes too we have to make assertions that will give us some of the power to bring about change, and this can be a little bit risky. We struggle to find a balance between love and power; between supporting the people of the neighborhood in claiming the power it deserves and getting better resources and learning how to undergird the community in love, of getting underneath and serving in a community so that transformation takes place from the bottom.[20]

The founder of Abundant Life is a single white woman in her early forties named Amy Sherman. Community development has been Sherman's life's work and calling since she finished her doctorate in political science in the early nineties. She believes that places like Abundant Life, where the poor and excluded are shown respect and kindness, offer a "foretaste of the Kingdom of God," a promise of the kingdom's "awesome and glorious" fullness, and "a preview of the coming attraction, the Kingdom of God in all its glory, beauty and wholeness"—not just for the poor but for all who take part.[21] Sherman does not need a primer on doctrine to instruct her on the meaning of eschatology. The inevitable frustrations of community building and the challenges of fostering hope in distressed areas offer a daily lesson in waiting for wholeness. Still, Sherman believes that God is continuing "to break the Kingdom into this world, to build His Kingdom," and that the people who take part in the work of mercy and justice experience the kingdom in palpable ways.[22] "The Kingdom of God has begun," explains Sherman, who lives in the Prospect neighborhood and suffers from chronic pain as a result of an automobile accident. She says,

> Jesus inaugurated it. It is now. But it is also 'not yet.' We wait and long in our still-broken world for its consummation. But while we wait, it is the task of the Church—Christ's Body—to continue to proclaim the good

news of the Kingdom, and to witness to it, to serve as foretastes of it. God is continuing to break the Kingdom into this world; He is building His Kingdom. And we are called to participate in that work and announce it to others, to bear witness to it in our callings. We are to be citizens of the Kingdom of God, to look different than citizens of the kingdom of this world. As citizens of the Kingdom of God, we are to be doing the work of the Kingdom—a work of justice, of love, of healing, of hope and transformation. We are called to give people foretastes of the coming Kingdom.[23]

~

Spencer Perkins, the son of John and Vera Mae Perkins, together with a white student from Middlebury College whose father had come south as a student volunteer in 1964, lived in an intentional interracial community called Antioch in Jackson, Mississippi, until Spencer's death in 1998. Antioch existed as a kind of evangelical Freedom House, "a very informal, disorganized, free-floating, seat of the pants, build the road as you walk, kind of thing," the white student Chris Rice said.[24] Antioch operated out of an eight-bedroom house left in shambles in the wake of suburban flight and surging crime. In addition to running a magazine devoted to racial reconciliation and urban healing, Perkins and Rice coauthored the influential book *More Than Equals: Racial Healing for the Sake of the Gospel*, and lectured on college campuses and church groups on Christian community and race relations.[25]

Rice says of his years as Spencer's organizing partner:

Our lives were completely synchronized, teaching, writing, living together, bringing people in and teaching them the principles and lessons learned through Voice of Calvary. The focus of our work was really the work of conversion, what I would call persuasion. It was not political and legal advocacy, which is extremely important. But our calling was to go from community to community, from church leader to church leader, seeking to persuade them, primarily from the Scriptures, as well as from our life together and from the lessons we had learned, to lead them through the same conversion we had gone through as African Americans and white Americans; to lead them into a mission together, not just to build relationships but to do something new in the world.

It's hard work. When you live in community you become very wary of each other's shit; you know each other's shit well, you get tired of talking about each other's shit, and you'd just rather not deal with the shit anymore. Spencer and I discovered all this in ways that drove our friendship to a crisis.[26]

One of their central convictions as "reconciliation partners" was that the civil rights movement's greatest legacy to black and white southerners was its ability to display a distinctive form of Christian community. "The civil rights movement was an overwhelming success," Perkins and Rice wrote in *More Than Equals.* "But it failed to inspire our nation to move beyond integration to reconciliation."[27] When the movement lost its anchor in the church, it began to splinter into activist groups whose spiritual visions were no larger than concerns for their own flourishing, and this proved devastating, since people are not inclined toward social relocation, economic redistribution, or racial reconciliation unless they see their own life stories in a larger theological narrative. The motivation to move beyond integration to reconciliation flows from a theologically specific belief in God. Rice says,

The day Spencer died of a heart attack, we had been talking about a culture of grace and the need to reach for new practices of grace in our lives. We had discovered in our spiritual journeys and in our lives together that the Gospel is about God's love that is unearned and undeserved. We had discovered the power of grace. Without doing anything we are beloved. And as we began to understand that, we began to understand that only as we are filled with that unconditional grace, and as we are changed by grace and God, can we offer ourselves back to each other. The reservoir of grace has to come from God. That is what we give to a world in pain. Not only does grace establish the paradigm for what God does for us, it is also the paradigm for what we are supposed to do to each other. We are supposed to give that kind of love back to each other through a life of grace.[28]

~

Many others have joined the Christian community development movement as well. A white businessman and Vietnam veteran named Bob Lupton volunteered in Jackson and moved to Atlanta to launch a community-building ministry in the neighborhoods of Grant Park and East Lake. Lupton and his partners have since established a medical center, a clothing cooperative, a daycare center for the working poor, and a housing rehabilitation program.[29] Lupton explained his motivation in terms of a "theology of community" based on Jesus's answer to the question, "Who is my neighbor?" given in his Parable of the Good Samaritan. "The community into which Christ invites us is one of interdependence. We are called to mutual sharing and the discovery of gifts Christ has concealed in the unlikeliest among us. And to those who consider themselves leaders, our Lord offers humility—

the salvation of the proud that comes from learning to receive from the least, who are the greatest in the kingdom."[30] In a lifetime spent in the inner city, Lupton has gained a deep and practical understanding of the sources that sustain redemption, reconciliation, and beloved community. "I have seen God take the broken, deformed things of this world, bless them with new life and sanctify them for his special purpose. From a broken tree, God provides shade in the summer. From a deeply scarred youth, he forms a person of unusual compassion and understanding, a model of hope to the disheartened of the inner city . . . And I am humbled to see that out of the twistedness of my wounds, he designs for me a special place of service."[31]

Desire Street Ministries in New Orleans fashions itself as an incarnational community "focused on indigenous leadership development," which seeks to revitalize violent and oppressive neighborhoods through spiritual and community development. The streets that intersect the project—Abundance, Benefit, Pleasure, Treasure—have seen hundreds of the neighborhood's sons and daughters killed in recent decades. The typical family living in the projects consists of a single mother with three children and an annual income below $6,000.[32] Founder Mo Leverett explains the vision of the Desire Street organizers as "the imitation of Christ"; that is, learning "to see the neighborhood become everything that it can become through the power of the gospel of Jesus Christ."[33] The spiritual disciplines that sustain the work have enabled organizers in New Orleans to build community with the poor and excluded in more sustained ways than the SNCC organizers who had worked decades earlier in the slums of the crescent city. The white volunteers and staff members share apartment buildings, transportation, meals, resources, and the experiences of daily life with the residents of the neighborhood, and more than half of all staff positions are held by local residents. "I want to be involved in seeing the vision of Christ's kingdom advanced as far and as deep and as wide as possible," Leverett says, "especially in areas where we have neglected our Christian responsibilities—in pockets of poverty where great injustices have occurred."[34]

In the Bronx, Ray Rivera launched the Latino Pastoral Action Center (LPAC) and a comprehensive range of "inner-city holistic ministries" as a way of building community among Latino and other urban communities. Rivera is an unlikely combination of Latino Pentecostal, converted at the age of fifteen in a storefront church in East Harlem, and Reformed minister ordained in the Christian Reformed Church, a Dutch Calvinist denomination headquartered in Michigan. The "miracle at 170th Street" includes health centers, drug rehabilitation programs, youth projects, women's centers, homeless shelters, housing development and construction, AIDS programs, Christian academies, small businesses, a community service center, and a weight room featuring a mural of a muscular Jesus with pumped-up disciples. Rivera bases his community building and organizing on the theological principles of liberation, healing, community, and transformation and explains the work of the LPAC as a vital part of Christian spiritual formation. "We are called to be transformed in to the image of Christ through daily devotion and practices which foster spiritual growth daily. Yet we must remember that we will never arrive at our destination until Jesus returns."[35]

In Philadelphia, the fellowship of the Simple Way was born when a few college students read an article in the local newspaper about thirty poor families who had moved into an abandoned cathedral in the city. The students learned that the city government and Archdiocese had given the families eviction notices, and they registered their protest by moving into the Cathedral and barricading the doors with the families. A sign was hung over the front door of the church that read: "How can you worship a homeless man on Sunday and ignore one on Monday?" Although no one was spared eviction and the cathedral was eventually condemned, the fellowship of the Simple Way emerged from the protest as a "Christ-centered community of peacemakers."[36] Eventually the Simple Way purchased a home on Potter Street and waited for action, seeking neither to create a church nor a commune but rather to incarnate the spirit of servant-minded availability in an urban environment. Surrounded by more than 700 vacant commercial buildings, 15,800 vacant lots, and 27,000 abandoned houses, members were soon operating a community center, a thrift store, a child-care and tutoring program, and job-training programs. The students studied, analyzed, and visited such experiments as Voice of Calvary, Jesus People USA, the Bruderhof, the Missionaries of Charity, and the Catholic Worker. Like theological pranksters on a social mission, the fellowship purchased a double-decker bus, intending to run a coffeehouse and café on the top deck and a cooperative store and postal service for homeless people at the bottom, but the bus broke down on a bridge in New Jersey and was never repaired. Through their daily work and nonviolent protest of military and corporate power; through the liturgy of arrests, trial, and incarceration; through the practice of the common purse and a lot of "hanging around" with their neighbors in the recesses of the urban ghetto, the members of the Simple Way make themselves available to the needs of the poor, bearing witness to the difference between the kingdom of God and "the American empire."

As the Christian community-building movement expanded and activist communities flourished throughout the nation, organizations were formed that blurred the lines between the sacred and the civil, with lumbering names and acronyms like the civil rights groups of the sixties. In addition to the Christian Community Development Association (CCDA), these include the National Fellowship of Housing Ministries (NFHM); Entrepreneurial Training Centers (ETC); City Builders and the Fresno Leadership Foundation (FLF); the Inner City Christian Fellowship (ICCF); Voices in the Wilderness (VIW); the Pastors Development Ministry (PDM); Wheels of Justice (WOJ); the Mustard Seed Associates (MSA), World Impact, Love Inc., Hope, Inc. In addition, the movement features its own journals, newspapers, and Web-zines as well as organizing manuals, theological studies of poverty, globalization and geographical space, and autobiographical narratives of lives reborn in compassionate service.

A photograph published in the *Washington Post* shortly before George W. Bush took office featured the president in conversation with a group of American religious leaders. The *Post* intended the photograph to illustrate President Bush's appeal to a new generation of black religious leaders, and the faces were a welcome sight to many participants in recent church-based activism.[37] Nonetheless, the notion that Gene Rivers, Cheryl Sanders, and John Perkins (respectively, a Pentecostal social radical, a womanist evangelical, and a black pacifist whose favorite senator is Hilary Clinton) would somehow be easier to placate than Jesse Jackson and Al Sharpton was comical.[38] (The group was not invited back.) In fact, as the idea of the faith-based initiative has taken rough form at the federal level, its planners have steadily refrained from endorsing the Christian community-building movement as represented by CCDA—as well as by other faith-based organizing traditions, such as the Pacific Institute for Community Organization (PICO) and the Industrial Areas Foundation (IAF)—and preferring instead general affirmations of community service, the good and decent and politically useful provision of goods and services to the underprivileged by congregations and religious agencies.[39] Community building and community organizing, on the other hand, too often require the politically troubling practices of resistance and reform and push toward a deeper identity of person and community than that of nationhood: all humanity created in God's image, redeemed from its fallenness by the "great event of the Cross."[40] The three thousand Christian activists who met at the 2003 conference of the CCDA in New Orleans—black, white, Latino/Latina, Asian American, and Native American—condemned the invasion of Iraq and the "new American hegemony."[41] Shane Clairborne of the Simple Way shared details of his recent trip to Iraq and meetings with Iraqi Christians, who expressed their confusion that the church in the United States had failed to take a united stance against the war. Indeed what we find in these abandoned and desolate spaces of America are Christians engaged in a set of distinctive social practices that stand in judgment on national idolatry and greed.

Furthermore, participation in the experiments in community-building partnerships more often than not promotes an appreciation for greater government involvement, even as it raises awareness of the scale of poverty and exclusion in America. In his seminal speech before the National Association of Evangelicals in Dallas on March 7, 2001, shortly before his departure from Washington and his controversial farewell to the "Mayberry Machiavellis" of the White House, the former director of the Federal Office of Faith-Base Initiatives, John DiIulio explained: "Even if all 353,000 religious congregations in America doubled their annual budgets and devoted them *entirely* to the cause of social services, and even if the cost of government social welfare programs was magically cut by one-fifth, the congregations would barely cover a year's worth of Washington's spending on [social] programs and never even come close to covering the program costs."[42] Religious and private institutions do not have the resources to carry the burden of social compassion alone; to place that burden on religious institutions is "to abdicate the legitimate responsibility of government."[43] For these reasons, a new appreciation for the scope of the social problem has led many volunteers to redefine the purpose of their mission. As one conservative Protestant student working in a community-building initiative explained, "God is at work in the city but not in the way I expected. I thought I would find him in the big details of life. But instead the city wrecks your head and messes with your theology."[44] A year later, the student was a resident of the Catholic Worker House in San Diego.

On an unusually cold Saturday in November, a hundred people gather in the Jackson State University baseball stadium to rally for racial unity in Mississippi. "Grace is Greater Than Race," announces the banner on the stage behind the pitcher's mound. On this night, however, with the small crowd huddled together against the cold amidst an ocean of empty seats, it seems more likely that there is nothing greater than the desire to make a swift retreat to warm homes. The frozen ground and darkened score board offer a grim forecast of the long winter ahead. Two gospel groups work hard to put an upbeat spin on the evening, but the weak response of the audience and problems with the taped R & B instrumental track only reinforce a mood of disappointment. A city-wide gathering held in the early summer had brought 35,000 people to old Memorial Stadium.

Six leaders of an organization called Mission Mississippi stand behind a podium at home plate. The event offers little evidence that the organization will inspire a "sweeping ministry of reconciliation in Christ" throughout the magnolia state as its literature promises. When one of the speakers apologizes in advance for the abbreviated comments of the main speakers, the audience offers its heartiest applause of the night.

The first testimony is given by Dick Bends. "I married a very Christian lady who kind of set me straight in a lot of areas," Bends says. "I came home one night and asked her, 'What would you think if I asked two black men and their wives to come have dinner with us?' I had never done this before and didn't know quite what to do. So my wife says, 'Maybe you should just ask them and we'll see what happens.' And so I did and they accepted and we became good friends. I encourage more of us to do more of this kind of thing." [45]

The second testimony comes from an African American pastor named Daniel Crowley. Crowley recalls a godly mother who endured the indignities of Jim Crow even while admonishing her children to love and forgive. "In the midst of all she had to give up on a daily basis, she still taught us to love." Crowley tells the audience about the day he finally realized how much he hated white people. It happened one afternoon during his senior year in high school. He was walking from his home to a store when a white teenager in a speeding car threw a cup of ice at him. The ice cut and bruised Crowley's face, and he felt his humiliation give way to rage. "That was the straw that broke the camel's back. I began to hate my sisters and brothers of a different race."[46] Crowley then asks the crowd to join him in singing a song about racial unity in Christ.

After a few verses, Dolphus Weary takes the microphone. Weary is the executive director of Mission Mississippi, a position he has held since leaving his position as head of Voice of Calvary in Mendenhall, and as he has done countless times he tells the story of his childhood in Braxton, Mississippi, and his early education in the realities of white supremacy. "I could never understand sitting at my mother's feet how the white church people could do the things they did. You see my mother had the privilege of knowing her grandmother, and many times my mom was able to hear stories about black life in rural Mississippi, personal stories about people having lynching parties and people she knew who had been lynched; and I could never understand how they did it; I could understand how the heathens could do it; but I could never understand how a people could go out and have a lynching party on Friday night and Saturday night, and then go into church on Sunday morning and sing, 'Amazing Grace How Sweet the

Sound' or 'What a Friend We Have in Jesus' or 'How Great Thou Art' or 'How Love Lifted Me.' I could never understand that."[47]

As soon as Weary was able to make his own decisions, he tells the crowd, he left Mississippi, never to come back. He accepted a basketball scholarship at a Christian college in Los Angeles and set his sights on a lifetime away from the South. But, like Perkins, Weary did come back, because he wanted to be a part of the work of building beloved community in the Deep South. "God has been showing me over the years a little something about race: if you label somebody as less than a human being, then you'll think it's OK to lynch them and to beat them and to do anything you want to them because they are less than human. I want you to know that it doesn't matter what kind of label we give people, when Jesus said that it's finished on the cross, he meant that that every label has been removed."[48]

Mission Mississippi began as a "prayer movement" in Jackson when a group of fifteen people agreed to meet once a week for breakfast in the unlikely setting of a police station. Sitting in metal chairs in a room of cinder-block walls, the "prayer warriors" ate donuts and sipped coffee from styrofoam cups. In time, the prayer breakfasts were moved to the Salvation Army headquarters in northeast Jackson.

The heart of Mission Mississippi's vision is fostering reconciliation between black and white Christians through "relationship building" and "attitudinal change."[49] Partnerships include twice-weekly prayer breakfasts, picnics in downtown Jackson, conferences on Christian unity, youth retreats, clergy appreciation banquets, evangelistic crusades, and the "Two and Two Together Restaurant Days," when restaurants offer a 22 percent discount to all parties made up of at least two black and two white people. All participants of Mission Mississippi, white and black, are asked to sign a "personal covenant of racial reconciliation in Christ," acknowledging all Christians as brothers and sisters in the Lord, asking God "to reveal any unbiblical attitudes . . . toward anyone because of his or race, and repenting," and "working to overcome the sinful effects of racial prejudice and encouraging . . . reconciliation efforts." Mission Mississippi organizers believe that through these partnerships and biracial arrangements the churches of Mississippi will one day become "owners of the vision of reconciliation within the Body of Christ."[50]

Although Mission Mississippi's official numbers are impressive, comprising hundreds of participating congregations and tens of thousands of white and black church members from across the ecumenical spectrum—from Christ the King Catholic Church to the Living Hope Pentecostal Ministry—the emotionally uplifting work of "Reconciliation 101" has come to an end, and with it the pleasant season of handshakes, smiles, and pats on the back.[51] The more demanding curriculum of "Reconciliation 201" is evidenced in the small shivering crowd in the Jackson State baseball stadium.

On this bitter November night, Dolphus Weary seems more mindful of the long road ahead than excited by the prospects of victory:

> What does it mean that we are a Christian now, a new creation? Is the same grace that saved us strong enough to break down the barriers of race that separate us? It is time for grace to rise above our race. Hattiesburg, Biloxi, Meridian, Columbus, Tupelo, Oxford, Grenada, Greenville, Vicksburg, Jackson, Laurel. Reconciliation is not an easy thing. Getting together once a year won't do it. Rallies like this won't do it. But you can put your suffering at the foot of the cross, where Jesus died for all your pain. Who will take the first step? Who will be vulnerable? Who will take the risks?[52]

~~

Martin Luther King Jr. spoke of the "spiritual movement in Montgomery," Clarence Jordan of the "God-movement" in southeast Georgia, Fannie Lou Hamer of the "New Kingdom in Mississippi," John Perkins of the "quiet revolution" of Christian community building, Mark Gornik of "the *shalom* of the city"—together these Christians point us to the reality that stands behind beloved community and gives purpose to lifetimes spent in service to poor and excluded people, the reality that cuts through all these human movements as their hidden sense and motor.[53] These contemporary retrievals of the spiritual movement toward "redemption, reconciliation and the creation of beloved community" demonstrate the vital role of spiritual nourishment in the work of mercy and justice, not as a substitute for material sustenance but as the condition of justice.[54] As Chris Rice said, "Communities like ours are hardly normative and they are never going to be normative, but their influence is disproportionate to their numbers. I just think of the hundreds and thousands of people who were touched through the work of Voice of Calvary in various ways: by coming and living with us for a while. These are places of deep conversion, places where the creation of allies is happening, places where Christians are learning not so much how to solve the race and other social problems but how to be truly church. I think there is lot of power in that."[55] The civil rights movement had extended the gesture of reconciliation, only eventually to withdraw it in the face of hateful rejection; but the new Christian radicals are finding the strength to keep the arms of mercy open, even in the face of restitution shirked and due reparations withheld.[56]

CHAPTER 8

The Contours of an Activist Faith for the Twenty-first Century

The pursuit of beloved community is not finally about the redemption of America's soul, nor even about the achievement of interracial community. To the Christians in our story, it is rather about bearing witness to the Prince of peace in a violent and suffering world.[1] The theologian Lesslie Newbigin reminds us that Jesus "did not write a book but formed a community."[2]

The beloved community may then finally be described as a gift of the kingdom of God introduced into history by the church, and thus it exists within the provenance of Christ's mystery in the world. When the beloved community remembers the gift, its witness is strengthened as its energy for service is renewed; when it celebrates the gift in praise and proclamation, the beloved community exists as the church, which it has always been in its essence. One could say that the relationship between church and beloved community is mutually enriching, even as the church remains at all times theologically prior. In other words, the church establishes the hidden meaning of beloved community even as beloved community makes visible that meaning in ways the church may often not.[3] At the same time, the beloved community enables the "real history" of the world to be glimpsed and touched, so that for a moment we are able to understand—or if we have forgotten, then we are reminded—that such "real history" is the motor that drives "so-called history" onward.[4] As SNCC's John Lewis once said of the mass meetings, "[They] *were* church, and for some who had grown disillusioned with Christian otherworldliness, they were better than church."[5] Time and again in the work of building beloved community, women and men caught up in a pentecost of compassion exclaim: *Man, this is like church, only better.* In a photograph by Danny Lyon of the Mississippi Freedom Democrats Vote of 1964, men and women with their hands raised in a chapel appear to be singing and praying, but in fact they are voting.

While the *church* as a worshipping community exists for the specific purposes of confessing, proclaiming, and worshipping Jesus Christ as Lord, the beloved community quietly moves from its historical origins into new and unexpected shapes of communion and solidarity. To be sure, the church has an obligation to nurture and fortify the beloved community, even though it often fails in this task. But the church's failure, its concessions to expediency and comfort, does not limit God's action in the world. At such times when the church chooses the easy way over the narrow way, God may nurture and fortify the beloved community through the activity of the Holy Spirit. Beloved community may then become a source of knowledge and conviction for the church, which the church in turn must acknowledge and appropriate in humility. But beyond humility, Christians should rejoice in the fact that when the church defaults on its mission in the world, the Spirit places the beloved community in the embracing arms of the kingdom of God.

In this manner, the Christian regards the peaceable reign of God as the hidden meaning of all movements for liberation and reconciliation, the hidden meaning that "brings us together for these days as strangers and yet as friends" (as the theologian Karl Barth wrote in 1919).[6] We should not collapse the kingdom into the church, nor should we diminish the full energy of the church to radiate outward into a gathering more inclusive than the confessing body. As we have observed throughout the pages of this book, beloved community is a way of talking about the redemptive and reconciling spaces whose real history is the church but which cannot be contained by the church or brought fully under its management. Beloved community overflows the boundaries of the church in a way analogous to St. Augustine's description of the divine love overflowing the triune God in the creation of the world. The logic of the church (as one might say), like that of the beloved community, moves always and everywhere beyond itself toward the peaceable reign of God on earth.[7] For this reason, we should also note that the Christian church has no monopoly on affirmations of the human; that movements, agencies, and persons outside the church often understand and appreciate affirmations of human dignity with greater attention to the detail and scope of their application in the world. (Who could doubt, for example, that Amnesty International operates with greater attention to human suffering than the

Foreign Mission Board of the Southern Baptist Convention, which regards its mission as the saving of lost souls from eternal damnation?)

Importantly, the theologian Dietrich Bonhoeffer pondered this matter of Christians and "good people" in his late meditations on justice. Bonhoeffer, a Lutheran pastor and dissident, had joined an organization in the German resistance called the *Abwehr*, and his writing, ponderous now in its intent, strains toward exceedingly difficult theological notions in a fragmented and unfinished beauty. For Bonhoeffer, those who come to the work of mercy and justice from places outside the church are drawn by a power that the church most eloquently bespeaks. The "children" of the church, who have left the church for reasons that are not only understandable but sometimes noble, and who have gone their own way in the world, return to their mother.[8] They do not return to their mother out of guilt or weakness, or out of an anxious realization that they could not make it on their own; whatever need they feel is based on shared concern for humanity. "During the time of their estrangement their appearance and their language had altered a great deal, and yet at the crucial moment the mother and the children once again recognized one another," Bonhoeffer writes. "Reason, justice, culture, humanity and all the kindred concepts sought and found a new purpose and a new power in their origin."[9]

The church should not be envious of her children, but should listen to them and should learn lessons as they catch a glimpse of a better future under a different banner than Christ. Indeed Christians should receive the discovery with humility and with gratitude for the opportunity to participate in a common human struggle for a just world; the church's recognition of "good people" should rather chasten Christian ambitions to impose the church's language on every human conflict. It is also true that the children may sometimes remind the church that its vision of shalom, unilaterally realized in the historical world, concludes in narcissistic renderings of its own will.[10] Still, as Bonhoeffer explains, everything that moves forward toward the overcoming of division and hostility moves at the same time backward to the reconciliation of all reality in Jesus Christ. In each and every case, resisting the powers of disintegration and division requires seeing the world in clearer perspective. The real history of the world is not defined by the macho clanking of the war machine; the real history is illuminated in the beloved community of God. Therefore, the story of the beloved community shows us the way in which the defenders of such endangered values as tolerance, reason, humanity, generosity, and justice enter into alliance and comradeship with Christians.

The church should then welcome its children home, as well as all those who come to the work of mercy and justice out of different faiths and convictions (and thus do not need to be called the children of the church), those who tend the fallow soil of earth and build hope for the future. The church should welcome its children and its partners with open arms. As Clarence Jordan once said in a speech weeks before his death, "It is not for the church to select the friends of her husband, Jesus Christ."[11] Certainly the church can use all the help it can get. "Our Christian calling does not make us superior to other men," wrote Thomas Merton, nor does it "entitle us to judge everyone and decide everything for everybody. We do not have the answers to every social problem, and all conflicts have not been decided beforehand in favor of our side. Our job is to struggle along with everybody else and collaborate with them in the difficult, frustrating task of seeking a solution to common problems, which are entirely new and strange to us all." [12]

Still, for all the remarkable discoveries gained from their sojourns in the world, the children must not be alarmed to learn that the mother knows their names. The mother knows them in ways they do not know themselves— the way a loving mother knows a child. The children must reckon with the theological conclusion that all who suffer for a just cause, all who risk peace and the preferential option for nonviolence, belong to the kingdom of God. "The operations of God's life-giving and life-affirming Spirit are universal," the theologian Jürgen Moltmann wrote in his luminous book, *The Spirit of Life: A Universal Affirmation*, "and can be recognized in everything which ministers to life and resists its destruction."[13]

Therefore, as Christians build beloved communities in, through, and outside the church, they must remain humbled by the camaraderie of unbelievers and non-Christians, grateful for their passion, and inspired (if not intrigued) by their pilgrimages in service, even as Christians continue to proclaim exuberantly the story of Jesus as the source of their own compassion and mercy. Christians must never cease preaching the good news of Jesus Christ as the source of compassion and mercy, and they must not be reluctant to explain their solidarity with the poor and the downtrodden as the story of the word made flesh. And while not all of us will be called to live in the Oak Park housing projects of Oakland, or in Baltimore's Sandtown, or in an intentional interracial community in a Mississippi barrio, we must confess that our faith begins and ends in places of exclusion and struggle. Our sojourn into a violent and hurting world is shaped by the memory of the Christ who was born in a stable because there was no room for him at the inn.

So we must acknowledge as Christians that the beloved community owes its energies and its convictions to the church, even when the beloved community learns and speaks others' languages and even when it turns its back on the church (in situations of historical necessity, personal hurt, or simple arrogance). The point bears repeating that the inner history of the church, like that of the beloved community, moves always and everywhere toward the peaceable reign of God on earth.

It is in this framework that Victoria Gray Adams once described the civil rights movement as "the journey toward the establishment of the Kingdom of God." The theological genius of the movement was its ability to ground the pursuit of beloved community in a bold and exuberant theology of reconciliation. "That's how I understand it now and that's how I understood it then," Gray said.

> We were seed people; no matter how bleak the terrain looked out there, we were planted for a rich harvest. And it was the church houses themselves out of which we had to move; these were the center of our lives. We didn't have much of anything really except the church, and as we put our faith in these, they were burned down. But the church was there for us; the church as the representation of the spirit of love—of God. We were a seed people and a spirit-people; I don't care whether you call yourself a Christian, Jew or Muslim. What happened back there in the 1960's with ordinary people could not have happened without an understanding of ourselves as spirit-people.[14]

The kingdom grounds, frames, and surrounds the pursuit of beloved community, gives it permanence in eternity that it never possesses in time (although for the time it remains visible, it opens onto eternity), gives it a memory that sharpens focus, inspires action, and sustains hope. For the kingdom of God originates in God's revolution, which is movement in the most basic sense: God's own inner and eternal movement, the trinitarian movement that precedes and cuts through all human movements as their hidden history and momentum, the creative origin of all human movements toward human liberation and flourishing.

We hope then for the redemption of the world, which we can hardly believe to be true. Our hope is pure miracle and gift, and we tend it with the discipline of one who would turn dry soil into an abundant garden. The Christian philosopher Søren Kierkegaard thought of faith as the most difficult artwork, and yet the most exquisite. The hope that reaches to us from the future is the future of our redemption, "a new heaven and a new earth" (Revelation 21:1). The hope that we must nurture is the hope that all will be made whole in the history of redemption and that together we will join hands and learn to live in the sobering light of God's promises. It may seem miraculous (to the Christian) that others come to the work of justice and mercy under other names than Jesus Christ; but that is no less a miracle than redemption itself. Truly the scandal of the cross is not that some may be saved from perishing, but that all have been redeemed.[15]

"There is nothing in all the world greater than freedom," said Dr. King.[16] Yet freedom is a light whose source is God. It illuminates not by covering over, like the hideous fluorescence of totalitarian space; freedom's light breaks pale over creation like the flickering of morning stars, like daybreak. The light of God is shattering and splintered. Christians dare not obscure the enveloping light, wherever freedom breaks in, by insisting that it is really darkness that we seek, shadow regions of piety covering telluric passion like camouflage for craven souls. The light of God illuminates the unjust spaces of the world in photographic clarity even as it reveals the fragility and loveliness of the human being and humanity's longing for beloved community.[17] Certainly the light of God may at times appear like the flash of a legal advocate's camera, illuminating the conditions of migrant workers in a substandard dwelling on a Virginia apple orchard, illuminating new regions of discipleship and responsible action.[18] "You are the light on a hill," Jesus says to his disciples. The disciples are commissioned as illuminations of divine love in a world of unjust ugliness.[19]

"Light is not only a divine gift," writes Mark Gornik, "it is the image that the prophet Isaiah uses to explain the impact of a faithful community in a world where the poor are crushed. . . . The people of God were to be a light among the nations (Isa. 60:1–3), their way of life a centripetal drawing to the peaceable and beautiful city of God (Isa. 2:1–5). But this light is God's glory, refracted through faith as costly discipleship that renounces rivalries and violence while doing what is peaceable and good."[20]

We hope for the sake of the broken world. We hope that the world may be healed and made whole. The hope that reaches to us from the future is a hope born in the past in the event of the cross and resurrection; the triumph of Calvary and the great event of Easter form an arch of renewing freshness from past to present to future and include us in an open and ever-extending circle. The hope born in the past is the promise of the redemption of the world. In the meantime, the Christian's hope, as well as the imaginative stress of envisioning the world made whole, enables moral discipline and discernment. As the young theologian Willis Jenkins writes, "The function of Christian witness is to show the world its perspective in God, and by so doing to bring isolated creatures into communion."[21]

Let us then stand in solidarity with the poor and the excluded, remembering that faith's practices are not intended to expand our pleasure or produce novelty. Behavior pleasing to God makes a simple claim: caring for the lonely and the poor and being a people attentive to "the fatherless and widows in their affliction."[22] Let us throw ourselves into humdrum tasks and the ordinary work of mercy and justice. (Small towns and rural areas are often more intractable to change than cities, but we remember that the story of the beloved community is also a story about the courage of ordinary men and women in inauspicious places.) Let us act boldly against the powers of death that surround us and reclaim from the cult of insipid godliness the courage to offend the pious and the proud. Let gratitude and the humility of participation shape our devotion to life. Let us resolve to make and keep others free, and let us resist the urge to colonize God for our group's needs even as we seek to keep redemptive spaces open. Let us live with passionate worldliness in the brilliant and fleeting time of our mortal life, and let our witness to peace grow out of the convictions of our faith, the audacity of our hope, and the generosity of our love. Let us never forget that the community of Christ exists as a structure with four sides open to the world.[23]

If Christians live according to these convictions, they will live in a manner more romantic than the romanticists and more humanist than the humanists, for they will see and feel the holy in the commonplace and in the wretched place alike.[24] The kingdom of God may be peculiar to itself, "in its promise as well as its revelation," though without doubt it does not and should not remain peculiar to itself: Christians must demonstrate the kingdom's central theme—"God is with us!"—in concrete acts of "being there" for others. Indeed, what Christians find in the nature of the triune God is that God as Father, Son, and Holy Spirit is a being for and with the other. If Christians live according to these truths and convictions, they will also and most certainly act out of a vivid sense of gratitude to God. Gotthold Lessing once remarked that the grateful thought raised to God is the perfect prayer. Gratitude lifts us out of our natural instinct to find fault and to belittle others. Gratitude is more than thanks to God for the good things. Gratitude reshapes the self in its relations to others by releasing the other from our compulsions of truth. A Christian community should be a body of people "with gratitude to spare," as theologian Lesslie Newbigin writes, and this gratitude should spill over the theological and social boundaries of the church into care and compassion for the neighbor, and as a care and compassion that frees rather colonizes the other.[25]

Therefore we should pray for the wisdom to discern when our inaction serves humanity better than our action. Do Christians in North America really believe that the world is God's creation, and that reconciliation and redemption are his work to accomplish? Then let us have the courage and the humility to recognize that God is most certainly tired of all our vanity and our talk. "God will surely not be embarrassed if you do not blow your trumpet," wrote the nineteenth-century peacemaker Christoph Blumhardt. "He has trumpets, too."[26] Ours is nation that could use a lesson in stillness. [27]

We are finally concerned with the idea of the movement itself, which on one hand appears as a synchronicity of a million unpredictable forces forming themselves against a long-endured humiliation, but which suddenly—or perhaps over difficult periods of struggle and longing—creates new spaces of freedom and growth. We are not only talking about Montgomery, Americus, and Jackson but about Barmen, Warsaw, Johannesburg, and Tiananmen Square, indeed about "the world of God breaking through from its self-contained holiness and appearing in secular life," in Barth's words.[28] We must learn how to perceive the living God who is building a new world in unexpected places and shapes; indeed, we must learn what it means to enter the new world of God. In short, we must relearn the meaning of being a Christian. For if Jesus Christ is Lord of the church and over all creation, powers, and principalities, as Christians believe, then our first order of business must be to learn again how to participate in that gift. This means too that the world would surely be more humane if we were to understand our role as participatory rather than manipulative.[29] But let us not for a moment conceal from ourselves the fact that obedience to this vision—our actual acceptance of what the Bible proposes: "Come to me all you who are weary and burdened, and I will give you rest"—is a step into space, "an undertaking of unknown consequences, a venture into eternity."[30] Christian discipleship leads one into the most passionate worldliness and the experience of life's polyphony, its beauty, anguish and complexity.

Therefore, the secularist criticism of the Christian faith as racially and culturally privileged needs serious revision. When one steps into the church, even into the most racially homogenous congregation, one steps into a transglobal association of astonishing diversity, into the deepest interracialism. One might be correct to complain of a privileged congregation that it too much reflects its social location; but that same congregation ministers to the lonely, to the depressed, and to the bereaved, even as it quietly reevaluates its mission to the world, often increasing its financial gifts to antipoverty work at home and abroad in response to testimonials and sermons. The Sunday morning rituals of Starbucks and the reading of the *New York Times* still have no offering for the poor. Of course, there are congregations filled with racists and scoundrels, but imagine how sorry these folk would be if instead of rolling their eyes over the Sermon on the Mount and singing "Amazing Grace," they stayed home and watched Bruce Willis movies. There are a million good reasons not to go to church, and yet let us be clear on one thing: Eleven o'clock Sunday may be the most segregated hour of the week as far as any particular parish goes, but it is the most integrated hour of the week as far as the kingdom goes.[31] In church we are taken up, perhaps even against our will, into a fellowship of astonishing variety and difference. In church, we are taken into "Christ-time," as SNCC's Charles Sherrod nicely put it, and given the hope that our fragile and infrequent experiences of reconciliation will one day become an eternal feast.[32]

So go ahead, join the Eucharistic feast of God. Go to church. Preferably one where you're not being told you're going to hell—even if you deserve it—and preferably one that doesn't sing the national anthem at the offertory or demonize Palestinians in a premillennialist sweep. Go to church where God is celebrated as the creator and lord of life, where the good news of God's overflowing love permeates the congregation's understanding of itself and the world. It does not matter whether the preacher is a liberal or an evangelical, a Protestant or a Catholic, an orator or a rock-and-roller, educated or uneducated, as a long as the hearts and minds are opened to the peace that passes all understanding. Go to church and let the beloved world of God slowly transform your life in compassion, mercy, and grace.

There is a resurgence of moral energy in many of the universities of North America most often fueled by religious conviction and inspired by the social movements of the past. A new generation of Christian student leaders and activists gives us reason to hope that better days lie ahead: young men and women who spend spring breaks building houses in rural and urban areas, organize on behalf of undocumented workers and single mothers and abused children, form interracial prayer groups and freedom rides, develop networks of caring and compassion, cook meals in hospitality houses, devote their Saturdays to block parties in poor neighborhoods, and campaign on behalf of HIV/AIDS sufferers in the United States and abroad. May they never relinquish responsibility for the future to the men in high places who presume that the paradigm of war is the only way to peace, or at least to the prosperity they crave. And may we all be inspired by the story of the beloved community to long for a better country, and may we dare to dream again.

Acknowledgments

It occurred to me several years ago that if you are a southerner, white, and Christian—and I am all of those—you owe the credibility of your faith to the courage and conviction of your black brothers and sisters. Without their witness, your own religious claims ring hollow; without their sacrifices, your piety becomes self-referential and shrill; and without their devotion, your pursuit of holiness lacks the scrutiny of historical contrast that prepares the way for repentance and revival. The power, authenticity, and sacrificial spirit of the African American Christian witness energizes your own words and actions in ways you may not understand, but should. So while it has often been said that white southerners stole reconstruction and gave the Negro Jesus; the Negro took that Jesus and gave it flesh and blood. This book emerges as an expression of gratitude for the courage and conviction of black church people in the South and should be read first and foremost as an exercise in Christian apologetics, an apologetics of lived experience, cast in historical narrative.

As the director of the Project on Lived Theology at the University of Virginia, it has been my privilege to work alongside a talented and inspiring group of theologians, scholars, activists, and religious leaders. This book is very much the product of the conversations and pedagogical innovations generated in these extraordinary exchanges of scholar and practitioner, and I am grateful to those who have contributed to the work: Mark Gornik, Omar McRoberts, Victor Anderson, Susan Glisson, Ellen Armour, Wallace Best, Stephen Ray, John Milbank, Heather Warren, Stephen Fowl, Grace Elizabeth Hale, Shawn Copeland, Barbara Holmes, Amy Laura Hall, Luis Pedraja, Christine Pohl, Houston Roberson, Ted Ownby, Tracy K'Meyer, Michael Cartwright, J. Cameron Carter, Mary McClintock Fulkerson, Lauren Winner, Don Davis, Gerald Schlabach, Ralph Luker, Timothy

Tseng, Manual Vasquez, Sondra Wheeler, Eugene McCarraher, John Kiess, Bruce and Gardenia Beard, Laura Brown, Nicole Hurd, George Telford, Brian vander Wel, Richard Wills, and Barbara Skinner. Chris Coble and Craig Dykstra of the religion division at the Lilly Endowment not only have made possible the financial support without which the Project on Lived Theology would not exist but also have helped shape the intellectual mission of this venture, illuminating productive avenues of inquiry and collaboration as well as keeping the programs grounded in social and congregational life. Working alongside these two theological visionaries has been the most rewarding experience of my professional life. Many other scholars who care deeply about the social integrity of their research and writing entered into conversations with me at various points, and in turn gave shape and substance to the work: Cheryl Sanders, Stanley Hauerwas, James Cone, Charles Reagon Wilson, Merald Watkins, Miroslav Volf, Linda Thomas, Larry Rasmussen, Keith Miller, Kelton Cobb, Thomas Slater, Daniel Smith, Robert Coles, Jung Ha Kim, John de Gruchy, and Taylor Branch.

This book could not have been written without the generous cooperation of numerous civil rights veterans and contemporary community builders who took the time to share their theological worldviews and their obser- vations on social justice and organizing. The names of these remarkable individuals appear throughout the book, but I would like to offer special thanks to Ed King, Victoria Gray Adams, Will Campbell, Bob Zellner, John Perkins, Lawrence Guyot, John Lewis, Duncan Gray Jr., Cleveland Sellers, Bob Moses, Laverne Stokes, Amy Sherman, Rydell Payne, Lee Stuart, Russell Jeung, Alicia Paul, Ray Rivera, Gene Rivers, Dolphus Weary, Reggie and Anna Robbins, Chris Rice, Spencer Perkins, Joe Szakos, Matthew Daloisio, and Amanda Walker.

In addition to all those who granted interviews and corresponded with me, thanks are due also to the archivists and librarians at the Martin Luther King Jr. Library and Archives; the Morland Springarn Research Center at Howard University; the Historical Commission of the Southern Baptist Convention; the McCain Library and Archives at the University of South- ern Mississippi; the Mississippi State Department of Archives and History; the Alabama Department of Archives and History; the State Historical So- ciety of Wisconsin; the Library of Congress; the Hargrett Rare Book and Manuscript Library, University of Georgia Libraries; the Alderman Library and Special Collections of the University of Virginia; the Southern Histor- ical Collection at the University of North Carolina at Chapel Hill; the Karl Barth Research Center at Princeton Theological Seminary; the Union Theological Seminary Library in New York; and the Billy Graham Center

Archives at Wheaton College. Thanks as well to Faith Fuller, producer and writer of the wonderful documentary film *Briars in the Cottonpatch*, who helped locate Koinonia photographs at the Habitat for Humanity International headquarters in Americus, Georgia. I am especially honored to have the photography of Danny Lyon, Burt Glinn, Herbert Randell, Flip Schulke, and Sylvester Jacobs grace the middle pages of this book. Sylvester Jacob's beautiful collection, *Portrait of a Shelter*, as well as a conversation with him many years ago in Huemoz, Switzerland, formed my first impressions of beloved community and remain to this day the most decisive.

I would also like to thank those institutions and individuals who invited me to present sections of the research: Dan Capper at the University of Southern Mississippi; Charles Wilson at the University of Mississippi; Christopher Edley, Gary Orfield, and Holly Lebowitz at the Civil Rights Project at Harvard University; the Society of Ethical Culture in New York City; Dan Mathews at Trinity Church, Wall Street; Van Gardiner at the Cathedral of the Incarnation in Baltimore; the Parrish Lectures at Baylor University; the Leadership Lecture Series at Mississippi College; the Nachbar Lecture at Loyola College in Baltimore; the African American Clergy Group of Memphis; Samy Naguib at the Summerhill Summit on Racial Reconciliation in Atlanta; Scott Stearman at the International Church of Paris; Kristine Lalonde at Randolph-Macon Women's College; David Weaver-Zercher at the Messiah College Conference on Spirituality and Social Justice, and the late Catherine Clarkson, Director of the Center on Religious Freedom at Virginia Wesleyan College. I wish to extend my heartfelt appreciation to Gilbert Fenwick, whose probing meditations on salvation and sanctification during my seminars at the Maryland State House of Corrections illuminated the depth and promise of the Christian doctrine of reconciliation in unforgettable and vivid ways. May Mr. Fenwick somehow find the mercy he deserves in the merciless world of the American penal system.

Alan Jacobs, Jennifer Seidel, Ted Ownby, Lauren Winner, Mark Gornik, and Karen Wright Marsh made detailed comments on the entire manuscript and vastly improved the book as a result; and for their generosity, insights, and helpful criticisms I am deeply grateful. I owe hearty thanks to my tenacious research assistants, not only for taking care of many tedious tasks but even more for their energy and inspiration: Peter Slade, Jennifer McBride, Katie Kennedy Whitworth, and Sarah Azaransky. My fellow travelers in Theological Horizons supported my research and writing in a variety of tangible ways and kept the lines of encouragement open. My parents, Bob and Myra Marsh, remain dear friends and a wellspring of kindness and unfailing support. I thank my agent, Carol Mann, for believing in the manuscript and working her magic in its behalf and for having the good sense never to take my self-pity too seriously. In Chip Rossetti at Basic Books, I found a wonderful editor whose intelligence, perspicuity, and friendliness were central in bringing the manuscript to life. Liz Maguire, the publisher of Basic Books and Counterpoint, offered encouragement and helpful advice at several crucial stages of the writing. I also wish to thank Joe Bonyata, the editorial production director at the Perseus Books Group for the kindness and patience with which he has helped move the manuscript through the various stages of production.

My colleagues in the Department of Religious Studies make the University of Virginia a rewarding and enjoyable place to work and teach, and I am grateful for their kindness and inspiration. My department chair, Harry Gamble, has supported my research and the work of the Project on Lived Theology, as has Ed Ayers, Dean of the College of Arts and Sciences, whose commitment to the moral integrity of intellectual life is reflected in his academic leadership and vocation as a scholar.

My love and respect for my wife, Karen Wright Marsh, are difficult to express adequately here and are perhaps better rendered in the flow of family and abiding romance. Still, I wish to remind her in writing of a simple fact spoken too rarely, that her passion for life and our journey together are my greatest inspiration. Our children, Henry, Will, and Nan, shared in the adventure of the book, asking questions about the characters and events and offering their judgments on religion, race, and politics in conversations around the kitchen table or beside the woodstove. I have long promised myself that I will never become the scholar whose children know him only as the strange man thumping around the basement office; and I happily accept all the rough edges of my professional life in exchange for wholehearted investment in my children's well-being.

Finally, this book is dedicated to my students, so many of whom hear the story of the beloved community and resolve to live according to a different standard than materialistic culture, who not only imagine a better world but take their astonishing gifts and talents to the difficult work of restoring hope in distressed places. Their moral and spiritual energy is a gift to us all as we face the uncertain years ahead.

Notes

INTRODUCTION

1. Martin Luther King Jr., *The Papers of Martin Luther King Jr.*, vol. 3, ed. Stewart Burns, Susan Carson, Peter Holloran, and Dana L. H. Powell (Berkeley: University of California Press, 1996), p. 452.

2. King, *The Papers*, vol. 3, p. 136.

3. Rowan Williams, *On Christian Theology* (Oxford: Blackwell Publishers, 2000), p. 286.

4. Thomas Merton, *Faith and Violence* (South Bend: University of Notre Dame Press, 1968), p. 131.

5. Martin Luther King Jr., "An Experiment in Love," in *A Testament of Hope: The Essential Writings of Martin Luther King Jr.*, edited by James M. Washington (San Francisco: HarperCollins Paperback, 1986), p. 20.

6. The preachers and televangelists who spread the American civil religion, despite their claims to the Bible's inerrancy, always seem to demur on the literal truth of Jesus's message, that a peaceable kingdom has entered into time and history in the "great epic" of the cross and resurrection and that Christians are called to inhabit it.

7. "Handbill, Albany Nonviolent Movement," *Debating the Civil Rights Movement, 1945–1968*, edited by Steven F. Lawson and Charles Payne (Lanham, Maryland: Rowman & Littlefield, 1998), p. 141.

8. Ibid.

9. "The Student Nonviolent Coordinating Committee (as revised in conference, April 29, 1962)," The Charles Sherrod Papers, file 24, State Historical Society of Wisconsin.

10. Ibid. John Lewis, SNCC's chairman in 1965, illustrated the spiritual link between the two generations in describing the sources of his own activism: "So many black church ministers talked about the way over yonder and the afterlife. But when I heard Dr. King preaching on the radio one Sunday afternoon, I was amazed that he did not talk about the pearly gates and the streets paved with gold. He was concerned about the streets of Montgomery, the highways and byways of America" (John Lewis, interview by the author).

11. Ibid.

12. John Lewis, correspondence, March 1964, SNCC Papers.

13. Os Guinness, *Dust of Death: A Critique of the Counter Culture* (Downers Grove, Illinois: Intervarsity Press, 1976).

14. In his review of Howard Zinn's book for the journal *Studies on the Left*, Tom Hayden described the "source of SNCC's special character" as "its origins in the experience of Negro oppression." Movement organizers derived their strength and vision from places far removed from "urban industrial society," indeed, from places where southern blacks had learned not only to bear but to interpret their suffering and to hope for a better future. "The movement takes root in places which testify tragically to the flaws of American morality and promise," Hayden writes. Hayden did not mention the black church, but he should have, for it was the church's realism about human limitation and sinfulness that chastened utopianism even as it tempered pessimism by its affirmation of the Spirit's deep workings in social struggle. "The honesty, insight and leadership of rural Negroes demonstrate to the students that their upbringing has been based on a framework of lies." Those lies would no doubt include a failure to understand the movement's "origins" and "disciplines" as well as an exaggeration of the importance of white radicals. The civil rights movement had "turned itself into the revolution we hoped for," said Zinn wisely, "and we didn't have much to do with its turning at all."

15. Claybourne Carson, *In Struggle: SNCC and the Black Awakening of the 1960s* (Cambridge: Harvard University Press, 1981), p. 305.

16. Stephen Carter writes that belief in God "matters to the community of resistance because people behave differently if they believe God to be before them and within them and around them. That idea of behaving differently is one of the gifts that the church must spread. We must spread it because we cannot wait a hundred years for the next great upsurge of activity or the next great radical transformation of society. . . . I am thinking of genuine sacrifice, about letting something be at stake." [Stephen L. Carter, "The Freedom to Persist," *Christianity Today*, June 12, 2000, vol. 44, no. 7, p. 58.]

17. Nonetheless, religion's social utility is no insignificant matter. As Father Andrew Greely has noted, "Frequency of church attendance and membership in church organizations correlate strongly with voluntary service. People who attend services once a week or more are approximately twice as likely to volunteer as those who attend rarely if ever." Even a third of persons who volunteer for specifically secular activities also relate their service "to the influence of a relationship based in their religion." Andrew Greely, "The Other Civic America: Religion and Social Capital," *American Prospect*, May–June 1997, pp. 70, 72. Or, as George Gallup Jr. has observed, "churches and other religious bodies are the major supporters of voluntary services for neighborhoods and communities. Members of a church or synagogue tend to be much more involved in charitable activity, particularly through organized groups." Gallup, "Religion in America," op. cit., p. 2." [Diiulio]. John Diiulio and Ram. A. Cnaan's research is the touchstone for assessments of the civic value of faith in the North American context. Diiulio states "For example, based on 3-hour site visits and 20-page questionnaires covering some 215 different social services administered at 401 of Philadelphia's roughly 2,000 community-serving congregations (on the way to a complete census of congregation services), Professor Cnaan and his associates report that over 90 percent of urban congregations provide social services, from preschools to prison ministries, from food

pantries to health clinics, from literacy programs to day-care centers, and so much more; the replacement value of their services in Philadelphia alone is a very conservatively estimated quarter-billion dollars a year; their primary beneficiaries are poor neighborhood children and youth who are not members, and whose families are not members, of the congregations that serve them; urban community-serving congregations are actually slightly more likely to partner with secular nonprofits than they are to collaborate with each other; and almost none of the urban community-serving ministries make entering their buildings, receiving their services, or participating in their programs in any way contingent upon any immediate or eventual profession of faith, or any performance of religious rites or rituals, of any kind." John Diiulio, "Compassion in Truth and Action: How Sacred and Secular Places Serve Civic Purposes and What Washington Should—and Should Not—Do to Help," speech before the National Association of Evangelicals, March 7, 2001. See also Ram A. Cnaan and Gaynor I. Yancey, "Our Hidden Safety Net," in E. J. Dionne and John J. Dilulio Jr., eds., *What's God Got to Do with the American Experiment?* (Washington, D.C.: Brookings Institution, 2000), chap. 21; Ram A. Cnaan et al., *The Newer Deal: Social Work and Religion in Partnership* (New York: Columbia University Press, 1999); and Cnaan, *Keeping Faith in the City: How 401 Religious Congregations Serve Their Neediest Neighbors*, Center for Research on Religion and Urban Civil Society, CRRUCS Report 2000–1. University of Pennsylvania, Philadelphia, PA, March 20, 2000.

18. Strange things happen when a generation abandons particularity for perpetual freedom, concern for concrete social reform for cosmic realignment, community building for coalition building, the transformation of the self for the emancipation from self. It may be too much for conservative critics to blame the sixties celebration of relevance and pluralism, its subordination of scholarship to the struggle for justice, as well other maladies of the counterculture, for corrupting true learning and for unraveling the "moral bonds holding society together." Nonetheless, a student revolution that began in the South as an affirmation of national unity, religious community, the integrity of family, and common human flourishing concluded with its repudiation of these very attachments. As a mood of interior skepticism combined with the celebration of different cultures—with difference itself a virtue—the university curriculum (that is to say, the humanities) became defined by a continual straining for a universal authenticity bracingly unforgiving of all those sinful habits which Americans had confessed throughout the decade. Afloat "on a sea of boundless subjectivity," the cultural left embraced the plight of women, minorities, the Third World, and the impoverished masses as one might embrace the esoteric rituals of an exclusive cult: the left delivered judgment without the possibility of repentance. See Benjamin R. Barber, *A Passion for Democracy: American Essays* (Princeton: Princeton University Press, 1998).

19. The phrase is Dietrich Bonhoeffer's from *Letters and Papers from Prison*; it was used to describe the passionate this-worldliness of genuine Christian faith.

20. Clayborne Carson, "Martin Luther King, Jr., and the African-American Social Gospel." In *African-American Christianity*, edited by Paul E. Johnson, 159–177. (Berkeley: University of California Press, 1994. Reprinted *African-American Religion: Interpretive Essays in History and Culture*, ed. by Tomothy E. Fulop and Albert J. Raboteau. New York: Routledge, 1997), p. 162.

21. Merton writes, "The American racial crisis which grows more serious every day offers the American Christian a chance to face reality about himself and recover his fi-

delity to Christian truth, not merely in institutional loyalties and doctrinal orthodoxies (in which no one has taken the trouble to accuse him of failing) but in recanting a more basic heresy: the loss of that Christian sense which sees every other man as Christ and treats him as Christ." *Faith and Violence*, p. 143.

22. Ibid.

23. A black Presbyterian minister and activist gave eloquent expression to this point in a 1963 letter. The church has been "silent too frequently," wrote Eddie Hawkins, "and even when it has spoken, it has not used its own distinctive language to stress . . . the moral dimension of the issue." Cited in James Findlay, *Church People in the Struggle* (New York: Oxford University Press, 1993), p. 76.

CHAPTER 1

1. "Recommendations to the Dexter Avenue Baptist Church," in Martin Luther King Jr., *The Papers of Martin Luther King Jr.*, vol. 2, *Rediscovering Precious Values, July 1951–November 1955*, edited by Clayborne Carson, Ralph E. Luker, Penny A. Russell, and Peter Holloran (Berkeley: University of California Press, 1994), p. 294.

2. As Richard Lischer explains, the sermon more closely approximates the classic sermon, "The Symmetry of Life," which was preached by the nineteenth century Episcopal bishop, Phillips Brooks. Brooks says, "There are, then, three directions or dimensions of human life to which we may fitly give these three names, Length and Breadth and Height. The Length of a life, in this meaning of it, is, of course, not its duration. It is rather the reaching on and out of a man, in the line of activity and thought and self-development . . . It is the push of a life forward to its own personal ends and ambitions." Quoted in Richard Lischer, *The Preacher King: Martin Luther King Jr. and the Word That Moved America* (New York: Oxford University Press, 1995), p. 97.

3. Martin Luther King Jr., "The Three Dimensions of a Complete Life," sermon delivered on January 24, 1954, although the published text is based on King's April 9, 1967, version. See *A Knock at Midnight*, ed. Clayborne Carson and Peter Halloran (New York: IPM/Warner Books, 1998).

4. Lischer, *The Preacher King*.

5. Houston Bryan Robertson, "Fighting the Good Fight: A History of Dexter Avenue King Memorial Baptist Church, 1865–1977" (unpublished dissertation, University of North Carolina, 1997), p. 8.

6. Quoted in Robertson, "Fighting the Good Fight," p. 6.

7. Quoted in Zelia S. Evans with J. T. Alexander, *The Dexter Avenue Baptist Church, 1877–1977* (Montgomery: Dexter Avenue Baptist Church, 1978), p. 14.

8. Robertson, "Fighting the Good Fight," p. 13.

9. Clayborne Carson, "Introduction," in King, *The Papers*, vol. 2, p. 28.

10. Ibid., p. 29.

11. Coretta Scott King, *My Life with Martin Luther King Jr.* (New York: Holt, Rinehart and Winston,1969), p. 39.

12. Joseph C. Parker Sr. to King," in King, *The Papers*, vol. 2, p. 257.

13. Ibid., p. 258.

14. J. David Garrow, *Bearing the Cross: Martin Luther King Jr., and the Southern Christian Leadership Conference* (New York: Vintage, 1988), p. 48.

15. J. Pius Barbour to King, in King, *The Papers*, vol. 2, p. 565.

16. Ibid., p. 33.

17. King, *The Papers*, vol. 2, p. 260.

18. Quoted in Taylor Branch, *Parting the Waters: America in the King Years, 1954–1963* (New York: Simon and Schuster, 1988), p. 112. When King asked the pulpit committee about the size and quality of the membership, Robert Nesbitt was quick to reply, "About two-thirds of the Alabama State College faculty attends church at Dexter. There are many other professional persons in the congregation. The principal of one of the largest schools also worships at Dexter." Quoted in Wally G. Vaughn and Richard W. Wills, eds., *Reflections on Our Pastor* (Dover, MA: The Majority Press, 1999), p. 4.

19. J. Mills Thornton III, *Touched by History: A Civil Rights Tour Guide to Montgomery, Alabama* (no publication record), p. 5.

20. "Recommendations to the Dexter Avenue Baptist Church," in King, *The Papers*, vol. 2, p. 291. "The committee shall keep before the congregation the importance of the N.A.A.C.P. The membership should unite with this great organization in a solid block. This committee shall also keep before the congregation the necessity of being registered voters. Every member of Dexter must be a registered voter." In *Stride Toward Freedom*, King wrote of his interest in the committee, presenting himself as a kind of preacher-activist who hit the ground running. He said, "As an expression of my concern with such problems as these [discriminatory voter registration practices], one of the first committees that I set up in my church was designed to keep the congregation intelligently informed" (San Francisco: Harper & Row, 1983), p. 30.

21. Stephen B. Oates, *Let the Trumpet Sound: The Life of Martin Luther King Jr.* (New York: Harper & Row, 1982), p. 58.

22. Ibid., p. 39.

23. In spring of 1954, the WPC had met twice with Montgomery's city commission and had discussed the complaints of the black community regarding segregated buses. These meetings led to minor changes in bus company policy, namely, that buses stop at every corner in African American neighborhoods. See Aldon D. Morris, *The Origins of the Civil Rights Movement* (New York: Free Press, 1984), p. 53.

24. Jo Ann Robinson, *The Montgomery Bus Boycott and the Women Who Started It: The Memoir of Jo Ann Gibson Robinson* (Knoxville: University of Tennessee Press, 1987).

25. Branch, *Parting the Waters*, p. 93.

26. King, quoted in Garrow, *Bearing the Cross*, p. 46.

27. DeWolf, quoted in Ted Poston, "Fighting Pastor, Martin Luther King," *New York Post*, April 11, 1956.

28. Steven Millner, "The Montgomery Bus Boycott: Case Study in the Emergence and Career of a Social Movement," in Garrow, *The Walking City: The Montgomery Bus Boycott, 1955–1956*, edited by David J. Garrow (Brooklyn, New York: Carlson Publishing, 1989), p. 433.

29. Thornton, *Touched By History*, p. 3.

30. Jack Bass, *Taming the Storm: The Life and Times of Judge Frank M. Johnson Jr., and the South's Fight over Civil Rights* (New York: Doubleday, 1993), p. 98.

31. Quoted in Carl Grafton and Anne Permaloff, *Big Mules and Branch Heads: James E. Folsom and Political Power in Alabama* (Athens: University of Georgia Press, 1985), p. 188–189.

32. Quoted in King, *The Papers*, vol. 2, p. 33.

33. Ralph Luker, interview by the author.

34. Quoted in Robertson, *Fighting the Good Fight*, p. 191.

35. Evans, *The Dexter Avenue Baptist Church*, p. 64.

36. Quoted in Garrow, *Bearing the Cross*, p. 38.

37. Septima Clark, *Ready from Within: A First Person Narrative*, edited with an introduction by Cynthia Stokes Brown (Trenton, NJ: Africa World Press, 1990), pp. 30–34.

38. Morris, *The Origins of the Civil Rights Movement*, p. 51.

39. Quoted in Stewart Burns, ed., *Daybreak of Freedom: The Montgomery Bus Boycott* (Chapel Hill: University of North Carolina Press, 1997), p. 9.

40. Quoted in Garrow, *Bearing the Cross*, p. 14.

41. Ralph David Abernathy, *And the Walls Came Tumbling Down* (New York: Harper & Row, 1989), p. 136.

42. Quoted in Abernathy, *And The Walls Came Tumbling Down*, p. 136.

43. Garrow, *Bearing the Cross*, p. 27.

44. King cited in *Montgomery Advertiser*, December 11, 1955.

45. King, *The Papers*, vol. 2, p. 73.

46. Ibid., p. 75.

47. The phrase is borrowed from the theologian Karl Barth, whose influence on King remains underappreciated.

48. "From that night forward," wrote Richard Lischer, "King and the black church community forged an interpretative partnership in which they read the Bible, recited it, sang it, performed it, Amen-ed it, and otherwise celebrated the birth of Freedom by its sacred light." *The Preacher King*, p. 198. The power resides finally in the meeting, in the way the spiritual energies of the protest are conjured in the space between preacher and congregation.

49. Branch, *Parting the Waters*, p. 142.

50. Donie Jones, quoted in Henry Hampton and Steve Fayer, eds., *Voices of Freedom: An Oral History of the Civil Rights Movement from the 1950s through the 1980s* (New York: Bantam Books, 1990), p. 24.

51. In this manner, King's career stands in continuity with Pauline understanding of apocalyptic struggle. J. Louis Martyn's excellent commentary on Galatians illuminates the cosmic dimensions of St. Paul's perception of Christian witness in the world in a manner familiar to King. "[God's] dispatch of the Spirit of Christ into the believers' hearts turns them all into soldiers active on the Spirit's field of battle. The martial, cosmic dimension of Paul's apocalyptic applies, then, to the church; and for that reason Paul can speak of the church itself both as God's new creation and as the apocalyptic community called to the front trenches in God's apocalyptic war again the powers of the present age. There, and only there, are the churches living in the real world, for it is there that the creation is being made what it now is by God's liberating invasion, an invasion that, in making things right, brings about a fatal separation from—a death to— the old cosmic." *Galatians* (New York: The Anchor Bible, 1997), p. 102.

52. "Letter to the National City Lines, Inc.," in Martin Luther King Jr., *The Papers of Martin Luther King Jr.*, vol. 3, *The Birth of a New Age, December 1955–December 1956*, edited by Stewart Burns, Susan Carson, Peter Holloran, and Dana L. H. Powell (Berkeley: University of California Press, 1996).

53. Quoted in Garrow, *Bearing the Cross*, p. 24.

54. *The Montgomery Advertiser*, December 9, 1955. The *Montgomery Advertiser* reassured white readers, "The Rev. M. L. King Jr. pointed out that his group is not interested in changing present segregation laws but he asked for modifications of practices under the law."

55. *Montgomery Advertiser*, December 9, 1955.

56. Ibid.

57. *Montgomery Advertiser*, December 15, 1955. The same letter offered a glimpse into the posturing of some white customers, which King had either been ignorant of or refrained from exposing. "I have been on many an uncrowded bus and have seen Negroes having to stand when there were open seats because some stupid white has a seat toward the rear of the bus and will not move forward to permit the Negro to sit."

58. Garrow, *Bearing the Cross*, p. 28.

59. *Montgomery Advertiser*, December 12, 1955.

60. Branch, *Parting the Waters*, p. 144.

61. *Montgomery Advertiser*, December 12, 1955.

62. See Abel Plenn, "Report on Montgomery a Year After," *New York Times Magazine*, December 29, 1957, pp. 11, 36–38. "A victim of such persecution was the reference librarian at the Montgomery Public Library, Miss Juliette Morgan—a sensitive, delicate young woman from a fine old Alabama family." Taylor Branch explained in more detail: "Morgan's letter brought down upon her a prolonged harassment by young people who threw rocks through her window, insulted her on the streets, and played tricks on her in the library. Her flighty sensitivity only provoked them to do worse. A little more than a year later, she would be found poisoned in her house, an apparent suicide. By way of explanation, whites would stress her emotional vulnerability or alleged mental problems, while Negroes remained certain that she had been persecuted to death on account of the . . . letter." *Parting the Waters*, p. 144.

63. *Montgomery Advertiser*, December 13, 1955.

64. *The Papers*, vol. 2, p. 150.

65. Reinhold Niebuhr, quoted in *Reinhold Niebuhr: Theologian of Public Life*, ed. Larry Rasmussen (Minneapolis: Fortress Press, 1991), p. 55.

66. Quoted in Garrow, *Bearing the Cross*, p. 43. King had praised Niebuhr for having the presence of mind to see through the naïve optimism of Protestant liberalism, which adhered to an evolutionary model of human progress. "This particular sort of optimism has been discredited by the brutal logic of events," King said in "Contemporary Continental Theology" (The Papers, vol. 2, pp. 113–139). Reinhold Niebuhr on the North American scene and Karl Barth in Europe emerged as the two most vocal critics of Protestant liberal optimism in mid-twentieth century theology, and King appreciated both men's courage to retrieve the doctrine of sin from its psychocultural reductions. Not only had the Christian faith succumbed to the spirit of the age—the exhilarating prospects of unlimited human progress—but it had become condemned to uncritical subservience to the prevailing structures and powers. "Man's inner experience did not provide a firm enough ground for resistance to these phenomena," noted King. Niebuhr argued that the pacifist tradition shares with liberalism a general confidence in the human capacity to transcend self-interest and pride—as well as a peculiar naïveté about the intent and effect of non-violent resistance. Non-violent resistance ultimately cannot live up to its ideals; it cannot yield "perfect proofs of a loving temper" and thus

remains blind to its own aggressive impulses and inherently violent social affects. Coercive force must remain a part of the strategic arsenal of justice. Niebuhr, *Theologian of Public Life*, p. 65.

67. Clayborne Carson, "The Boycott that Changed Dr. King's Life," *New York Times Magazine*, January 7, 1996. The Fellowship of Reconciliation, or FOR, was the Christian pacifist organization founded in the United States during World War I. Glenn Smiley, who had been imprisoned in 1944 as a conscientious objector, wrote in his "Report from the South" in winter 1956: "[The Fellowship of Reconciliation] should step up its participation in the race struggle in the South, as non violence is the essential element if social change to be brought about without widespread resentment. The Fellowship of Reconciliation should also encourage interracial prayer meetings and discussion groups in the South." Smiley continued, "This seems like a small item but since in many tension areas there is no contact between white and colored citizens on a prayer or discussion level, it might be a means of breaking up the log jam." Glenn Smiley, "Report from the South," Martin Luther King Jr. Papers, Boston University.

68. King, *Stride Toward Freedom*, pp. 121–22.

69. Quoted in King, *The Papers*, vol. 3, p. 181.

70. Branch, *Parting the Waters*, p. 155.

71. Carl Rowan, *Breaking Barriers* (New York: Little, Brown and Company, 1991), p. 140.

72. King, *Stride Toward Freedom*, p. 126.

73. Branch, *Parting the Waters*, p. 156.

74. L. D. Reddick, "The Bus Boycott in Montgomery," in Garrow, *The Walking City*, p. 77.

75. Reddick, "The Bus Boycott in Montgomery," p. 77.

76. Quoted in Gilliam, "The Montgomery Bus Boycott of 1955–1956" in *The Walking City*, edited by David J. Garrow, p. 258.

77. Branch, *Parting the Waters*, p. 157.

78. Quoted in Garrow, *Bearing the Cross*, p. 55.

79. Ibid., p. 157.

80. Stewart Burns, *Daybreak of Freedom: The Montgomery Bus Boycott*, edited by Stewart Burns (Chapel Hill: University of North Carolina Press, 1997), p. 2.

81. *Montgomery Advertiser*, cited in Robert Graetz, *A White Preacher's Memoir: The Montgomery Bus Boycott* (Montgomery: Black Belt Press, 1998), p. 93.

82. Quoted in Garrow, *Bearing the Cross*, p. 55.

83. Quoted in Bass, *Taming the Storm*, p. 103.

84. Garrow, *Bearing the Cross*, p. 55.

85. B. J. Simms, *The Walking Tour*, p. 581.

86. Quoted in Garrow, *Bearing the Cross*, p.55.

87. Quoted in Graetz, *A White Preacher's Memoir*, p. 93.

88. *Montgomery Advertiser*, December 13, 1955.

89. Martin Luther King Jr., *The Autobiography of Martin Luther King Jr.*, ed. Clayborne Carson (New York: Warner Books, 1998), p. 74.

90. Ibid.

91. Quoted in Branch, *Parting the Waters*, pp. 160–161.

92. King, *Autobiography*, p. 76.

93. Ibid., p. 77.

94. Ibid., p. 76.

95. Ibid., p. 77.

96. Quoted in Garrow, *Bearing the Cross*, p. 56.

97. Ibid.

98. King, *Autobiography*, p. 77.

99. Garrow, *Bearing the Cross*, p. 59.

100. Psalms (King James Version).

101. King, *Autobiography*, p. 76.

102. Ibid., p. 77.

103. Ibid.

104. Ibid., p. 78.

105. Ibid.

106. King, "An Autobiography of Religious Development," in *The Papers of Martin Luther King Jr.*, Vol. 1, ed. Clayborne Carson, Ralph E. Luker, and Penny A. Russell (Berkeley: University of California Press, 1992), p. 361.

107. King, *Autobiography*, p. 106.

108. King, "An Autobiography," p. 362.

109. Ibid. See editors' introduction to *The Papers*, vol. 1, for a helpful summary of King's studies at Crozer.

110. Garrow, *Bearing the Cross*, p. 58.

111. Morris, *The Origins of the Civil Rights Movement*, p. 59.

112. As the theologian Lewis Baldwin explained, "The fact that he experienced the 'vision in a kitchen' after his liberal training at Crozer Theological Seminary and Boston University shows that the spiritual resonances of his heritage in the South become eminently more important than his theological education in preparing him to lead his people against the evil forces of racism." Lewis V. Baldwin, *There Is a Balm in Gilead: The Cultural Roots of Martin Luther King Jr.* (Minneapolis: Fortress Press, 1991), p. 189.

113. King, "An Autobiography," p. 364.

114. King, *Autobiography*, p. 15.

115. Quoted in Clayborne Carson, "Martin Luther King Jr., and the African-American Social Gospel Tradition," p. 162.

116. Ibid., p. 161.

117. King, cited in Carson, "African American Social Gospel Tradition," pp. 9, 11. Protestant liberals like Paul Tillich and Henry Nelson Wieman, the subjects of King's doctoral dissertation, recast the traditional doctrine of God to satisfy the cultural, philosophical, and therapeutic needs of Euro-American moderns, deriding, unwittingly but with cynical effect nevertheless, the exquisite mysteries of African American belief. "Both Tillich and Wieman reject the conception of a personal God," King says, "and with this goes a rejection of the rationality, goodness, and love of God in the full sense of the words." Ibid., p. 9.

118. Branch, *Parting the Waters*, p. 162.

119. Ibid.

120. "In the middle of the fire we are healed and restored, though never taken out of it," explains the theologian Rowan Williams in his book, *The Wound of Knowledge: Chris-*

tian Spirituality from the New Testament to St. John of the Cross (Cambridge, MA: Cowley Publications, 1979, p. 182). "To want to escape the 'night' and the costly struggles with doubt and vacuity," says Williams, "is to seek another God from the one who speaks in and as Jesus crucified" (p. 182).

121. Quoted in *The Papers*, vol. 3, p. 130.

122. Quoted in Garrow, *Bearing the Cross*, p. 54.

123. King, *The Papers*, p. 108.

124. "Notes on MIA Mass Meeting at First Baptist Church," in *The Papers*, vol. 3, p. 114.

125. King, *Stride Toward Freedom*, p. 136.

126. King, *Autobiography*, p. 79.

127. Ibid.

128. King, *The Papers*, vol. 3, p. 115.

129. Robinson, *The Montgomery Bus Boycott*, p. 132.

130. King, *Stride Toward Freedom*, p. 138.

131. Mrs. Pinkie S. Franklin, quoted in *The Papers*, vol. 3, p. 116.

132. Marcus Garvey Wood, quoted in *The Papers*, vol. 3, p. 129.

133. King, *The Papers*, vol. 3, p. 136.

134. Quoted in Simms, *The Walking Tour*, p. 580.

135. See Jean Lassere, *The Gospel and War*, trans. Oliver Coburn (Scottsdale, PA: Harold Press, 1962).

136. King, *Stride Toward Freedom*, p. 82.

137. Importantly, historians Charles Payne and Timothy Tyson indicate in their important work that more research needs to be done on the degree to which the black organizing tradition at times depended on "the attitude of local people toward self-defense" as a necessary dimension of its success. Nevertheless, the tradition of nonviolent direct action taught by King reached toward a different moral end. In the story of the civil rights movement, we see something remarkable: that many of the men and women who made up the civil rights movement in the South responded to terrorism by a massive show of nonviolent force. The scholar Aldon Morris writes that "nonviolence was practically unheard-of in Southern black communities before the civil rights movement." King's "commitment" to pacifism was not a commitment to nonviolent non-resistance (as practiced by Mennonites and other members of the historic "peace churches" and recently promoted by the theologian Stanley Hauerwas as the consistent "ethic of the Cross"), but to nonviolent direct action. The strategies and purposes of nonviolent direct action changed in ways appropriate to the social situation at hand, and indeed all were in some way intended to provoke and to unsettle the other. This leaves King open to the Niebuhrian critique (which Clarence Jordan would make from Koinonia Farm) that actions intended to provoke violence, or actions that may provoke violence, cannot themselves be called nonviolent. There is philosophical substance to this critique; still, if we say that turning the other cheek is implicitly violent then all we have really said is that we live in a violent world and that peace will often be met with a sword. In any case, King's commitment to nonviolence was neither dogmatic nor morally innocent; it was shaped in a variety of provocative and strategically shrewd forms. Perhaps it lacked moral purity and consistency. And it remains open to further critical questions; nonetheless, he remained committed to the realization of the "power" of Christian love in lived social

and political existence. And the various ways such love was embodied or enacted in social organizing and (yes) coercive action demonstrate not so much the compromises King was forced to make but the resilience and elasticity of love to transform oppressive structures apart from violent aggression. See also Greg Moses's excellent study of King's philosophy of nonviolence, *Revolution of Conscience: Martin Luther King Jr. and the Philosophy of Nonviolence* (New York: The Guilford Press, 1997).

138. Carol Polsgrove, *Divided Minds: Intellectuals and the Civil Rights Movement* (New York: W. W. Norton, 2001), p. 46.

139. Cited in Polsgrove, *Divided Minds*, p. 43.

140. See Polsgrove's essential chapter "Northern Reservations" in *Divided Minds*, p. 42.

141. Polsgrove, *Divided Minds*, p. 43.

142. Ibid., p. 46.

143. Reinhold Niebuhr cited in Polsgrove, *Divided Minds*, p. 46.

144. Quoted in Polsgrove, *Divided Minds*, p. 47.

145. Ibid., p. 46.

146. King, *The Papers*, vol. 2, pp. 276–277. Post-liberal critics of Reinhold Niebuhr such as Stanley Hauerwas add theological detail to the same point. "Christ was also the symbol of sacrificial love for Niebuhr, but the very language of symbol was used to protect against any need to make classical christological claims that require trinitarian displays of who God is. So in spite of Niebuhr's reputation as one who attempted a recovery of orthodoxy, his account of God remained more theist than Christian—that is, a theism combined with a sentimental Christ. Niebuhr may well be the greatest representative of a theology shaped to make America work. But if that is the case it is a deep judgment of such theology just to the extent that Christians lost the reality of God found in cross and resurrection." Stanley Hauerwas, *A Better Hope*, p. 34.

147. King, *The Papers*, vol. 2, p. 150.

148. Quoted in Lischer, *The Preacher King*, p. 215. See also King, *Strength to Love* (Cleveland: William Collins, 1963), p. 50.

149. Joseph Bettis, "Theology and Politics: Karl Barth and Reinhold Niebuhr on Social Ethics after Liberalism," *Religion in Life* 48, no. 1 (Spring 1979): p. 60.

150. King cited in *The Papers*, vol. 3, pp. 273–274.

151. Garrow, *Bearing the Cross*, p. 64.

152. King, quoted in Garrow, *Bearing the Cross*, p. 65.

153. Cited in Garrow, *Bearing the Cross*, p. 74.

154. *The Papers*, vol. 3, p. 200.

155. Ibid.

156. Ibid., p. 230.

157. *The Papers*, vol. 3, p. 202.

158. Quoted in Garrow, *Bearing the Cross*, p. 76.

159. David Garrow, *Bearing the Cross*, p. 77.

160. Through it all, Johnson remained a member of the First Baptist Church of Montgomery and would keep his letter there. But in 1961, when an interracial group of visitors was denied entrance to the sanctuary on Sunday morning, he stopped attending regular services, and his wife became a Unitarian. Throughout the South, Unitarian and Unitarian Universalist Churches welcomed all races and were the exception to the

rule of the closed church; even though the sensibilities of the Swedenbourgian tradition struck most black southerners as unfamiliar. Bass, *Taming the Storm*, p. 27.

161. *Encyclopedia of African-American Civil Rights*, edited by Charles D. Lowery and John F. Marszalek (Westport, CT: Greenwood Press, 1992), p. 283.

162. Bass, *Taming the Storm*, p. 110.

163. "[Frank] Johnson had the most devout patriotism of anybody I've ever known," said his friend and law clerk, Sidney Fuller (quoted in Bass, *Taming the Storm*, p. 113). The Johnson court's ruling was just the beginning of a series of enormously influential decisions it would offer. Journalist Frank Bass noted, "They struck down segregation and discrimination in almost every facet of Alabama life" (*Taming the Storm*, p. 116).

164. Bass, *Taming the Storm*, p. 112.

165. Ibid., p. 113.

166. Quoted in Garrow, *Bearing the Cross*, p. 80.

167. *The Papers*, vol. 3, p. 328.

168. Ibid., p. 328 (my emphasis).

169. Ibid., p. 417.

170. Ibid., p. 418.

171. Ibid., p. 328.

172. Ibid., pp. 462, 17.

173. Quoted in Lischer, *The Preacher King*, p. 123. Or as Dietrich Bonhoeffer wrote from Tegel concentration camp in one of his final letters before his execution in the concentration camp at Flossenburg: "It is certain that we may always live close to God and in the light of his presence, and that such living is an entirely new life for us; that nothing is then impossible for us, because all things are possible with God; that no earthly power can touch us without his will, and that danger and distress can only drive us closer to him. . . . In Jesus God has said Yes and Amen to it all, and that Yes and Amen is the firm ground on which we stand." Dietrich Bonhoeffer, *Letters and Papers from Prison* (New York: Macmillan, 1972), p. 391.

174. King, *The Papers*, vol. 3, p. 327.

175. In Martin Luther King Jr., *A Testament of Hope: The Essential Writings and Speeches of Martin Luther King Jr.* (San Francisco: Harper, 1986), p. 17.

176. Ibid., p. 24.

177. King, *The Papers*, vol. 1, p. 249.

178. Ibid., p. 249.

179. Quoted in Garrow, *Bearing the Cross*, p. 68.

180. King, *A Testament of Hope*, p. 17. To speak of Gandhi's sacrifices as "parables of justice," as I have, invokes the unlikely ally of Karl Barth, the Swiss theologian and father of the so-called theology of crisis, who apropos of this description, in the late volumes of his *Church Dogmatics*, talks about certain "parables of the Kingdom," words and actions not directly associated with the Christian proclamation but which in their particular coming-into-being become genuine forms of Christian expression. These parables have to do with "true words which are not spoken in the Bible of the Church" but which have to be heard as true in relation to the Word of God—true because they bear witness to the reach and majesty of the incarnation—in the lowest depths He has triumphed, in the supreme heights He rules at the right hand of the Father." Parables of the Kingdom are possible because God rules supreme in the "depths" and in the "heights," and the

majesty of God's reign overflows the church onto regions of existence otherwise unbap-
tized. The "sphere of His dominion and Word is in any case greater than that of their
prophecy and apostolate, and greater than that of the *kerygma*, dogma, cultus, mission
and whole life of the community which gathers and edifies itself and speaks and acts in
their school." Karl Barth, *Church Dogmatics*, IV/3, trans. G. W. Bromiley (Edinburgh:
T & T Clark, 1961) p. 116. Barth's formulation breaks with liberal Protestant notions of
the essential divinity of the human in his claim that humanity derives its dignity precisely
from the one divinity, the God of Israel and Jesus Christ, who invites sinful humanity
into His saving love in grace. Barth says, "If we recognize and confess Him as the One
who was and is and will be, then we recognize and confess that not we alone, nor the
community which, following the prophets and apostles, believes in Him and loves Him
and hopes in Him, but . . . all men and all creation derive from His cross, from the reconciliation accomplished in Him, and are ordained to be the theater of His glory and
therefore the recipients and bearers of His Word" (p. 117). Gandhi's words register this
kind of power in King's theology (as perhaps they do in Barth's as well), for the words of
"the little brown man from India" in turn "lead the community more truly and pro-
foundly than ever before to Scripture"(p. 114).

   Still, we must take some caution in comparing King and Barth, because Barth's
dialectical theology was often critical and sometimes caricatured by King's mentors,
sometimes written off as the piety of a fideist. In his Boston University studies, King,
too, indulged at times in the fashionable stereotyping of Barth, and one would not really
expect anything less. King was a graduate student working with a faculty suspicious of
the new European scene, and his assessment is plausible, though unoriginal, in the
context of Barth's dialectical writings of the years 1919–1931. But by 1955, Barth had
moved to a position that resolved the kinds of conflicts stemming from his earlier
description of revelation as pure act. In 1948, Barth spoke of his "supratemporal"
characterization of God as a theological exaggeration; "although I was confident to treat
the far-sidedness of the coming kingdom of God with absolute seriousness, I had no
such confidence in relation to its coming as such." And in 1960, he would write in his
book *The Humanity of God* (Richmond: John Knox Press, 1960) that he had overstated
his criticisms of nineteenth-century experiential theology and that it was now time to
accord to "that earlier theology, and the entire development culminating it" a "greater
historical justice than appeared to us possible and feasible in the violence of the first
break-off and clash." Yet despite King's ragged interpretation, the intent of Barth's
defiant "Nein" to Protestant liberalism is exceedingly important in helping him clarify
the drift, if not the intent, of his own theological frame of reference. No doubt, King's
academic vocabulary bears the imprimatur of mid-twentieth-century Protestant
American thought. Boston University retained many of the original convictions of the
Protestant liberal tradition in its approach to theological studies. The Boston
personalist school considered itself to be a "species of Personal Idealism" that valued the
human person as the "ontological ultimate" and personality as "the fundamental ex-
planatory principle." In this manner, a doctrine such as the incarnation was understood
not as the miraculous event of the Word made flesh but as a symbol bearing lessons
about a person of consummate will and devotion; that "only a person of holy love could
do what God has done in Christ," as the Boston religious philosopher John Lavely
explains. This kind of blurring of the difference between the divine and human—and at

the same time unraveling of the trinitarian nature of God—represents the very tradition against that Barth makes his famous protest. Still, the question of Barth's influence—or at least the Barthian resonances, of King's thought—is appropriate. Like many young theological minds, King was taken by Barth's shattering critique of liberalism. King had already begun to discern theologically the naïveté of liberalism's hopes, lessons personally evidenced in his childhood in the Jim Crow South, even in the childhood of a fairly protected middle-class boy. "We in the Anglo-Saxon world," King wrote in a graduate student essay, "securely relying upon our vast natural resources, our highly developed science and technology, and our fairly stable social institutions, have been thinking and talking far too glibly about the Kingdom of God as of something that we might hope to 'bring in' by our own human efforts. Half unconsciously, we have been confusing the ancient hope of the coming of God's Kingdom with the modern doctrine of progress. Have not we depended too much on man and too little on God?" King confesses that "maybe man is more of a sinner than liberals are willing to admit." Perhaps humanity should also admit that "many of the ills of the world are due to plain sin." King said, "The tendency on the part of some liberal theologians to see sin as a mere 'lay of nature' which will be progressively eliminated as man climbs the evolutionary ladder seems to me quite perilous." For "only the one who sits on the peak of his intellectual ivory tower looking unrealistically with his rosy colored glasses on the scene of life can fail to see this fact."

181. Quoted in Oates, *Let the Trumpets Sound*, p. 101.

182. Ibid., p. 102.

183. Ibid., p. 110.

184. King, *Stride Toward Freedom*, p. 162.

185. King, *The Papers*, vol. 3, p. 452.

186. King discovered the church not only as "a center of difference," as Stephen L. Carter writes, but as "a center of resistance" (*Christianity Today*, June 12, 2000, p. 58). The ecclesial zone of resistance and reconciliation was a church on the move: When local congregations supplied the boycott with their own vehicles to help facilitate the car pool, the "rolling churches" overflowed the geographical boundaries of the parish. Dominic J. Capeci Jr., "From Harlem to Montgomery: The Bus Boycotts and Leadership of Adam Clayton Powell Jr. and Martin Luther King Jr.," in Garrow, *The Walking City*, p. 311. "Most of the dispatch stations were located at the Negro churches, which cooperated by opening their doors early each morning so that the waiting passengers could be seated. Many of these churches provided heat on cold mornings and coffee to start the day." Morris, *The Origins of the Civil Rights Movement*, p. 58. Montgomery is an exercise in Christian hospitality. The church doors were open, invitations were sent, and generosity was extended. Yet the spiritual movement in Montgomery extended a gesture of reconciliation to whites, and whites didn't know what to do with it. The movement of Montgomery would become institutionalized, codified into national organization forms, and go about changing larger structures of injustice; but reconciliation as a gesture of Christian hospitality remained undeveloped in the civil rights movement.

187. King, *The Papers*, vol. 3, p. 458.

188. Drafted by the Quaker activist Glenn Smiley, the "Suggestions" admonished those who planned to ride the buses the next morning to maintain "a calm and loving

dignity" and recommended that they not "deliberately sit by a white person, unless there is no seat."

189. Quoted in Garrow, *Bearing the Cross*, p. 82; and Burns, *Daybreak of Freedom*, p. 327. Although the Montgomery movement's rhetoric had a "seductive gentleness," as James Farmer says, their action was "sinewy and tough." James Farmer, *Lay Bare the Heart* (New York: Signet, 1998), p. 185. It was a demonstration, too, that the beloved community did not stand or fall on some future act of God "to which human beings can contribute little or nothing except an attitude of prayerful expectancy." R. S. Barbour, *The Kingdom of God and Human Society*, edited by R. S. Barbour (Edinburgh: T & T Clark, 1993), p. xii. "The bus protest is not merely in protest of the arrest of Rosa Parks," King and numerous other black ministers declared in their manifesto, "To the Montgomery Public." The boycott "is the culmination of a series of humiliating incidents over a period of many years. It is an upsurging of a ground swell that has been going on for a long time. Our cup of tolerance has run over." King, *The Papers*, vol. 3, p. 91.

190. King, "Statement on Ending the Bus Boycott," in *The Papers*, vol. 3, p. 487. Most often protest and reconciliation appear as dialectical twins who reunite as rivals rather than as friends, different goals that sometimes intersect and cross-pollinate but usually diverge and clamor for attention. But in Montgomery, protest and reconciliation were part of the same process, the working out of the "concept of love" in social existence. Civil rights successes would be easier to come by than reconciliation; reconciliation was slow and difficult to gauge and did not promise the satisfactions of political organizing. Reconciliation could not be measured by standards of political achievement. The two trajectories of protest and reconciliation are not mutually exclusive, as the Montgomery story shows; yet as they extend from Montgomery into the next decades of congregational activism, they forge different visions and hopes for the beloved community. Thus the question: Is it possible to move from protest to reconciliation?

191. Quoted in *Encyclopedia of African-American Civil Rights*, p. 482.

192. John Howard Yoder, *For the Nations: Essays Public and Evangelical* (Grand Rapids: William B. Eerdmans Publishing, 1997), p. 126.

193. Quoted in Michael Eric Dyson, *I May Not Get There With You: The True Martin Luther King Jr.* (New York: The Free Press, 2000), p. 128.

194. See Lischer, *The Preacher King*, and Ralph Luker's groundbreaking essay, "The Kingdom of God and Beloved Community in the Thought of Martin Luther King Jr.," in *Ideas and the Civil Rights Movement*, ed. Ted Ownby (Jackson: University Press of Mississippi, 2001).

195. Josiah Royce, *The Problems of Christianity* (Chicago: University of Chicago Press, 1968), p. 196.

196. King, *The Papers*, vol. 3, p. 201.

197. Ibid., p. 462, 17.

198. "Religion and the Impasse in Modern American Social Thought," in Eugene McCarraher, *Christian Critics* (Ithaca: Cornell University Press, 2000), pp. 14–16.

199. King, *The Papers*, vol. 3, p. 328 (my emphasis).

200. King, *Testament of Hope*, p. 279.

201. See my article "The Civil Rights Movement as Theological Drama: Interpretation and Application," *Modern Theology*, 18, no. 2 (April 2002): pp. 231–250. On an im-

portant but slightly unrelated matter, it is worth noting that in recent years historians have been trying to "decenter the movement" by deemphasizing King; but a theological analysis of the movement properly returns King to the center. (My thanks to Ted Ownby for clarifying this point.)

CHAPTER 2

1. See Tracy Elaine K'Meyer, *Interracialism and Christian Community in the Postwar South: The Story of Koinonia Farm* (Charlottesville: University Press of Virginia, 1997); Marguerite Guzman Bouvard, *The Intentional Community Movement: Building a Moral World* (Port Washington, NY: Kennikat Press, 1975); and Martin B. Duberman's excellent narrative of the Black Mountain experiment, *Black Mountain: An Exploration in Community* (Garden City, NY: Anchor Press, 1973).

2. Martin Luther King Jr., *The Papers of Martin Luther King Jr.*, vol. 3, *The Birth of a New Age, December 1955–December 1956*, edited by Stewart Burns, Susan Carson, Peter Holloran, and Dana L. H. Powell (Berkeley: University of California Press, 1996), p. 347.

3. See K'Meyer, pp. 4–6.

4. Ernest Morgan, quoted in King, *The Papers*, vol. 3, p. 348.

5. Martin Luther King Jr., *The Papers of Martin Luther King Jr.*, vol. 2, *Rediscovering Precious Values, July 1951–November 1955*, edited by Clayborne Carson, Ralph E. Luker, Penny A. Russell, and Peter Holloran (Berkeley: University of California Press, 1994), p. 355.

6. Martin Luther King Jr., *The Papers of Martin Luther King Jr.*, vol. 4, edited by Susan Carson, Adrienne Clay, Virginia Shadron, and Kieran Taylor (Berkeley: University of California Press, 2000), p. 123.

7. In recent years, the deacons of Dexter Avenue Baptist have closed the church archives to scholars as a matter of policy, making impossible the determination of a matter so simple as the history of committee formations.

8. Martin Luther King Jr. to Clarence Jordan, April 8, 1958. Clarence Jordan Papers, Hargrett Rare Book and Manuscript Library, University of Georgia Libraries.

9. Ibid.

10. Martin Luther King Jr., *Stride Toward Freedom* (San Francisco: Harper & Row, 1983), pp. 21–22.

11. Clarence Jordan, "Notes for Dexter Series," March 24, 1958, Clarence Jordan Papers. Clarence Jordan, like King, had been influenced by the social gospel of Walter Rauschenbusch, the Baptist pastor and theologian who sought to retrieve the doctrine of the kingdom of God from the individualism of late Victorian piety. Yet Jordan, like King, had learned important lessons in theological humility by observing certain pitfalls in the social gospel, most notably the fact that the social gospel theologians brought to their vocations overly optimistic assessments of human goodness and historical progress, imagining beloved community as a historical inevitability. Rauschenbusch would not go so far as to describe the kingdom of God as a religious expression of American exceptionalism. The prospects of realizing the kingdom of God in America might be sunny, but they were not inevitable. Rauschenbusch was rather convinced that social progress depended on the church's willingness to engage the pressing issues of

the day; and as a pastor and denominational leader, he knew that church renewal was no historical necessity. Nonetheless, Rauschenbusch believed that the present age was alive with religious and social progress and that the rediscovery of the kingdom of God made possible a new spirit of civic munificence and international brotherhood. But by 1958, at the height of a violent season of terrorist attacks and coordinated economic threats from white civic and business leaders, Jordan had given up hope of "christianizing the social order." He understood and accepted the situation of the church's character as pilgrim and "peculiar people." He was not even sure the community would be able to survive the winter. The world had changed too—two world wars since Rauschenbusch's death—such that honest reckoning with the century's lessons confronted one with the inescapable fact of human evil.

12. Walter Rauschenbusch, *A Theology for the Social Gospel* (Nashville: Abingdon Press, 1945), p. 135.

13. Ibid., p. 141.

14. Ibid., p. 142.

15. The lectures were held at Ralph Abernathy's First Baptist Church.

16. Matthew 13:33 (New International Version).

17. Clarence Jordan, *Sermon on the Mount* (Valley Forge, PA: Judson Press, 1952), p. 90.

18. King to Clarence Jordan, May 12, 1958, Clarence Jordan Papers.

19. Melvin Watson, quoted in Clayborne Carson, "Introduction," in King, *The Papers*, vol. 2, p. 31.

20. Melvin Washington, quoted in King, *The Papers*, vol. 2, p. 31.

21. Clarence Jordan, "What is the Kingdom of God?" *The High Call* (Summer 1950): p. 29–30.

22. Ibid.

23. Galatians 3:26–28 (King James Version).

24. Quoted in Dallas Lee, *Cotton Patch Evidence* (New York: Harper & Row, 1971), p. 6.

25. Lillian Smith, *Killers of the Dream* (New York: W. W. Norton, 1949).

26. Lee, *Cotton Patch Evidence*, p. 8.

27. Ibid., pp. 7–8.

28. James Wm. McClendon Jr., *Biography as Theology: How Life Stories Can Remake Today's Theology* (Nashville: Abingdon, 1974), p. 115.

29. Lee, *Cotton Patch Evidence*, p. 10.

30. Clarence Jordan to his mother, July 3, 1932, Clarence Jordan Papers.

31. Ibid., March 4, 1933.

32. Clarence Jordan, "My Call to the Ministry," Clarence Jordan Papers.

33. McClendon, *Biography as Theology*, p. 114.

34. Quoted in P. Joel Snider, *The "Cotton Patch" Gospel: The Proclamation of Clarence Jordan* (Lanham, Maryland: University Press of America, 1985), p. 10.

35. Clarence Jordan, "Is It An Impossible Job?" *Young People*, August 12, 1956.

36. Clarence Jordan to his mother, n.d., Clarence Jordan Papers.

37. Ibid., n.d.

38. Ibid., July 9, 1934.

39. Ibid., October 1934.

40. Ibid., December 30, 1941,

41. Florence Jordan, "Biographical Sketch," Clarence Jordan Papers.

42. Quoted in Lee, *Cotton Patch Evidence*, p. 16.

43. Henlee Hulix Barnette, "The Southern Baptist Seminary and the Civil Rights Movement: From 1859–1952," *Review and Expositor* 93 (Winter 1996): pp. 77–126. Weatherspoon had been a member of the racially progressive Social Service Commission of the Southern Baptist Convention since 1929. When he became chairman of the organization in 1943, he rattled conservatives in the denomination by writing in his report to the convention, "Have we adopted irretrievably the Germanic principle?" In 1950, he fought successfully for the integration of the seminary and, in 1954 he provoked the wrath of Baptist segregationists far and wide by lobbying successfully for the denomination's support of *Brown vs. Board* at the annual Southern Baptist Convention—just weeks after the Supreme Court decision.

44. Jordan was also influenced by Christian labor organizer Howard Kester, who worked with the Southern Tenant Farmworkers Union and also served as a field investigator for the NAACP and the Committee on Economic and Racial Justice. Kester's theological critique of the southern church's "great act of apostasy" in endorsing slavery and Jim Crow laid the foundation of Jordan's lifelong polemic. Kester had written, "The church, both high and low, merged its intellect and its soul with the established order; it adapted itself to the exigencies of time and circumstances and when faced with a supreme test it had no prophetic utterance to make . . . The church remains more of a social institution—lightly respected by all but not deeply revered by any—than a religious institution." Howard Kester, "The Fellowship of Southern Churchmen: A Religion for Today," *Mountain Life and Work*, April 1939, p. 3. As executive secretary of the Fellowship of Southern Churchmen, Kester had spent five years traveling around the country from Virginia to Texas engaged in such services as "the nerve-wracking one of investigating lynchings and organizing sharecropping," "presenting the grievances of the people to church, university, civic and governmental bodies," "facing mobs and hostile audiences," and "seeing an impoverished, exploited, and almost hopeless people throw off their yoke and grapple with a new spirit and insight with their own problems." Howard Kester, "Annual Report of Howard Kester," Committee on Economic and Racial Justice, Howard Kester Papers, University of Virginia Special Collections. The historian Andrew Chancey notes that members of the Louisville Koinonia had corresponded with Howard Kester as early as October 1940 and had attended sessions when Kester lectured at the Baptist seminary in March 1941. In March 1942, Kester offered seminars on the "Church and Social Reconstruction" at Wakefield, the intentional Christian community where Jordan's future partner in ministry, Martin England, was currently living. Kester had been pleased with the response to his lectures among Southern Baptists and was confident that the new organization called the Fellowship of Southern Churchman was "off to a good beginning." In the summer of 1943, Kester and Jordan would lead a seminar together on the church and race relations. Kester grew to admire the young Southern Baptist seminarian, who shared his alternative theological vision of the South. When Kester resigned his position as secretary of the organization in 1943, he wrote Jordan and asked whether he might be interested in taking the job. Jordan declined the position but was honored that one of his theological heroes had regarded him worthy of the post. Andrew Chancey, *Race, Religion and Reform: Koinonia's*

Challenge to Southern Society (unpublished doctoral dissertation, University of Florida, 1998), p. 40.

45. Mark Newman, *Getting Right with God: Southern Baptists and Desegregation, 1945–1995* (Tuscaloosa: The University of Alabama Press, 2001), p. 8.

46. J. B. Lawrence cited in Foy Valentine, *A Historical Study of Southern Baptists and Race Relations, 1917–1947* (New York: Arno Press, 1980), p.137.

47. Clarence Jordan, correspondence, October 6, 1941, Clarence Jordan Papers.

48. Ibid.

49. Snider, *"Cotton Patch" Gospel*, p. 12.

50. Clarence Jordan, correspondence, April 11, 1941, Clarence Jordan Papers.

51. Ann Louise Coble, *Cotton Patch for the Kingdom* (Scottsdale, PA: Herald Press, 2002), p. 46.

52. Clarence Jordan, quoted in Coble, *Cotton Patch for the Kingdom*, p. 48.

53. Ibid., p. 47.

54. Ibid., p. 49.

55. Snider, *"Cotton Patch" Gospel*, p. 12.

56. Martin England, quoted in K'Meyer, *Interracialism and Christian Community*, p. 36.

57. Martin England, quoted in David Stricklin, *A Genealogy of Dissent: Southern Baptist Protest in the Twentieth Century* (Lexington, KY: The University Press of Kentucky, 1999), p. 55.

58. In April of 1956, nearly five months into the bus boycott, England wrote King in Montgomery. England offered his fellow Crozer alumnus a gentle reminder that the most important part of nonviolent protest was the steadfast refusal to humiliate the opposition. "You must know better than I do how much easier it is to defeat segregationists than to transform them," England wrote. The enemy must be transformed, not embarrassed or ridiculed. England had in mind a recent newspaper report describing an emerging attitude of vindication among some of the Montgomery boycotters. "Nonviolence is such a powerful tool," England added, "that when its advocates discover its strength, they may be tempted to use it for the same ends for which others use violence; to conquer the opponent, rather than redeem him . . . God grant that you and your associates may have the love that will lead those who now oppose you to cry out, like the Philippian jailer, 'Men and brethren, what must we do to be saved?'" (in King, *The Papers*, vol. 3, p. 233). King certainly understood the importance of England's concerns, having set for his own leadership of the Montgomery protest high standards of civility and respect. Still, the letter calls attention to unresolved questions in King's civil rights ministry about the nature and scope of Christian social protest in Montgomery. First and foremost, Baptist pastors have the obligation to preach the Gospel, and while preaching must undoubtedly inspire faithful witness in society, it must never replace a minister's primary mission of calling the nations to repentance and the believer to Christ-like living. England was communicating to King the vision of Clarence Jordan for civil rights: The beloved community must always hug the prophetic margins of the dominant culture as a witness to its distinctive message, rather than engage the social order in direct acts of reform and protest as a player in the networks of worldly power.

59. Andrew Chancey reports that of Sumter County's total population in 1940 of 24,502, 61.2 percent was African American, and in the town of Americus, the county seat, just over half (4,855) of the 9,281 residents were black. Chancey, "Race, Religion

and Reform," p. 49ff. Martin England later noted that the decision to locate in Sumter County had been carefully considered. "We had explored the idea of Christian community in our talks, often and long. . . . We also believed we would find a higher proportion of desperately poor people in Southeast Alabama and Southwest Georgia . . . We visited Tuskegee Institute in Alabama, then went across into Sumter County, Georgia, where we found the tract of land which became Koinonia Farm." Henlee Barnette, "Clarence Jordan: A Prophet in Blue Jeans," lecture presented at Southern Baptist Seminary," April 1983, Louisville, Kentucky.

60. Quoted in Barnette, "Prophet in Blue Jeans," p. 8.

61. Coble, *Cotton Patch for the Kingdom*, p. 69.

62. England, quoted in Stricklin, *A Genealogy of Dissent*, p. 61.

63. Lee, *Cotton Patch Evidence*, p. 1.

64. Clarence Jordan, "Christian Community in the South," Clarence Jordan Papers.

65. Ibid., p. 29.

66. Clarence Jordan, quoted in Lee, *Cotton Patch Evidence*, p. 32.

67. K'Meyer, *Interracialism and Christian Community*, p. 51.

68. The Bruderhof community movement began in Germany after World War I, when Eberhard Arnold, a theologian and pastor, left Berlin for the village of Sannerz. The Bruderhof became an intentional community dedicated to Christian spiritual formation and peacemaking. In 1937, the community was targeted by the Gestapo and its members were either arrested or expelled from the country. Some members created settlements in the jungles of Paraguay. In 1954, a Bruderhof community was established in Rifton, New York, and today the Bruderhof's membership numbers more than 2,500, with communities in the United States, England, Australia, and Germany. The Bruderhof practice of admonishing a brother or sister in love meant speaking directly to each other of areas in their lives that needed improvement, and while this practice may have had some biblical backing, it was not in keeping with southern manners and its disarming indirectness. Some Koinonians pushed for closer affiliation with Bruderhof and other historic Anabaptist communities; in fact, Koinonia joined the Fellowship of Intentional Communities in the early 1950s and took part in its conferences and reunions. But Clarence Jordan never really cared much for the Bruderhof model, and quietly made sure that Koinonia kept an arm's distance between its purposeful disorganization and the Bruderhof's earnest and regimented structure. When he visited the Forest River Colony in Inkster, North Dakota, in 1955, he was appalled to learn of the Hutterite practice of punishing the sons and daughters who ventured beyond the community and then returned in hopes of being received by their families. Had the Hutterites never heard of the parable of the Prodigal Son—about the father who welcomed his rebellious son home with open arms and of the resentful brother bent on punishment? "There is no scriptural basis for this," Jordan said. During a visit to the Hutterites, it was suggested to Jordan that his clean-shaven face was a sign of certain vanity. Jordan responded again by pointing to the pages of the New Testament. "If you can show me that Christ wants me to have a beard, I'll not only grow it—I'll not even trim it as you fellows do. I'll grow it to my knees" (Lee, *Cotton Patch Evidence*, pp. 94–97).

69. Quoted in Coble, *Cotton Patch for the Kingdom*, p. 96.

70. Quoted in K'Meyer, *Interracialism and Christian Community*, p. 69.

71. K'Meyer, *Interracialism and Christian Community*, p. 59.

72. Ibid., p. 60.

73. Jordan, correspondence, January 12, 1951.

74. Barnette, "Prophet in Blue Jeans."

75. Clarence Jordan, *Kingdom Building: Essays from the Grassroots of Habitat*, edited by David Johnson Rowe and Robert William Stevens (Habitat for Humanity, 1984), p. 17.

76. Clarence Jordan, quoted in "Dreams Into Deeds: Celebrating 50 Years of Koinonia," *Sojourners*, p. 19. Clarence Jordan Papers.

77. Chancey, *Race, Religion and Reform*, p. 107.

78. Ibid., p. 112.

79. The phrases are those of Mississippi attorney Tom Brady, author of the 1954 diatribe *Black Monday: Segregation or Amalgamation . . . America Has Its Choice* (Winona, Mississippi: Association of Citizens' Councils, 1955).

80. Chancey, *Race, Religion and Reform*, p. 112.

81. *Koinonia Farm Newsletter,* no. 13, April 24, 1957, Clarence Jordan Papers.

82. Lee, *Cotton Patch Evidence*, p. 131.

83. *Koinonia Farm Newsletter,* no. 18, Clarence Jordan Papers.

84. Chancey, *Race, Religion and Reform*, p. 130.

85. Dorothy Day, quoted in Paul Elie, *The Life You Save May Be Your Own: An American Pilgrimage* (New York: Farrar, Straus, and Giroux, 2003), p. 246.

86. Clarence Jordan, "The Effect of the Christian Community on the World," in Jordan, *Sermon on the Mount*, pp. 23–28.

87. Clarence Jordan, *The Cotton Patch Version of Matthew and John* (Clinton, NJ: 1970), p. 22.

88. Jordan, *Sermon on the Mount*, p. 25.

89. Jordan, quoted in Lee, *The Cotton Patch Evidence*, p. 225.

90. Jordan, *Sermon on the Mount*, p. 28.

91. Ibid., p. 90.

92. K'Meyer, *Interracialism and Christian Community*, p. 127.

93. Clarence Jordan, in *Plenty to Share*, documentary film directed by Gayla Jamison.

94. Christoph Blumhardt, *Action in Waiting* (Farmington, PA: The Plough Publishing House, 1998), p. 23.

95. K'Meyer, *Interracialism and Christian Community*, p. 151.

96. Charles Sherrod, interview by Tracy K'Meyer.

97. K'Meyer, *Interracialism and Christian Community*, p. 151.

98. Howard Thurman, the chaplain at Boston University during King's student years, opened up his congregation's spacious rooms on Larkin Street in San Francisco as a haven for exhausted workers from the southern theater; and yet still Thurman is sometimes criticized for failing to take a more visible role in the movement.

99. Ed King, interview by the author. My thanks to Ed King for sharing this observation with me.

100. Christine Pohl, *Making Room: Recovering Hospitality as a Christian Tradition* (Grand Rapids, MI: William B. Eerdmans Publishing, 1999), p. 183.

101. Edwin King provided this description of Koinonia legacy. Interview by the author, September 1, 2003.

102. Hosea Williams brought his SCOPE project to Americus in 1965 in the form of a selective buying campaign, even though local civil rights workers had advised him

against it. Jordan was critical of the SCLC-sponsored plan, as were SNCC representatives. SNCC's Willie Ricks said, "We've been operating in Americus for three years, and now we've got to figure out how to clean up the mess Dr. King will leave behind." Quoted in J. David Garrow, *Bearing the Cross: Martin Luther King Jr., and the Southern Christian Leadership Conference* (New York: Vintage, 1988), p. 440. Randolph Blackwell and Andrew Young insisted that the SCOPE initiative was poorly run and relied on inexperienced volunteers. Blackwell explained his concerns in a memorandum to King and Abernathy: "The SCOPE project as it presently exists should be brought [to] an end just as soon as it possibly can without inviting public inquiry. . . . It has cost freedom contributors ten times what it should have. In my candid opinion, the project has degenerated in the main to an experiment in liquor and sex, compounded by criminal conduct, no less than a series of reported rapes." Quoted in Garrow, *Bearing the Cross*, p. 441.

103. Quoted in K'Meyer, *Interracialism and Christian Community*, p. 161.

104. Clarence Jordan, untitled manuscript, May 17, 1968, Clarence Jordan Papers.

105. Clarence Jordan to Craig Peters, October 23, 1967, Clarence Jordan Papers.

106. Clarence Jordan, *The Substance of Faith and Other Cotton Patch Sermons*, edited by Dallas Lee (New York: Association Press, 1972), p. 99.

107. Jordan, *The Substance of Faith*, p. 99.

108. Peter 5:8 (King James Version).

109. See James Cone, *Black Theology, Black Power* (New York: Seabury Press, 1969); and Vincent Harding, "Black Power and the American Christ," in *Black Theology: A Documentary History, 1966–1979*, edited by Gayraud S. Wilmore and James H. Cone (Maryknoll, New York: Orbis Books, 1979), pp. 35–43. Harding wrote, "If judgment stands sure it is not primarily upon SNCC that it will fall, but upon those who have kidnapped the compassionate Jesus—the Jesus who shared all he had, even his life, with the poor—and made him into a profit-oriented, individualistic, pietistic cat who belongs to his own narrowly defined kind and begrudges the poor their humiliating subsistence budgets. These Christians are the ones who have taken away our Lord and buried him in a place unknown. . . . The time of singing may be past. It may be that America must now stand under profound and damning judgment for having turned the redeeming love of all men into a white, middle-class burner of children and destroyer of the revolutions of the oppressed" (p. 41).

110. Martin Luther King Jr., "Letter from Birmingham City Jail," in *Testament of Hope: The Essential Writings and Speeches of Martin Luther King Jr.*, edited by James M. Washington (San Francisco: HarperCollins Paperback, 1986), p. 300.

111. Jordan, *Sermon on the Mount*, p. 90.

112. Jordan exemplifies the way in which most American fundamentalists have not not taken their own most basic convictions seriously, succumbing instead to the seductions of insatiable ambition and American power.

113. Clarence Jordan, "Thy Kingdom Come—On Earth?" *High Call*, Summer, 1950, p. 31.

114. Jordan, *Sermon on the Mount*, pp. 90–92. It may be that Jordan's biggest threat to the southern Christian establishment was not his belief in the equality of the races, or his experiment in communal living, but his relentless effort to demonstrate that southern white evangelicalism was built on an ancient Christian heresy. Southern evangeli-

cals were docetic to the core, a doctrine that regarded the human nature and suffering of Jesus Christ as a disguise rather than as the real incarnation of God. The natural world was essentially degrading, the docetists believed, and thus God could not have assumed the properties of human nature and suffered in the body as the Church fathers claimed—Jesus Christ as truly God, truly human. God must have simply disguised himself in the flesh of Jesus. Jordan asked: How else could the theological error of southern evangelicalism be explained than that an ethereal Christ has replaced the wordly Jesus? "When God became man," says Jordan, "we didn't know what to do with him." Jordan, *Substance of Faith*, p 19. But if the teachings of Jesus have become irrelevant to life in the social order, then we find ourselves groping for other ideas and experiences that we can endow with religious meaning: race, tradition, money, nationhood, war. Entombing Jesus into our own image, we quash the freedom of the spirit, but we also protect ourselves from the bodily demands of faith.

115. Quoted in Susan Glisson, "Life in Scorn of the Consequences: Clarence Jordan and the Roots of Radicalism in the Southern Baptist Convention" (masters thesis, University of Mississippi,1994), p. 36.

116. Charles Sherrod, quoted in Stephen G. N. Tuck, *Beyond Atlanta: The Struggle for Racial Equality in Georgia, 1940–1980* (Athens and London: The University of Georgia Press, 2001), p. 178.

117. Charles Sherrod, interview by Tracy K'Meyer.

118. Jordan to his son, February 27, 1966, Clarence Jordan Papers.

119. See Millard Fuller's wonderful book *Love in the Mortar Joints: The Story of Habitat for Humanity*, coauthored with Diane Scott (Piscataway, NJ: New Century Publishers, 1980), as well as his *Theology of the Hammer* (Macon, Georgia: Smyth and Helwys, 1994). The daughter who sang at Jordan's funeral, Faith Fuller, has recently produced an extraordinary documentary film, *Briars in the Cottonpatch*.

CHAPTER 3

1. Charles Sherrod, "For the Student Interracial Ministry," Charles Sherrod Papers, State Historical Society of Wisconsin.

2. Carson, *In Struggle: SNCC and the Black Awakening of the 1960s* (Cambridge, MA: Harvard University Press, 1981), p. 11.

3. Ibid., p. 11.

4. SNCC, "What Is SNCC? Philosophy," *Student Voice* 1 (June 1960).

5. Nash, quoted in Carson, *In Struggle*, p. 21.

6. Diane Nash, quoted in Cheryl Lynn Greenberg, ed., *A Circle of Trust: Remembering SNCC* (New Brunswick, NJ: Rutgers University Press, 1998), pp. 18–19.

7. The description is Reverend Edwin King's (unpublished lecture, University of Virginia, April 2003).

8. Carson, *In Struggle*, p. 1.

9. Carson, *In Struggle*, p. 1. Carson would not agree with my claim about the theological character of SNCC's radicalism. He argues that as early as 1963, SNCC's radicalism had assumed a "secular rather than a religious tone."

10. Victoria Gray Adams, Lecture, Conference on Lived Theology and Civil Courage, University of Virginia, June 13, 2003.

11. See my theological narrative of Mrs. Hamer in *God's Long Summer: Stories of Faith and Civil Rights* (Princeton: Princeton University Press, 1997).

12. Fannie Lou Hamer, quoted in Edwin King, "Go Tell It On the Mountain," *Sojourners* 11, no. 11 (December 1982): p. 87.

13. Howard Zinn, quoted in Greenberg, *A Circle of Trust*, p. 28.

14. The belief was strongly felt, and even more strongly expressed, through song, testimonial, preaching, and witness, that God was there, in the exhilaration, tedium, and chaos of the movement, in the endless meetings and debates, working in and through persons, communities, and actions toward a world more just, merciful, and humane, in the big steps and in the small as well. "Our faith is incurably optimistic and unyieldingly realistic," read Sherrod's mission statement for the "Nonviolent Movement" of southwest Georgia. "Handbill, Albany Nonviolent Movement," in Steven F. Lawson and Charles Payne, eds., *Debating the Civil Rights Movement, 1945–1968*, edited by (Lanham, MD: Rowan & Littlefield, 1998), p. 141. Many SNCC members engaged the world as if the purpose of life were the reenactment of divine love in human social existence. Still, the enfleshened church, like the black freedom church upon which it was based, did not need to wrap up the outsider in the ecclesial vestments of the sanctuary. "Incarnate historical life," as the liberation theologians insist, "when lived in solidarity with the poor, is intrinsically spiritual. Jon Sobrino, *Spirituality of Liberation: Toward Political Holiness* (New York: Maryknoll, 1985), p. 4. SNCC as the church in action grounded the movement's larger, sometimes global perspectives, in local struggles and in their particular stories. In her excellent study of SNCC, historian Wesley Hogan describes the black freedom church as the second wellspring of the civil rights struggle alongside the black organizing tradition. "It fostered the spirit of resistance, providing through the examples of people in the Old and New Testament an inspiration, hope and sustenance for a full humanity—despite the outward hold of slavery and segregation. The Freedom Church also fostered what civil rights activist James Lawson called the forces of spiritual and moral revolution, where despite the indignities and inhumanities suffered at the hands of whites, African Americans could gather together to pursue 'relationships of rightness, of compassion, of care.' At base, the Black Freedom Church was both a spirit and an institution, promoting and transmitting to future generations of African Americans, as philosopher Cornel West defined it, 'a sense of respect for others, a sense of solidarity, [and] a sense of meaning and value which would usher in the strength to battle against evil.'" Wesley Hogan, *"Radical Manners": The Student Nonviolent Coordinating Committee and the New Left in the 1960s* (doctoral dissertation, Duke University, 2000), p. 27.

15. These factors also include the mobilization of white student energies toward anti-war activism, the burgeoning women's liberation movement, the search for new religious experiences and an alternative consciousness, and a host of other personal and social liberation movements and experiments. Not to be forgotten too is the persisting segregation of the southern white evangelical church, which decidedly had not accepted the movement's invitation to build beloved community as a divine word of conviction and edification. D.C. See Doug McAdam, *Freedom Summer* (New York: Oxford University Press, 1976), pp. 171–178; Sara Evans, *Personal Politics: The Roots of the Women's Liberation in the Civil Rights Movement and the New Left* (New York: Random House,

1979); Steven M. Tipton, *Getting Saved from the Sixties: Moral Meaning in Conversion and Cultural Change* (Berkeley: University of California Press, 1982).

16. John Lewis, quoted in Carson, *In Struggle*, p. 170.

17. Stanley Wise, staff meeting, May 11, 1966, SNCC Papers, Martin Luther King Jr. Center, Atlanta, GA.

18. "Assumptions about SNCC," SNCC Papers.

19. Richard King, *Civil Rights and the Idea of Freedom* (New York: Oxford University Press, 1992), p. 166.

20. Bob Moses, quoted in "Minutes of the Meeting of the SNCC Executive Committee, December 27–31, 1963," SNCC Papers.

21. Julian Bond, lecture, University of Virginia.

22. Victoria Gray Adams, quoted in Greenberg, *A Circle of Trust*, p. 77.

23. John Lewis, interview by the author.

24. Jane Stembridge to Bob Moses, SNCC Papers.

25. Ibid.

26. Bob Zellner, "Notes of a Native Son," *Southern Exposure* 9, no. 1 (Spring 1981).

27. Bob Moses, quoted in Hogan, "Radical Manners," pp. 76–77.

28. Mary King, quoted in Greenberg, *A Circle of Trust*, p. 25.

29. Bob Moses, quoted in Hogan, *"Radical Manners,"* p. 100.

30. Jane Stembridge to Max Heirich, July 28, 1969, SNCC Papers.

31. Ibid.

32. Ned Option to Bob Moses and Casey Hayden, memorandum, SNCC Papers. This was not always a popular strategy.

33. Jane Stembridge, *I Play Flute and Other Poems* (New York: Seabury Press, 1966), p. 30.

34. Ibid., p. 128.

35. Tom Hayden, quoted in Greenberg, *A Circle of Trust*, p. 3.

36. Joyce Ladner, "Summer Project '64," Joan Trumpauer Mulholland Papers, private collection, p. 26.

37. "Mississippi Faces Drive for Rights," *New York Times*, May 17, 1964.

38. John Lewis with Michael D'Orso, *Walking with the Wind: A Memoir of the Movement* (New York: Simon & Schuster, 1998), p. 86.

39. Elizabeth Sutherland, ed., *Letters from Mississippi* (New York: McGraw-Hill, 1965), p. 226.

40. Sherrod, quoted in Hogan, *"Radical Manners,"* p. 144.

41. Hogan, *"Radical Manners,"* p. 145.

42. Mike Miller, memorandum to SNCC national staff, October 23, 1964, SNCC Papers.

43. "Minutes Student Nonviolent Coordinating Committee Meeting," November 25–27, 1960. SNCC Papers.

44. Ibid.

45. John Lewis, "Statement by John Lewis, Chairman, Staff Meeting, February 1965," SNCC Papers.

46. Action sometimes makes the best crucible for thought," Carol Polsgrove writes in her essential book on intellectuals and the civil rights movement, *Divided Minds: Intel-*

lectuals and the Civil Rights Movement (New York: W. W. Norton, 2001). "We may find, as the movement did, that we think best in the open air, on our feet" (p. 246).

47. Marion S. Barry Jr., Correspondence with Mr. Jonathan Swartz, August 16, 1960, SNCC Papers.

48. Mary King, quoted in Greenberg, *A Circle of Trust*, p. 26.

49. Chuck McDew, quoted in "Spiritual and Moral Aspects of the Student Nonviolent Struggle in the South," in *The New Student Left*, edited by Mitchell Cohen and Dennis Hale (Boston: Beacon Press, 1966), p. 51.

50. Ibid., p. 56.

51. Ibid.

52. Casey Hayden, *Deep in Our Hearts: Nine White Women in the Freedom Movement*, edited by Constance Curry et al. (Athens: University of Georgia Press, 2000), p. 342.

53. Marion Barry to Mr. Jonathan Schwartz, August 16, 1960, SNCC Papers.

54. Hayden, *Deep in Our Hearts*, p. 342.

55. Carson, *In Struggle*, p. 299. SNCC's acceptance of armed resistance violence arose in the context of its debate on the use of guns, which was waged with increased intensity in the spring and summer of 1965. The disagreement cut through familiar lines with John Lewis taking the side of the Christian pacifists and Stokely Carmichael declaring that, "We are not King or SCLC." Carmichael's justifications often traded on King's unacknowledged dependence on the armed protection of federal and state police—the same criticism Clarence Jordan had made—and betrayed his own refined instincts for self-protection. "[King and SCLC] don't do the kind of work we do nor do they live in the areas we live in." Stokely Carmichael, "Executive Committee Meeting, Holly Springs, Mississippi." In other words, a late night excursion down Highway 49 might be more than enough to convince the black clergymen of the value of a handgun. Other SNCC members sought training in judo and karate and marksmanship. By the following year, Carmichael's pragmatic argument would evolve into a bold endorsement for violence in the mantra of liberation from white oppression by any means necessary.

56. Thomas Merton, *Faith and Violence* (South Bend: University of Notre Dame Press, 1968), p. 143. Dietrich Bonhoeffer, the German theologian and resistance activist, observed after his year at Union Theological Seminary that the Protestant church in North America performed a "Protestantism without Reformation": the result, Bonhoeffer concluded, was that "the person and work of Jesus Christ . . . sink into the background and in the long run remain misunderstood, because [Jesus Christ] is not recognized as the sole ground of radical judgment and radical forgiveness." Dietrich Bonhoeffer, "Protestantism without Reformation, "in *No Rusty Swords: Letters, Lectures, and Notes, 1928–1936*, ed. Edwin H. Robertson, p. 117. The standard of the person and work of Jesus Christ is compromised by competing loyalties, none more assertive than race and nationhood. It is worth wondering whether Bonhoeffer—had he lived to see it unfold—would have regarded the civil rights movement as seeds of the Reformation of the Protestant Church in North American, a moment of divine judgment and chastening, which has never grown to full colors.

57. McDew, *The New Student Left*, p. 56.

58. Ibid., p. 55.

59. Ibid.

60. Howard Zinn, *SNCC: The New Abolitionists* (1964; repr. Cambridge, MA: South End Press, 2002), p. 18.

61. Sutherland, *Letters from Mississippi*, p. 50.

62. Ibid., p. 49–50.

63. Ibid., p. 23.

64. Ibid.

65. Sutherland, *Letters from Mississippi*, p. 51 (emphasis mine).

66. Ibid., p. 50.

67. Howard Zinn, quoted in Carson, *In Struggle*, p. 17.

68. Ed King, "The Herrons and the Beloved Community," unpublished paper, Edwin King Papers.

69. Quoted in Anne Cooke Romaine, "The Mississippi Freedom Democratic Party through August, 1964" (M.A. thesis, University of Virginia, 1970).

70. Richard King, *Civil Rights and the Idea of Freedom*, p. 99.

71. Ibid.

72. Bob Zellner, quoted in Carson, *In Struggle*, p. 302.

73. Charles Sherrod, quoted in Carson, *In Struggle*, pp. 57–58.

74. Charles Sherrod, quoted in Richard King, *Civil Rights and the Idea of Freedom*, p. 144.

75. Sherrod, quoted in Carson, *In Struggle*, p. 58.

76. Charles Sherrod, "Minutes of the Meeting of the SNCC Executive Committee, December 27–31, 1963," SNCC Papers.

77. Julian Bond, quoted in Carson, *In Struggle*, p. 62. Because Sherrod's theological convictions grounded him in the everyday life of a community with all its joys and frustrations, he understood that SNCC would never become a "perfect circle" but would remain always a "broken fellowship"—broken like the body of Christ itself. Sherrod imagined SNCC as a social witness of the church proclaiming the message that only when "we have welcomed the slave as a peer" in an "overflowing cup of witness" shall the table of fellowship become the Lord's table, the "welcome table." Charles Sherrod, "Union's Welcome Table," Union Theological Seminary, February 24, 1966, SNCC Papers. Like Jordan, Sherrod also believed that devotion to the church and its teachings on nonviolence established the context for building redemptive community. But Sherrod departed from Jordan on the matter of how the church should relate itself to the social order, preferring instead the model of the "church militant," which King had retrieved from the Christian tradition in the Montgomery protest. The movement church had the power to overcome white supremacy in the South by creating dramas that challenged civil authority as well as by fortifying the commitment to interracial organizing.

78. Hogan, "*Radical Manners*," p. 119.

79. Moses, quoted in "Minutes of the Meeting of the SNCC Executive Committee, December 27–31, 1963," SNCC Papers.

80. Amzie Moore, quoted in Eric R. Burner, *And Gently He Shall Lead Them: Robert Parris Moses and Civil Rights in Mississippi* (New York: New York University Press, 1994), p. 206.

81. Bob Moses to Jane Stembridge, SNCC Papers.

82. Sutherland, *Letters from Mississippi*, p. 15.

83. "Resume of the Inquiry Regarding Robert Parris Moses, Conscientious Objector," SNCC Papers.

84. Ibid.

85. Burner, *And Gently He Shall Lead Them*, p. 16.

86. Moses, quoted in Carson, *In Struggle*, p. 17.

87. Carson, *In Struggle*, p. 25.

88. Ibid., p. 26.

89. Bob Moses to Jane Stembridge, SNCC Papers.

90. Jane Stembridge, to Bob Moses, SNCC Papers.

91. Ibid. The two young dissidents saw the world from a similar perspective: They were rebels discontent with American society and also with the middle-class black leadership of the Southern Christian Leadership Conference.

92. That task he left to more gregarious souls like Fannie Lou Hamer, who once confronted her minister during the Sunday morning service in her Baptist church on his reluctance to take a stand. "Pharaoh was in Sunflower County!" Mrs. Hamer said. "Israel's children were building bricks without straw—at three dollars a day! . . . And you, Reverend Tyler, must be Moses! Leadin' your flock out of the chains and fetters of Egypt—takin' them yourself to register—*tomorra*—in Indianola!" Tracy Sugarman, *Stranger at the Gate* (New York: Hill and Wang, 1966), p. 121.

93. Edwin King, *Life in Mississippi*, unpublished manuscript, Edwin King Papers.

94. Moses, quoted in "Minutes of the Meeting of the SNCC Executive Committee, December 27–31, 1963," SNCC Papers.

95. See Richard King, *Civil Rights and the Idea of Freedom*, pp. 147–148. As one SNCC document indicated, the Freedom schools would provide "an educational experience for students which will make it possible for them to challenge the myths of our society, to perceive more clearly its realities and to find alternatives—ultimately new directions for action." Richard King, *Civil Rights and the Idea of Freedom*, p. 148. The Freedom schools represented parallel or alternative institutions that would not only help remedy the state's grotesquely inadequate educational system for black children, but would further inspire a new sense of human worth in these children and adults and expand the horizons of knowledge and experience.

96. Robert Moses with Charles E. Cobb Jr., *Radical Equations: Civil Rights from Mississippi to the Algebra Project* (Boston: Beacon Press, 2001), p. 62.

97. Ibid., p. 69.

98. Ibid., p. 66.

99. See my profile of Sam Bowers in *God's Long Summer*.

100. Ed King, quoted in William H. Chafe, *Never Stop Running: Allard Lowenstein and the Struggle to Save American Liberalism* (New York: Basic Books, 1993), p. 180.

101. Moses, *Radical Equations*, p. 62.

102. "Report of Leonard Edwards," SNCC Papers.

103. Moses, *Radical Equations*, p. 69.

104. Howard Zinn, "Executive Committee Meeting, August 11–13, 1961," SNCC Papers.

105. "The General Condition of the Mississippi Negro," October 1963, SNCC Papers.

106. Ibid.

107. Moses, *Radical Equations*, p. 71.

108. John Dittmer, *Local People: The Struggle for Civil Rights in Mississippi* (Urbana: University of Illinois Press, 1994), p. 205.

109. Donaldson, quoted in Dittmer, *Local People*, p. 205.

110. The phrase is Ernst Borinski's, the Holocaust survivor and sociologist at Tougaloo College in Jackson. (See Greenberg, *A Circle of Trust*, p. 9.)

111. Zinn, *SNCC: The New Abolitionists*, p. 251.

112. Moses, quoted in "Minutes of the December 27–31, 1963 Meeting," SNCC Papers.

113. Chafe, *Never Stop Running*, p. ix.

114. "Minutes of the Meeting of the SNCC Executive Committee," Student Nonviolent Coordinating Committee, March 29, 1964.

115. The board of trustees at Berea College nixed the idea of a training session in Kentucky and the session moved to Oxford, Ohio.

116. The quoted phrase is from Douglas Renick. In 1962, an initiative was launched called the Student Interracial Ministry. The SIM fashioned together a network of black churches, mostly in North Carolina but also in Tennessee and Mississippi, each of which would host a white pastoral intern. White Protestant seminarians were assigned to black churches for a summer of ministerial service, assisting the senior pastor in preaching, pastoral care, and administration. At the end of July, the seminarians wrote one-page reports of their work to date. The reports offer a fascinating vista into a time more optimistic than ours about the prospects of ecclesial innovations in social progress and racial unity. Douglas Renick, volunteering from Union Theological Seminary at the Davie Street Presbyterian Church in Raleigh, North Carolina, described his "dawning realization that we are alike and essentially one people." Renick confessed he had no answer to the difficult practical questions concerning the mechanics of social change, especially of whether nonviolent direct action would prove an effective strategy for breaking down the barriers of segregation. Yet over the course of the summer the white seminarian had become convinced that if racial reconciliation were to take place in American society, it would fare best in the context of the church. "I am convinced that the reconciliation that occurs within the Christian community is the deepest and most permanent of reconciliations." Renick's estimation was hardly sanguine; for the "path of reconciliation" was not without thorns and thistles; indeed it will surely "take longer and is probably more difficult because the reconciliation is between persons and not between the application of national and state laws." But the church is the only place where the sources of forgiveness and reconciliation are so highly developed as to be able to address with healing power and conviction the traumas of cruelty, hatred, and oppression ingredient to the human story. Charles Sherrod Papers.

117. Moses, *Radical Equations*, p. 74.

118. Dittmer, *Local People*, p. 209.

119. James Forman, quoted in Carson, *In Struggle*, p. 99.

120. John Lewis, interview by the author.

121. Fannie Lou Hamer, "Foreword," in Sugarman, *Stranger at the Gate*, p. xi.

122. Moses, *Radical Equations*, p. 72.

123. Ibid.

124. Bob Moses, quoted in Burner, *And Gently He Shall Lead Them*, p. 129.

125. Hamer, quoted in Carson, *In Struggle*, p. 99. Clayborne Carson claims that most of the supporters of the proposed Summer Project were veteran SNCC volunteers (p. 99). In her study, *A Case of Black and White: Northern Volunteers and the Southern Freedom Summers, 1964–1965* (Westport, CT: Greenwood Press, 1982), Mary Aickin Rothschild adds, "Fannie Lou Hamer believed that the 'bridge' built between white volunteers and black children was one of the greatest achievements of the summers. Never again would southern blacks be so separated from the white community. Likewise, the white community simply could not continue to maintain many of the myths about the 'necessity' of separation of the races, which, of course, had never existed anyway when there was work to be done" (p. 172).

126. Cited in Cleveland Sellers with Robert Terrell, *The River of No Return: The Autobiography of a Black Militant and the Life and Death of SNCC* (Jackson: University Press of Mississippi, 1990), p. 56.

127. SNCC document cited in Sellers, *River of No Return*, p. 56.

128. Sellers, *River of No Return*, p. 51.

129. "Freedom Schools—Final Report, 1964," SNCC Papers.

130. Joyce Ladner, "Summer Project '64," p. 26, SNCC Papers.

131. Bob Moses, in Connie Field and Marilyn Mulford, *Freedom on My Mind*, documentary film.

132. Marshall Ganz, in *Freedom on My Mind*.

133. Willie Peacock, in *Freedom on My Mind*.

134. "Assumptions Made by SNCC," SNCC Papers.

135. Ed Brown, "Interview with Tom Dent," Tom Dent Oral History, Amistad Research Center, Tulane University.

136. Sellers, *River of No Return*, p. 111.

137. Jack Newfield, *A Prophetic Minority* (New York: A Signet Book, 1966), p. 72.

138. See Sara Evans, *Personal Politics: The Roots of Women's Liberation in the Civil Rights Movement and the New Left* (New York: Vintage Books, 1980); and Carson, *In Struggle*, p. 144.

139. Zellner, "Minutes of November 8, 1964 Staff Meeting," SNCC Papers, Martin Luther King Jr. Archives.

140. SNCC, "Minutes of November 8, 1964 Staff Meeting," SNCC Papers, Martin Luther King Jr. Archives.

141. Sellers, *River of No Return*, p. 117. See also the discussion in John W. De Gruchy, *Christianity and Democracy: A Theology for a Just World Order* (Cambridge: Cambridge University Press, 1995), pp. 13–34, 131–164.

142. SNCC, "Minutes of November 8, 1964."

143. Ibid.

144. Carson, *In Struggle*, p. 145.

145. "SNCC Staff Assumptions," SNCC Papers.

146. Ibid.

147. See Evans, *Personal Politics*, pp. 90–94.

148. Dittmer, *Local People*, p. 326. See also Burner, *And Gently He Shall Lead Them*, pp. 217–223.

149. Hogan, *"Radical Manners,"* p. 626.

150. Carson, *In Struggle*, p. 152.

151. See Sellers, *River of No Return*; and George M. Fredrickson, *Black Liberation: A Comparative History of Black Ideologies in the United States and South Africa* (New York: Oxford University Press, 1995), pp. 277–318.

152. Student Nonviolent Coordinating Committee memo, cited in "Appendix: Student Nonviolent Coordinating Committee," FBI Papers; "Report from the Chairman, 5 May, 1967," SNCC Papers.

153. "Report from the Chairman, 5 May, 1967," SNCC Papers.

154. Ibid. Certainly there had been many hints earlier in the decade of this transcendent narcissism—maybe even more than a hint. One student volunteer had exclaimed in the summer of 1964: "It was incredible. We were it! We were at the center of everything! We were making history all the while flying by the seat of our collective pants. What a rush! Were we full of ourselves? You bet. Did it feel great? Fuck, yes!" McAdam, *Freedom Summer*, p. 200. Yet in the southern towns, the black church, like a mother comforting an excited child, embraced these breakthroughs and ecstasies, these stratagems for authenticity and utopian aspirations, gave them a name and a history.

155. "Conclusions and Recommendations," SNCC Papers.

156. "Minutes of the Central Committee Meeting, June 10, 11, & 12, 1966," SNCC Papers.

157. John Lewis, "Statement by John Lewis, Chairman, Staff Meeting, February 1965," SNCC Papers.

158. Ephesians 6:11–12 (King James Version).

159. The church offered Christians training in spiritual warfare. Paul believed that the saving effect of the cross involved not only the atonement of humanity's sin but the overcoming of the entire cosmos contained in the reign of Adam. J. Louis Martyn, *Theological Issues in the Letters of Paul* (Nashville: Abingdon Press, 1997), p. 136. Martyn writes, "What is gone with the crucifixion of the cosmos is not simply circumcision, but rather both circumcision and uncircumcision, and thus the distinction of Jew and Gentile. Or, to take the matter to its root, what has suffered eclipse is not simply the Law, but rather the cosmos that had at its foundation both the Law and the Not-Law" (p. 136). Sin enslaved and enclosed, like the oppressive reign of Jim Crow. By contrast, Paul understood salvation as Christ's liberation of humanity from the enslaving forces of the cosmos and adoption into the family of God. "Wherefore thou art no more a servant, but a son; and if a son, then an heir of God through Christ," he wrote. The civil rights movement from the Pauline perspective then is about God's reform of the closed Adamic society, the cancellation of the old Jim Crow law in the new freedom movement of the kingdom. Which is not say that Fannie Lou Hamer was not thoroughly disgusted with the whole Democratic establishment. "We didn't come all this way for no two seats," she had said. But like most of the local church people representing the Freedom Democrats (and unlike most of the younger SNCC staffers), Hamer kept a steady head in her estimation of racial progress. She did not need Atlantic City to convince her that "the white man is not going to give up his power to us." Fannie Lou Hamer, "To Praise Our Bridges," in *Mississippi Writers: Reflections of Childhood and Youth*, vol. 2, ed. Dorothy Abbot (Jackson: University Press of Mississippi, 1986), p. 327. Atlantic City broadened that realism by teaching her that racism "is not Mississippi's problem, but America's"—

that the "enemy was not just the usual suspects, the bigots, klansmen and good old boys who preserved the southern caste system but "the powers in high places." Edwin King, "Go Tell It On the Mountain," p. 87. But Fannie Lou Hamer refused the refuge of despair; resignation was not an acceptable option when the demands of poverty were staring you in the face.

160. Carson, *In Struggle*, p. 149.

161. Quoted in Sellers, *River of No Return*, p. 131.

162. Ibid., pp. 131-132.

163. Jim Mansonis, "Student Nonviolent Coordinating Committee," December 27-31, 1963, SNCC Papers.

164. Malcolm X, *Malcolm X Speaks* (New York: Grove Press, 1965), p. 107.

165. Leslie Burl McLemore, *The Mississippi Freedom Democratic Party: A Case Study of Grass-Roots Politics* (Ph.D. dissertation, University of Massachusetts, 1971), p. 128.

166. Edwin King, unpublished manuscript, Edwin King Papers.

167. Edwin King, interview by the author.

168. Newfield, *Prophetic Minority*, p. 73.

169. John Lewis, interview by the author; see also Sean Wilentz, "The Last Integrationist," *The New Republic*, July 1, 1996, pp. 19-26.

170. James Peck, "Black Racism," *Liberation*, October, 1966, p. 31.

171. Joyce Ladner, "What 'Black Power' Means to Negroes in Mississippi," *TRANSaction* 5 (November 1967): p. 202.

172. Ralph McGill, quoted in Carson, *In Struggle*, p. 226.

173. Lewis, quoted in Jack Nelson, "*Los Angeles Times* Report," July 29, 1966, SNCC Papers.

174. Newfield, *Prophetic Minority*, p. 75. But Lewis had also come a long way from home. The stuttering boy who once preached salvation to the doomed chickens in his back yard coop in lower Alabama had made a few adjustments to his own ideas about discipline. When Joyce Ladner ran into him at a 1966 Thanksgiving party in Atlanta, she was flabbergasted by his new man-on-the-town demeanor. She wrote to a friend, "John Lewis has changed considerably on the question of morals. He is walking around (when he gets a sniff of liquor under his belt) talking about how long his dick is. Can you believe it! I was so shocked and tickled that I laughed for hours." Joyce Ladner, correspondence, personal collection.

175. Evelyn Marshall, secretary to Stokely Carmichael, to Mr. Dick Janson, December 21, 1966, SNCC Papers. Newfield, *Prophetic Minority*, p. 72.

176. Ibid., p. 75.

177. "We are all suffering from race fatigue," Rice and Perkins wrote in their 1993 book, *More Than Equals: Racial Reconciliation for the Sake of the Gospel* (Downers Grove, IL: Intervarsity Press, 1993). "The civil rights movement has run its course, and we've gotten just about all you can expect to get from a political movement," p. 30.

178. "Central Committee Meeting Notes and Decisions of May, 1967," SNCC Papers.

179. Ibid.

180. Bob Zellner, interview by the author. Was the exclusion of whites a mistake? An SNCC working paper drafted in the fall with Zellner's help described the difficulty of gaining the trust of poor whites in Itawamba County in northeast Mississippi, where

COFO had spent two months talking and listening as preparation for encouraging "the poor white people to provide a basis for political organization." The paper provides a description of the plight of the poor white that calls to mind the heartbreaking images of Walker Evans's photographic studies of poor southern whites in James Agee's *Let Us Now Praise Famous Men*. "For poor whites, poverty is something to be ashamed of," the paper read. "Their pressing needs are economic needs . . . They are very cynical about politics as a means of solving their economic problems. They want direct solutions: cooperatives, new industries, loans, etc. They are open to the idea of unions, but to many even unions look like a lot of talk without much in the way of tangible results. Many do not want unions because they know that the runaway factories would just run somewhere else to get cheap labor." The COFO organizers in Itawamba County had noticed that poor whites, when discussing race issues informally and without knowing that their interlocutors were part of the civil rights movement, displayed more openness to biracial initiatives than middle-class whites. "They think Negroes ought to have the vote, at least in their area." (The white folk of Itawamba County had little to fear since they made up 95 percent of the population). However, once the poor whites learned that SNCC and COFO were civil rights groups, "then people did not open their doors when we came back, or they went for their guns or the telephone." The working paper then recommended that COFO and SNCC members who worked with whites "dissociate themselves" voluntarily from their organizations. Dissociation might be difficult given the state's close surveillance of civil rights workers, but it was the preferred policy.

181. H. Rap Brown, "A Letter from Prison from H. Rap Brown," February 21, 1968. SNCC Papers.

182. "Prosecution Dropped in SNCC Case," *Washington Post*, September 11, 1968.

183. Julius Lester, *Look Out, Whitey: Black Power's Gon' Get Your Mama* (New York: Dial Press, 1968). Carmichael's defection to the Panthers left in ruins his organization called Black United Front, which he had founded as a coalition of black militant organizations in January of 1968 during a break in the world tour.

184. Robert Maynard, "SNCC Falters Without Carmichael," *Washington Post*, September 20, 1968.

185. Helmut Thielicke, *Between Heaven and Earth: Conversations with American Christians*, translated and edited by John W. Doberstein (New York: Harper & Row, 1965), p. 122.

186. Ibid., pp. 124–25.

187. Ibid., p. 133.

188. Stokely Carmichael, "What We Want," *The New York Review of Books*, September 1966, pp. 6–7.

189. Ibid.

190. Carl Oglesby, quoted in Os Guiness, *The Dust of Death: A Critique of the Counter Culture* (Downers Grove, Ill.: InterVarsity Press, 1973), p. 102.

191. Mike Miller, "Memo to SNCC National Staff, October 23, 1964," SNCC Papers.

192. Ibid.

193. Ibid.

CHAPTER 4

1. John Lennon, quoted in Os Guinness, *The Dust of Death*, p. 77.

2. Thomas Merton, quoted in Paul Elie, *The Life You Save May Be Your Own: An American Pilgrimage* (New York: Farrar, Straus and Giroux, 2003), p. 406.

3. Martin Luther King Jr., "Eulogy for the Martyred Children," *A Testament of Hope: The Essential Writings and Speeches of Martin Luther King Jr.*, edited by James M. Washington (San Francisco: HarperCollins Paperback, 1986), p. 221.

4. Martin Luther King Jr., "I Have a Dream," *A Testament of Hope*, p. 217.

5. Michael Eric Dyson, *I May Not Get There With You: The True Martin Luther King Jr.* (New York: The Free Press, 2000), p. 128.

6. King, quoted in John Howard Yoder, *For the Nations: Essays Public and Evangelical* (Grand Rapids, MI: William B. Eerdmans Publishing, 1997), p. 144.

7. Martin Luther King Jr., "A Time to Break Silence," in *A Testament of Hope*, pp. 232, 241.

8. Ibid., p. 242.

9. Taylor Branch, lecture, University of Virginia, Spring 2003. See also James H. Cone, *Martin and Malcolm and America: A Dream or a Nightmare* (Maryknoll, New York: Orbis Books, 1992), pp. 295–311.

10. Noam Chomsky, *Understanding Power: The Indispensable Chomsky* (New York: The New Press, 2002), p. 95.

11. Thomas Merton, *Faith and Violence* (South Bend: University of Notre Dame Press, 1968), p. 122.

12. Joan Didion, *Slouching Towards Bethlehem* (New York: the Modern Library, 2000), p. 76.

13. Friedrich Nietzsche, *The Gay Science*, trans. Walter Kaufmann (New York: Vintage Books, 1973), section 125.

14. Didion, *Slouching Towards Bethlehem*, p. 56.

15. Dan Wakefield, *New York Times Book Review*, July 21, 1968, p. 8.

16. Didion, *Slouching Towards Bethlehem*, p. 75.

17. See Richard Rorty, *Contingency, Irony and Solidarity* (Cambridge: Cambridge University Press, 1989), p. 101.

18. Didion, *Slouching Towards Bethlehem*, p. 51.

19. Ibid., p. 52.

20. Ibid., p. 67.

21. Ibid., p. 193.

22. Ibid., p. 76.

23. Ibid., p. 132.

24. Ibid., p. 133.

25. Ibid., p. 130.

26. Richard Rorty, *Achieving Our Country: Leftist Thought in Twentieth-Century America* (Cambridge: Harvard University Press, 1999).

27. Ibid., p. 35. Rorty insists that the reformist Left is better remembered by such progressive era thinkers and public intellectuals as John Dewey and Herbert Croly. Croly laments the "equivocal foundation" on which any nation in the world rests "so

long as the great majority of the poor in any country are inert and are laboring without any hope in this world." And he gives voice to a distinctively American socialism—"a more highly socialized democracy"—based on Christian principles of shared wealth in which public life, as Croly writes in his book *Progressive Democracy* (New York: Macmillan, 1915), "like the faith of St. Paul, finds its consummation in a love which . . . [is] a spiritual expression of the mystical unity of human love." These progressive intellectuals would also include members of the social Gospel movement, Rorty's maternal grandfather, the Baptist theologian Walter Rauschenbusch, and the Wisconsin economist and theologian Richard Ely, whose book *Social Aspects of Christianity* (New York: T. Y. Crowell, 1899) argues that industrial capitalism has produced the "farthest and deepest reaching crisis known to human history." Rauschenbusch, like his allies Croly and Ely, preached tirelessly against the "servants of Mammon," who "drain their fellow men for gain" and "who have cloaked their extortion with the gospel of Christ." See Walter Rauschenbusch, *The Theology for the Social Gospel* (New York: Macmillan, 1919).

28. Rorty, *Achieving Our Country*, p. 66.

29. Ibid., p. 68.

30. Ibid., p. 68.

31. Ibid., p. 36.

32. Ibid., p. 37.

33. Rorty says, "To step into the intellectual world which some of these leftists inhabit is to move out of a world in which the citizens of a democracy can join forces to resist sadism and selfishness into a Gothic world in which democratic politics has become a farce. It is a world in which all the daylit cheerfulness of Whitmanesque hypersecularism has been lost, and in which 'liberalism' and 'humanism' are synonyms for naivete—for an inability to grasp the full horror of our situation." *Achieving Our Country*, p. 96. See also Mark Edmondson, *Nightmare on Main Street: Angels, Sadomasochism, and the Culture of the Gothic* (Cambridge, MA: Harvard University Press, 1997).

34. Rorty, *Achieving Our Country*, p. 94. Herbert Marcuse made a similar point in his influential 1964 book, *One Dimensional Man*, "In the absence of demonstrable agents and agencies of social change, the critique is thrown back to a high level of abstraction. There is no ground on which theory and practice, thought and action meet." Herbert Marcuse, *One-Dimensional Man: Studies in the Ideology of Advanced Industrial Society* (Boston: Beacon Press, 1964), p. xlv.

35. Rorty, *Achieving Our Country*, p. 93. Rorty says, "Even though what these authors 'theorize' is often something very concrete and near at hand—a current TV show, a media celebrity, a recent scandal—they offer the most abstract and barren explanations imaginable."

36. Rorty says, "To form [such alliances] will require the cultural Left to forget about Baudrillard's account of America as Disneyland—as a country of simulacra—and to start proposing changes in the laws of a real country, inhabited by real people who are enduring unnecessary suffering, much of which can be cured by government suffering." *Achieving Our Country*, p. 99.

37. Rorty, *Achieving Our Country*, p. 102.

38. Ibid., p. 102.

39. Richard Rorty, *Philosophy and Social Hope* (London: Penguin Books, 1999), p. 208.

40. Terence Powderly, quoted in June Rossbach Bingham, *Courage to Change: An Introduction to the Life and Thought of Reinhold Niebuhr* (New York: Charles Scribner's Sons, 1961), p. 135.

41. Bingham, *Courage to Change*, p. 135.

42. Quoted in Anthony Dunbar, *Against the Grain: Southern Radicals and Prophets, 1929–1959* (Charlottesville: University Press of Virginia, 1981), p. 258.

43. Howard Kester, quoted in John Egerton, *A Mind to Stay Here: Profiles from the South* (New York: Macmillan, 1970), p. 86.

44. Howard Kester, *Revolt Among the Sharecroppers* (New York: Covici Friede Publishers, 1936), p. 26.

45. Guinness, *Dust of Death*, p. 379.

46. Ibid., p. 367.

47. Nicholas Wolterstorff, *Until Justice and Peace Embrace* (Grand Rapids, MI: William B. Eerdmans Publishing, 1983), p. 11.

48. James W. Gaffney, review of *Dust of Death*, in *America*, March 31, 1973, p. 292.

49. Guinness, *Dust of Death*, p. 20.

50. Ibid., p. 22.

51. Quoted in Guinness, *Dust of Death*, p. 23.

52. Guinness, *Dust of Death*, p. 140.

53. Ibid., p. 146.

54. Herbert Marcuse, *One-Dimensional Man: Studies in the Ideology of Advanced Industrial Society* (Boston: Beacon Press, 1964), p. 10, cited in Guinness, Dust of Death. Guinness acknowledges that the counterculture is not a monolithic unity but "contradictory in its complexity," rolling like "a relentless river of amorphous people, trends, fashions, ideals and aspirations."

55. See Michael S. Hamilton's helpful article, "The Dissatisfaction of Francis Schaeffer," *Christianity Today*, March 3, 1997. Hamilton writes, "This small, intense man from the Swiss mountains delivered a message unlike any heard in evangelical circles in the mid–1960's. At Wheaton College [where he delivered the lectures that became his first book, *The God Who Is There*], students were fighting to show films like Bambi, while Francis was talking about the films of Bergman and Fellini. Administrators were censoring existential themes out of student publications, while Francis was discussing Camus, Sartre and Heidegger. He quoted Dylan Thomas, knew the artwork of Salvador Dali, listened to the music of the Beatles and John Cage. . . . Francis Schaeffer tore down the gospel curtain that had separated evangelicals from contemporary cultural expression, giving Christian object lessons in how to interpret sculpture, music painting, and literature as philosophical statements of the modern mind."

56. Jean-Paul Sartre, "Preface," in Franz Fanon, *The Wretched of the Earth*, translated by Constance Farrington (New York: Grove Press, 1968), p. 14. Fanon responded by exposing the hidden logic of the European will as the psychotherapeutic deployment of force, which became at the same time the framework of his own recommendation. The "new man" and his "new concepts" set afoot on Europe is but the "old man" and "old concepts" with darker complexion.

57. Guinness, *Dust of Death*, preface.

58. Ibid., p. i.

59. Arthur Blessitt, quoted in "Is God Making a Comeback?" *Time* magazine, December 26, 1969.

60. Guinness, *Dust of Death*, p. 329.

61. Guinness, *Dust of Death*, p. 375.

62. Ibid., p. 29. By way of example Guinness explained that the church must resist the perverse logic that shapes such confused notions, favored by most conservative Christians in North America, that "a man who was openly convicted by his peers for the crime of wiping out almost a whole Asian village, including children, be allowed to live in near freedom with presidential favor, whereas a man of intense religious and moral convictions, convicted only of pouring dove's blood on state papers, was harshly sentenced."

63. "Counter-Culture and More," *Times Literary Supplement*, September 7, 1973, p. 1034.

64. In his discussion of capital punishment, he argued that with a properly high view of the human—and avoiding "the mistake of stressing only what the Bible teaches"—capital punishment can not only be justified theologically but can also be regarded as an affirmation of the created dignity of humankind in the image of God. Guinness's radical Christian fits in a bit too comfortably with the worldview of political conservatives in North America.

65. In 1970 Francis Schaeffer, the L'abri founder, had written that "one of the greatest injustices we do to our young people is to ask them to be conservative," but in Schaeffer's 1981 *Christian Manifesto*, he began claiming that with "the conservative swing in the United States in the election of 1980 . . . there is a unique window open." In 1970 he had warned Christians of the dangers of wrapping Christianity in the American flag, but in the *Christian Manifesto* he surprised his students, many of whom were looking for a way out of oppressive American fundamentalism, by praising Jerry Falwell's Moral Majority for opening the window of conservative politics. Michael S. Hamilton, *Christianity Today* 41, no. 3 (March 3, 1997): p. 22.

66. Guinness, *The Dust of Death: The Sixties Counterculture and How It Changed America* (Wheaton, Ill.: Crossway Books, 1994), p. 381.

67. Michael Hamilton writes, "The major departure in [Schaeffer's new work] was its extended look at legalized abortion as a case study in arbitrary government and the imminent threat of authoritarianism. Schaeffer had always opposed abortion, but the matter only became prominent in his work after 1973, when the U.S. Supreme Court declared abortion a constitutional right. Beginning in 1977, Schaeffer began devoting his full attention to the issue. 'If you want to understand Operation Rescue,' says Randall Terry, the anti-abortion group's founder once wrote, 'you have to read Schaeffer's *Christian Manifesto*.'" Hamilton, *Christianity Today* 41, no. 3 (March 3, 1997): p. 22.

68. Edwin King interview by the author.

69. Ibid.

CHAPTER 5

1. John Dittmer, *Local People: The Civil Rights Movement in Mississippi* (Urbana: University of Illinois Press, 1994), p. 424.

2. Will D. Campbell, interview by the author.

3. Martin Luther King Jr., *Where Do We Go from Here? Chaos or Community* (New York: Harper & Row, 1967), p. 100.

4. John Herbers, *The Lost Priority: What Happened to the Civil Rights Movement in America* (New York: Funk and Wagnalls, 1970), p. 207.

CHAPTER 6

1. John Perkins, *A Quiet Revolution: The Christian Response to Human Need* (Pasadena, CA: Urban Family Publications, 1976), p. 86.

2. John Perkins, quoted in Spencer Perkins, "Body Punches," unpublished essay, courtesy of Spencer Perkins.

3. Spencer Perkins, "Body Punches," unpublished essay, courtesy of Spencer Perkins.

4. Spencer Perkins, "I'm on the Freedom Side," unpublished essay, courtesy of Spencer Perkins.

5. Ibid.

6. *Perkins vs. State of Mississippi* (January 1972) p. 13. Federal Reporter 455, 2nd series (1972).

7. For a well-researched and riveting account of the day, see Philip Yancey, "Mississippi Ambush," *Campus Life* 32, no. 10 (May 1975): p. 41ff.

8. *Perkins vs. the State of Mississippi.*

9. John Perkins, *Let Justice Roll Down* (Ventura, California: Regal Books, 1976), p. 160.

10. Ibid.

11. John Perkins, interview by the author.

12. Neal McMillan, *Dark Journey: Black Mississippians in the Age of Jim Crow* (Urbana: University of Illinois Press, 1989), p. 306. "Local white men burned with resentment because of black soldiers who came back from service to their country with a new sense of their personal dignity," biographer Stephen Berk explains. White Mississippians even sought at times to "blot out the memory of the war" as a preemptive move against black protest. Stephen E. Berk, *A Time to Heal: John Perkins, Community Development, and Racial Reconciliation* (Grand Rapids, MI: Baker Books, 1997), p. 38.

13. John Perkins, *Let Justice Roll Down*, p. 21.

14. Ibid., p. 22.

15. Ibid.

16. John M. Perkins and Thomas A. Tarrants III, with David Wimbish, *He's My Brother: A Black Activist and a Former Klansman Tell Their Stories* (Grand Rapids, Michigan: Chosen Books, 1994), p. 33.

17. Pellagra was a disease of poverty caused by deficiency of niacin in the diet, with a range of devastating symptoms including skins rashes, severe nervous dysfunction, and mental symptoms.

18. John Perkins, *Let Justice Roll Down*, p. 23.

19. A shotgun rested on the front seat of the car. Mississippi law allowed a person to carry a concealed weapon if the person had "good and sufficient reason to apprehend a serious attack from any enemy," and Perkins had plenty of good reasons to be concerned about his safety. He had grown accustomed to a daily diet of harassing

phone calls and death threats. "It was widely known in Mendenhall," he said, "that there were people offering thousands for dollars to kill me." *John M. Perkins vs. State of Mississippi.* But the code's provisions were aimed to protect white against black, as Perkins discovered when he was soon charged with resisting arrest for claiming his innocence.

20. *Perkins vs. the State of Mississippi*, p. 19.

21. John Perkins, interview by the author.

22. *Perkins vs. the State of Mississippi.*

23. John Perkins, *Let Justice Roll Down*, p. 164.

24. Spencer Perkins, "Philippi," unpublished essay, courtesy of Spencer Perkins.

25. John Dittmer, *Local People: The Struggle for Civil Rights in Mississippi* (Urbana: University of Illinois Press, 1994), p. 21.

26. John Perkins, *Let Justice Roll Down*, p. 168.

27. In 1967, John and Vera Mae were one of the only four black families in town that sent their children to a white public school under the federal supervision of the Freedom of Choice Plan. The Perkinses' children understood the importance of their action and were courageous in their single-mindedness, but they weren't spared traumatic physical and psychological abuse that would last a lifetime. Spencer explained, "There was one white boy the first week who talked to me and he was treated so bad that he never talked to me again. So for two years I never talked to any of the other students. And you never really got used to. You know how when you have something you're afraid of and every time you think of it your heart just pounds. That happened for years. I'd be home playing and think about having to go to school and I'd get frozen in fear." Spencer Perkins, interview by the author.

28. Spencer Perkins, "Philippi," unpublished essay, courtesy of Spencer Perkins.

29. Remarkably, Spencer would become one of the pioneers of the evangelical racial reconciliation movement of the 1990s and coauthor of the book *More Than Equals: Racial Healing for the Sake of the Gospel* (Downers Grove, IL: Intervarsity Press, 1997). Still, just months before his fatal heart attack in 1999 at the age of forty-two, Spencer would tell an interviewer that his daydreams were often filled with avenging plots on white racists. He described a novel he wanted to write about a young African American who retaliated for the murder of his father by tracking down the white killers one by one and subjecting them to a slow and painful death. Spencer Perkins, interview with the author.

30. Berk, *A Time to Heal*, p. 19. See also the profile of Perkins and Voice of Calvary Ministry by Randall Balmer, *Mine Eyes Have Seen the Glory: A Journey into the Evangelical Subculture in America* (New York: Oxford University Press, 2000), pp. 176–192.

31. John Perkins, interview by Christopher Easly and Paul Erickson, courtesy of the Billy Graham Center Archives, Wheaton College, Illinois.

32. John Perkins, *A Quiet Revolution*, p. 26.

33. McMillan, *Dark Journey.*

34. Dittmer, *Local People*, p. 2.

35. Dittmer, *Local People*, p. 2.

36. John Perkins, *Let Justice Roll Down*, p. 53.

37. John Perkins, *A Quiet Revolution*, p. 17.

38. John Perkins, *Let Justice Roll Down*, p. 56.

39. Ibid., p. 63.

40. Spencer Perkins, "Freedom of Choice," unpublished essay, courtesy of Spencer Perkins.

41. Spencer Perkins, interview by the author.

42. Vera Mae Perkins, cited in John Perkins, *The Quiet Revolution*, p. 24.

43. John Perkins, *A Quiet Revolution*, p. 17.

44. Berk, *A Time to Heal*, p. 60.

45. John Perkins, *Let Justice Roll Down*, p. 68.

46. Ibid.

47. Ibid., p. 70.

48. Berk, *A Time to Heal*, p. 78.

49. John Nelson Darby, cited in Cartwright, "Wrestling with Scripture: Can Euro-American Christians and African-American Christians Learn to Read Scripture Together?" in *The Gospel in Black and White: Theological Resources for Racial Reconciliation*, ed. Dennis Okholm (Downers Grove, IL: Intervarsity Press, 1997), p. 97.

50. John Perkins, *Let Justice Roll Down*, p. 79.

51. John Perkins, "The Christian Community: Breaking the Cycle of Poverty," John M. Perkins Papers, John M. Perkins Foundation, Jackson, MI.

52. Fred Alexander, editorial, *Freedom Now* 2, no. 1 (1965): p. 3. Fred Alexander was one of Perkins's fellow black evangelicals in the 1960s. His magazine *Freedom Now*, founded in 1965, sought to reclaim mainline evangelicalism's tradition of social engagement.

53. John Perkins, "Voice of Calvary Source Document," John M. Perkins Papers. "The problem of poverty is the lack of committed, indigenous, Christian leadership," Perkins said, and thus civil rights activism and social reform were not a part of their early call.

54. Spencer Perkins, interview by the author.

55. Perkins operated with the sensibility of any good fundamentalist Christian, which accounts for his ambiguous place in civil rights historiography.

56. John Perkins, *Post-American*, John M. Perkins Papers.

57. John Perkins, *A Quiet Revolution*, p. 62.

58. Berk, *A Time to Heal*, p. 98.

59. John Perkins, interview by Paul Erickson, Billy Graham Center Archives.

60. Archie Buckley, in John Perkins, *A Quiet Revolution*, p. 50.

61. John Perkins, *A Quiet Revolution*, p. 51. Walker was a deacon in the Oak Ridge Church and a farmer.

62. Joel A. Carpenter, *Revive Us Again: The Reawakening of American Fundamentalism* (New York: Oxford University Press, 1997), p. 39.

63. John Perkins, *A Quiet Revolution*, p. 70.

64. Gordon Aeschliman, *John Perkins: Land Where My Father Died* (Ventura, California: Regal Books, 1987), p. 53.

65. John Perkins, interview by Paul Erickson, Billy Graham Center Archives.

66. John Perkins, *A Quiet Revolution*, p. 74.

67. Spencer Perkins, "Philippi."

68. Spencer Perkins, interview by the author.

69. John Perkins, interview by Paul Erickson, Billy Graham Center Archives.

70. Earlier in the twentieth century the evangelical theologian Carl F. H. Henry had criticized dispensationalism because it allowed only a very minor place for any sort of Christian witness other than personal soul winning. Carpenter, *Revive Us Again*, p. 202.

71. John Perkins, *Let Justice Roll Down*, p. 222.

72. Ibid., p. 198.

73. James C. Cobb, *The Most Southern Place on Earth: The Mississippi Delta and the Roots of Regional Identity* (New York: Oxford University Press, 1992), p. 113.

74. Charles M. Payne, *I've Got the Light of Freedom: The Organizing Tradition and the Mississippi Freedom Struggle* (Berkeley: University of California Press, 1995), p. 43.

75. John Perkins, *Let Justice Roll Down*, p. 200.

76. John Perkins, *He's My Brother*, p. 130.

77. John Perkins, *Let Justice Roll Down*, p. 205

78. Ibid., p. 174.

79. Ibid., p. 205.

80. John Perkins, interview by Paul Erickson, Billy Graham Center Archives.

81. Ibid.

82. John Perkins, *Let Justice Roll Down*, p. 206.

83. John Perkins, *He's My Brother*, p. 132.

84. Ibid., p. 133.

85. Dolphus Weary, *"I Ain't Comin' Back"* (Wheaton, Illinois: Tyndale House Publishers, 1990), p. 91.

86. Berk, *A Time to Heal*, p. 192.

87. "A Day in the Life of a Black Fundamentalist," *Eternity*, September 1971, p. 24.

88. "Spotlight on Herbert Jones," *The Voice* 2, no. 2 (March/April 1975), John M. Perkins Papers.

89. Artis Fletcher, quoted in Aeschliman, *John Perkins*, p. 58.

90. *Philippians* 2 (King James Version).

91. John Perkins, *Radix*, March–April 1977, p.7.

92. "Voice of Calvary Ministries: Statement of Faith," John M. Perkins Papers.

93. Stokely Carmichael, quoted in Jack Newfield, *A Prophetic Minority* (New York: Signet Book, 1966), p. 81.

94. John Lewis, "Staff meeting February 1965." SNCC Papers, Martin Luther King Jr. Center, Atlanta, GA. Importantly, Perkins offered an affirmative to the question John Lewis had once asked in SNCC meeting: "Is it possible for Negroes and whites in this country to engage in certain political experiment such as the world has never yet witnessed and in which the first condition would be that whites consented to let Negroes run their own revolution, giving them the necessary support, and being alarmed at some of the sacrifices, and difficulties that this would involve."

95. John Perkins, "An Interview," *Post-American*, March 1975, p. 15.

96. John Perkins, *A Quiet Revolution*, pp. 219–220.

97. Ibid., p. 209.

98. Alan Boesak, *Black and Reformed* (Johannesburg, South Africa: Skotaville Publishers, 1984), p. 32.

99. Charles Sherrod, "Southwest Georgia Project, Winter Report," Charles Sherrod Papers, State Historical Society of Wisconsin, Madison, WI.

100. John Perkins, *A Quiet Revolution*, p. 166.

101. Ibid., p. 167.

102. *The Four Spiritual Laws* were a popular evangelistic tract written by Bill Bright, the founder of Campus Crusades for Christ, International. Approximately 1.5 billion copies of *The Four Spiritual Laws* have been printed since the tract was written in 1965.

103. Ibid., p. 166.

104. Ibid., p. 167.

105. Weary, *"I Ain't Comin' Back,"* p. 90.

106. Deborah Lesure, "Thriftco Grand Opening Fulfilling an Urgent Need," *Jackson Advocate*, September 20-26, 1979.

107. Berk, *A Time to Heal*, p. 271.

108. The story of how these commitments were met with frequent frustration and complications is beautifully told by Chris Rice in his memoir, *Grace Matters: A True Story of Race, Friendship and Faith in the Heart of the South* (San Francisco: Jossey Bass, 2002).

109. John Perkins, quoted in Ralph Beebe, "Voice of Calvary," *Evangelical Friend*, November 1979, p. 3.

110. John Perkins, interview by the author, December 3, 2003.

111. John Perkins, "A Community Organizer," in *Peacemakers: Christian Voices from the New Abolitionist Movement*, ed. Jim Wallis (San Francisco: Harper & Row, 1983), p. 123.

112. John Perkins, interview by the author, December 3, 2003. As it turned out, white southern fundamentalists in Mississippi could have cared less that Perkins shared their dispensationalist views. In their minds he was just another black troublemaker. Coming of age spiritually in the cheerful evangelical world of southern California had not prepared him for the conflicts he would encounter between dispensationalism's concern for the world to come and black Mississippians' desperate need for social progress here and now. "The fundamentalists hang Jesus up in the sky," Perkins would say. "The meaning of his life is not worked out in daily life." John Perkins, quoted in Will Norton, "An Interview with John Perkins," *Christianity Today*, p. 21.

113. Credentials Committee Transcript, Democratic National Convention, Joseph Rauh Papers, Library of Congress.

114. John Perkins, "Stoning the Prophets," *Sojourners*, February 1978, p. 8.

115. Ibid.

116. John Perkins, *A Quiet Revolution*, p. 35.

117. Ibid., p. 141.

118. The term is mine, but the spirit is Perkins's.

119. John Perkins, "Is Affirmative Action Biblically Correct?" *Journal of Christian Ministry* 13, no. 3 (1995).

120. John Perkins, *A Quiet Revolution*, pp. 140-141.

121. Ibid., p. 220.

122. John Perkins, *A Quiet Revolution*, p. 218. Perkins believed in capital ownership and always recoiled when members of peace churches proposed that Voice of Calvary implement the practice of the common purse. Voice of Calvary existed to foster black economic empowerment: The operations of free enterprise and redistribution of wealth through reparations could be brought to unity in prophetic Christianity.

123. John Perkins, *A Quiet Revolution*, p. 152.

124. Perkins's friend Senator Mark Hatfield had made a similar point: "If each church or synagogue took over the responsibility of 18 families—a total of 72 adults and children——who are eligible for welfare today, there would not be any need for the existing federal or state welfare programs to families." Mark Hatfield, quoted in John Perkins, *Radix*, March–April 1977, p.7.

125. "Note from the Desk of Billy Graham," John M. Perkins Papers. The Southern Baptist evangelist Billy Graham introduced Perkins at several rallies as "the miraculous result of what happened when one man decided to make Christ's love real amid the hatred and bigotry of the Deep South." Doug Coe is the head of the International Fellowship Foundation, whose influence runs deep among both Republicans and Democrats in Washington.

126. Not all national evangelical leaders shared Colson's and Hatfield's enthusiasm. Harold Ockenga, president of an influential evangelical seminary in Massachusetts, was furious when Perkins criticized free-market capitalism in a lecture, and he responded in a public statement to the disgruntled board members who had heard about Perkins's remarks, "I don't think there's any exploitation of the black race in America today." Harold Ockenga, quoted in Titus Presler, "Perkins Visit 'Impetus' for Criticism," *The Paper* (Student Publication of Gordon-Conwell Theological Seminary), John M. Perkins Papers. Further, when the progressive evangelical journal *Freedom Now* published an issue in 1966 exploring the matter of Martin Luther King's Christian faith, the response of many white fundamentalists betrayed the subculture's convenient otherworldliness on civil rights matters. According to these readers, the civil rights movement stood in direct opposition to Jesus, who led "a Bible-centered movement with a solid stand for Christian separation from the world's ways." Garry L. Preston, Springfield, Ohio, letter to the Editor," *Freedom Now* 2, no. 4 (1966): p. 6. *Freedom Now*'s cautious endorsement of King was the first sympathetic treatment of the civil rights leader in an American evangelical publication, although the editors found him evasive on doctrinal matters, claiming drolly that "nowhere does he tell us about the shed blood of Christ or about our need for redemption." Still, the editors of *Freedom Now* were grateful for King's vision of beloved community and commitment to nonviolence. "By the grace of God the civil rights movement is led by a man who recognizes that vengeance is not his." The lead articles had asked, "Is Dr. Martin Luther King Jr. a Communist?" and "Is Dr. Martin Luther King Jr. a Fundamentalist?" and answered both cases in the negative. *Freedom Now* 2, no. 3 (July 1966).

127. In 1978 the *New York Times* reported on the emergence of an "evangelical left," mentioning the publications *The Other Side* and *Sojourners*, as well as Evangelicals for Social Action and Evangelicals for Social Concerns. "While several factors—among them pluralism, upward mobility, secularism and relativism—have reformed the evangelical movement to some extent, the inculcation of countercultural attitudes has left the clearest mark" (Kenneth A. Briggs, "Evangelical Christian Movement Being Reshaped by Radical Wing; Faith and Social Activism Evangelical Movement Changing, *New York Times*, July 16, 1978).

128. The sobering fact was that Mississippi in 1980 bore many familiar patterns of the once legally segregated South. The churches remained segregated; and most white families had fled the public schools to one of the start-up academies in the suburbs.

Perkins and his troops might have been hard at work building beloved community in the excluded neighborhoods of west Jackson, but elsewhere in the magnolia state a person could be called a liberal for expressing a fondness for *Sanford and Sons*, public schools, or William Faulkner. Some Jackson television stations reserved the right to preempt network programs that aired "northern" views on race, as happened one summer morning when a black sociologist named Charles King appeared on the *Phil Donahue Show*. A sociology professor at Georgia State University, King had been standing in front of a chalkboard furiously drawing graphs, diagrams, and flowcharts to make a point about white supremacy in America. Suddenly—as if it were still 1963—the broadcast was interrupted with the message, "Sorry, cable trouble." Over the course of the civil rights years, Jackson's two major network affiliates made it a matter of policy to preempt television programming when race was the focus. But the sight of the message in 1981 did not bode well for the forces of racial progress. The confederate flag was also making a comeback, mounted on the back window of pickup trucks or flying outside gas stations, gun shops, and restaurants. "There is a neo-confederate sentiment afoot," wrote one former Mississippian to his son in the North. The Citizens Council reappeared in the form of the Council of Concerned Citizens with the endorsements of prominent white leaders in the state. Not to be forgotten, the summer of 1980 brought presidential hopeful Ronald Reagan to the Neshoba County Fair, where the California governor stole the hearts of the white Democratic south with a speech in praise of state's rights, not once mentioning the civil rights workers murdered in 1964 a few miles away. From that day forward, the Republican Party became the majority party in the Deep South.

129. Bill Lowery, quoted in "We Are to Be Instruments of Reconciliation," *The Reconciler*, John M. Perkins Papers.

130. John Perkins, "Address of the Christian Community Development Association," New Orleans, November 12, 2003.

131. See the prescient 1969 article, "In Defense of the Steeple," by Duncan M. Gray Jr., in which the rector of St. Peter's Episcopal Church in Oxford and later Bishop of Mississippi explained why he was not yet ready to throw up his hands in despair over the local church. "There are yet many resources to be tapped in the parish church for witnessing to and making effective the reconciliation of men to God and men to men. More the point, the parish church may be the one place where this can be done in any final or meaningful way." *Katallagete, Journal of the Committee of Southern Churchmen* 2, no. 1 (Winter 1968–1969), pp. 29–31.

132. *A Quiet Revolution* (Voice of Calvary Ministry newspaper), First Quarter 1997.

133. "Empty Pew: Why W. Doesn't Go to Church," Amy Sullivan, *New Republic*, October 11, 2004, pp. 14–16.

134. But Perkins does not spare criticism of black religious and civic leadership when he thinks leaders speak presumptuously on behalf of the poor. He insists that some of the most uncharted mission fields in the world are poor black communities in the United States, and he finds pernicious the claim of certain African American intellectuals and academics that white involvement is necessarily patronizing. These academics, he thinks, happily ensconced in middle-class lives, are out of touch with the residents of poor communities, who almost without exception respond as gratefully to white compassion as to black. He laments the decline of a demanding moral vision among black political leaders, the decline of the language of sacrifice and reconciliation. "The Civil Rights Move-

ment gave people a sense of focus. They knew what the communities needed and they created plans for change. The new leaders are just sort of reacting to what happens and they don't have any central focus on their own." John Perkins, interview by the author. He also laments the frequent equivocations among political and civil rights leaders regarding the sources of black crime, which may have metaphorical roots in slavery and oppression but are more immediately constitutive of a shocking lack of respect for life among a coterie of young African Americans raised without structures of moral accountability. "But I can't imagine [King] living through the sixties and seventies," Perkins said. "Had he not been killed by a white person, he would have been killed by a black person—a dope pusher or gang leader—because of his message. At times I have had to cross a line where living was no longer worth it and dying would have been a relief. King crossed that line, and he was too committed to humanity ever to go back." John Perkins, "What Would He Be Today?" *Christianity Today*, April 8, 1988, p. 42.

135. John Perkins, quoted in Aeschliman, *Land Where My Fathers Died*, p. 167.

136. John Perkins, "The Oneness of Believers," *Freedom Now* 1, no. 3 (December 1965): p. 4.

137. John Perkins, "A Community Organizer," in Wallis, *Peacemakers*, p. 124.

138. John Perkins, "The Hope and Cost of Reconciliation," Voice of Calvary Ministries, John M. Perkins Papers.

139. Ibid.

140. John Perkins, "Integration or Development," *The Other Side*, 1974.

141. Further, while SNCC waged war against an often faceless enemy of legal inequity and white terror, Perkins reached out the hand of friendship to Christians across the tracks, offering them a place where reconciliation and hospitality could be experienced, and he has kept the hand of friendship extended even when it is unreciprocated. SNCC's focus on organizing for power in poor and excluded neighborhoods had too often concluded in the vilification of white antagonists and indifference to the sources—and social power—of forgiveness and reconciliation.

142. John Perkins, *A Quiet Revolution*, p. 223.

CHAPTER 7

1. Mark Gornik, *To Live in Peace: Biblical Faith and the Changing Inner City* (Grand Rapids, MI: William B. Eerdmans Publishing, 2002), p. 171.

2. John Kiess, "A New Song in Sandtown," unpublished undergraduate thesis, University of Virginia, 2001.

3. Gornik, *To Live in Peace*, p.171.

4. Gornik, *To Live in Peace*, p. 238.

5. Laverne Stokes, conversation with Workgroup on Lived Theology and Community Building, University of Virginia, December 16, 2000.

6. Russell Jeung, "Toward a Theology of Organizing," lecture, University of Virginia, June 12, 2003.

7. Russel Jeung, "The Rich Young Guy," Web site of the Project on Lived Theology, University of Virginia, http://livedtheology.org (accessed August 2004).

8. Laura Counts, "Oak Park Tenants Invest in Housing," *Oakland Tribune*, August 13, 2001.

9. Jeung, "Toward a Theology of Organizing."

10. Gene Rivers, "The Responsibility of Evangelical Intellectuals in the Age of White Supremacy," in *The Gospel in Black and White: Theological Resources for Racial Reconciliation*, edited by Dennis L. Okholm (Downers Grove, IL: Intervarsity Press, 1997), p. 13.

11. Gene Rivers, quoted in John Leland, "Savior of the Streets," *Newsweek*, June 1, 1998, p. 25.

12. Omar M. McRoberts, *Streets of Glory: Church and Community in a Black Urban Neighborhood* (Chicago: University of Chicago Press, 2003). As sociologist Omar McRoberts observes, "[From] Harvard Yard emerged a church of Black intellectuals who believed not only in the need for transformative social activism but in the literal truth of the Bible, ascetic Holiness living, and glossolalia, the aural footprint of the Holy Spirit" (p. 119).

13. Gene Rivers, quoted in Wendy Murray Zoba, "Separate and Equal," *Christianity Today*, February 5, 1996.

14. Ibid.

15. Gene Rivers, quoted in McRoberts, *Streets of Glory*, p. 119.

16. Zoba, "Separate and Equal."

17. Ibid.

18. Rydell Payne, lecture, University of Virginia, Project on Lived Theology, April 22, 2003.

19. This profile is based on John Kiess's analysis in "From Prospect Avenue: The Work of Abundant Life Ministries," *The Jericho Road* 2, no. 5 (December 2001), Christ Episcopal Church, Charlottesville, Virginia.

20. Rydell Payne, interview by the author.

21. Amy Sherman, presentation to the Theology of Community Building Workgroup, University of Virginia, October 13, 2001, http://livedtheology.org (accessed August 2004).

22. Ibid. Urban sociologist Daphne Spain has written of the "redemptive places" created at the turn of the twentieth century to relieve American cities of the tremendous pressures of rapid demographic change. Daphne Spain, "Redemptive Spaces: Charitable Choice and Welfare Reform," *Journal of the American Planning Association* 67, no. 3 (Summer 2001): p. 249. Redemptive places included boardinghouses, hotels, dining halls, vocational schools, and settlement houses, and they offered a range of services from libraries, playgrounds, kindergartens, health care, and English language classes. The Young Women's Christian Association (YWCA) established boardinghouses for the supervision of white women; while the National Association of Colored Women (NACW) formed vocational schools to teach African American women the skills they would need to survive in cites. The Salvation Army offered food, clothing, and a place to stay for new arrivals in American cities. These and other charitable organizations were located in ordinary buildings; "redemptive places" occupying "vernacular space" (p. 253). We might call the new experiments in beloved community of the Christian community development movement "reconciling spaces," geographically precise locations where the civil rights movement's vision of beloved community is kept alive through shared theological hopes and acts of mercy.

23. Sherman, presentation to the Theology of Community Building Workgroup, October 13, 2001.

24. Chris Rice, presentation to the Workgroup on Theology and Race, University of Virginia, February 24, 2001.

25. Spencer Perkins and Chris Rice, *More Than Equals: Racial Healing for the Sake of the Gospel* (Downers Grove: Intervarsity Press, 1993), p. 17.

26. Rice, presentation to the Workgroup on Theology and Race.

27. Ibid., p. 17.

28. Rice, presentation to the Workgroup on Theology and Race, University of Virginia, February 24, 2001.

29. They also helped coordinate the ambitious community development initiative in Summerhill. Until the late sixties, Summerhill had been a thriving and integrated middle-class neighborhood a mile south of the Georgia capitol building, but the construction of two bisecting interstate highways and the Fulton County Stadium with its connecting roads and massive parking lots required the demolition of more than two thousand homes. As families and businesses left, gang members, drug dealers, and pimps took their place. From a population of 39,000 in 1968, by the time the International Olympic Committee named Atlanta the site of the 1996 games only 2,700 residents were left in Summerhill. What distinguished the Summerhill project from other urban renewal initiatives were two interconnected goals: the intention of the white and black suburban organizers to move to the neighborhood and the creation of multiclass blocks. In addition to the mixed-income community, the plan called for rehabbing several hundred homes, revitalizing a local black business district and social services, and opportunities for interracial fellowship.

30. Robert D. Lupton, *Theirs Is The Kingdom: Celebrating the Gospel in Urban America* (San Francisco: Harper, 1989), pp. 6–7.

31. Ibid., p. 13. The Christian community-building movement, Lupton observes, "seem to be flowing around" rather than through the institutional church, as the work most often emerges of house churches, fellowships, intentional communities, church/parachurch hybrids, and other nontraditional structures. "The members and leaders of these groups are mostly young people who are turned off by the blandness of institutional church, yet who are willing to make radical personal sacrifices for the sake of the gospel."

32. Mo Leverett, "The Lost Art of Redemptive Suffering," lecture, Trinity Presbyterian Church, Charlottesville, Virginia, February 23, 2003.

33. Mo Leverett, quoted in Katharine Bothner, "Bringing Joy Out of Suffering: Battling the Powers of Evil with the Power of the Gospel to Restore Inner-City New Orleans," research paper, University of Virginia, 2003.

34. Ibid.

35. Roy Rivera, presentation to the Theology of Community Building Workgroup of the University of Virginia, Bronx, NY, March 13, 2001.

36. Shane Claiborne, "The Simple Way," lecture delivered to the Christian Community Development Association, New Orleans, November 15, 2003.

37. See account of this meeting, "My Meeting with the President-Elect," *Christianity Today* Web site, December 22, 2000, http://www.christianitytoday.com (accessed August 2004).

38. Sociologist Richard Wood has shown in his study of the Pacific Institute for Community Organization (PICO) that faith-based community-building initiatives

among the poor and excluded often become "sociopolitical critics of government," quite a contrast to "the religious right's emphasis on individual and legislatives moral change." Richard L. Wood, *Faith in Action: Religion, Race and Democratic Organizing in America* (Chicago: University of Chicago Press, 2002), p. 4.

39. For a first-rate study of the Pacific Institute for Community Organization (PICO) see Wood, *Faith in Action*, p. 4; and for a superb account of the Industrial Areas Foundation, see Mark R. Warren, *Dry Bones Rattling: Community Building to Revitalize American Democracy* (Princeton: Princeton University Press, 2001).

40. Martin Luther King Jr., *The Papers of Martin Luther King Jr.*, vol. 3, ed. Stewart Burns, Susan Carson, Peter Holloran, and Dana L. H. Powell (Berkeley: University of California Press, 1996), p. 328.

41. Shane Claiborne, "Notes of the 2003 CODA Meeting," courtesy of Margaux Stuart.

42. John DiIulio, speech delivered at the National Association of Evangelicals, Dallas, Texas, March 7, 2001.

43. According to Independent Sector data, in 1996 the total revenue for congregations was $81.2 billion. In 1995, Washington expended $204 billion on Medicaid, Supplemental Security Income, housing assistance, food and nutrition, and other aid to low-income citizens (see Gary Burtless et al., "The Future of the Social Safety Net," in Robert D. Reischauer, ed., Setting Budget Priorities [Washington, D.C.: Brookings Institution, 1997], p. 79). Hypothetically, even if the revenue for congregations were doubled to $162 billion, and if federal spending were cut by one-fifth to $160 billion, that would represent only the federal share of social welfare program costs—the states spent nearly $70 billion in 1995 on Medicaid alone; see John J. DiIulio Jr. and Richard P. Nathan, "Introduction," in Frank Thompson and John J.DiIulio Jr., eds., *Medicaid and Devolution: A View From the States* (Washington, D.C.: Brookings Institution, 1998), p. 4.

44. Alicia Paul, correspondence with the author, July 1995.

45. "Grace is greater than race," remarks transcribed by Peter Slade, November 20, 2000.

46. Ibid.

47. Weary, "Grace is greater than race." Portions of this citation were taken from Weary's address at First Baptist Church, Jackson, MI.

48. Ibid.

49. Dolphus Weary, interview by the author.

50. Mission Mississippi, "History," www.missionmississippi.org (accessed July 2004).

51. Dolphus Weary, interview by the author.

52. Weary, "Grace is greater than race."

53. Timothy Gorringe, *Karl Barth: Against Hegemony* (Oxford: Oxford University Press, 1999), p. 49.

54. Rod Sider, "Among White Evangelicals," *Boston Review*, April/May 2001.

55. Chris Rice, presentation to the Workgroup on Theology and Race, University of Virginia, February 24, 2001.

56. John Perkins, *Resurrecting Hope: Powerful Stories of How God Is Moving to Reach our Cities* (Ventura, California, 1995), p. 19.

CHAPTER 8

1. See Arthur C. Cochrane, *The Mystery of Peace* (Elgin, IL: Brethren Press, 1986); and Walter Brueggemann, *Peace* (St. Louis: Chalice, 2001).

2. Lesslie Newbigin, *The Gospel in a Pluralistic Society* (Grand Rapids: William B. Eerdmans Publishing Company, 1989), p. 227.

3. Quoted in Bruce McCormack, *Karl Barth's Critically Realistic Dialectical Theology: Its Genesis and Development, 1909–1936* (New York: Oxford University Press, 1995), p. 144.

4. McCormack, *Karl Barth's Critically Realistic Dialectical Theology*, p. 144.

5. John Lewis, interview by the author.

6. Karl Barth, *The Word of God and the Word of Man*, translated by Douglas Horton (Gloucester, MA: Peter Smith Publishers, 1978), p. 274.

7. Barth, *Word of God*, p. 297. Beloved community and the church may serve this purpose well, although the church somehow endures all its confusions, living amidst a fallible but purposeful series of divine actions and evidences, whereas the beloved community appears and disappears in relation to discrete social needs.

8. Dietrich Bonhoeffer, *Ethics* (New York: MacMillan, 1955), p. 178.

9. Bonhoeffer, *Ethics*, p. 178.

10. The Old Testament scholar, Walter Bruggemann, writes, "As a vision of an assured future, the substance of shalom is crucial, for it can be a resource against both despair and an overly eager settlement for an unfinished system. But when that vision of the future becomes 'present tense,' and any present order is equated with that future, *shalom* inevitably results in a self-congratulatory distortion of the present." Bruggemann, *Peace*, p. 5.

11. Clarence Jordan, *Christian Century*, Clarence Jordan Papers, University of Georgia, Athens, GA.

12. Thomas Merton, *Faith and Violence* (South Bend, IN: University of Notre Dame Press, 1968), pp. 142–143.

13. Jürgen Moltmann, *The Spirit of Life: A Universal Affirmation*, translated by Margaret Kohl (Minneapolis: Fortress Press, 1992), p. xi. Clark Pinnock offers a similar meditation on spirit: "Spirit is perfecter, then, of the creation of which Jesus is the highest expression. Spirit is at work in history, first bringing humankind into existence and then moving it toward the goal of union. Spirit is the power released to bring the divine plans to completion. He is Spirit of creation and new creation, concerned with creating community and bringing about the Kingdom. Spirit is the power by which this present age will be transformed into the kingdom and which ever works to bring about ultimate fulfillment. As the power of creation, the Spirit does not call us to escape from the world or from history but keeps creation open to the future." Clark Pinnock, *Flame of Love: A Theology of the Holy Spirit* (Downers Grove, IL: Intervarsity Press, 1996), p. 61.

14. Victoria Gray Adams, interview by the author.

15. See Hans Urs von Balthasar, *Dare We Hope That All Men Shall Be Saved?* (San Francisco: Ignatius Press, 1988). The Jesuit theologian Balthasar writes, "We might, however, make it quite clear to ourselves how outrageous it is to blunt God's triune will

for salvation, which is directed at the entire world ('God wants all men to be blessed'), by describing it as 'conditonal' and calling absolute only that divine will in which God allows his total will for salvation to be thwarted by man" (p. 25). See also Karl Barth's magisterial volume *Church Dogmatics*, vol. 2 (Edinburgh: T & T Clark, 1961), in which he rewrites the doctrine of double predestination by enfolding all reality into the triumph of God's irresistible grace.

16. Martin Luther King Jr., "Facing the Challenge of a New Age," *The Papers of Martin Luther King Jr.*, vol. 3, ed. Stewart Burns, Susan Carson, Peter Holloran, and Dana L. H. Powell (Berkeley: University of California Press, 1996), p. 54.

17. Henri de Lubac, *The Discovery of God*, translated by Alexander Dru (Grand Rapids, MI: William B. Eerdmans Publishing, 1956). "Man is of absolute value," writes the French theologian, Henry de Lubac, "because he is illuminated by a ray of light from the face of God" (p. 190).

18. I have in mind the advocacy work of the Virginia Center for Farm and Immigrant Workers. See Matthew Whelan's remarkable field report, "When a Stranger Resides with You: Migrant Farm Workers and the Gift of Food," Project on Lived Theology, University of Virginia, http://livedtheology.org (accessed August 2004).

19. See John DeGruchy, "Holy Beauty: A Reformed Perspective on Aesthetics within a World of Unjust Ugliness," Project on Lived Theology, University of Virginia, http://livedtheology.org/pdfs/deGruchy.pdf (accessed July 2004).

20. Mark R. Gornik, *To Live in Peace: Biblical Faith and the Changing Inner City* (Grand Rapids, MI: William B. Eerdmans Publishers, 2002), p. xx.

21. Willis Jenkins, paper presented at the American Academy of Religion, November 19, 2003, Atlanta.

22. The *Epistle of St. James* 1:27, New International Version.

23. Barth, *Word of God*. The Christian martyr Dietrich Bonhoeffer, reflecting on his camaraderie with atheists and humanists in the German resistance and the nazification of the *Deutsche Kristen*, offered late in his life this remarkable insight: "In earlier times the church could preach that a person must first become a sinner, like the publican and the harlot, before he could know and find Christ, but we in our time must say rather that before a person can know and find Christ he must first become righteous like those who strive and who suffer for the sake of justice, truth and humanity." Bonhoeffer, *Ethics*, p. 182. Bonhoeffer says further, "Jesus gives His support to those who suffer for the sake of a just cause, even if this cause is not precisely the confession of His name" (p. 181).

24. Barth, *Word of God*, p. 303.

25. Newbigin, *The Gospel*, p. 228.

26. Christoph Blumhardt, quoted in Joseph Bettis, "Theology and Politics: Karl Barth and Reinhold Niebuhr on Social Ethics after Liberalism," *Religion in Life*, 1979, p. 61.

27. Bettis, "Karl Barth and Reinhold Niebuhr," p. 60. The life of authentic faith can itself be excruciatingly dull and prosaic, and of frustrations it has no end. St. James writes in his epistle in the New Testament that genuine religion is "to visit the fatherless and widows in their affliction, and to keep [oneself] unspotted from the world" (James 1:27). This admonition to care for the lonely and the poor and to maintain personal discipline offers the simple promise of behavior pleasing to God. Faith stretches

out human ambition in impossibly awkward angles. For example, our preferential option for nonviolence may not always achieve results consistent with its ideals. We live in a fallen world and risk is an inevitable part of faithful action. Still, those of us who live by the teachings of Jesus, and by the examples of such witnesses as King, Gray, Sherrod, Jordan, Dorothy Day, Bonhoeffer, and Gandhi, must understand that the gun will never bring peace; that violence can never reveal the true grain of the universe; and that the disposition toward the peaceful resolution of conflict must always guide our actions as we journey together with God through this world of such great beauty and of such heartbreaking violence.

28. Barth, *Word of God*, p. 286.

29. Bettis, "Karl Barth and Reinhold Niebuhr, p. 60.

30. Barth, *Word of God*, p. 32.

31. In recent years, Clarence Jordan's description of the Kingdom of God as rich diversity has been further confirmed by the astonishing growth of the global church. As Philip Jenkins writes in his essential work, *The Next Christendom: The Coming of Global Christianity*, "[The] center of gravity has shifted inexorably southward to Africa, Asia, and Latin America. Already today, the largest Christian communities on the planet are to be found in Africa and Latin America. If we want to visualize a 'typical' contemporary Christian, we should think of a woman living in a village in Nigeria or in a Brazilian *favela*," (New York: Oxford University Press, 2002), p. 2.

32. Charles Sherrod, "The Missionary: A New Image," 1966, Charles Sherrod Papers, State Historical Society of Wisconsin, Madison.

Selected Bibliography

Abernathy, Ralph David. *And The Walls Came Tumbling Down*. New York: Harper & Row, 1989.

Aickin, Mary. *A Case of Black and White: Northern Volunteers and the Southern Freedom Summers, 1964–1965*. Westport, CT: Greenwood Press, 1982.

Anderson, Victor. *Beyond Ontological Blackness: An Essay on African American Religious and Cultural Criticism*. New York: Continuum, 1995.

Arnold, Eberhard. *God's Revolution: Justice, Community, and the Coming Kingdom*. Farmington, PA: The Plough Publishing House, 1997.

Arrowsmith, William. *Antonioni: The Poet of Images*. New York: Oxford University Press, 1995.

Baldwin, Lewis V. *There is a Balm in Gilead: The Cultural Roots of Martin Luther King Jr*. Minneapolis: Fortress Press, 1991.

Balthasar, Hans Urs von. *Dare We Hope That All Men Be Saved?* Translated by David Kipp and Lothar Krauth. San Francisco: Ignatius Press, 1988.

Barber, Benjamin R. *A Passion for Democracy: American Essays*. Princeton: Princeton University Press, 1998.

Barbour, R. S. *The Kingdom of God and Human Society*. Edinburgh: T & T Clark, 1993.

Barth, Karl. *Church Dogmatics*. Vol. 4, Part 2, *The Doctrine of Reconciliation*. Translated by G. W. Bromiley. Edinburgh: T & T Clark, 1961.

_____. *The Humanity of God*. Richmond: John Knox Press, 1960.

_____. *The Word of God and the Word of Man*. Translated by Douglas Horton. Gloucester, MA: Peter Smith, 1978.

Bass, Jack. *Taming the Storm: The Life and Times of Judge Frank M. Johnson Jr. and the South's Fight over Civil Rights*. New York: Doubleday, 1993.

Belfrage, Sally. *Freedom Summer*. New York: The Viking Press, 1965.

Berk, Stephen E. *A Time to Heal: John Perkins, Community Development, and Racial Reconcilation*. Grand Rapids: MI: Baker Books, 1997.

Bingham, June Rossbach. *Courage to Change: An Introduction to the Life and Thought of Reinhold Niebuhr*. New York: Charles Scribner's Sons, 1961.

Blake, Casey Nelson. *Beloved Community: The Cultural Criticism of Randolph Bourne, Van Wyck Brooks, Waldo Frank, and Lewis Mumford*. Chapel Hill: University of North Carolina Press, 1990.

Blumhardt, Christoph. *Action in Waiting.* Farmington, PA: The Plough Publishing House, 1998.

Boesak, Alan. *Black and Reformed.* Johannesburg, South Africa: Skotaville Publishers, 1984.

Bonhoeffer, Dietrich. *Discipleship.* Translated by Barbara Green and Reinhard Krauss. Minneapolis: Fortress Press, 2001.

_____. *Ethics.* New York: Macmillan, 1955.

_____. *Letters and Papers from Prison.* New York: Macmillan, 1972.

Bonino, Jose Miguez. *Doing Theology in a Revolutionary Situation.* Philadelphia: Fortress, 1975.

Branch, Taylor. *Parting the Waters: America During the King Years, 1954–1963.* New York: Simon & Schuster, 1988.

_____. *Pillar of Fire: America in the King Years, 1963–1965.* New York: Simon & Schuster, 1998.

Burner, David. *Making Peace With the 60s.* Princeton: Princeton University Press, 1996.

Burner, Eric R. *And Gently Shall He Lead Them: Robert Parris Moses and Civil Rights in Mississippi.* New York: New York University Press, 1994.

Burns, Stewart, ed. *Daybreak of Freedom: The Montgomery Bus Boycott.* Chapel Hill: University of North Carolina Press, 1997.

_____. *To the Mountaintop: Martin Luther King Jr.'s Sacred Mission To Save America, 1955–1968.* San Francisco: Harper Collins, 2004.

Campbell, Will D. *Brother to a Dragonfly.* New York: Seabury, 1977.

_____. *Race and the Renewal of the Church.* Philadelphia: Westminster Press, 1962.

Camus, Albert. *Resistance, Rebellion and Death.* Translated by Justin O'Brien. New York: Alfred A. Knopf, 1961.

_____. *The Rebel: An Essay on Man in Revolt.* Translated by Anthony Bower. New York: Vintage Books, 1991.

Carmichael, Stokely. "What We Want," *The New York Review of Books* 7, no. 4 (September 22, 1966).

Carmichael, Stokely, and Charles V. Hamilton. *Black Power: The Politics of Liberation in America.* New York: Random House, 1967.

Carpenter, Joel A. *Revive Us Again: The Reawakening of American Fundamentalism.* New York: Oxford University Press, 1997.

Carson, Clayborne. *In Struggle: SNCC and the Black Awakening of the 1960s.* Cambridge, MA.: Harvard University Press, 1981.

_____. "The Boycott that Changed Dr. King's Life," *New York Times Magazine,* January 7, 1996.

Chancey, Andrew. "Race, Religion and Reform: Koinonia's Challenge to Southern Society." Unpublished doctoral dissertation, University of Florida, 1998.

Chappell, David L. *A Stone of Hope: Prophetic Religion and the Death of Jim Crow.* Chapel Hill: University of North Carolina Press, 2004.

Chafe, William H. *Never Stop Running: Allard Lowenstein and the Struggle to Save American Liberalism.* New York: Basic Books, 1993.

Chomsky, Noam. *Understanding Power: The Indispensable Chomsky.* New York: The New Press, 2002.

Clark, Septima. *Ready from Within: A First Person Narrative.* Edited with an introduction by Cynthia Stokes Brown. Trenton, NJ: Africa World Press, 1990.

Clendenning John. *The Life and Thought of Josiah Royce*. Madison, WI: University of Wisconsin Press, 1985.

Cnann, Ram A. *Keeping Faith in the City: How 401 Religious Congregations Serve Their Neediest Neighbors*. Center for Research on Religion and Urban Civil Society (CR-RUCS). Philadelphia: University of Pennsylvania, March 20, 2000.

Coble, Ann Louise. *Cotton Patch for the Kingdom*. Scottsdale, PA: Herald Press, 2002.

Cochrane, Arthur C. *The Mystery of Peace*. Elgin, IL: Brethren Press, 1986.

Cohen, Mitchell, and Dennis Hale, eds. *The New Student Left*. Boston: Beacon Press, 1966.

Cone, James H. *Black Theology, Black Power*. New York: The Seabury Press, 1969.

_____. *My Soul Looks Back*. Maryknoll, New York: Orbis Books, 1986.

_____. *Martin and Malcolm and America: A Dream or a Nightmare*. Maryknoll, NY: Orbis Books, 1992.

Connolly, William E. *Why I Am Not a Secularist*. Minneapolis: University of Minnesota Press, 1999.

Cox, Harvey. *God's Revolution and Man's Responsibility*. Valley Forge, PA: The Judson Press, 1965.

Curry, Constance, ed. *Deep in Our Hearts: Nine Women in the Freedom Movement*. Athens, GA: University of Georgia Press, 2000.

Davies, Alan. *Infected Christianity: A Study of Modern Racism*. Kingston: McGill-Queen's University Press, 1988.

Deats, Paul, and Carol Robb. *The Boston Personalist Tradition in Philosophy, Social Ethics, and Theology*. Macon, GA: Mercer University Press, 1986.

De Gruchy, John W. *Christianity and Democracy: A Theology for a Just World Order*. Cambridge: Cambridge University Press, 1995.

Delbrel, Madeleine. *We, the Ordinary People of the Streets*. Translated by David Louis Schlinder Jr. and Charles F. Mann. Grand Rapids, MI: William B. Eerdmans Publishing, 2000.

De Lubac, Henri. *The Discovery of God*. Translated by Alexander Dru. Grand Rapids, MI: William B. Eerdmans Publishing, 1956.

Didion, Joan. *Slouching Towards Bethlehem*. New York: The Modern Library, 2000.

Dittmer, John. *Local People: The Struggle for Civil Rights in Mississippi*. Urbana: University of Illinois Press, 1994.

Dunbar, Anthony. *Against the Grain: Southern Radicals and Prophets, 1929–1959*. Charlottesville: University Press of Virginia, 1981.

Dunbar, Leslie. *A Republic of Equals*. Ann Arbor: University of Michigan Press, 1966.

Dyson, Michael Eric. *I May Not Get There with You: The True Martin Luther King Jr*. New York: The Free Press, 2000.

Egerton, John. *A Mind to Stay Here: Profiles from the South*. New York: Macmillan, 1970.

_____. *Speak Now Against the Day: The Generation before the Civil Rights Movement in the South*. New York: Alfred A. Knopf, 1994.

Elie, Paul. *The Life You Save May Be Your Own: An American Pilgrimage*. New York: Farrar, Straus, and Giroux, 2003.

Ellul, Jacques. *The Presence of the Kingdom*. Translated by Olive Wyon. New York: Seabury Press, 1967.

Evans, Sara. *Personal Politics: The Roots of Women's Liberation in the Civil Rights Movement and the New Left*. New York: Vintage Books, 1980.

Evans, Zelia S., with J. T. Alexander. *The Dexter Avenue Baptist Church, 1877–1977.* Montgomery, AL: Dexter Avenue Baptist Church, 1978.

Fanon, Franz. *The Wretched of the Earth.* Preface by Jean-Paul Sartre. Translated by Constance Farrington. New York: Grove Press, 1968.

Findlay, James F., Jr. *Church People in the Struggle: The National Council of Churches and the Black Freedom Movement, 1950–1970.* New York: Oxford University Press, 1993.

Flynt, Mark. *Alabama Baptists: Southern Baptists in the Heart of Dixie.* Tuscaloosa and London: The University of Alabama Press, 1998.

Forman, James. *The Making of Black Revolutionaries.* New York: Macmillan, 1972.

Frady, Marshall. *Martin Luther King Jr.* New York: Viking Book, 2002.

Fuller, Millard. *The Theology of the Hammer.* Macon, GA: Smyth & Helwys Publishing, 1994.

Gandhi, Mahatma. *The Essential Gandhi.* Edited by Louis Fischer. New York: Vintage Books, 1983.

Garrow, J. David. *Bearing the Cross: Martin Luther King Jr. and the Southern Christian Leadership Conference.* New York: Vintage Books, 1988.

Garrow, David J., ed. *The Walking City: The Montgomery Bus Boycott, 1955–1956.* Brooklyn, NY: Carson Publishing, 1989.

Gitlin, Todd. *The Sixties: Years of Hope, Days of Rage.* New York: Bantam, 1987.

Gornik, Mark. *To Live in Peace: Biblical Faith and the Changing Inner City.* Grand Rapids, MI: William B. Eerdmans Publishing, 2002.

Gorringe, Timothy. *Karl Barth: Against Hegemony.* Oxford: Oxford University Press, 1999.

Graetz, Robert A. *A White Preacher's Memoir: The Montgomery Bus Boycott.* Montgomery, AL: Black Belt Press, 1998.

Gray, Fred. *Bus Ride to Justice: Changing the System by the System.* Montgomery, AL: Black Belt Press, 1995.

Greenberg, Cheryl Lynn, ed. *A Circle of Trust: Remembering SNCC.* New Brunswick, NJ: Rutgers University Press, 1998.

Guiness, Os. *The Dust of Death: A Critique of the Counter-Culture.* Downers Grove, IL: Intervarsity Press, 1973.

Hale, Grace Elizabeth. *Making Whiteness: The Culture of the South, 1890–1940.* New York: Vintage Books, 1999

Hampton, Henry, and Steve Fayer. *Voices of Freedom: An Oral History of the Civil Rights Movement from the 1950s through the 1980s.* New York: Bantam Books, 1990.

Hauerwas, Stanley. *A Better Hope: Resources for a Church Confronting Capitalism, Democracy, and Postmodernity.* Grand Rapids, MI: Brazos Press, 2001.

The Hauerwas Reader. Edited by Michael G. Cartwright and John Berkman. Durham: Duke University Press, 2001.

_____. *With the Grain of the Universe: The Church's Witness and Natural Theology.* Grand Rapids, MI: Brazos Press, 2001.

Havel, Vaclav. *Living in Truth.* London: Faber and Faber, 1987.

Hegel, Georg Wilhelm Friedrich. *Introduction to the Philosophy of History.* Translated by Leo Rauch. Indianapolis: Hackett Publishing Company, 1988.

_____. *Lectures on the Philosophy of Religion.* Volume 3. Edited by Peter C. Hodgson. Translated by R. F. Brown, P. C. Hodgson, and J. M. Stewart. Berkeley: University of California Press, 1985.

Herbers, John. *The Lost Priority: What Happened to the Civil Rights Movement in America?* New York: Funk and Wagnalls, 1970.

Hodgson, Peter C. *God in History: Shapes of Freedom.* Nashville: Abingdon Press, 1989.

Hoffer, Eric. *The True Believer: Thoughts on the Nature of Mass Movements.* New York: Harper & Row, 1989.

Hogan, Wesley. "Radical Manners: The Student Nonviolent Coordinating Committee and the New Left in the 1960s." Doctoral dissertation, Duke University, 2000.

Holmes, Barbara A. *Joy Unspeakable: Contemplative Practices of the Black Church.* Minneapolis: Fortress Press, 2004.

Horst, Mark. "The Unfinished Agenda of the Civil Rights Movement." *The Christian Century*, April 27, 1994, pp. 446–448.

Horton, Miles, with Judith Kohl and Herbert Kohl. *The Long Haul: An Autobiography.* New York: Doubleday, 1991.

Horton, Walter Marshall. *Contemporary Continental Theology: An Interpretation for Anglo-Saxons.* New York: Harper & Brothers, 1938.

Jordan, Clarence. *The Cotton Patch Version of Matthew and John.* Clinton, NJ: Association Press, 1970.

_____. *The Cotton Patch Version of Paul's Epistles.* Clinton, NJ: Association Press, 1968.

_____. *Sermon on the Mount.* Valley Forge, PA: Judson Press, 1952.

_____. *The Substance of Faith and Other Cotton Patch Sermons.* New York: Association Press, 1972.

Kavanaugh, John F. *Following Christ in a Consumer Society: The Spirituality of Cultural Resistance.* New York: Maryknoll, 1992.

Kelly, Thomas R. *A Testament of Devotion.* San Francisco: HarperSanFrancisco, 1992.

Kester, Howard. *Revolt among the Sharecroppers.* New York: Covici Friede Publishers, 1936.

King, Charles H. Jr. *Fire in My Bones.* Grand Rapids, MI: William B. Eerdmans Publishing, 1983.

King, Coretta Scott. *My Life with Martin Luther King Jr.* New York: Holt, Rinehart and Winston, 1969.

King, Martin Luther, Jr. *The Autobiography of Martin Luther King Jr.* Edited by Clayborne Carson. New York: IPM/Warner, 1998.

_____. *The Papers of Martin Luther King Jr.* Vol. 1. Edited by Clayborne Carson, Ralph E. Luker, and Penny A. Russell. Berkeley: University of California Press, 1992.

_____. *The Papers of Martin Luther King Jr.* Vol. 2. Edited by Ralph E. Luker, Penny A. Russell, and Peter Holloran. Berkeley: University of California Press, 1994.

_____. *The Papers of Martin Luther King Jr.* Vol. 3. Edited by Stewart Burns, Susan Carson, Peter Holloran, and Dana L. H. Powell. Berkeley: University of California Press, 1996.

_____. *The Papers of Martin Luther King Jr.* Vol. 4. Edited by Susan Carson, Adrienne Clay, Virginia Shadron, and Kieran Taylor. Berkeley: University of California Press, 2000.

_____. *Stride Toward Freedom: The Montgomery Story.* San Francisco: Harper & Row, 1983.

_____. *A Testament of Hope: The Essential Writings and Speeches of Martin Luther King Jr.* Edited by James M. Washington. San Francisco: Harper, 1986.

_____. *Where Do We Go From Here? Chaos or Community.* New York: Harper & Row, 1967.

King, Mary. *Freedom Song: A Personal Story of the 1960s Civil Rights Movement*. New York: Quill, 1987.

King, Richard. *Civil Rights and the Idea of Freedom*. New York: Oxford University Press, 1992.

K'Meyer, Tracy Elaine. *Interracialism and Christian Community in the Postwar South: The Story of Koinonia Farm*. Charlottesville: University Press of Virginia, 1997.

Ladner, Joyce. "What 'Black Power' Means to Negroes in Mississippi." *TRANS-action* 5 (November 1967).

Lawson, Steven F. "Freedom Then, Freedom Now: The Historiography of the Civil Rights Movement." *The American Historical Review* 96, no. 2 (April 2, 1991).

Lawson, Steven F., and Charles Payne, eds. *Debating the Civil Rights Movement, 1945–1968*. Lantham, MD: Rowman & Littlefield, 1988.

Lee, Dallas, *Cotton Patch Evidence*. New York: Harper & Row, 1971.

Lewis, John, with Michael D'Orso. *Walking with the Wind: A Memoir of the Movement*. New York: Simon & Schuster, 1998.

Lischer, Richard. *The Preacher King: Martin Luther King Jr. and the Word That Moved America*. New York: Oxford University Press, 1995.

Lowery, Charles D., and John F. Marszalek. *Encyclopedia of African-American Civil Rights*. Westport, CT: Greenwood Press, 1992.

Luker, Ralph, "The Kingdom of God and Beloved Community in the Thought of Martin Luther King Jr." In *Ideas and the Civil Rights Movement*, edited by Ted Ownby. Jackson: University Press of Mississippi, 2001.

Lupton, Robert D. *Theirs Is the Kingdom: Celebrating the Gospel in Urban America*. San Francisco: Harper, 1989.

Malcolm X. *Malcolm X Speaks*. New York: Grove Press, 1965.

Marcuse, Herbert. *One–Dimensional Man: Studies in the Ideology of Advanced Industrial Society*. Boston: Beacon Press, 1964.

Marsden, George M. *Fundamentalism and American Culture: The Shaping of Twentieth-Century Evangelicalism, 1870–1925*. New York: Oxford University Press, 1980.

Marsh, Charles. "The Beloved Community: An American Search." In *Religion and Civil Rights*, edited by Gary Orfield and Christopher Edley. New York: The Century Foundation Press, 2000.

_____. "The Civil Rights Movement as Theological Drama: Interpretation and Application." *Modern Theology*, April 2002.

_____. "Human Community and Divine Presence: Dietrich Bonhoeffer's Theological Critique of Hegel." *Scottish Journal of Theology* 45, no. 2 (December 1992), pp. 427–448.

_____. *God's Long Summer: Stories of Faith and Civil Rights*. Princeton: Princeton University Press, 1997.

_____. "In Defense of a Self: The Postmodern Search for a Theological Identity." *Scottish Journal of Theology*, Fall 2002.

_____. "One, Two, Three, What Are We Praying For?" *The Baltimore Sun*, February 2, 1991.

_____. "Rorty among the Theologians," *Books and Culture*, July 2000.

_____. "A Theology for Community Service," *Loyola Magazine*, Fall 1996.

Martyn, J. Louis. *Galatians*. New York: The Anchor Bible Dictionary, 1997.

_____. *Theological Issues in the Letters of Paul*. Nashville: Abingdon Press, 1987.

McAdam, Doug. *Freedom Summer*. New York: Oxford University Press, 1988.

McCarraher, Eugene. *Christian Critics: Religion and Its Impasse in Modern American Social Thought*. Ithaca: Cornell University Press, 2000.

McClendon, James William., Jr. *Biography as Theology: How Life Stories Can Remake Today's Theology*. Nashville: Abingdon Press, 1974.

McCormack, Bruce. *Karl Barth's Critically Realistic Dialectical Theology: Its Genesis and Development, 1909–1936*. New York: Oxford University Press, 1995.

McMillen, Neil. *The Citizens' Council: Organized Resistance to the Second Reconstruction, 1954–1964*. Urbana: University of Illinois Press, 1971.

_____. *Dark Journey: Black Mississippians in the Age of Jim Crow*. Urbana: University of Illinois Press, 1989.

McRoberts, Omar M. *Streets of Glory: Church and Community in a Black Urban Neighborhood*. Chicago: University of Chicago Press, 2003.

Merton, Thomas. *Faith and Violence*. South Bend, IN: University of Notre Dame Press, 1968.

Milbank, John. *Theology and Social Theory: Beyond Secular Reason*. Oxford: Blackwells, 1993.

Miller, Keith D. *Voice of Deliverance: The Language of Martin Luther King Jr. and Its Sources*. Athens, GA, and London: University of Georgia Press, 1998.

Mills, Kay. *This Little Light of Mind: The Life of Fannie Lou Hamer*. New York: Dutton, 1993.

Mills, Nicolaus. *Like a Holy Crusade: Mississippi 1964—The Turning of the Civil Rights Movement in America*. Chicago: Ivan R. Dee, 1992.

Mills, Thornton J., III. *Dividing Lines: Municipal Politics and the Struggle for Civil Rights in Montgomery, Birmingham, and Selma*. Tuscaloosa: The University of Alabama Press, 2002.

Moltmann, Jürgen. *Theology of Hope*. Translated by James W. Leitch. New York: Harper & Row, 1967.

_____. *The Spirit of Life: A Universal Affirmation*. Translated by Margaret Kohl. Minneapolis: Fortress Press, 2003.

Moody, Anne. *Coming of Age in Mississippi*. New York: Doubleday Publishing, 1968.

Morris, Aldon D. *The Origins of the Civil Rights Movement: Black Communities Organizing for Change*. New York: Free Press, 1984.

Moses, Greg, *Revolution of Conscience: Martin Luther King Jr. and the Philosophy of Nonviolence*. New York: The Guilford Press, 1997.

Newbigin, Lesslie. *The Gospel in a Pluralistic Society*. Grand Rapids, MI: William B. Eerdmans Publishing, 1989.

Newfield, Jack. *A Prophetic Minority*. New York: Signet Book, 1966.

Newman, Mark. *Getting Right with God: Southern Baptists and Desegregation, 1945–1995*. Tuscaloosa: The University of Alabama Press, 2001.

Niebuhr, Reinhold. *Moral Man in Immoral Society: A Study in Ethics and Politics*. New York: Scribner, 1960.

_____. *The Self and the Dramas of History*. New York: Charles Scribner's Sons, 1955.

Noll, Mark A. *The Old Religion in a New World: The History of North American Christianity*. Grand Rapids, MI: William B. Eerdmans Publishing, 2002.

Oates, Stephen B. *Let the Trumpets Sound: The Life of Martin Luther King* Jr.. New York: Harper & Row, 1982.

Ownby, Ted. *Subduing Satan: Religion, Recreation and Manhood in the Rural South, 1865–1920.* Chapel Hill: University of North Carolina Press, 1990.

Padover, Saul K., ed. *Sources of Democracy: Voices of Freedom, Hope and Justice.* New York: McGraw-Hill, 1973.

Payne, Charles M. *I've Got the Light of Freedom: The Organizing Tradition and the Mississippi Freedom Struggle.* Berkeley: University of California Press, 1995.

Pearson, Hugh. *The Shadow of the Panther: Huey Newton and the Price of Black Power in America.* Reading, MA: Addison-Wesley Publishing, 1994.

Percy, Walker. *Signposts in a Strange Land.* Edited by Patrick Samway. New York: Farrar, Straus and Giroux, 1991.

Perkins, John. *Beyond Charity: The Call to Christian Community Development.* Grand Rapids, MI: Baker Books, 1993..

_____. *Let Justice Roll Down.* Ventura, CA: Regal Books, 1976.

_____. *A Quiet Revolution: The Christian Response to Human Need.* Pasadena, CA: Urban Family Publications, 1976.

_____. *Resurrecting Hope: Power Stories of How God Is Moving to Reach Our Cities.* Ventura, CA: Regal Books, 1995.

Perkins, Spencer, and Chris Rice. *More Than Equals: Racial Healing for the Sake of the Gospel.* Downers Grove, IL: Intervarsity Press, 1997.

Pinnock, Clark H. *Flame of Love: A Theology of the Holy Spirit.* Downers Grove, IL: Intervarsity Press, 1996.

Pohl, Christine. *Making Room: Recovering Hospitality as a Christian Tradition.* Grand Rapids, MI: William B. Eerdmans Publishing, 1999.

Polsgrove, Carol. *Divided Minds: Intellectuals and the Civil Rights Movement.* New York: W. W. Norton, 2001.

Rauschenbusch, Walter. *Christianity and the Social Crisis.* Boston: Pilgrim Press, 1907.

_____. *A Theology for the Social Gospel.* New York: Macmillan, 1919.

Rice, Chris. *Grace Matters: A True Story of Race, Friendship, and Faith in the Heart of the South.* San Francisco: Jossey-Bass, 2002.

Rivers, Gene. "The Responsibility of Evangelical Intellectuals in the Age of White Supremacy." In *The Gospel in Black and White: Theological Resources for Racial Reconciliation.* Edited by Dennis L. Okholm. Downers Grove, IL: Intervarsity Press, 1997.

Robertson, Houston Bryan. "Fighting the Good Fight: A History of Dexter Avenue King Memorial Baptist Church, 1865–1977." Doctoral dissertation, University of North Carolina, 1997.

Robinson, Jo Ann. *The Montgomery Bus Boycott and the Women Who Started It: The Memoir of Jo Ann Gibson Robinson.* Knoxville: University of Tennessee Press, 1987.

Rorty, Richard. *Achieving Our Country: Leftist Thought in Twentieth-Century America.* Cambridge: Harvard University Press, 1998.

_____. *Contingency, Irony and Solidarity.* Cambridge: Cambridge University Press, 1987.

_____. *Philosophy and Social Hope.* London: Penguin Books, 1999.

Royce, Josiah. *The Problem of Christianity.* Chicago: University of Chicago Press, 1968. First published 1913.

_____. *The Sources of Religious Insight*. New York: Charles Scribners Sons, 1912.

Rowan, Carl. *Breaking Barriers*. New York: Little, Brown and Company, 1991.

Saunders, James Robert, and Renae Nadine Shackleford. *Urban Renewal and the End of Black Culture in Charlottesville, Virginia*. Jefferson, NC: McFarland & Company, 1998.

Saunders, Stanley P., and Charles L. Campbell. *The Word on the Street: Performing the Scriptures in the Urban Context*. Grand Rapids, MI: William B. Eerdmans Publishing, 2000.

Schlabach, Gerald W. *And Who Is My Neighbor? Poverty, Privilege and the Gospel of Christ*. Scottdale, PA: Herald Press, 1990.

Sellers, Cleveland, with Robert Terrell. *The River of No Return: The Autobiography of a Black Militant and the Life and Death of SNCC*. Jackson: University Press of Mississippi, 1990.

Sharpe, Dores Robinson. *Walter Rauschenbusch*. New York: Macmillan, 1942.

Silver, James. *Mississippi: The Closed Society*. New York: Harcourt, Brace and World, 1963.

Smith, Kenneth L., and Ira G. Zopp Jr. *Search for the Beloved Community*. Valley Forge, PA: Judson Press, 1974.

Smith, Lillian. *Killers of the Dream*. New York: W. W. Norton, 1949.

Sobrino, Jon. *Spirituality of Liberation: Toward Political Holiness*. New York: Maryknoll, 1985.

Stembridge, Jane. *I Play Flute and Other Poems*. New York: Seabury Press, 1966.

Stricklin, David. *A Genealogy of Dissent: Southern Baptist Protest in the Twentieth Century*. Lexington, KY: University Press of Kentucky, 1999.

Sugarman, Tracy. *Strangers at the Gates*. New York: Hill & Wang, 1966.

Sutherland, Elizabeth, ed. *Letters from Mississippi*. New York: McGraw-Hill, 1965.

Taylor, Charles. *Hegel and Modern Society*. Cambridge: Cambridge University Press, 1979.

Thielicke, Helmut. *Between Heaven and Earth: Conversations with American Christians*. Edited and translated by John W. Doberstein. New York: Harper & Row, 1965.

Thurman, Howard. *With Head and Heart: The Autobiography of Howard Thurman*. New York: Harcourt Brace Jovanovich, 1979.

_____. *Jesus and the Disinherited*. Richmond, IN: Friends United Press, 1981.

Tillich, Paul. *The New Being*. New York: Charles Scribner's Sons, 1955.

Tipton, Steven M. *Getting Saved from the Sixties: Moral Meaning in Conversation and Cultural Change*. Berkeley: University of California Press, 1992.

Tutu, Desmond Mpilo. *No Future Without Forgiveness*. New York: Doubleday, 1999.

Valentine, Foy D. *A Historical Study of Southern Baptists and Race Relations, 1917–1947*. New York: Arno Press, 1980.

Vaughn, Wally G., and Richard W. Wills. *Reflections on Our Pastor: Dr. Martin Luther King Jr. at Dexter Avenue Baptist Church, 1954–1960*. Dover, MA: The Majority Press, 1999.

Volf, Miroslav. *Exclusion and Embrace: A Theological Exploration of Identity, Otherness and Reconciliation*. Nashville: Abingdon Press, 1996.

Von Hoffman, Nicholas. *Mississippi Notebook*. New York: David White Company, 1964.

Warren, Heather A. *Theologians of a New World Order: Reinhold Niebuhr and the Christian Realists, 1920–1948*. New York: Oxford University Press, 1997.

Warren, Mark R. *Dry Bones Rattling: Community Building to Revitalize American Democracy*. Princeton: Princeton University Press, 2001.

Weary, Dolphus. *"I Ain't Coming Back."* Wheaton, IL: Tyndale House Publishers, 1990.

West, Cornel. *Prophesy Deliverance!: An Afro-American Revolutionary Christianity*. Philadelphia: Westminster, 1982.

Williams, Rowan. *On Christian Theology*. Oxford: Blackwell Publishers, 2000.

_____. *The Wound of Knowledge: Christian Spirituality from the New Testament to St. John of the Cross*. Cambridge, MA: Cowley Publications, 1979.

Wilson, Charles R. *Baptized in Blood: The Religion of the Lost Cause, 1865–1920*. Athens: University of Georgia, 1980.

Wolterstorff, Nicholas. *Until Justice and Peace Embrace*. Grand Rapids, MI: William B. Eerdmans Publishing, 1983.

Wood, Richard L. *Faith in Action: Religion, Race, and Democratic Organizing in America*. Chicago: University of Chicago Press, 2002.

Wuthnow, Robert, and John H. Evans. *The Quiet Hand of God: Faith-Based Activism and the Public Role of Mainline Protestantism*. Berkeley: University of California Press, 2002.

Yoder, John Howard. *For the Nations: Essays Public and Evangelical*. Grand Rapids, MI: William B. Eerdmans Publishing, 1997.

_____. *The Christian Witness to the State*. Scottdale, PA: Herald Press, 2002.

Zinn, Howard. *SNCC: The New Abolitionists*. Cambridge, MA: South End Press, 2002. First published 1964.

ARCHIVES

Alabama Department of Archives and History. Montgomery, AL.

Martin Luther King Jr. Papers. Boston University.

Billy Graham Center Archives. Wheaton College, IL.

Historical Commission of the Southern Baptist Convention. Nashville, TN.

Charles Sherrod Papers. State Historical Society of Wisconsin. Madison WI.

Clarence Jordan Papers, Hargrett Rare Book and Manuscript Library, University of Georgia, Athens, GA.

Edwin King Papers. Private collection.

Edwin King Papers. Tougaloo College Special Collections Library. Jackson, MS.

Joan Trumpauer Mulholland Papers. Private collection.

John M. Perkins Papers. John M. Perkins Foundation. Jackson, MS.

SNCC Papers. Martin Luther King Jr. Center. Atlanta, GA.

Special Collections Library. Alderman Library. University of Virginia.

Special Collections. University of Southern Mississippi.

Tracy Sugarman Oral History Archives. Private collection.

Index